THE WINDS OF CHANGE

MANAGING CELTIC FC 1991-2005

Alex Gordon

Forewords by Billy McNeill and Davie Hay

Published by CQN Books, 2015.

First published in the United Kingdom in 2015 by CQN Books
ISBN 978-0-9934360-1-7

A catalogue for this book is available from the British Library
and the Irish Library in Dublin.

Cover & page design and typesetting by Stephen Cameron
for CQN Books.

Edited by David Faulds. Printed in the UK by CPI Books.

A special thank you to everyone in the
Celtic Quick News community and the wider Celtic family.
Please visit www.celticquicknews.co.uk

A FOUR LEAF CLOVER

With a four leaf clover on my breast,
And the green and white upon my chest,
It's such a joy for us to see,
For they play football the Celtic way

It's been ten years, long time indeed,
We stood with pride and we took defeat,
Our beloved team, our ancient ground,
Has been rebuilt, a club reborn.

With a four leaf clover on my breast,
And the green and white upon my chest,
It's such a joy for us to see,
For they play football the Celtic way

McCann he rode the winds of change,
And the things he brought will long remain,
A phoenix rising, a house of steel,
And 60,000 Celtic dreams

With a four leaf clover on my breast,
And the green and white upon my chest,
It's such a joy for us to see,
For they play football the Celtic way

The work is done and the stage is set,
The Celtic dream can now be met,
In a sea of dreams, we're here today,
Let's sit and watch the Champions play

Written by SANDY and PETER DEVERS

DEDICATION

This is for Gerda, because she deserves it.

ACKNOWLEDGEMENTS

David Faulds deserves special mention for sterling work above and beyond, as usual, as Editor of this work. Well done, David!

A cheer, too, for Paul Brennan, Founder of Celtic Quick News, for his professionalism and support throughout.

Seoc Colla, who was always there to jog a memory or two and make a valid suggestion.

John Shand, whose professional help was inestimable.

Of course, I cannot overlook those two wonderful legends, Billy McNeill and Davie Hay. A pleasure to work again with such committed Celtic men.

All the others, too, who gave their time. I cannot name you all, but you know who you are. Much appreciated, my friends.

And a massive thank you, once again, must go to Celtic supporters home and abroad and to all the posters and readers on www.celtiquicknews.co.uk

Keep the faith.

SUNDAY FEBRUARY 27, 1994. A DAY OF IMFAMY

Alex Gordon left his desk at the Sunday Mail for the last time on February 8, 1994. He had worked for the Daily Record/Sunday Mail for 27 years but could take no more.

In his previous book Caesar & The Assassin, published by CQN Books in November 2014, Gordon was able to draw upon his very close friendships with both Billy McNeill and Davie Hay to get their insights into managing Celtic after Jock Stein.

Alex is old school. He never once hid his affection for Celtic and in his final days as the sports editor of Scotland's biggest selling newspaper he fought tooth and nail to prevent a gimmick appearing in the paper.

Indeed Gordon point blankly refused to allow the 'story' to appear on the back page while he was there.

It was therefore no surprise to Alex Gordon when 19 days after he walked out, the editor of the Sunday Mail sanctioned the story and it appeared on the back page. There was a hearse outside Celtic Park ready to bury Celtic Football Club.

Alex Gordon was disgusted, just like the rest of the Celtic support.

In The Winds of Change, Gordon picks up the story in 1991 when Billy McNeill has just been removed for the second time as Celtic manager. He takes us through 14 seasons and 8 managers in what is a rollercoaster of a read. Sit down, recall the lows and enjoy the highs. This is The Winds of Change.

David Faulds
Editor

CONTENTS

BILLY McNEILL

Celtic Manager: 1978/83. Honours:
3 League Championships, 2 Scottish Cups, 1 League Cup
1987/91: 1 League Championship, 1 Scottish Cup

It is often said an individual can leave Celtic Football Club, but Celtic Football Club will never leave an individual. If anyone knows how true that sentiment is, it must be me.

I don't mind admitting the club broke my heart on a May day back in 1991 when they told me, in a fairly blunt manner, that I was no longer manager of Celtic, my services, in effect, were no longer required. That was one of the absolute lowest points of my career. When I was given the news I was left numb, a horrible feeling.

In August that year - almost two weeks short of three months since I lost the job of my dreams - I was wishing Liam Brady, my successor, the very best of luck before his Celtic managerial debut against my old adversary Jim McLean, the Dundee United manager, in the opening Premier League game of the 1991/92 Premier League season at Tannadice.

Why not? I may not have been the Celtic manager any longer, but I was still a Celtic supporter. And I was as delighted as anyone that Liam got off to a winning start at what had always been a tricky venue for my club. I say 'my' because that's the way it has always felt.

I was manager of Manchester City and Aston Villa in between my two spells at Parkhead, but it never felt the same as when I was on duty at Celtic.

How could it be? It's true - Celtic Football Club never leaves you.

DAVIE HAY

Celtic Manager: 1983/87.
Honours: 1 League Championship, 1 Scottish Cup

At long last I can reveal Liam Brady might have been at Celtic four years before he was installed as Billy McNeill's replacement in 1991.

Obviously, I didn't know it at the time, but the axe was about to fall on yours truly and I would be out of a job in the summer of 1987.

Prior to that, though, I was drawing up a roster of possible transfer targets and the Republic of Ireland international's name was on that list. I was aware, at the age of thirty-one, he was showing an interest in returning to the UK at the end of his seventh year in Italy. He was with Ascoli at the time and I knew Celtic could afford him. I also reckoned he had at least another two years in his legs.

I admired Liam as an intelligent midfielder and I thought he would bring a bit of experience and know-how to the team. I could imagine him teaming up with Paul McStay and providing a foil for the likes of Roy Aitken and Peter Grant. Being from Dublin, there was already a Celtic connection and I believed he might fancy a few years in the green-and-white hoops. It certainly wasn't outwith the realms of possibility.

Unfortunately, I never got the opportunity to firm up my initial interest. West Ham had a bid of £100,000 accepted by Ascoli in March 1987 and Liam returned to London to spend three years at Upton Park before retiring.

I was as surprised as anyone when he was named Celtic manager. There can be no doubt about his playing credentials, but, as he admitted later, Celtic are not a club for a first-time team boss. No amount of ability out on a football pitch can prepare you for a job of that magnitude.

Unfortunately, Liam, like others, was about to find that out the hard way.

PROLOGUE
STORM CLOUDS ON A SUNNY DAY

It seemed wholly inappropriate that Celtic Park should be bathed in glorious sunshine on the morning Billy McNeill was given the news he was out of a job. It was May 22 1991, almost four years to the day since he was invited back for a second stint as Celtic manager to guide the club with exuberance and expertise through their triumphant Double-winning Centenary Year.

The radiant setting in the east end of Glasgow looked more germane for a singalong carnival than a savage sacking. Outside, sweetness and light; inside, pandemonium in Paradise.

McNeill, in ruthless fashion, had been sacrificed by a panicking board who would suffer an identical and ignominious fate as their club legend in the not-too-distant future when an unlikely juggernaut by the name of Fergus McCann swept away the debris at the club.

As this extremely proud individual, holding his emotions in check, granted on-the-spot interviews in the midst of a media scrum on the steps at the front door at Celtic Park, the mood among the public onlookers was blackening with every passing moment. A Celtic board member, who had consented to the removal of Billy McNeill as the club manager a couple of hours earlier, smiled wanly at his ex-employee as he made his way past him and through the gathering throng en route to a swift and, no doubt, welcome getaway.

Suddenly, without warning, the director was confronted by an irate observer who, it was evident, wasn't quite in agreement with the actions taken by him or the other five members of the decision-makers at the club. McNeill acted swiftly. Instinctively, he shot out an arm to come between startled individual and would-be inquisitor. 'Now, now, there's no need for that,' he said. 'We're all disappointed, let's leave it at that.'

It was a remarkable and spontaneous display of guardianship by one human being to protect another. In an instant, the sting had been taken out of an awkward moment and the Celtic director had the good grace to look embarrassed as he shuffled off towards his car.

No-one who understood the qualities within McNeill would have been one bit taken aback by his selfless act. He had just lost the job he loved and possessed enough savvy to realise he had reached the inevitable and indisputable point of no return. There would be no third comeback to his spiritual home for the club's most iconic captain. It was all over. 'I think I should have been treated with a little more respect,' he reflected years later. It was a masterly understatement from McNeill.

To this backdrop of bedlam, Celtic, without a plan and devoid of direction, set about looking for a new manager, their eighth appointment in one hundred and three years. It would be a colossus of a task to follow giants such as Willie Maley, Jimmy McStay, Jimmy McGrory, Jock Stein, Davie Hay and, of course, Billy McNeill, who had been in charge on two occasions. Only the unfortunate McStay, the custodian between the war years of 1940/45, failed to win a trophy. Among them, the other five contributed seventy-four pieces of silverware.

The next six Celtic managers would muster a mere four for their efforts over a disastrous nine-year period as fate hit the pause button on success at Parkhead. The notable exception was Wim Jansen, who, in his solitary year, stylishly delivered the League Championship and a League Cup in season 1997/98.

Twenty-eight days after Billy McNeill's departure, the directors, promising a bold, exciting future, unveiled his successor, a sportsman of some repute who had never managed at any level in football. Liam Brady had more than illustrated his pedigree as a distinguished midfielder with the Republic of Ireland as well as club sides such as Arsenal, Juventus and Inter Milan. The question, of course, was: Could he deliver as a manager?

No soothsayer could have predicted the rocky rollercoaster Celtic were about to embark upon over the next fourteen years as Brady was succeeded, in rapid succession, by Lou Macari, Tommy Burns, Wim Jansen, Jozef Venglos, John Barnes, Kenny Dalglish, in a caretaker capacity, and Martin O'Neill.

Undoubtedly, it was the most turbulent, tumultuous, topsy-turvy period in the history of the club. It was a time when Celtic teetered on the very brink of extinction; an age where they would come within two hours of achieving a second European trophy in the most spectacular of circumstances; a term of lost causes; a stage of total domestic dominance.

The contrasts were strikingly vivid. For every Henrik Larsson, there was a Wayne Biggins; for every Martin O'Neill, there was a John Barnes; for every Chris Sutton, there was a Tony Cascarino; for every Alan Stubbs, there was a Rafael Scheidt, for every Lubomir Moravcik, there was a Martin Hayes; for every breathtaking high, there was a depressing low. It was the best of times, it was the worst of times.

This is the story of that utterly remarkable span of time in the history of Celtic Football Club.

CHAPTER ONE

LIAM BRADY: DEALING WITH PRESSURE

It's early afternoon on Friday July 16 1993 and the Brother Walfrid restaurant at Celtic Park is as hectic as an oasis. In the welcome solitude, I have been invited to share a table with Liam Brady, the Celtic manager of two years and twenty-seven days. I like the softly spoken Dubliner; he's intelligent, thoughtful and articulate.

As Sports Editor of the Sunday Mail, the biggest-selling newspaper in Scotland at the time with close to a three-million readership, I got to know Brady shortly after his appointment as Billy McNeill's replacement. Back on June 19 1991, the accomplished seventy-two times capped Republic of Ireland midfielder looked the perfect fit for Celtic Football Club. A first time manager, certainly, but one with a sound footballing philosophy.

As a player, his sheer quality shone through with his every caress of a football. Brady was an elegant, attacking, subtle creator in the hurly-burly environment of congested midfields. It was a career that was to begin at Arsenal with a first team debut at the age of seventeen in 1973 and, a mere six years later, see him deservedly crowned the English Footballers' Player of the Year. A season later, Brady embarked on a captivating journey to Italy where he beguiled the fans of Juventus, Sampdoria, Inter Milan and Ascoli for seven years before returning to London to wind down his career at West Ham United, removing his debonair skills from the football field at the age of thirty-four.

There was no argument, Liam Brady was a class act; an authoritative, ambitious individual with the pedigree, hopefully, to put his stamp on a football club desperate to return to valued traditions.

That was then and this is now. Brady, almost suffocated by relentless squabbling within the walls of Celtic Park, is struggling. The club is in the shadow of their bitterest foes, Rangers. The Celtic manager is only too cognizant of the fact the team have endured consecutive barren years during his albeit brief period in charge. However, two years of non-success at this club constitutes a full-blown crisis. Brady accepts he is under awesome pressure.

There are the usual rumblings in the background insisting Brady is about to walk. I am well aware these suggestions are not too wide of the mark. The Celtic manager is clearly frustrated and, years later, told me he was on the brink of chucking it a few times during that particular summer. At this stage, though, with a new season on the horizon, the position is clear. It is either resign or remain and try to change it. Brady chose the latter.

The Celtic manager is now thinking positively. He is also talking expansively. Not for the first time he tells of a role that is clearly physically, mentally and emotionally draining. 'You can't fathom the sheer magnitude of this job or the size of this club until you are actually involved in it,' he admits. 'You think you can, but, believe me, you can't. The demands are with you night and day. You look at our support on a matchday, home or away, and you realise you have to cope, you have to produce. It's my job to put a formation out on the pitch that will entertain and, most importantly, be successful. So, of course, it hurts that it hasn't happened.' Significantly, and with a twinkle in his eyes, he adds, 'Yet.'

Brady is looking forward to the forthcoming three-game tour of Italy and then the friendly game against Sheffield Wednesday on July 31, which will be the season's curtain-raiser at Celtic Park. The Yorkshire club are managed by Trevor Francis, his team-mate of two years at Sampdoria. The Irishman produces a photograph of himself and Francis, a pre-match pose in the colours of their Italian club. 'This may be helpful,' he says as he passes the snap across the table. Undoubtedly, this will seem like a small illustration of the man's professionalism, but it indicates his anticipatory thinking.

We have organised an interview to publicise the encounter and he has sought out an image which will sit perfectly with the feature. These days, of course, a couple of clicks of the keyboard will produce such photographs; that was not the case back in 1993. The Daily Record and Sunday Mail would not have possessed such a snap among their library files. It would have meant the Picture Editor getting on the case and scouting one down, either from a London agency or an Italian newspaper. That could be time consuming. Brady eliminated the problem by producing a snap from his own collection.

At this stage in his pre-campaign plans, I am aware he has long identified a genuine signing target. Pat McGinlay had been involved in a wrangle with Hibs over his contract for about a year and it has now just expired. Pre-Bosman, the player wasn't permitted to simply walk away while the Edinburgh club held his registration. At this stage, though, Brady remains resolute and is confident of pushing the deal through before the competitive action gets underway with an opening league encounter coming up fast against Motherwell at Fir Park on August 7.

I am also in possession of the facts of a lot of feverish activity going on in the background in what must surely rank as one of the most bizarre transfers in the history of the club. Celtic, like any other, are well versed in the cloak-and-dagger shenanigans that will always be part and parcel of such intriguing developments. I should know what I am talking about - I was instrumental in the deal from day one.

McGinlay was anxious to quit Hibs that summer. Or, more accurately, he was desperate to join Celtic. Quite by chance, we met at the christening of a mutual friend's son on the south side of Glasgow in December 1992 and I was introduced to him as the Sunday Mail's Sports Editor. McGinlay, without preamble which I later discovered was his normal point-blank style, asked, 'Can you get me to Celtic?' I explained I was on reasonably good terms with the manager, but I didn't think Liam Brady would race out and sign a player on my recommendation. I would leave such persuasive actions to a svelte-tongued agent, eager to collect their fifteen per cent. McGinlay was undeterred. 'Will you drop my name in his ear?' This wasn't at all unusual and McGinlay certainly wasn't the first - nor the last - who would make such a request. I assured him I would. The last words McGinlay said to me as he left that day were, 'Now, don't forget.' I nodded my head.

By remarkable coincidence, I was chatting to Brady in the Celtic manager's office a week or so later and he informed me he was searching for a 'box-to-box player. Someone like Manchester United's Bryan Robson.'The bulb went on above my head; I hadn't forgotten McGinlay's plea. Brady acknowledged he was well aware of the capabilities of the player who had performed well when Hibs had beaten Celtic home and away the previous season. He had played with distinction, too, against Rangers, scoring two goals in his side's 4-3 reverse in Edinburgh in January. However, the manager was non-committal. I thought that was the end of the matter.

Unexpectedly, one morning at the Sunday Mail sports desk about a month later, my telephone shrieked to life. I picked up the receiver and the genteel Irish lilt on the other end of the line was immediately recognisable. Hibs had played a midweek game against Partick Thistle and won 3-0 with an incognito Brady, flat cap, woolly scarf and coat collar turned up, sitting in the Firhill stand. It didn't harm McGinlay's case that he knocked in two goals that chilly February evening in Maryhill. Clearly, Brady had been impressed. Until that point there had been no link with Celtic and the player. I was given the green light to break the story of the club's initial interest, but, obviously, the information could not come directly from anyone at Parkhead. Undoubtedly, the Hibs hierarchy would have interpreted that as a deliberate attempt to unsettle their player. It was a game every club played with each other.

My next move was to get in touch with McGinlay. He was absolutely delighted with the news, but, once again, you have to play what amounts to a Machiavellian role in these delicate matters. And, so, on February 21, the Sunday Mail readers were gazing at an exclusive back page story concerning Celtic and McGinlay. The headline, in big, bold print, roared: PAT'S MY BHOY; the sub-deck was: Celts line up McGinlay.

The headline was actually stronger than the story which can often be the case. It read:

'Pat McGinlay will almost certainly be quitting Hibs when his contract expires in the summer.

'And Celtic are likely to be first in the queue to sign the talented goalscoring midfielder.

'Parkhead manager Liam Brady was impressed when he watched McGinlay score two goals in the Easter Road side's 3-0 win over Partick Thistle on Tuesday. The player has never hidden his admiration of Celtic.

'He said last night: "I am concentrating 100 per cent on Hibs at the moment. I am putting all the transfer talk behind me. But I will be looking closely at my situation when my contract expires. I am 25 and I have to safeguard my family's future."

'McGinlay, signed on a free transfer from Blackpool six years ago, rejected new terms from Hibs last season. He is valued at around £500,000, but cash-strapped Celtic believe they will have the money available for McGinlay when they offload some of their own players.'

I had deliberately quoted the Hibs player, which I knew would keep the daily newspapers away from him while seeking his reaction to a breaking story. It's an old ploy, but it works. Brady would have been an outstanding poker player, so nothing would emanate from his corner. However, the main thing was the transfer was in motion; slow motion, maybe, but the wheels were turning. Celtic already had the exquisitely-gifted double-act of Paul McStay and John Collins supplying the guile in midfield and Brady had made up his mind that McGinlay would be his ideal 'box-to-box player'. He was being forced to wait until the end of the season before signing the midfielder. Then it would be the responsibility of an independent tribunal to set a precise transfer fee. It was obvious McGinlay wasn't going to move elsewhere, but nerves can be a little stretched and situations can become fraught with anxiety when these possible transfers become sagas.

Brady was in 'disguise' again when, unannounced and unnoticed, he slipped in and out of Easter Road at the beginning of March to witness Hibs losing 2-1 to Aberdeen. McGinlay, scorer of his side's goal, again impressed with his energy and endeavour against opponents who were a notch above those at Partick Thistle the last time the Celtic boss had watched the player. There were no transfer window restrictions in place at the time, of course, but it was clear to all Brady had no money of any consequence to spend on strengthening his squad. The tired, old 'biscuit tin' jibes were still in full flow, to the dismay of some and to the delight of others. There is little doubt, though, Brady, if the cash had been available, would have signed McGinlay long before the end of the season.

And so the drama rumbled on in the background with only a handful of individuals aware of what was developing. In fact, McGinlay and his wife Mags were sitting on the sofa in my front room one evening while Brady and Celtic were in Italy as they attempted to get rid of the close season rust. The player, with two young daughters to support, had been informed by Hibs they would stop paying his wages, but he would still remain their property. Extraordinarily, this was legal procedure back then. The tension must have been unbearable for the McGinlays. I told them they had to remain strong and that Brady had things in hand. Easy for me to say as my future wasn't on the line.

We had dinner at the local restaurant and came back to my place simply to shoot the breeze. The player couldn't take it any more. 'You've got to speak to Liam Brady,' he said. 'When?' I asked. 'Now!' replied a clearly exasperated McGinlay. 'He's in Italy,' I protested. 'Have you got his hotel phone number?' enquired McGinlay. 'As a matter of fact I have,' I answered. 'Please phone him. Now!' 'Pat, it's almost eleven o'clock in Bergamo and the game against Atalanta is tomorrow. He might not welcome a phone call.'

This went on for about ten minutes and I could see the strain on the player and his wife. I had the full Celtic touring itinerary so I located the number, got through to the hotel switchboard and asked for Mr Brady, of Celtic Football Club. I was informed he was in the foyer with a couple of club officials. They very helpfully hooked me up with the manager. He wasn't one bit fazed by the phone call or, I hasten to add, surprised. I explained the situation developing in my front room.

He informed me the club would be back in four days' time after the third game against Napoli and things would begin moving at pace. He reminded me, 'We need to get cash in, but I think I've got that covered.' I relayed the information to McGinlay. He still looked more than just a tad concerned. In all honesty, I couldn't blame him. A crucial piece of the jigsaw was still missing; money.

Joe Miller would soon be on his way back to Aberdeen. Celtic's 1989 Scottish Cup goalscoring hero had been hindered by injury in his last year at the club. Miller also believed he was being played out of position on the right wing during his fleeting first team appearances. I was in Brady's office when he was involved in a cat-and-mouse phone call with an individual - he was never identified - and it was clear the manager would not part with Miller to the Pittodrie club for anything less than £400,000. That was the fee and there was no room for manoeuvre. At one stage, Brady smiled and winked. I knew the £400,000 was in the bag. Now, with the club in funds, it was just a question of getting McGinlay on board and leaving it to the tribunal to determine a fee.

As anticipated, they eventually settled on £400,000 and that cash was transferred in an instant to Hibs. The Edinburgh club weren't happy, of course. They were demanding half-a-million pounds for a player who hadn't cost a penny to sign, had given six years service, had never been a top earner and was a stranger to international squads. Eventually, after the usual posturing, the furore passed and McGinlay could get on with his new career at Celtic. By the way, an agent got the full percentage for the player's transfer. I neither received nor wanted a penny. I got the story and, as a newspaperman, that was all I was looking for.

I emphasise the tale as an indication of how dramatically things had changed at the club. In the previous two years, Liam Brady was allowed to break the Celtic transfer record twice in twelve months. He paid out £1.1million for Tony Cascarino from Aston Villa and, at the start of the following season, spent £1.5million in bringing Stuart Slater to the club from West Ham. Both, it must be admitted, were resounding flops. Tony Mowbray, a name that would make its presence felt later in Celtic history, cost £1million when he joined from Middlesbrough and, through unfortunate and unforeseen circumstances on and off the pitch, he never quite made into the club's Hall of Fame, either.

Right at the start, though, it had to be admitted Celtic were taking a risk with Liam Brady, an individual blessed with awesome vision with the ball at his feet, who had never managed a football club before at any level. Also, Brady was the first manager who had never played for the club. The fans were assured by the board Celtic were moving into a new era, this was the way forward. When Billy McNeill took his leave, the board, remarkably, had no-one in mind to take his place. For the first time in the club's history, the powerbrokers awaited applications for the prestigious post. Many doubted the wisdom of this procedure, but, as ever, were willing to give it a chance.

Eventually, the list of hopefuls was trimmed to four. Tommy Craig, the previous assistant manager to McNeill and Davie Hay, threw his cap into the ring. Frank Stapleton, the former Manchester United and Arsenal marksman who had represented the Republic of Ireland seventy times, also did enough to convince the board he was worthy of an interview. Ivan Golac was a surprise candidate. The Yugoslav had managed Partizan Belgrade to their implausible 1989/90 UEFA Cup success over Celtic after scoring four goals in Glasgow in the second leg. They lost 5-4 on the night, but advanced on goal difference after a 6-6 aggregate stalemate. Those were the men Brady had to overcome in his bid to be named the seventh individual to manage Celtic in the club's history. Not one of them had ever donned the green and white hoops. The club were indeed breaking new ground.

Bizarrely, the board decided to hold all four interviews on the same day. Brady later called it a 'mind-boggling' decision. Who could argue? The candidates, in a very public manner, were given designated slots for their meetings with the selection panel and Brady, Stapleton, Golac and Craig, although he had been around long enough to have an inkling, must have been more than just a tad bemused to see the media circus camped on the Celtic Park doorstep as they came and went at their appointed hours.

Brady was invited back for a private meeting with club chairman Jack

McGinn and Chief Executive Terry Cassidy. He took along his solicitor and recalled, 'I asked a lot of questions. In the first, they had been doing the asking. They offered me the job, I accepted and I was the centre of attention by the time I got back to London. The fact I was the new Celtic manager had already been on national news. I think I got the job because the field of runners and riders didn't have great track records, without being disrespectful to any of them. Frank Stapleton was one of them who, like myself, was keen to get into management. Tommy Craig had the disadvantage of having been there and again, in a kind of overt political stance by the board, they wanted to move away from what had been to something new.'

Brady, in fact, kept Craig as his No.2 while bringing in his former Irish team-mate Mick Martin, a man of many clubs including Manchester United and Newcastle United. Martin's role was that of first team coach. It was an interesting ensemble that took their seats in the dug-out at Tolka Park on July 20 for the game against Shelbourne, the first of four friendlies against Irish opposition as the new-look Celtic management made its debut. Around 10,000 fans squeezed into the ground to witness the moment, a 3-0 canter for Celtic with Tony Cascarino making his debut. Two goals from Charlie Nicholas and one from Stevie Fulton sealed the victory with both teams going through the basic motions.

Three days later, Brady gave Cascarino a second outing and rotated attackers such as Jacki Dziekanowski, Andy Walker, John Hewitt and Gerry Creaney against Cork City. Astoundingly, Celtic drew a blank as they capitulated 2-0 to their opponents, who were managed by former Celt Mike Conroy. Brady, in an instant, realised he had a job on his hands. A goalless draw with Dundalk followed and the mini-tour was wrapped up with a 2-0 win over Shamrock Rovers where Cascarino netted his first goal for the club with Nicholas adding the other.

Brady returned to Highbury on July 30 for the Testimonial Match for Arsenal defender Paul Davis and admitted later he was 'utterly astonished' at the support from the Celtic fans. It was estimated 10,000 had turned up to swell the 30,000 crowd, but those in London on the night remain convinced the away support actually dwarfed that of the home fans. It was exciting fare for one of these occasions where no-one wants to sustain an injury of any sort with a new season only weeks away.

Nicholas, former darling of the North Bank, bamboozled goalkeeper David Seaman with an effort that dipped onto the crossbar before opening the scoring in the eleventh minute. Arsenal, the English champions, came back to level through Alan Smith three minutes after the turnaround and Lee Dixon snapped up the rebound from a Pat Bonner penalty save to shoot his side into the lead in the seventieth minute. It ended all-square when Dariusz Wdowcyzk zoomed an unstoppable long-range free-kick high past the helpless Seaman. Brady had one remaining fixture to fulfil as he prepared his team for the campaign ahead - an August 4 meeting with Spurs in front of a crowd of 23,365 at Celtic Park. John Collins claimed the only strike of the occasion in the fourth minute in what, in truth, was a fairly pedestrian performance from both teams.

Now it was time for the real deal; Brady's competitive managerial baptism for Celtic. It was an intriguing situation as he took his team to Tayside for the opening Premier League encounter against Dundee United at Tannadice on August 10. The Irishman stepped into the dug-out for minute one of his new career while Jim McLean, just a few yards along the touchline, was in his twentieth year as manager of United. The contrasts couldn't have been more stark. A crowd of 16,535 were shoe-horned into the ground with Brian McGinlay being handed the refereeing duties.

Brady chose his formation carefully against a team that had completed the previous season in joint third place alongside the Hoops on forty-one points. Pat Bonner, Brady's former Republic of Ireland team-mate, got the nod in goal with Chris Morris, Derek Whyte, Dariusz Wdowcyzk and Anton Rogan as the back four. With Paul McStay injured, the mid-three were Stevie Fulton, Peter Grant and John Collins and, in an exceptionally adventurous formation, Tommy Coyne, Tony Cascarino and Charlie Nicholas were the three-man strike-force.

Within seventeen minutes Tannadice was rocking; Celtic were two goals ahead and displaying some devastating and intricate offensive football. The opening goal arrived in the ninth minute and, while it wasn't the product of any silky soccer or strategies from the training ground, it was still welcoming. Rogan hurled in a long throw from the left, Cascarino made a nuisance of himself in the penalty box, Coyne flicked it on and Nicholas, only a couple of yards out, steered a header beyond Alan Main. Coyne doubled the advantage with a measured right-foot shot from outside the box with the ball flying low in at the keeper's left hand post. Referee McGinlay then awarded United a penalty-kick ten minutes later when he spotted an infringement in the box as Celtic defended a left-wing corner-kick. Michael O'Neill made no mistake with an expertly-taken effort that soared high to Bonner's left as the keeper took off for his right.

Just on half-time, though, Collins restored the visitors' two-goal lead, Now, this was a beauty. Collins created it with a swift pass inside to Gerry Creaney, on for the limping Cascarino in thirty-eight minutes, and he laid a return pass into the tracks of the midfielder who launched a left-foot twenty-five yard drive into the top corner. A platoon of custodians couldn't have kept that effort out of the net. Jim McLean, the longest-serving manager in the league, decided on a more direct approach after the turnaround. He replaced Hamish French with Mixu Paatelainen and no-one in the ground believed it was to add culture to his forward line. The Finn was an old-fashioned battering-ram of a centre-forward and he lined up with Duncan Ferguson, another front player who would never win awards for finesse.

Within four minutes United were back in the game and Brady must have winced at the ease at which they scored. The defence made a mess of attempting to clear a routine shy chucked in from the left. The ball eventually dropped invitingly for O'Neill to fire low past Bonner. Alarmingly, it was all-square in the sixty-eighth minute. David Bowman lobbed over an angled ball from the right and Ferguson, virtually unchallenged in front of goal, rose to sizzle a header beyond Bonner. Clearly, after an excellent start, things were not going according to plan. In the midst of the impending wreckage, Brady looked calmness personified as he surveyed the scene and sized up the situation from the touchline.

It was obvious Paatelainen and Ferguson were creating havoc with their up-and-at-'em approach. It wasn't easy on the eye, but United, to be fair, now had twenty-two minutes to turn the contest completely on its head. Whyte and Wdowczyk, two ball-playing central defenders, were being rag-dolled. Brady couldn't miss the red flags and, in the seventy-second minute, he put on Mike Galloway for Fulton and the substitute raced directly into the middle of the Celtic rearguard to shore up the defence. It worked a treat. Four minutes from time Collins nailed the points when Creaney headed down into his path and his first-time left-foot drive thundered past the desperately-diving Main.

'If all the games are going to be like that, then we are in for a helluva season,' summed up Brady, almost breathless at the finish. The new Celtic manager, though, had just witnessed the uneven mix that had cost Billy McNeill his job that summer. Exciting and extravagant going forward; frustrating and exasperating in defence. The midfield was a lot happier on the front foot, too. Celtic could score goals, but, as Brady had just experienced, they could chuck them in with a frightening generosity at the other end, too. In the following fifteen league games, Bonner picked the ball out of his net on fifteen occasions. Crucially, two goals conceded came in the opening Old Firm game of the season as Rangers triumphed 2-0 at Parkhead in August and he was beaten again in the 1-1 draw at Ibrox in November.

Cultured central defender Paul Elliott had already been sold to Chelsea in the summer without Brady's knowledge, but the club tried to balance that by bringing in Gary Gillespie from Liverpool. It is often quoted that the tall, graceful Scot cost Celtic £925,000, but, in effect, he was signed without a transfer fee being paid. Injury had wrecked the thirty-one-year-old's career at Anfield and Liverpool were keen to offload him to any club who would pick up his wages. Celtic agreed and, unfortunately, the player continued to be plagued by setbacks at Parkhead. He played in five successive games around the beginning of the season, making his debut against his former club

Falkirk in August, a 4-1 stroll for the Hoops in which he scored one of his two goals for the club. He missed the next two games, came back for three and was sidelined again. It was the story of his frustrating stay at the club he had always claimed were his 'boyhood favourites'. He turned out sixty-nine times in a three-year period and never did himself justice in the green-and-white hoops.

In desperation, Brady tried a new double-act with Brian O'Neil partnering Mike Galloway for an October 19 meeting with Falkirk at Brockville. The new pairing misfired with disastrous consequences as Celtic lost 4-3. Barry Smith, an untested seventeen year old, was introduced for the first time as the Celtic manager shuffled his defence, still searching for a settled formula. Clearly, the debutant wasn't the answer to even a fraction of the problem. Smith, in fact, made only twenty appearances in four years at the club before being released. Midfielders Paul McStay, with two, and John Collins took on the mantle of scorers while their opponents gleefully bundled the goals behind Pat Bonner.

The situation transferred from grey to jet black for Brady three nights later when he presided over Celtic's worst-ever result in Europe. The 5-1 mauling against Neuchatel Xamax was only surpassed in Gordon Strachan's first competitive game as the club's manager when they collapsed 5-0 to Artmedia Bratislava in a Champions League qualifier in 2005. In Switzerland, fourteen years earlier, Brady could only stare into the headlights of certain European doom. To say his formation was shambolic would be kind. He deployed Daruisz Wdowcyzk behind Derek Whyte and Mark McNally in a new-look central defence and it back-fired horribly. Three goals adrift before the interval, Celtic were being humiliated by a team of journeymen who would be dismantled 4-1 on aggregate in the following round by Real Madrid. The next goal would be absolutely critical and yet the defence was wide open when Hossam Hassan, who scored four on the night, latched onto a long high ball and fired past a badly-positioned Pat Bonner. The keeper didn't look too clever, either, sixteen minutes from time when he allowed a low shot to squirm from his grasp and Hassan delightedly tucked the gift into the inviting net.

Tony Cascarino's performance against the Swiss defied description. A 6ft 3in, thirteen-stone striker being pushed and bullied by the opposition was not what Brady expected when he broke the transfer record to sign him in the summer. The flop frontman put it this way. 'When I wasn't giving the ball away, I was tripping over myself. Liam pulled me off in the second-half. The fans had a real go as we walked off the pitch. Liam was incensed in the dressing room. His team had played shamefully. His first managerial signing was making a mockery of him. "What the hell is going on, Tony? You were a disaster. I've never seen you play so badly."'

Cascarino uttered the immortal retort, 'Yeah, I dunno. I was just crap.' No-one bothered to argue.

And yet Brady believed Brian O'Neil's superbly-headed consolation goal could yet provide the springboard to launch Celtic to an unlikely comeback triumph in Glasgow a fortnight later. 'If we get an early goal, it will change the complexion of the game completely,' he reasoned. 'There's still a chance we can do something here.' And he would have got his wish if it hadn't been for the waywardness of Charlie Nicholas, presented with a penalty-kick opportunity in only four minutes. It was inconceivable that such a gifted ball-playing performer could actually miss the entire target from twelve yards, but Charlie did it with some aplomb, his dreadful effort skied so high it was more of a threat to the floodlights than it was the Neuchatel goalkeeper. The Swiss knew it was going to be their night thereafter and even a second-half counter from Joe Miller hardly knocked them out of their stride. In the end, alas, it was a futile attempt by Celtic.

There is little doubt the defeat did a lot to affect Brady's credibility with the support. They had witnessed the team concede four to an ordinary Falkirk team on the Saturday and then throw five into the net against an average Swiss side three days later. The manager was savvy enough to realise he was already looking down the barrel of a gun. Neuchatel had been only his nineteenth competitive game in charge and, even for a fledgling manager, the honeymoon period was well and truly over. Suddenly, his tactics were being scutinised and the word 'naive' was coming to the fore regularly.

It had been a similar story when the League Cup run came to an abrupt halt in the first week of September against Airdrie at Broomfield. Celtic had beaten Morton 4-2 at Cappielow and Raith Rovers 3-1 in Glasgow to reach the third round. Airdrie, on their tight, awkward pitch which virtually eliminated wing play, were always a tough proposition. Brady, still looking for a goal from the club's most expensive signing Cascarino, kept faith with the Irish international and teamed him with Nicholas. After extra-time, it was still goalless and it went to the dreaded penalty-kick showdown. Celtic's kickers were wasteful and the club tumbled into the competition's obscurity after losing 4-2.

Brady knew he urgently required an injection of steel in the middle of his backline. The man he believed would provide the answer was a twenty-seven-year-old no-frills back-four operator by the name of Tony Mowbray, who had previously played his ten-year career at Middlesbrough. A cheque for £1 million was signed and Mowbray made a solid debut in a 2-1 win over Aberdeen in Glasgow on November 9. Eoin Jess silenced the 36,837 fans with the opening goal in the eleventh minute, but Charlie Nicholas levelled three minutes later and substitute Gerry Creaney got the winner shortly after the hour mark.

A week later, Celtic crashed 3-1 against Hearts at Tynecastle. It was their fifth league defeat of the season and, worryingly, it looked as though the battle for the title would be buried under the rubble of mediocrity before the turn of the year. And so, unfortunately, it proved. An inadequate team, lacking inspiration, limped along towards the turn of the year shedding points in stalemates against Motherwell (2-2), Hibs (0-0), Dundee United (1-1) and Aberdeen (2-2). However, they believed they could salvage something from a desperate situation when Rangers were Parkhead's first-footers on the opening day of 1992. A crowd of 51,383 was in attendance for what was a must-win game for the Hoops.

Brady would regularly scoff at the lack of the traditional luck of the Irish when he needed it most and he did deserve some sympathy after a 3-1 defeat on this occasion. Rangers were in the enviable situation of being able to field a team with seven players costing £1 million or more while Celtic still had the awful Cascarino lumbering around up front, basically getting in his team-mates' way. It was heading for a goalless first-half when Dale Gordon, on the right, picked out an unguarded Hateley, deep in the danger zone with a calamitous defence spreadeagled. The Englishman botched his shot and struck the ball into the ground. It bounced once and, uncannily, fell to McCoist right in front of goal and he couldn't miss.

There was a lifeline, though, when Tony Mowbray thundered a header past Goram from a corner-kick and the game tilted in the favour of Brady's men. With thirteen minutes to go, Cascarino made his only genuine telling contribution to the game. Unfortunately, it was Rangers who benefited. He sent a reckless pass inside which was intercepted by John Brown who switched it in front of McCoist. The Ibrox raider never required too much persuasion to go sprawling inside a penalty area and he did so again under a challenge from keeper Gordon Marshall, bought from Falkirk for £270,000 to replace Pat Bonner six games earlier. Referee George Smith, from Edinburgh, bought into the penalty shout and pointed to the spot. Hateley dispatched it low past Marshall to his right. A minute into injury time, Brown sauntered forward, Derek Whyte and Co backed off and invited him to have a go. He did just that and with a swish of his left boot he thumped a drive into the net via the left hand post.

The match official booked four players, all from Celtic, in what was hardly a roughhouse occasion. Marshall, for his tussle with McCoist, Mike Galloway, Mark McNally and Mowbray. The last named could hardly complain about his yellow card. He dived into Hateley and left him in a heap on the muddy surface. As one TV commentator put it, 'That tackle from Mowbray wasn't so much late as posthumous.'

Brady, stubbornly, refused to throw in the towel. Celtic were now trailing the Ibrox side by ten points and were also adrift of Hearts who were due in Glasgow three days later. 'There's still a chance,' urged the manager. Ninety minutes later, the league race, as far as Celtic were concerned, was over. The Tynecastle side, under the cosh for most of the first-half, scored two goals in a minute and went onto win 2-1.

The dozy back lot contributed heavily once again to the team's misery. Just before the hour mark, Chris Morris and McNally got involved in some suicidal passing just outside their own penalty box. The defenders were treating the ball like a live hand grenade and John Robertson intervened, passed wide to Tosh McKinlay who picked out Scott Crabbe and his curling effort completely eliminated the stretching Marshall. Sixty seconds later, the keeper was fishing the ball out of the net after Robertson had set up John Millar. John Collins pulled one back near the end, but, once again, the Celtic fans streamed out of the ground in silence while 7,000 Hearts fans whooped it up. Cascarino never started another game for the club and was swapped for Chelsea left-back Tommy Boyd in February.

Brady now had seventeen largely meaningless league games to look forward to. That hadn't been in the script back at Tannadice in August. Remarkably, the team, with the pressure off, embarked on a sixteen-game unbeaten run until the last match of the campaign when they went down 2-1 against Hibs at Easter Road. The highlight, naturally enough, was the 2-0 victory over Rangers at Ibrox in March; Brady at last tasting the joys of an Old Firm win. Even better, it was thoroughly deserved against a Walter Smith team that was odds on to stretch their unbeaten run to twenty games.

The heavens opened over Govan that grey afternoon, but nothing could put a dampener on an illuminating Celtic performance. Charlie Nicholas got the breakthrough goal with a scorching first-time drive from the edge of the box after Nisbett had frantically headed a Chris Morris cross into his tracks. Nicholas belted it with his right foot and the rain water was shaking loose off the net behind Goram before he could move. That pulverising effort in the thirty-second minute gave the visitors the initiative at the interval, but, in truth, they could have been three in front at that stage. Gerry Creaney missed with a badly-placed header from close range and Tommy Boyd, making his first appearance in the hectic Glasgow derby, might have netted when he sneaked in at the far post to get on the end of a Nicholas right-wing cross, but he screwed his effort off target from six yards. Even this early in his Hoops career, it was evident scoring goals was not going to be the defender's forte.

Three minutes before the hour mark, the Celtic supporters were taunting their Rangers counterparts with chants of 'Easy...Easy' after Brady had witnessed his team doubling their lead. Paul McStay drifted in from the old inside-right position, shrugging off Spackman, before sliding a pass in front of Creaney. He moved away from John Brown, steadied himself and then rifled a low right-foot shot away from Goram. Celtic controlled the encounter throughout and Gordon Marshall had one of his easiest afternoons of the term.

Nicholas said, 'Liam Brady simply told us to go out and play. He knew we could do this, turn it on against Rangers. He told us to have no fears. Listen, we've lost here 5-1 and 4-0 in recent years and there must have been a dread about coming back to Ibrox. But after this win we'll be looking forward to returning to Ibrox.'

It was an impressive display from Celtic and had the fans wondering of what might have been if the ball had bounced for them earlier in the campaign. In the end, though, eight defeats and ten draws consigned them to third place, ten points adrift of their old foes and one behind Hearts when it was still two points for a win and one for a draw.

Once again, the Scottish Cup looked the club's best bet for silverware. Charlie Nicholas put it this way, 'The Cup is so important because around January time in the past we've been out of running for the title. We've built our hopes on winning the trophy and this year is no different. I would say this has been my best season since 1983 and, having won two Cups with Aberdeen, I want to win the Cup with Celtic. There's a unity among the players, a good spirit in the dressing room and we think we're capable of doing something to help Celtic get back on top.'

Hat-tricks from Gerry Creaney and Tommy Coyne helped Celtic breeze past the first hurdle, Montrose losing 6-0 at Parkhead on January 25. Creaney and Coyne were on target again when Dundee United were dismissed 2-1 on a Tuesday evening in February in Glasgow. There were just five minutes remaining and, with the score deadlocked at 1-1, Joe Miller delivered a peach of a cross from wide on the right. Coyne's timing was impeccable as he rose above friend and foe to scorch a header into the far corner. Creaney had claimed the opener in the twenty-fifth minute when Tannadice keeper Guido van de Kamp blundered as he flapped at a left-wing corner-kick from Mike Galloway. The Dutchman gave it the bar of soap treatment and Creaney nodded in from practically under the crossbar. United's reply was instantaneous when Mixu Paatelainen steered a close-range drive past the motionless Gordon Marshall.

Creaney was unstoppable in the tournament and fired in two more in the 3-0 victory over Morton in the home quarter-final. The striker, who, sadly, never realised his true potential and would have his moments of friction with Brady, took his total to six with a simple tap-in for the sixth minute opener and a blistering right-foot drive from outside the box for the second just before the turnaround. John Collins killed off the brave part-timers with a third after pouncing on a slack passback from Graham Ogg and sliding the ball under the advancing David Wylie,

Celtic went into the semi-final draw with Rangers, Hearts and Airdrie. Brady was desperate to play Rangers in the Scottish Cup Final, totally convinced his team would beat anything Walter Smith put up against them. The Irishman saw that possibility as being afforded the opportunity to bring down the curtain on a testing campaign with a bit of a flourish and to give the supporters some optimism for a new campaign. Unfortunately, the semi-final paired them with the men from Ibrox. And what an encounter that turned out to be at storm-lashed Hampden Park on the evening of March 31. The stark facts show that Rangers won 1-0 with a goal from McCoist after playing with ten men for eighty-three minutes. That doesn't tell you half the story.

David Robertson was red-carded in the seventh minute for clattering into Joe Miller, the left-back clearly a solemn believer of stopping his man at all costs. The Celtic winger had neatly dummied the ball and was poised for a run down the touchline before he was crudely dumped on the sodden turf. Referee Andrew Waddell had no alternative but to point Robertson in the direction of the dressing room. Celtic attacked with a gusto, but, frustratingly, couldn't make their possession pay dividends for huge chunks of the first-half. There was little doubt Brady would be having words with the players at the interval.

It got worse, though, when McCoist netted right on the half-time whistle. He first-timed a low pass from Stuart McCall from twelve yards and Gordon Marshall threw himself to his right to get a touch to the shot. Agonisingly, it swept beyond him, kissed the inside of the right-hand post and rolled into the net. It was an eager Celtic that kicked off the second-half. Brian O'Neil sent in a rasping long-range drive that took a slight deflection before zipping past a static Andy Goram only to smack against the base of the upright and rebound to safety. Paul McStay also left the Rangers keeper standing with a ferocious eighteen-yarder, but this time the ball battered the crossbar.

However, the most contentious decision went against Celtic when John Brown clearly scythed down John Collins as the midfielder wriggled into a shooting position in the penalty area. The match official had an excellent view of the incident and, incredibly, waved play on. Former Rangers skipper Terry Butcher, who had left the club six months beforehand to join Coventry City, was in the Sky commentary box that evening. His verdict? 'I thought that was a clear-cut penalty-kick.' Waddell might have been the only man at the national stadium who thought there had been no infringement. Minutes later it was all over and Celtic were out. The entire campaign was as good as over with that emphatic shrill of Waddell's whistle. There was sympathy for Brady and the players, but the nagging thought persisted that Celtic should have done so much better against opposition who had to face playing almost the entire game a man short.

As the season rolled to a halt, first-time manager Brady now fully realised what dug-out veterans meant when they oft repeated, 'Success as a team boss will always come down to two things - results and transfers.' The results hadn't gone Celtic's way, that was obvious. And a lot was made of Tony Cascarino, the club's £1.1 million signing. Celtic fans had to wait until October 5 for his first goal for the club after coming on as a sixty-sixth minute substitute for Charlie Nicholas against Hearts at Parkhead. Two minutes after his appearance, he rolled the ball into an empty net for the clinching goal in the 3-1 win. Five minutes later, he was sent off by referee Jim McCluskey after elbowing Tynecastle defender Craig Levein in the face. It appeared the London-born player could do no right in the green and white.

He scored four goals - one against Rangers in the 1-1 draw at Ibrox in November - in thirty appearances and was quoted as saying, 'Celtic played too much football to suit my game.' It was a ludicrous statement from Cascarino, but he got it right when he said, 'I was banging away the goals for fun in training, but that's no good, is it? As soon as I got on the park on a Saturday, I couldn't hit a cow's backside with a banjo.'

In fairness to Brady, he put himself under as much close examination as Cascarino when he persuaded the board to write the cheque for a player who had scored a mere twelve goals in fifty games for Aston Villa which was not an inspiring statistic for an out-and-out striker. Brady had also been the player's agent for a spell, so must have been confident of his major signing providing the goods. He got that wrong. But, while Brady and Cascarino were scrutinised, across the Clyde, Walter Smith would be given a blank chequebook and paid out £6.85million in signing six players with £2.2million alone going on Alexei Mikhailichenko from Sampdoria. Stuart McCall (Everton), Dale Gordon (Norwich City), Andy Goram (Hibs), David Robertson (Aberdeen) and Paul Rideout (Notts County) were also shipped in.

The football world now knows where such profligacy eventually led the club, but that was hardly Liam Brady's concern at the time. The Celtic manager had enough to occupy his thoughts after a gruelling and intense introduction to life in the dug-out.

CHAPTER TWO
THE BRADY BUNCH

Liam Brady beamed as he ushered Stuart Slater, Andy Payton and Rudi Vata into Parkhead on the same day in mid-August 1992. He introduced the trio and exclaimed, 'This is now my Celtic team.' The words were well intentioned, but, by the end of his second tumultuous season, they had a distinctly hollow ring to them.

Attacking midfielder Slater became the club's latest record signing at £1.5million when he joined from West Ham United. The Irishman, who knew the player from his latter playing days at the London club, enthused, 'Stuart is an exciting individual who will get bums on seats and bums up off seats.' It wasn't the most eloquent endorsement of the player's talents, but, clearly, Brady believed he had delivered a signing coup. Thirteen months later Slater was sold to Ipswich Town for half of Celtic's initial outlay.

Payton was a striker who, in fact, had interested Billy McNeill at one stage before choosing to remain in England and sign for Middlesbrough after leaving Hull City the previous year in a £750,000 deal. He was a straight swap for Republic of Ireland right-back Chris Morris who had been popular with the support, particularly during the double-winning Centenary Year. Payton's season-long stay at Ayresome Park hadn't been a success and he was more than happy to pack up and cross Hadrian's Wall to sample Scottish football when Brady made his move. The versatile Vata's route to the east end of Glasgow was slightly more circuitous when he became one of seven Albanian internationals who decided to defect after a European Championship tie against France in Paris the previous March.

Derek Whyte commanded a £900,000 transfer fee when he joined Morris at Middlesbrough. The versatile Whyte, who could play left-back and centre-half, had been introduced to the first team as a seventeen year old by Billy McNeill in 1986 and was all set to commit his future to the club when his contract was close to expiring. I chatted with Whyte in a Glasgow hotel and this normally happy-go-lucky character was grim-faced on this occasion. He told me he wanted to stay at Celtic, but the board's terms had been 'insulting' while adding, 'I feel like I have just been kicked in the balls.' I caught his drift.

Brady had made no inroads during the summer on the transfer front while he spent the bulk of his time attempting to persuade Paul McStay to sign a new long-term contract at the club. The midfielder known as 'The Maestro' had excelled for Scotland during the European Championship Finals in Sweden with undeniably fine displays against world champions Germany, European title holders Holland and the remnants of the fractured USSR, calling itself CIS, (Commonwealth of Independent States). The Scots lost the first two encounters, but McStay was unstoppable against the CIS and netted a wonderful long-range effort as Andy Roxburgh's side triumphed 3-0.

During that summer's most avidly followed guessing game, I was kept up to speed about the teams casting envious glances in the direction of the Hoops captain. There was genuine interest from Italy, Germany and France, but, McStay, about to become a first-time father, wasn't going to be easily swayed. Despite the team's indifferent form and their lack of silverware success, McStay still saw himself as a Celtic player. Brady went to work and I was invited to the Celtic boardroom one afternoon to be told the exclusive news that McStay had agreed a new contract. Brady got his man, McStay got his wishes and I got the story. Everyone was happy, for the time being.

During the summer, Rangers, attempting to win five championships in a row, had added to their squad by paying £2.4million to Marseille for England international midfielder Trevor Steven, curiously only one year after selling the player to the French club for more than double that fee. Walter Smith was happy enough to spend £1.3million to bring back central defender Dave McPherson from Hearts and £300,000 to Motherwell for keeper Ally Maxwell as a back-up to Andy Goram. Brady realised he couldn't possibly compete at those prices.

There were no extravagant promises from the manager as Celtic went into a campaign in the realisation the previous three years had been a vacuum as far as trophies were concerned. The opening league confrontation was against Hearts in Edinburgh. Peculiarly, four of the club's opening six Premier encounters were away from home. After Tynecastle, there was a midweek trip to Pittodrie, back-to-back home games against Motherwell and Dundee United and then trips to Ibrox and Broomfield. The Celtic bosses voiced their concern, but the powers-that-be once again blamed the dreaded computer.

No matter. Celtic got off to a winning start on August 1 when Craig Levein diverted the ball past his own keeper Henry Smith for the only goal of the game. There was the odd sight of Roy Aitken clattering into Celtic players the following Wednesday. The powerhouse, affectionately known as 'The Bear' by the Hoops followers, had signed for Aberdeen a mere two years after leaving Parkhead for Newcastle. Davie Hay, then the St Mirren manager, ambitiously brought him back to Scotland after only one season on Tyneside. The Dons then lured him north and were happy to set him loose on his former colleagues. Gerry Creaney hit Celtic's goal in a creditable 1-1 draw. It was far too early for rampant optimism, but three points from a possible four after visits to Tynecastle and Pittodrie augured well.

And then Motherwell took a point at Parkhead. Tony Mowbray opened the scoring and Celtic looked comfortably in cruise control. Davie Cooper produced one fine crossball all afternoon and it caused consternation in the Celtic defence. Steve Kirk rose to flight a header past Gordon Marshall and a point was carelessly discarded. On the same day, Rangers struggled to a goalless stalemate against Hibs at Easter Road. A week later, Celtic were top of the Premier League, the first time they had occupied that spot for an extremely long and excruciating period.

Two opportunist goals from Gerry Creaney, playing alongside Andy Payton for the first time, toppled Dundee United 2-0 in Glasgow while their Ibrox adversaries were being shredded 4-3 by newly-promoted Dundee at Dens Park. Coincidentally, Brady's former Arsenal team-mate Graham Rix, at the age of thirty-four, was the most accomplished performer on the pitch. Now all eyes were on the first Old Firm skirmish of the season at Ibrox on August 22.

Stuart Slater would have to be a content with a spot on the substitutes' bench before making a second-half appearance in place of Payton. There was still no sign of Rudi Vata - by now nicknamed, imaginatively, 'Holy' by the support - who was not deemed to be fully match-fit by Brady. The encounter was tied at 1-1 when the full-time whistle brought a halt to the action. Celtic, for the second successive occasion at the home of their greatest rivals, had more than acquitted themselves. There was an assured look about the team and, but for a momentary lapse in concentration in defence, they could have celebrated another victory on enemy soil.

Gerry Creaney just about lifted the roof off the net when he put Celtic ahead in the fifty-third minute. A Mark McNally cross from the right was deflected into the air by John Brown and the striker's timing was impeccable as he raced through the heart of the defence to hit the ball with a ferocious dunt as it dropped at his feet a mere six yards out. Andy Goram didn't move a muscle. With twenty-one minutes to go, the defence clocked off when Peter Huistra was allowed to race down the left wing and hurl over a back post cross which was knocked down by Mark Hateley and Ian Durrant, with no green-and-white jerseys in the vicinity, was allowed to first-time a drive high past Gordon Marshall.

Celtic had the opportunity of completing six league games of the season while remaining unbeaten when they travelled to take on the troublesome Airdrie at ramshackle Broomfield. The signs looked good with Paul McStay and John Collins in charge in the middle of the park while the home side's keeper John Martin was the busiest player on the field with a handful of superb saves. Andy Payton opened the scoring while claiming his first goal for the club in the twentieth minute with a whizzbang effort following a long, deep ball from Dariusz Wdowczyk. Brady was confident enough on the hour mark to shove on Slater for Joe Miller, but calamity struck three minutes later when the home side levelled. John Boyle drove a low shot past Marshall and, try as they might, Celtic could not get a winner on a ground where they rarely flourished. It might have been some consolation at the end of the campaign when Airdrie were relegated.

Amazingly, the draw saw Brady's men slump from the pinnacle to fourth place. Dundee United moved into pole position on nine points, Rangers, Hearts and Celtic all had eight points, but the men from Govan and Gorgie had better goal differences. Brady was discovering the fine margins between success and failure in the beautiful game. Interestingly, he left Tommy Coyne and Charlie Nicholas at home to play for the reserves on the same afternoon. Coyne netted two and Nicholas another in a 5-1 win. Also on the scoresheet was Rudi Vata, working his way into top team contention at a steady rate.

Celtic eased into September and goals from Collins (2) and Creaney gave them a 3-1 success against St Johnstone in Glasgow, but, without warning, they lost two of their next three encounters. Making matters worse was the fact that both games were in front of their own support at Parkhead. The 3-2 defeat from Hibs was simply unacceptable, a disgraceful surrender. Brady's team were strolling to both points until the occasion turned on its head in the sixty-fifth minute when the Edinburgh side levelled at 2-2 and, seven minutes from the end, the visitors were gifted a ridiculous third. Manager Alex Miller was delighted to learn afterwards it was the first time since the mid-sixties Hibs had managed to score more than two goals in the east end of Glasgow.

Dariusz Wdowcyzk, with what was now becoming a trademark free-kick, bamboozled veteran keeper John Burridge with a near-post effort, but that was nullified when a wayward header out of defence fell to Keith Wright and he drilled the equaliser past Gordon Marshall. Shortly after the interval, Paul McStay executed a perfect scissors-kick and once again Burridge was left scampering across his line as the ball found the net at his far post. Things were going so well until Celtic discovered the seemingly-inevitable banana skin.

Marshall made a complete hash of a passback from Tommy Boyd and looped the ball high up into the air. Darren Jackson raced in to put on the pressure and the shotstopper compounded his error by pulling his rival to the surface. It was a certain penalty-kick and Jackson swept his effort wide of Marshall. With seven minutes remaining, Stuart Slater, making his first start, gave the ball away deep in Hibs territory. One pass out, though, left Tony Mowbray in a one-on-one with Wright. The centre-back still looked favourite to clear his lines, but he allowed the Hibs striker to nip the ball round him, Marshall was less than convincing as he tried to take the ball off the opponent's toe. Wright squared it to Gareth Evans, whose first shot was blocked on the line by Wdowczyk. Unfortunately, it rebounded straight back to Evans who, on this occasion, made no mistake as he walloped the ball into the empty net. It was an awful way to lose the first league game of the campaign at the eighth hurdle.

Publicly, Brady said something along the lines of 'I'm disappointed and we know we should have done so much better.' Privately, he lambasted his players for a dire, feeble display and let them know it would not be tolerated. Some of his words, unfortunately, fell on deaf ears.

It was no surprise Pat Bonner returned to goal for the next game against Falkirk at Brockville a week later following Gordon Marshall's appalling performance against Hibs. However, it was hardly a grand reintroduction for the Irish international, now in the veteran stage at the age of thirty-four. He was forced to pick the ball out of the net four times, but was rescued when two goals from Gerry Creaney and others from Dariusz Wdowczyk, with a penalty-kick, Andy Payton and John Collins, in the last minute, gave Celtic an unlikely 5-4 triumph. Four days later, any hopes of joy in the League Cup were erased.

Celtic had reached the semi-final with wins over Stirling Albion (3-0), Dundee (1-0) and Hearts (2-1) and were within ninety minutes of Brady's first Cup Final in Scotland. Tony Mowbray had toiled against Hibs and Falkirk with the team conceding seven goals and his name was nowhere to be seen on the team sheet as Mike Galloway partnered Gary Gillespie in the heart of the defence against the Dons. It was not an inspirational pairing. Brady, laudably, went for flair in midfield with Slater, McStay and Collins his preferred combination against a strong, dour Pittodrie side with Roy Aitken again in their line-up.

One goal decided the tie and once again lamentable defending by the Celtic back lot contributed hugely to the downfall. Aberdeen won a corner-kick on the right just five minutes from the interval. It was no surprise that the ball was aimed at Mixu Paatelainen, the burly former Dundee United striker. What may have been surprising, though, was that the Finn, who did his best work in the air, wasn't picked up by any opponent. Gillespie may have been 6ft 3in, but he rarely attacked aerial threats, much preferring the ball at his feet. Paatelainen, untroubled and unhindered, was allowed to run from the eighteen-yard line to get his head to the ball to knock it fiercely past the unprotected Pat Bonner. John Collins scrambled it off the line, but, as luck would have it, the ball fell directly to Eoin Jess six yards out and he lashed it home.

Celtic huffed and puffed throughout the second-half, but to no avail. The Dons, with Alex McLeish and Aitken performing stoutly, held out for the victory. They carelessly undid all their hard work against Brady's men when they lost 2-1 in the Final to Rangers. Central defender Gary Smith, bewilderingly, launched himself at a left-wing cross to sizzle a header behind keeper Theo Snelders for the Ibrox club's winner six minutes from the end of extra-time. Jimmy McGrory would have been proud to have claimed that as one of his own.

After the League Cup exit, the pressure was piling on Brady. Mowbray was back in place three days later when Partick Thistle, who would complete the league campaign seven points away from relegation, came visiting. Unbelievably, they celebrated their first-ever Premier League triumph at the home of Celtic and, equally outrageously, their winning goal in a 2-1 victory came from yet another simple and straightforward corner-kick. Celtic weren't even into the third month of the season and the dark clouds were already gathering in the east end of Glasgow.

Bonner was beginning to look decidedly wobbly, especially at crossballs, and, predictably, the Firhill side took the lead when he was caught out at his near post as George Shaw knocked in a header. Payton levelled early in the second-half, Collins smacked the woodwork with a twenty-two yard free-kick, Boyd missed with a free header from six yards and, only five minutes from time, Thistle were practically invited to take the points across Glasgow. Davie Kinnaird swung in a left-wing corner-kick, Davie Irons nodded it down with Bonner flapping in no-man's land and Shaw prodded home from six yards. A crowd of 21,486 had been in attendance at the kick-off, but Celtic Park was a virtual ghost town by the end. The fans, having watched their team lose back-to-back home league games against Inferior opposition while enduring a League Cup banishment, streamed towards the exits as soon as Shaw's effort strangled itself in the net. It was obvious they had little faith in this line-up to turn things around. And so it proved.

Remarkably, in the midst of all this carnage, Celtic produced a truly magnificent performance in the UEFA Cup against Cologne in Glasgow on the last day of Black September. The Hoops were trailing 2-0 after the first round first leg defeat and it was obvious confidence was low among the players and the supporters. However, as can so often happen, both the individuals on the field and those on the terracings came together to ignite another epic European encounter under the lights at Celtic Park. The sound and the fury made an unexpected, but welcome, return. The Germans, with international Bodo Illgner guarding their goal, were confident of making progress and Head Coach Jorg Berger made all the expected noises when he arrived in Glasgow with his squad. 'We know Celtic are a good team, despite recent results. We will offer them every respect.'

Cologne were on the rocks before the half-time whistle after Celtic dramatically switched on the afterburners to score two goals in three minutes. In the thirty-sixth minute, the Bundesliga side failed to clear a left-wing corner-kick and Paul McStay volleyed an unstoppable left-foot drive past Illgner. Then it was Gerry Creaney's turn to deflect a powerful effort from John Collins into the net for the leveller. With eleven minutes remaining, Collins accepted a pass from Tommy Boyd, drifted past two challenges and rifled a shot low into the corner. Celtic Park was in bedlam. No-one - not even the most optimistic within the green and white ranks - saw this coming. It was the third time in twenty-four years Celtic had come back from two goals to win a European tie. Brady said, 'Prior to the first goal, we looked nervous and they were the better team. But goals change attitudes.'

When the draw for the second round was announced, Brady must have felt like searching for his birth certificate to make sure he was, in fact, born in Dublin. Once again, the fabled luck of the Irish deserted him. Having seen off one extremely dangerous Bundesliga opponent, Celtic were paired with another, Borussia Dortmund. This time there were to be no raucous celebrations at Parkhead. Brady, unfortunately, made history by becoming the first Celtic manager to preside over home-and-away defeats in Europe if you discount the Vienna Rapid farce. Swiss international striker Stephane Chapuisat was his side's main man and Brady made plans to keep him quiet. He had Tony Mowbray, Gary Gillespie and Brian O'Neil in central defence while, unusually, he elected to go with a lone striker, Gerry Creaney, in attack with Stuart Slater tucked in behind him.

The disciplined formation was working a treat until the seventy-first minute when that man Chapuisat managed to get clear of the reinforced rearguard to knock the only goal of the game behind Pat Bonner. However, that slender advantage was obliterated in only thirteen minutes in the second leg when Creaney netted, leaving future Rangers goalkeeper Stefan Klos helpless. However, the tie turned dramatically during four incredible second-half minutes. Old fox Ottmar Hizfeld, who won the Champions League with the German outfit in 1997 with Paul Lambert in midfield, switched things around to nullify the left-wing threat of Boyd and Collins. Chapuisat levelled in fifty-three minutes and Michael Zork added a quickfire second. Celtic exited on a 3-1 scoreline against, admittedly, quality opposition. The Germans went all the way to the UEFA Cup Final after dismissing Real Zaragoza (4-3), Roma (2-1) and Auxerre (6-5 on penalties after a 2-2 draw). Remarkably, they lost 3-1 at their fortress to Juventus in the first leg and succumbed 3-0 in Turin for an embarrassing record 6-1 aggregate defeat in the competition's Final.

The pressure on Brady and his players was relentless. Three days after the Borussia Dortmund elimination, Rangers were due at Parkhead for the second Old Firm derby of the campaign. If Celtic had a European hangover, they disguised it well. They ripped into their Ibrox foes right from the start and it was inconceivable that they should contrive to lose the game. Alas, they managed the unlikely feat after the defence went to sleep just after the half-hour mark. Earlier, Paul McStay had whipped in a low shot that left Andy Goram stranded, but Richard Gough extended his apparently-telescopic right leg to block the ball on the line. Shortly afterwards, Goram hurled himself high to his right to turn away a blistering free-kick from Dariusz Wdowcyzk. Rangers could hardly get out of their own half with their goal under siege.

And yet they sneaked up the pitch with Dale Gordon delivering a right-foot cross into the box that picked out McCoist. He cushioned a header into the path of the unmarked Durrant and he slid the ball underneath the exposed Pat Bonner. Stuart Slater took it upon himself to show he could be a £1.5million footballer during a sparkling second-half. He weaved inside and out, sizzling in from the left to leave defenders in his wake. He zipped past three challenges to smack a sixteen-yarder at goal. Once again, Goram was helpless. Once again, the ball flew agonisingly wide of the upright. The Rangers keeper then produced a marvellous save to tip a pile-driver from Slater to safety. The player, still looking for his first Celtic goal, looked determined to provide the goods at last. He then walloped in another drive from the edge of the box that clipped the crossbar on its way over. After a ferocious, one-sided second-half onslaught, Rangers clung onto Durrant's effort and took the points.

Liam Brady would not concede a thing - 'there's so much football still to be played' - but Celtic were losing ground in the race for the flag while Aberdeen, with Roy Aitken playing well, were emerging as the biggest threat to the Ibrox domination. In the next game, the Parkhead men had to rely on a goal four minutes from time by substitute Charlie Nicholas to rescue a point in a 1-1 draw with Dundee United at Tannadice and also preserve their marvellous unbeaten away league record that stretched to a year. Mike Galloway, inadvertently, had given the Tayside outfit the lead just before half-time when he turned the ball beyond Bonner.

Brady was correct, though. His Celtic team had no intention of throwing in the towel. They won four and drew one of their next five league games as they prepared to see out 1992. The only blip was a 2-2 draw with Aberdeen in Glasgow at the start of December where, at least, Slater scored his first goal for the club in his twenty-third appearance. His accurate low right foot shot arrowed in at Theo Snelders' left-hand post with the keeper motionless. The celebrations were short-lived, though, as the Pittodrie men came back to lead 2-1 at the interval. Eoin Jess, who made a habit of scoring against the Hoops, rattled in the equaliser with a drive across Bonner and Paul Kane capitalised on some horrendous defending by Mark McNally to blitz in a second. Rudi Vata was another to open his goal account with the leveller and Celtic were out of luck near the end when Creaney's well-placed header smacked against the base of the upright and bounced to safety.

Celtic, however, couldn't sustain the form and two back-to-back 1-0 defeats from Hearts at Tynecastle and Dundee United at Parkhead put them back on a shaky tightrope without a safety net in sight. They travelled across Glasgow to kick off 1993 with a January 2 meeting with league leaders Rangers. Brady's team were trailing by eight points and he knew he faced another must-win encounter. Without too many options, he selected the same line-up that had lost the previous week to Dundee United.

Andy Payton missed a sitter when he was one-on-one with Goram and fired the ball against the keeper. Gerry Creaney slid one wide of the upright with Joe Miller better placed for a pass. Tommy Boyd, up with the attack as usual, hit one just wide. In the thirty-fourth minute Rangers went up the park and scored the game's only goal. John Brown took a free-kick on the halfway mark and rolled the ball to Ian Ferguson. No-one picked up the midfielder as he took the opportunity to take a touch and then hit a cross practically onto the head of Hateley. He nodded it across the face of the six-yard line and Trevor Steven, arriving at pace, left Pat Bonner helpless with a searing header. At this stage, Liam

THE WINDS OF CHANGE

Brady must have been wondering where he could get hold of a player who could actually defend inside his own penalty area. Largely, Celtic controlled the second-half with Walter Smith content for his team to sit back and hit a vulnerable defence on the break. The nearest Celtic got to a reward for their efforts came just before the end when John Collins rolled the ball under Goram, but left-back David Robertson arrived at the last moment to scramble it clear.

'TEN AND OUT' roared the back page headlines in the following day's newspapers. Celtic were ten points adrift of the Ibrox side and a landslide behind on goal difference. Brady, though, was typically defiant. He made the valid assertion that his team had dropped five points from a possible six in the three Glasgow derbies and, with a little bit of fortune, the games quite easily could have gone the other way. The statistics told a simple story, though. Rangers had forty points, Aberdeen had thirty-five and Celtic had thirty. The Parkhead side had played twenty-five games, two more than the team from Govan and one ahead of the Dons.

The Scottish Cup adventure stalled and then sunk without trace at the second hurdle. The season was just coming out of the first week in February and, once again, it looked as though Celtic would merely be going through the formalities. The pressure on Brady was growing by the day. Celtic needed two goes to overcome Clyde in the opening round, drawing 0-0 away while a strike from Tommy Coyne separated the sides in the replay. Neither performance was lauded.

The hopes of the faithful were obliterated when Falkirk beat Celtic in the competition for the first time in their history. Once again, the club found it impossible to keep a clean sheet at Brockville. And veteran Pat Bonner had to take his share of the blame. He looked jittery and unconvincing throughout and had already been rescued midway through the first-half by a Mike Galloway clearance off the line after Neil Duffy outjumped the keeper to direct a Ian McCall free-kick towards the net. A minute from half-time, Bonner underlined that he hadn't learned his lesson and the home side took the lead when he failed to cut out a McCall corner-kick and this time Duffy's header rattled the rigging.

Strangely, Celtic, with Paul McStay and John Collins in the line-up, had little or no imagination as they attempted to rescue their season after the turnaround. Andy Payton came on to play up front alongside Tommy Coyne, but it made little difference. Seven minutes from the end, Falkirk scored again and there was no way back. Mike Galloway made a hash of a clearance from a routine Fraser Wishart free-kick and the ball fell nicely to the unmarked Eddie May who smashed it past Bonner. In the end, Celtic couldn't score a goal against the team with the worst defensive record in the league.

Cries of 'Sack the board' were now becoming common place wherever the team played. Fergus McCann and Brian Dempsey were attempting to force change and there was talk of them getting rid of Brady and appointing their own manager. Through all the turmoil, the Celtic team boss tried to remain focused. 'No, it wasn't pleasant,' he admitted. 'But I still had a job to do and I was doing it to the best of my ability.'

After the trauma of the Scottish Cup exit at Brockville, Celtic drew their next two league games - Aberdeen at Pittodrie (1-1) and Partick Thistle at Parkhead (0-0). Unexpectedly, they won their next six matches, among them were Rangers, toppled 2-1 in the east end of Glasgow. The fans whooped it up, of course, but, once the dust had settled, the league table that evening still showed the Ibrox men ten points ahead with a game in hand. However, that mattered little in the immediate aftermath of the encounter on March 20, which emerged as Brady's only win over the Ibrox men at Parkhead.

Walter Smith's outfit went into the confrontation with an unbeaten record forty-four games in domestic competition to preserve. Celtic, with nothing but pride to play for, displayed an urgency right from the off that had been strangely lacking in other outings throughout an erratic campaign. Frank McAvennie, a free agent after leaving West Ham for a second time and following an ill-fated three-game period at Aston Villa, had returned in January. It was a signing that underlined the lack of cash in the Celtic coffers. The thirty-four year old was actually photographed in the national press waving a Partick Thistle scarf while shaking hands on a deal with manager John Lambie at Firhill. Two days later he was a Celtic player.

Brady told me, 'I think Frank is worth a try. I believe he still has got goals in him. He won't play every week, but I think he could be a good squad member.' McAvennie said, 'I'm glad to be back, of course. I just hope John Lambie will forgive me. I couldn't turn down the opportunity of returning to Paradise.'

McAvennie, who had already scored two goals from his nine successive appearances, was in place at the kick-off for the visit of Rangers. The Celtic players were up for the challenge. Referee Douglas Hope waved away an early Andy Payton appeal for a penalty-kick when he was clearly brought down by John Brown. Stuart Slater slashed one past the upright and Payton had a remarkable miss from six yards after being picked out by a low left-wing cross from John Collins. Payton, once again displaying a lack of composure, rushed a shot wide and earned a verbal volley from the better-placed McAvennie, as ever, a willing worker.

Collins got the barrier-breaking goal in the thirty-seventh minute with a sweet strike from twenty yards after gathering a pass from Paul McStay, nimbly turning in a confined area and slamming a right foot drive away from Andy Goram. Shortly after the interval, Payton, who had earlier hit the bar, doubled the advantage in the simplest of fashions. Collins swung in a deep left-wing corner-kick and the Rangers defence stood back to allow Goram to come and collect the ball inside the six-yard box. Wires were crossed and Payton diverted the ball goalwards for his fifteenth strike of the season. A couple of minutes later, he was 'rewarded' by left-back David Robertson who rammed a left elbow into his face as they challenged for a high ball. The Celt had to go off as blood gushed from the wound. Eventually, he returned looking like an extra from 'Apocalypse Now'.

McAvennie was denied a third Celtic goal as he twisted away from McPherson to explode a right foot shot goalwards, but Goram pushed it away before being knocked over by the sheer velocity of the effort. With six minutes remaining, Hateley hit his side's consolation, a quick, low shot evading Pat Bonner at his right hand post. The Celtic dug-out bounced with delight at the final whistle, but one man remained stoically firm without a trace of a smile. Liam Brady knew a team that could perform like the one he had just witnessed should have been battling for a championship. Amid the joy, he wondered what the future held in store.

Two weeks after the well merited and equally well fought win over Rangers, Celtic lost 2-0 to Motherwell at Fir Park. The two performances, both in the starkest of contrasts, illuminated everything that was wrong with the team. It was a soulless second-half after going in at the interval two goals adrift. The first strike typified a hesitant, error-prone rearguard. Mark McNally panicked as a high ball dropped into the box. He misjudged his header back to Pat Bonner, who had strayed too far from his line. Stevie Kirk ran in to blast the ball into the gaping net for the easiest goal of his career.

The second came via the penalty spot in the fortieth minute, awarded after Tommy Boyd tangled with Dougie Arnott. TV pictures later showed it was a clear dive by the little striker, but Les Mottram, as inefficient a referee as it could be anyone's misfortune to find in football, pointed to the spot, booked the Celtic defender and Davie Cooper tucked it away to the keeper's left. Boyd was sent off near the end for a challenge on John Philliben. Admittedly, it was a late and desperate tackle and was worthy of a yellow card. He trudged off the field around the same time the visiting support was heading for the exits after witnessing a performance of total disarray.

Celtic won five of their remaining seven league games, drawing 1-1 with St Johnstone in Perth and losing 3-1 to Hibs in Edinburgh. Frank McAvennie scored in six of the matches, including winners against Falkirk, Aberdeen and Partick Thistle in successive weeks. The final league table made for depressing reading for anyone inclined towards Celtic. The team lost eight and drew twelve of their forty-four games to slump into third place on sixty points, a massive thirteen behind Rangers and four adrift of Aberdeen.

It left Liam Brady with plenty to ponder during the summer months, including the very real possibility of handing in his resignation. Of course, that would have constituted the admission of failure. The Irishman wasn't quite ready to take that route. Not at this stage, anyway.

CHAPTER THREE
THE END OF THE LINE

The last ball of the almost unendurable 1992/93 campaign was kicked in the midst of a jolly fanfare at Celtic Park on May 15 1993. Prior to the kick-off to the depressingly meaningless meeting with Dundee, the home supporters were invited by the board to come in fancy dress costumes to say farewell to the old Jungle before seats were installed.

Undoubtedly, the directors would have preferred to have kept whatever spare cash they possessed under lock and key in a vault, but they had little say in the matter after the Taylor Report in 1990, following the Hillsborough Disaster the previous year, dictated that every football ground in Scotland and England must be all-seated by the start of the 1994/95 season.

On the final day, though, the Jungle was awash with gaiety. Fans arrived dressed as lions, dragons, scarecrows, clowns and there was even a very special tiger. Later it was discovered, director Michael Kelly was inside the suit. Celtic greats trotted out, including Jimmy Johnstone and the rest of the European Cup-winning side, to wave merrily at the cavorting throng. There were pom-pom girls dancing around the centre circle and a huge inflatable pink elephant floated high above one of the goals. All very surreal for a club veering far too close to death throes. No-one seemed to care that goals from Paul McStay and Frank McAvennie gave Celtic a 2-0 win in a non-event encounter. It was a bizarre manner in which to bring down the curtain on another barren and joyless season.

Upon reflection, there was something quite remarkable about the scoreline. It transpired this was to be Liam Brady's final league victory at Celtic Park.

Two months and a day later, I found myself sitting opposite the Celtic manager in the tranquility of the Brother Walfrid Restaurant at Parkhead as he attempted to plot his way through another minefield. He had no money to spend and didn't mention he might be more than a shade envious that another manager across Glasgow, Walter Smith, had just paid a Scottish transfer record fee of £4million for Dundee United striker Duncan Ferguson and a 'mere' £1.2million for Gordon Durie from Spurs. Brady must have felt like the boxer in the ring with both hands tied behind his back.

However, he had been involved in a shake-up at managerial level by bringing in Joe Jordan as his assistant, ditching Mick Martin while moving Tommy Craig to the post of Youth Development Officer. Old Scotland international warhorse Jordan, affectionately known as 'Jaws', had been sacked as manager of Hearts at the end of the season after three years in charge of the Edinburgh outfit. He summed up, 'That's life, you get on with it. Nobody's going to listen to your sad stories.' Jordan, who had never hidden his admiration of Celtic, had got to know Brady during his career in Italy with AC Milan and Verona. Although he had been a striker during his playing days, Jordan's great strength in coaching was organising defensive systems. He was the role reversal of Jock Stein, a stonewall centre-half who concentrated on offensive formations.

After a wait of almost five months, Pat McGinlay was on his way with Joe Miller moving out to accommodate his £400,000 transfer fee. Twenty-four hours after completing the deal, McGinlay wore the green and white hoops for the first time in the 1-1 pre-season stalemate with Sheffield Wednesday on July 31 and was utilised as a second-half substitute in a 1-0 defeat in another friendly against Manchester United at Old Trafford three days later. A further - and welcome - £225,000 arrived from Bolton Wanderers who signed midfielder Stevie Fulton.

Brady was working with a threadbare squad, but was looking forward to turning things around. Moses probably found parting the Red Sea an easier task.

Celtic were sent to Fir Park for the opening fixture of the season against a Motherwell side who dodged the drop from the Premier League by only six points. Despite the boast of twelve months beforehand, this was hardly 'Brady's team'. Only two of the starting line-up - Stuart Slater and Frank McAvennie - had been brought to the club by the Irishman. Pat McGinlay started the game on the substitutes' bench. After thirty-eight minutes, Tommy McLean's team, whose main tactic appeared to be to try to bore the opposition into submission, were two goals ahead and Celtic were floundering. Dougie Arnott and Alex Burns were the players on target and Brady must have had that old familiar sinking feeling.

However, Slater threw the team a lifeline with a cracking right-foot shot just on half-time and McAvennie, following on from last season, grabbed an equaliser just after the hour mark. A crowd of 14,569 watched the action, but it was hardly champagne vintage. After only ninety minutes, it was clear this was heading for another campaign of toil.

Brady wasn't to know it, but he would only be in charge of the team for only nine more league games, a mere two of which were won. The Celtic players had to wait until the fourth match of the season before picking up a win bonus. There were draws against Hibs (1-1) and Rangers (0-0) before they beat Partick Thistle with a solitary effort from the unlikely source of Mark McNally at Firhill. However, that was swiftly followed by a 1-0 reverse against Aberdeen in Glasgow with the burly Mixu Paatelainen again terrorising the Celtic defence while scoring the winner. Brady's last league win as the club's manager came on September 11 in Fife where two first-half goals from Charlie Nicholas and two after the turnaround from Andy Payton gave the club an emphatic 4-1 triumph over Raith Rovers. The following week a strike from Gerry Creaney nullified a goal from Billy McKinlay as Celtic settled for a dismal 1-1 stalemate against Dundee United at Parkhead. The entertainment level never got anywhere close to the colourful display in Brady's managerial debut against the same opponents back in August 1991.

Massive disappointment was awaiting the Irishman and Celtic in midweek as the club prepared for the League Cup semi-final against Rangers, played at Ibrox with Hampden out of commission due to refurbishment. The clubs agree to toss a coin to decide the venue, either Parkhead or Ibrox. With Brady out of the country on club business, Joe Jordan stepped in to flip a coin with Walter Smith. The Celtic assistant called it right and thought the club had won a home tie. It was explained he had only earned the right to call first in the real thing. This time, unfortunately, he got it wrong and Rangers, without any input, were suddenly awarded a home tie.

Celtic, though, would have half of the tickets for a near-50,000 sell-out and, for the first time in history, the Rangers players would come out the tunnel to be confronted with a sea of green and white with the visiting support commandeering the Govan stand. I decided to give the Press Box a miss that evening and Liam Brady actually organised two tickets to be collected at the Ibrox reception. I received some strange looks in a cramped and exceptionally busy area when I was asked for the name on the envelope. The Celtic manager had told me the tickets would be in his name. I answered, 'Liam Brady' and the place, packed with Rangers fans, went exceptionally quiet. I took my seat in the centre of the stand and the atmosphere, as ever, was electrifying.

I knew exactly how much this game meant to Brady. He had seen Celtic lose two semi-finals the previous season and he was utterly determined not to suffer a third failure. If he could push the club to the Final, he believed he could source the springboard to success. First, though, he would have to dismiss Rangers. Celtic had reached the last four by overcoming Stirling Albion (2-0), Arbroath (9-1) and Airdrie (1-0). The goal storm at Gayfield, with Frank McAvennie and Andy Payton both hitting hat-tricks, was the worst result in Arbroath's history. Ironically, they were managed at the time by Celtic legend Danny McGrain, who quit the job the following season after fourteen months in charge.

On September 22 in Govan, the Celtic players had the opportunity to carve out their own piece of history. Brady and Jordan worked with the players during training in the lead-up to the confrontation and both were satisfied everyone was aware of the expectation levels. John Collins failed a late injury test, but, otherwise, it was a strong Celtic team. Alas, they blew it big-style. For the second successive season, they lost 1-0 in a semi-final to their fiercest rivals. Even worse, like the Scottish Cup defeat the previous term, they capitulated once again to ten men. With the tie goalless, Huistra was sent off five minutes into the second-half after aiming a wild kick at Tommy Boyd. Referee Douglas Hope couldn't miss the foolishness of the Rangers winger and had no hesitation in flashing a red card.

The Celtic support could sense a win on this occasion and were cheering wildly when Dariusz Wdowcyzk swung over an arcing right wing corner-kick with his left foot and Stuart Slater, unmarked at the far post, looped a header over Ally Maxwell only for Gary Stevens to knock his effort off the line. The optimism was short-lived, unfortunately, when Rangers took the lead in the sixty-fifth minute after some dire defending from Mike Galloway. Stevens pushed the ball fairly aimlessly down the right touchline and Galloway, yards ahead of the lurking Durrant, sauntered across to deal with the situation. The simple thing would have been to touch it out for a shy. Galloway, alarmingly, got his feet in a fankle, Durrant took control, launched a low ball across the face of the goal and Hateley prodded in the gift from six yards.

And yet Celtic still had twenty-five minutes to do something about it against a team with a player short. The best chance of the evening fell to Paul McStay, in the clear about twelve yards out, but the skipper, so often a hero, belted it high and wide with the ball flying into the Celtic supporters behind Maxwell's goal. And with that wild and wretched attempt went the team's hopes of levelling the tie and taking their toiling opponents to extra-time. A grinning Walter Smith said, 'That's our best performance of the season. You've got to give credit to Durrant for capitalising on the Celtic player's error.' Liam Brady kept his thoughts to himself.

I talked to him the following morning. He was as depressed as I had ever heard him. He didn't even attempt to hide the fact that the club hadn't played well and had let down the support. I made the point that Celtic had been keeping three players back late in the game when they were about to take corner-kicks. Tommy Boyd, Mark McNally and Galloway were strung along the halfway line against a lone Ranger, Hateley, who was absolutely spent and working off memory. Brady, without pointing the finger of blame at anyone, answered, 'Joe likes the defence to keep its shape.' I didn't reply. Celtic, with a man advantage, were actually a man short in their opponents' penalty area in these situations. It made no sense then and it makes none today. In the Brady era, mistakes were made and brutally punished.

Fourteen days after our private and off-the-record conversation, Brady handed in his resignation. I wasn't surprised.

On the Saturday after the Ibrox flop, a solitary goal from John Robertson gave Hearts a win over a poor and clueless Celtic, the club's second league defeat of the season. Photographs of Brady, grimacing as he watched his team stumble, were appearing on back pages of every newspaper. The pressure was unyielding. A week later, the Celtic players were serenaded with boos, jeers and cat-calls at the interval and full-time after another hapless performance, this time a goalless draw against Kilmarnock at Parkhead. Brady said, 'The fans gave us pelters and we deserved pelters. That's the second league game on the trot we have played really, really badly.'

It wasn't to get much better. In midweek, Celtic lost 2-1 to St Johnstone, who would eventually be relegated, and once again a cacophony of wailing disappointment spilled from the terracings from a support who had reached breaking point. A dejected Brady, sitting on the touchline with his head buried into his hands, knew the end of his Celtic managerial career was near. In fact, it was only an hour or so away.

The Perth defeat left the club ninth in the twelve-team Premier League. Celtic had picked up nine points from a possible twenty after ten games. They had claimed only two wins - both away from home - had lost three and drawn five. They had scored ten goals and conceded nine. However, it is worth looking at what was happening at Ibrox over the same period because Rangers were not racing away at the top. Far from it. They were a mere point better off than Celtic and had won three, lost three and drawn four with eleven goals scored and twelve conceded. Aberdeen, who had finished as runners-up the previous season, had amassed thirteen points after four wins, one defeat and five draws. So, despite an awful opening to the campaign, no-one could write off Celtic at that stage.

Brady, as studious a character as I've ever met in football, wouldn't have made up his mind in the spur of the moment to leave Celtic. Instinctively, though, he knew it was time to go. His resignation filtered through to the Press the following morning. A statement, apparently from the exiting manager, stated, 'After recent results and performances, I have decided to resign. A tremendous pressure surrounds the club at the moment - the management staff, players, board and supporters alike. It is my responsibility as manager that this should not affect the players. I have not been able to do this. I have taken the decision to stand down.' It read like a formation of words straight from the PR Department.

Kevin Kelly, who had taken over from Jack McGinn as chairman, followed the party line. He was quoted, 'Liam always conducted himself with great dignity as Celtic manager. He did the honourable thing by resigning.' Rather needlessly, his statement added the board would consider as 'a matter of urgency' the question of a permanent replacement.

It was a heaven-sent opportunity for Fergus McCann, smelling blood in the boardroom battle, to have his say. The Scots-born Canadian millionaire didn't hesitate to go into print. 'Perhaps the board should accept their responsibility for the current situation and do the honourable thing. Perhaps changes should be made at the top. Some of the directors should look at themselves for a change.'

Brady had no intention of facing the media at a Press Conference. I was aware he didn't have a lot of time for my fellow-hacks. He came off everyone's radar as they frantically searched for his whereabouts. I knew exactly where he was, but couldn't say or write a word. As a Sunday newspaperman in these situations, you have got to hope your story remains exclusive until Saturday after the dailies had exhausted their sources in the pursuit of the awol Irishman. Even then, you have to make sure your Sunday rivals don't get a sniff. I had every confidence Brady would not speak to anyone else, even if there was big money on offer for a so-called scoop.

Before I could get round to putting that story into print, came another bombshell from Parkhead twenty-four hours later. Joe Jordan, who was expected to step up and take charge of the team, suddenly quit. Why? There's been a fair amount of conjecture over the years. There's also been a fair amount of silence. It was obvious Jordan was extremely upset he wasn't immediately awarded the job as Brady's successor. My information at the time suggested the Celtic directors had already made an approach to Lou Macari, who was Stoke City's manager, with the offer of the post at his former team.

If that was the case, the men who occupied the Celtic boardroom were displaying a remarkable level of ignorance or, if you want to be kind, naivety. It was well known in football circles that Jordan and Macari were the best of pals, forging a friendship during their years as colleagues at Manchester United and also the Scotland international squad. Undoubtedly, Macari would have contacted his mate about the situation. For me, that would have sparked the reaction from Jordan on the Friday when he walked out of Celtic Park for the last time. He left saying simply, 'You've got to make these sort of calls.'

Coach Frank Connor, back at the club for a third time after being sacked as Davie Hay's assistant in 1983, was catapulted into the dug-out for the weekend home game against Dundee which the club won 2-1 with a late goal from substitute Pat McGinlay. A leaving present for Brady for making a dream come true?

As pre-arranged, I contacted Liam Brady in Dublin on Friday afternoon. As ever, he was courteous and focused. There was no problem with a 'first person 'exclusive. I wasn't surprised there was no mention of a fee for his time. Under the banner headline 'PARADISE LOST' I ghosted the story everyone else wanted. With Liam Brady's name on the tale, it read thus:

'I was sitting on the team bus on a stretch of the M9 on Wednesday night when I made the decision to quit as manager of Celtic. I had just watched the team lose 2-1 to St Johnstone and I was utterly dejected.

'I thought about that game - and the recent performances against Hearts and Kilmarnock - and I knew I couldn't shield the players from the pressures any longer. It was getting to me and it was getting through to them.

'I HAD TO GO.

'I approached the chairman Kevin Kelly and told him I had made up my mind to quit. He didn't even attempt to talk me into changing my mind.

'IT WOULD HAVE BEEN A WASTE OF TIME, ANYWAY!

'My mind was made up and, having come to such a momentous decision, I wasn't going to change it. It was the most difficult decision of my life. I leave Celtic with so many regrets. I would have loved to have given those wonderful fans a trophy. They deserved more than they got.

'But let's nail some of the rumours right now. I was NOT stabbed in the back by Joe Jordan or anyone else. I brought Joe to the club. He was my appointment, there can be no arguments on that.

'I HAD HOPED JOE WOULD GET THE JOB.

'I was amazed when I heard the news he had quit, too. Naturally, I can't go into that because I don't know the facts. I would like to say there were no running feuds with the board. I wasn't at their throats and they weren't at mine.

'Sure, money was tight. But I knew the situation at the club from day one. However, if anything, things got worse this year. Of course, the atmosphere could have been better. All the talk of the rebel takeover and so on kept on the pressure. It just never went away and it affected the club, the management and some individuals.

'And, yes, there was talk of the rebels putting in their own man as manager if they were successful. However, I stress I am NOT using that as an excuse. Things just didn't work out on the pitch. We didn't get results in my two years and that is what it is all about. No-one is more aware of Celtic's reputation than me. Okay, I didn't play for the club, but I was brought up in Dublin and the two teams everyone talked about were Celtic and Manchester United. Their flamboyance and style were well known. That was my aim. I wanted Celtic to continue to play with that flair.

'People have also been saying I was contemplating quitting after we lost to Rangers in the League Cup semi-final last month.

'BUT I CAN TELL YOU THERE IS NO TRUTH IN THAT.

'Yes, it was a huge blow losing that match at Ibrox...but I believed we could pick things up again. That wasn't to be. Obviously, I am sad that some of the transfers I made didn't work out. The name Tony Cascarino continually crops up, but I would like to point out he is currently in the Chelsea first team. Why didn't he do the business at Parkhead? I believe the unique pressure of being involved with a Glasgow team got to him.

'To understand just how stressful life can be in Glasgow as a sportsman you really have to sample it. You have to be a certain animal to cope. It took me at least a year to understand it. Tony just could not settle and I believe he is finding life a lot easier in England.

'The same goes for Stuart Slater. I was greatly disappointed he didn't match up to expectations at Parkhead. The boy oozes talent and I'm sure we'll see him do the business at Ipswich. And who could have predicted that Tony Mowbray would have picked up such a series of injuries after joining us? I think he missed about four games in ten years at Middlesbrough, but that's the way things go. You have to be philosophical about it.

'What does the future hold for Liam Brady? I'll sit down and think about that when the dust settles. I'll talk over everything with my wife Sarah and I'll spend some time with the kids.

'I MAY EVEN STAY IN SCOTLAND.

'I have made some very good friends during my stay at Parkhead. Who knows what is around the corner in this game? Would I think about becoming a manager again? Anything is possible. Again, I won't be making any rash decisions.

'I hasten to add that I did not run away from things in Glasgow. That is not my style. I was already scheduled to be in Dublin at Jury's Hotel this weekend. It is a beautiful place to get away from the rigours of life. There is a dinner I have agreed to go to tonight. And I'll probably stick around for the Republic of Ireland's World Cup-tie against Spain on Wednesday.

'Meanwhile, I am still trying to come to terms with the fact I am no longer manager of Celtic.

'THAT FACT HURTS, BELIEVE ME.

'But there is no bitterness on my part. I'm just sad that it didn't work out as planned. Good luck to Celtic and their marvellous fans in the future.

'They deserve the very best and I hope they get it.'

Five years later, I was penning a magazine feature on Liam Brady. I decided to update the story of his traumatic time at Parkhead. Once again, the Irishman was only too happy and willing to talk about his experience. Once more, he refused to hide behind a mountain of excuses. He said, 'Yes I admit I made mistakes. I was new to football management and Celtic were one heck of a club to start off with. There were things that didn't go right immediately and I made an error of judgement in the transfer market. I bought Tony Cascarino for £1.1 million and, unfortunately, he couldn't cope with the pressure that is always on Celtic players.

'Sadly, there was precious little time to turn things around at Parkhead. The pressure was simply relentless. It never went away. Rangers brought in plenty of players and some of them didn't exactly produce the goods, but you can get away with things like that when the team is winning and isn't under close examination or scrutiny.'

I was well aware Brady arrived in Glasgow in the summer of 1991 with every intention of maintaining the Celtic tradition of performing with exciting excellence. He continued, 'Yes, that was my ambition. The Celtic support deserved that sort of team, that is what I wanted to give them. I'll never forget my first game in charge – we won 4-3 against Dundee United at Tannadice. Scorelines like that would have kept those wonderful fans happy, I'm sure.

'I can recall some smashing games in my time there and I hope the Celtic fans appreciated what I was trying to achieve. There were never any problems in the dressing room. The players were happy and I was working flat-out to run the club properly as far as the football team was concerned.'

Brady sighed before continuing. 'There were so many divisions at Parkhead and, of course, it was a well known fact that the old board didn't have a lot of money to spend in the transfer market. There was friction around the place and that gets through to the players – of course it does. Anyone who says it doesn't has got it wrong. You name me one club who has performed well out on the park when there has been trouble at boardroom level. It was all so frustrating. The Celtic fans were so unhappy and disillusioned with the old board that they refused to back the team. That affected us, too.

'In my days, money was tight and I had to get it right with every player. There was no room for manoeuvre, no way of going out and buying another player if one purchase didn't work out. Stuart Slater was like Cascarino. There can be no doubting his class, anyone at West Ham would tell you how good he was when he played at Upton Park. He was a born entertainer, a typical Celtic player, if you like. However, it just didn't work for him in Glasgow. Once more the strain showed and he never displayed the talents we all knew he possessed and that was a pity. But Glasgow and playing for Celtic can do that to you.

'I've got to hold up my hands and say the pressure, without doubt, got to me, too. Of course, it did. You've got to ride the storm and, sadly, I couldn't manage it. That was why I had to resign.'

I made the point that Brady had been given little back-up from the board who had presented him with the job in the first place. They were too busy ducking for cover behind the sandbags to give a first-time manager much-needed guidance.

'It was a turbulent time,' recalled Brady. 'There can be little doubt about that. I had to cope with Terry Cassidy during my time and that was not a very pleasant experience, I can assure you. The trouble with Cassidy was that he was not a football man and, as such, did not understand football people.'

I enquired about the story that had come to my ears about a raucous slanging match in the office of the-then Chief Executive, who only kept the position for eighteen months. I had been informed the Celtic team boss left after having his forcible say to return to his office only yards away. His fax machine then kicked into action and a message came through stating, 'Please don't slam my door when you leave my office!' True or false?

Brady actually laughed. 'No, it wasn't quite like that, but I do have a file of memos from Cassidy. There are some classics in that collection. You never know, maybe some day I'll get them published as a book - it could be a best-seller! Yes, we had some stand-up rows, Cassidy and I. It did little for the morale of the place with things like that going on. I wanted to manage the side and do my level best to put out a team that deserved to wear the green and white hoops. Simple as that, but there was interference from every corner.

'When Cassidy eventually left, Celtic put in Michael Kelly to handle the club's Press Relations department and things didn't get any better. It all became a bit intense and it got to the stage that you had to continually look over your shoulder. So much for team harmony and pulling together. Yes, it was quite an experience managing Celtic Football Club!'

I asked Brady if he nurtured any regrets about taking the job in the first place. The reply was typically forthright. 'I had to give it a chance. Celtic are one of the big clubs of world football. You know, they talk about the luck of the Irish, but I didn't get much when I was there. We seemed to keep tripping over when it came to important hurdles. We played three semi-finals in my time and lost them all.

'I'm not going to start making excuses at this late stage, but a rub of the green would have helped us on all three occasions. We didn't get it and the results – all 1-0 defeats – are now in the history books.

'But we DID play an awful lot of good football and no-one can take that away from us. There was a lot on the plus side, as far as I was concerned. I would dearly have loved to have given the Celtic fans a trophy in my time there. The reason I moved out was to give someone else a crack at providing the goods. When it got near to the end for me it was a very, very difficult time. I was aware of what the Celtic fans wanted. I knew about their desires for the club because they matched my own. Unfortunately, it didn't work out.'

Brady summed up, 'Nowadays, my wife Sarah must enjoy seeing me without the added stress. Glasgow was an experience that I wouldn't have missed. However, it was tough, VERY tough, trying to cope with the in-fighting, boardroom takeover rumours and all that goes with managing a club such as Celtic.'

It could be debated that Brady was the right man in the right place at the wrong time. His vision for Celtic was the one any supporter would have encouraged. However, things can get slightly blurred when you are not contesting with your main rivals on a level playing field. Brady was forced to try to get the best out of some individuals who, deep down, he realised were not what he would call Celtic class. Walter Smith spent more on one player - Duncan Ferguson at £4million - than Brady spent during his entire stay at Parkhead. In his three close seasons at the club, Rangers lavished £16million in total in bringing in new talent. It was the sort of financial muscle Brady could only dream about.

The Irishman arrived at Celtic Park as a decent, dignified, cultured human being and left with those precious qualities intact. Two months after exiting Celtic, in mid-December 1993, Brady was appointed manager of Brighton in the old English Division Two. The club, like Celtic, were experiencing financial difficulties and were second bottom of the league at the time of the Irishman's arrival. He managed to get them to mid-table safety by the end of the season. They performed in much the same manner with the same outcome in his second term before he left the club by 'mutual consent' in November 1995. His managerial career was over at the age of thirty-nine.

Liam Brady's journey into football management should have been a monumental expedition. Instead, alas, it was merely an excursion.

CHAPTER FOUR
LOU MACARI: WELCOME TO A CRISIS

Lou Macari had a well-earned reputation as a gambler. He liked a flutter, he enjoyed taking risks. Perhaps, then, it was not surprising he rejected a lucrative five-year contract to extend his stay as Stoke City manager to return to Celtic as the replacement for Liam Brady on October 27 1993. Once again, Macari was willing to speculate. On this occasion, though, he called it spectacularly wrong and was out of a job eight months later.

Macari realised his old club were in a mess, on and off the pitch, and, by his own admission, he was 'parachuted into a crisis'. But he didn't hesitate in accepting the under-siege board's invitation to become the eighth individual to be named team boss of Celtic Football Club. Stoke City agreed £225,000 in compensation for Macari who was under contract following two successful years at the club. Ironically, Celtic had accepted an offer of £200,000 for the busy, little forward from Manchester United to prise him away from the east end of Glasgow in 1973. It was a record fee for a Scottish footballer at the time. Now, twenty years later, the board would be forced to pay £25,000 more to lure him back to his spiritual home.

Three days after the appointment, Macari was in the Ibrox dug-out to take his bow as the Celtic manager. A game against Rangers certainly didn't appear to faze this naturally effervescent character. On the day of the encounter, the television crews were waiting for him as he stepped out of Celtic's age-old HQ, Seamill Hydro, en route to Govan. He was asked for his thoughts. Smiling broadly, Macari answered, 'Really looking forward to going up there and getting plenty of stick.' As a Celtic player, the Rangers support rarely missed the opportunity to single him out for special 'treatment', but it hadn't bothered him then and, on the face of it, anyway, it appeared his attitude hadn't changed.

With sublime irony, Macari last kicked a ball as a Celtic player against Rangers on the same ground on January 6 1973 before his big-money move to Old Trafford ten days later. As a manager, he was hoping for better luck on this occasion. As a player, he went out a loser after Alfie Conn, who would later play for Celtic, netted the winner in the last minute. Macari didn't make a single change to the line-up selected by caretaker boss Frank Connor for the previous league game, a 1-1 draw with Hibs at Easter Road. Pat Bonner was in goal with a back four of Peter Grant, Gary Gillespie, Tony Mowbray and Tommy Boyd. Paul Byrne, a young Dubliner brought to the club by Liam Brady from Bangor, played wide right with a mid-line of Pat McGinlay, Paul McStay and John Collins. Gerry Creaney and Charlie Nicholas led the attack. Andy Payton and Brian O'Neil were on the bench.

The confrontation was evenly balanced until the Celtic rearguard committed an act of sheer folly in the sixty-seventh minute to allow poacher supreme McCoist far too much time and space in the penalty box. Those commodities were oxygen to the Ibrox striker. McCall whipped in a low cross from the left and, unforgivably, there was no-one anywhere near challenging distance of McCoist, only eight yards out. His first shot was blocked by Bonner, but he snapped up the rebound to ram it into the net.

Three minutes afterwards, Macari was doing a jig of joy on the Ibrox touchline as he celebrated the first goal of his managerial reign at the club. McGinlay, on the right forty yards out, slung a long diagonal high ball into the Rangers penalty area. Nicholas chased what looked like a forlorn cause as Ally Maxwell leapt and stretched above him. It looked a simple catch for the keeper. He must have had one eye on his Celtic opponent, though, as he fumbled the ball and dropped it behind Nicholas. Collins, reading the situation perfectly, stepped in, took control and, with a fair degree of nonchalance, swept the ball into the net.

The game was deep into injury time when substitute O'Neil, on for Nicholas in eighty-eight minutes, made a massive impact. Collins hurled over a right-wing corner-kick and once again Maxwell was in trouble. He jumped along with Payton and both missed. O'Neil, right behind them, rose toweringly and thumped in a glorious header from practically under the crossbar. Game over. Job done. Dream debut. Macari happy.

Sitting among the Celtic support that afternoon, behind the goal where Collins and O'Neil had just scored, were Fergus McCann, Brian Dempsey and other members of the consortium plotting feverishly and working overtime in their dogged and determined efforts to oust the current board. They were now known as 'McCann and his Rebel Gang' and Lou Macari couldn't have guessed the full significance the shift in balance within the corridors of power at Parkhead would have on his return to the club. For the time being, though, deep in the heart of enemy territory, he whooped it up with the rest of the Celtic contingent. However, Macari would also have been aware of McCann's thinking at the time. Only a couple of days beforehand, McCann, with undisguised disdain, proclaimed the appointment of Macari as 'nothing more than a publicity stunt'.

It didn't take long for the new man to sample defeat. Four days later, Sporting Lisbon inflicted a 2-0 reverse in the second leg of their UEFA Cup-tie in the Portuguese capital which obliterated Gerry Creaney's goal in the first game. Macari made history by becoming the third Celtic team boss to take charge of the club in only four European ties in the same season. Liam Brady saw the team stumble through the opening round, relying on an extra-time own goal in Glasgow to see off Young Boys of Berne 1-0 on aggregate and Frank Connor was in the Parkhead dug-out for the first leg against their eventual Portuguese conquerors.

Macari and the team came home to the now-mandatory and vehement anti-board demonstrations before the next game, a 3-0 win over Partick Thistle at Parkhead where Pat McGinlay (2) and Charlie Nicholas claimed the goals. Despite the ubiquitous 'Sack The Board' banners, director Michael Kelly still insisted, 'The Celtic fans are much more interested in what happens on the pitch than behind the scenes.' Only 21,629 bothered to welcome Macari back to Celtic Park that afternoon. A crowd of 47,942 witnessed the goalless draw in the first Old Firm meeting of the season in late August. A lot of bodies had gone awol.

Celtic then embarked on a three-game winless run, drawing with Aberdeen (1-1), Kilmarnock (2-2) and Hearts (0-0). Two goals from Pat McGinlay got the team back on track as they overcame Motherwell 2-0 in Glasgow where the attendance figure had shrunk alarmingly to 16,654. The fans were afforded their first glimpse of a less-than-slender Wayne Biggins, a thirty-three-year-old striker who had been brought to the club by Macari to score goals. Biggins had arrived from Barnsley in an exchange deal with Andy Payton, who never started a first team game under the new manager. It was reported Macari also paid £100,000 to land the journeyman forward who had netted only two goals in thirteen outings for the Yorkshire team that season. Payton had scored eleven goals in his debut campaign and, after one start and five substitute appearances, had collected two before the arrival of Macari.

A few years later, Payton's take on the transfer was interesting. He put it this way, 'He (Macari) brought Wayne Biggins up in a swap deal for me which was beyond belief as he didn't even score a goal for the (Celtic) reserves. I'm not singling out the player, I'm just looking at the two records and it's frightening, really.'

Biggins' nickname was 'Bertie', but he had earned a few more unkind monickers before he departed Celtic four months later. He started four games and came on as a substitute on six occasions before he returned back across the border with Stoke City, now managed by Joe Jordan, who, incredibly, forked out £125,000 for him. As one thoroughly frustrated Celtic fan put it, 'At least, you could say Biggins was the most consistent centre-forward we had at the club during that period. He failed to score a goal in each of his ten appearances. Now that's consistent.'

Macari's three other signings were equally less than inspiring and, unfortunately, accurately reflected the dire situation that pervaded at the club. Goalkeeper Carl Muggleton was twenty-six years old when he agreed a £150,000 move from Leicester City on January 11 1994. He had started his career at his local club in 1986, but had made only fifty-four first team appearances in seven years before arriving at Parkhead. The reason for that statistic was simple; Muggleton had been loaned to Chesterfield, Blackpool, Hartlepool, Stockport, Liverpool and Sheffield United in the intervening years. No-one took up the option to buy him.

He was brought in to put pressure on Pat Bonner and made his debut in a goalless draw against Dundee United at Parkhead on January 22. In fact, that was one of six consecutive league games where the Englishman kept a clean sheet. There were two more scoreless stalemates against Raith Rovers and Hibs with Celtic winning the others against Hearts (2-0), Kilmarnock (1-0) and St Johnstone (1-0). The one goal Muggleton conceded in the midst of that impressive run was enough to put Celtic out of the Scottish Cup and, effectively, end their season on January 29 1994 with sixteen league games still to be played.

Obviously, it was utterly crucial that Celtic did not slip when they were drawn against Motherwell at Fir Park at the first hurdle in the national competition. It was to be Muggleton's only appearance in the tournament, but the 1-0 loss could hardly be blamed on the goalkeeper as the Parkhead outfit meekly accepted their earliest exit from the competition since 1976. The game was a personal triumph for Tommy Coyne, who had been jettisoned by Liam Brady to Tranmere Rovers in March 1993. The striker returned to Scotland eight months later when Motherwell had a bid of £125,000 accepted.

Fir Park could be a grim, charmless, little ground at the best of times and it wasn't at its best during blustery conditions with an Arctic blast swirling around by the time Motherwell kicked off to set the game in motion. Both teams were jittery and apprehensive as the troublesome, stubborn wind dictated proceedings and, ultimately, played its role in the solitary goal. There were only eight minutes left to play when Tommy McLean's team were awarded a free-kick just yards from the edge of the box on their left. The players, friend and foe alike, jostled for positions expecting a flighted ball into the box. Instead, substitute

Stevie Kirk seemed to dig his toe into the ground as he took the kick and the ball flew knee-high into the box. It struck John Collins on the thigh and spun crazily into the air. The Celtic midfielder tried valiantly to rescue the situation, but somehow the wayward ball was flicked on to Coyne and he showed his typical predatory instinct by thrusting ahead of Tony Mowbray and the advancing Muggleton to glance a close-range effort into the net. The Celtic fans weren't holding their collective breath in anticipation of a lifeline when Macari, responding immediately to the loss of the goal, threw on Wayne Biggins for Paul Byrne.

The club had played six games in 1994 and had failed to win one. A Celtic player told me afterwards, 'We went into the Fir Park dressing room and the place was in silence. We were gutted. We knew that was it for the season. We showered and changed and there was no sign of the manager. We sat around wondering what was coming next. Surely, there would be an on-the-spot inquest? Instead, about an hour later, the boss stuck his head round the door and said, "Right, see you lot in training on Monday." And that was that. We expected a rollicking, but that was the extent of the manager's reaction.'

The board, though, didn't get off so lightly. A victory, or even a draw, might just have slowed the tempo of the matchday banner protests that constantly reminded the directors it would be in Celtic's best interests if they were elsewhere. A run in the Scottish Cup with the possibility of a first trophy in five years might have bought them some time. That luxury was not afforded them, though, the instant Coyne's deft effort sailed towards the net behind Muggleton. The 'Sack The Board' campaign stepped on the gas after the latest intolerable failure.

In this chaotic setting, Lee Martin, once an FA Cup-winning hero with Manchester United, arrived as Macari's third signing. Just days before his twenty-sixth birthday, he agreed a three-year deal. The left-back, who scored the Old Trafford side's winning goal at Wembley in the 1990 Cup Final replay victory over Crystal Palace, was out of contract when he arrived in late January. A tribunal ordered Celtic to pay a transfer fee of £350,000. Hardly money well spent for a player who broke a leg in a freak off-the-ball accident while playing against

Falkirk in October that year and would make only twenty appearances before being shipped off to Bristol Rovers.

The fourth and final signing was Willie Falconer who, depending on which source you listen to, was unwittingly instrumental in the final overthrow of Kevin Kelly and Co. The former Aberdeen striker arrived in a £350,000 deal from Sheffield United on February 10. Manager Macari didn't exactly give the twenty-seven year old a ringing endorsement after the move was completed. Whereas Brady was openly enthusiastic about Stuart Slater getting people out of their seats and onto their feet to applaud his latest signing's tantalising ability, Macari was less than enthusiastic about the skills of Falconer. The Celtic boss said something along the lines of he 'didn't expect him to set the heather on fire.' At least, you could reason he wasn't putting undue pressure on the new boy to deliver above expectations.

Before Falconer arrived and the Scottish Cup exit, it was obvious that Charlie Nicholas and Wayne Biggins were a match made in hell. There was no spark between the two frontmen, no understanding and no cohesion as the attack fired blanks. Celtic had two matches to play to see out November and a double from John Collins did the business in a 2-0 win over Raith Rovers in Glasgow. It wasn't a performance to get the heart pumping against a woeful Fife side who would win only six of their forty-four league games before disappearing from the top division. Although the displays were well short of scintillating, Celtic had still gone nine league games without defeat by the time they travelled to take on Dundee United at Tannadice on November 30. A goal eighteen minutes from time by Paddy Connolly blew apart the unbeaten sequence. Biggins came on as a second-half substitute for Nicholas to merely to confirm the points would remain on Tayside.

The second lowest league attendance of the campaign - 16,751 - bothered to witness the opening game of December, a 1-0 win over St Johnstone where Pat McGinlay got the goal. Someone likened the atmosphere within the vast bowl to that of a local library and even the winning goal in the sixty-ninth minute failed to rouse the spectators from their lethargy. Celtic had to settle for a 1-1 draw with Dundee at Dens Park a week later with Gerry Creaney hitting the equaliser. Biggins played the entire ninety minutes, but Paul Mathers, in the home side's goal, wouldn't have noticed.

The unfortunate Biggins would last until the sixty-eighth minute in the home fixture against Hibs before being replaced by Nicholas. Five minutes later, Paul McStay netted the only goal of the afternoon, but, once again, it hardly stirred the 16,793 fans shivering in the stands. Referee Les Mottram put everyone out of their agony and mercifully blew for time-up and 1993 was heading for the history books. It had been an eventful twelve months for Celtic. Those who cared about the football club must have wondered if there was any hope the corner might be turned in 1994.

Alas, menacing, stormy waters lay ahead and some rudderless ships would sink without trace.

Extraordinarily, as 1993 ticked down, Celtic had gone seven successive home games - six league and one UEFA Cup - without conceding a goal. The last player to put the ball behind Pat Bonner had been Dundee's Billy Dodds from the penalty spot in the fifty-fourth minute of his side's 2-1 defeat on October 9. The total amount of minutes without the loss of a goal? Exactly 666. Three sixes, the number of the Beast. Was it an omen?

Within three minutes of the traditional January 1 Old Firm scuffle, Rangers had managed something seven previous teams had failed to do and that was to puncture the Celtic rearguard at Parkhead. Not just once, but twice. Before the half-hour mark, they had added a third. The level of incompetence displayed by Gary Gillespie and Dariusz Wdowcyzk ensured they were never again allowed to form a partnership in Celtic's central defence. Gillespie appeared to have a chronic aversion to tackling and a distaste of tracking back and marking opponents. Wdowcyzk could, at least, point to the fact he delivered a mean free-kick. Embarrassingly, Mark Hateley and Gordon Durie bossed them both for a large chunk of the game as the Ibrox side eased reasonably comfortably to a 4-2 win.

Celtic kicked off and found themselves a goal behind in fifty-eight seconds. Gillespie, in a pressure-free situation, carelessly slid a misguided pass straight to Stuart McCall, about ten yards inside his own half. The midfielder didn't hesitate as he showed his foe how it should be done. He released a perfect ball behind the Celtic defence and Hateley, played onside by Peter Grant in his unfamiliar right-back position, simply raced into the void, drew Pat Bonner and clipped an arcing left-foot effort into the net. McCall enjoyed the moment so much he decided to stage a re-enactment in the third minute. Another direct pass straight through the heart of the rearguard saw his fellow-midfield man Neil Murray racing in on Bonner. The keeper did well to desperately thrust out a leg and divert the ball to his right, but Mikhailichenko, without a goal all season, was completely on his own as he first-timed a left-foot drive into the net.

Billy McNeill, wearing his matchday analyst's hat on the TV gantry, said sternly, 'Celtic are looking so uncomfortable at the back.' I'm not too sure those would have been the exact words he would have favoured had he been in the dug-out that day as the back lot fell apart. Gillespie once again displayed his distaste for the physical side of the game and Hateley was well aware of the fact as he clattered into him in the air and on the ground. It was like watching a battering ram take on a marshmallow. Wdowcyzk couldn't get to grips with the pace of Durie and it made for dire viewing for Celtic fans.

In the twenty-ninth minute, right-footed Gary Stevens, playing at left-back, teased over a cross to the back post. Hateley clambered all over Tommy Boyd, nodded into the path of Durie, whose sclaffed shot spun towards Mikhailichenko and the man who couldn't score in the previous four months knocked in his second of the afternoon. Lou Macari, who had never seen his team concede a goal in the east end of Glasgow, had now witnessed three fly past Bonner inside half-an-hour. He cut a grim figure standing beside the dug-out. At that point, he might have wondered about the wisdom of knocking back a cast-iron five-year contract offer from Stoke City two months beforehand.

There was also the unwelcome sight of one misguided individual making a beeline for Maxwell after the third goal had been tucked away. Presumably, he wasn't going in search of an autograph and the pitch invader was knocked to the ground before being bundled away by stewards. It was turning into anything but a Happy New Year for anyone with Celtic connections. And that included the sitting ducks, now insultingly known as the 'Biscuit Tin Board', who populated the home directors' box. The air was thick with venom and rage as the game ticked towards the interval. Vitriol flowed uncontrollably towards the clearly uncomfortable Celtic decision-makers. Unfortunately, it was more than just verbal abuse that rained down on the men who controlled the club. One complained of being struck by a missile. It was later revealed the 'missile' was, in fact, hastily-discarded confectionary in the shape of a Mars Bar. What must have possessed some poor, fevered individual to part with his half-time snack?

There was some relief when the onfield action got underway and John Collins scored two minutes into the restart. He capitalised on a cleverly-worked free-kick twenty-five yards out, gliding away from McCall before placing a left-foot shot of laserbeam accuracy low into Maxwell's far corner of the net. Suddenly, as though a switch had been thrown, the focus of the fans was back on the pitch; the directors welcoming the respite. Amazingly, Celtic almost pulled another one back when Charlie Nicholas, rolling back the years, twisted and turned away from Richard Gough to curl an impudent, angled swerving drive away from the helpless Maxwell, only to see the ball shudder against the crossbar and bounce to safety.

Davie Syme was making his final appearance in charge of an Old Firm collision before retiring at the end of the season following twenty-one years of mystifying decisions. There was no chance of this match official leaving the big-game stage without upsetting the Celtic support at least one more time and he pulled off the feat again when Gough hauled down Nicholas as the attacker wriggled free on the right. To everyone, apart from Syme and his linesman, it looked as though the Ibrox skipper was the last Rangers player between Nicholas and Maxwell. As the fuming home fans bellowed the time-honoured 'Off! Off! Off!', the referee was not to be swayed. He was content to book the defender for his last-man assault on the Celt. The ref pointed in the direction of John Brown to indicate he was, in fact, in a deeper position than Gough. Brown on a motorbike wouldn't have caught Nicholas running in flippers. An astonished Billy McNeill couldn't help himself. He informed the watching millions worldwide, 'That's typical of that referee just to give him a yellow card'. He didn't have to elaborate.

Wdowczyk's afternoon of anguish came to a premature halt when he limped off with a leg strain just after the hour mark. Wayne Biggins made his one and only appearance in this fixture and, nine minutes after his introduction, Rangers had once again extended their advantage to three. No fault could be levelled at the substitute, but the same could not be said for the lackadaisical Gillespie whose inadequate defensive awareness was exposed yet again. Unhindered, Durie was allowed to practically walk past Gillespie's frail challenge on the right by-line before slinging over a cross. The ball eventually fell to the feet of Kuznetsov and, from twenty-five yards, the Ukraine international took a touch before volleying a ferocious drive low past Bonner at his right-hand post.

Billy McNeill was heard to say, 'Oh, dear.' That didn't quite mirror the more colourful exclamations of the thousands bedecked in green and white in attendance that day. Nine minutes from the end, Mark McNally headed down a left-wing corner-kick and Nicholas stooped to nod in the second goal, but there was little doubt the points were already thundering their way towards Govan. The pea was still rattling around in Syme's whistle when the ire of the support once again descended upon the home directors' box. Things were getting nasty, but there was some consolation for Michael Kelly, James Farrell, Jack McGinn, David Smith and Chris White; they wouldn't be in the same position the next time Rangers came visiting. Fergus McCann would make sure they were long gone.

So, ninety minutes into a new year, the Premier League table showed Rangers on top with thirty-two points after twenty-five games. Celtic were four adrift with a game in hand. They promptly blew the opportunity of closing the gap when they lost 1-0 to Partick Thistle at Firhill. The Parkhead men were destined to finish outside the top two in the league for the fifth consecutive season. Disappointing doesn't begin to describe the ongoing situation.

Celtic completed a hat-trick of consecutive defeats when they collapsed 2-1 against Motherwell, fog descended to halt the next encounter against Aberdeen in Glasgow with the scoreline standing at 0-0. The game went on again in midweek and, after ninety smog-free minutes, it was still deadlocked. This time the conclusion was 2-2 and Wayne Biggins allowed the goalscoring duties to fall to Paul Byrne and Paul McStay on this occasion. The only other worthwhile thing to note on the night was the fact that Lee Martin made his debut for the club. A crowd of only 17,235 attended the goalless draw with Dundee United in Glasgow on January 22, the week before the Scottish Cup expulsion at Fir Park. Interestingly, the game against the Tannadice side in September had attracted 26,377. Celtic had shed 9,142 fans in four months.

After a dull goalless draw against trapdoor-bound Raith Rovers, Celtic beat Hearts 2-0 at Tynecastle for their first victory on their travels since Lou Macari's managerial baptism at Ibrox on October 30 the previous year. Charlie Nicholas claimed both goals and Willie Falconer made his debut and, as his boss had predicted so boldly, he 'didn't set the heather on fire'.

It was all unravelling off the field, though. The White, Kelly and Grant dynasty was edging ever closer to an ignominious exit. The 'Celts For Change' movement, a supporters' group set up to assist in overthrowing the board, were gathering momentum; their patience and resoluteness about to be rewarded. The families who had ruled the club for generations were now being propelled towards a dark place. Pressure was mounting and 'McCann and his Rebel Gang' were storming the barricades. The first day of March saw the pendulum swing away from an obstinate set of directors never to return.

Celtic were due to play Kilmarnock at Parkhead and a blanket boycott had been called for among the various supporters' groups. 'Celts For Change' hired an agency to place a person on each turnstile and count the number of fans going into the ground. Hardly a foolproof system, but one that might give an indication of how far the faith the support had in the board had sunk. Celtic needed an attendance of 10,000 as a break-even figure for the club to remain operationally viable on a matchday basis. The board released the 'official' crowd as 10,882 for the Tuesday night match while their nemesis insisted it was 8,225. There was little point in arguing over the figures; the board was doomed. Ironically, the followers who did bother to pay in that evening broke into sustained choruses of 'Sack The Board' throughout ninety minutes of inaction. Celtic won 1-0 with a deflected free-kick goal from John Collins in the last minute.

No-one seemed too interested in the actual events of the game in the following day's newspapers. The match was overwhelmingly eclipsed by historic events off the field.

CHAPTER FIVE
McCANN'S THE MAN

Lou Macari didn't know quite what to expect. The Celtic manager had been informed Fergus McCann, fresh from his dramatic takeover of the club late the previous evening, intended visiting the dressing room before the league encounter against St Johnstone at McDiarmid Park on the Saturday afternoon of March 5. Macari admitted, 'I was ready to meet and greet the new man in charge.'

According to Macari, though, he was blatantly ignored by McCann when he made his entrance. 'He never said a word to me,' is how Macari recalls the moment. 'He walked straight past me and acknowledged Charlie Nicholas, Packie Bonner and Paul McStay. Once he had said what he had to say, he went straight out again. As the manager of Celtic Football Club, you would have thought I'd be the first person he would come to see. Instead, he just brushed past me.'

Macari's card had been marked; clearly, he wasn't in McCann's long-term plans for the club. The team boss admitted to feeling 'immediately undermined.' In an uneasy atmosphere, Macari resolved to get on with the task at hand and focus completely on the team. I was at the game in Perth that afternoon and the revolution that had gone on behind the scenes was certainly a lot more intriguing than anything that was being displayed on the park. Celtic won 1-0 with a goal in eighty-five seconds from Paul Byrne after Saints keeper Andy Rhodes had fumbled a Charlie Nicholas cross at the winger's feet. A shade over eighty-eight minutes of general tedium followed while McCann and Brian Dempsey, who had played the role as a campaign manager, watched from the stand.

The previous evening, a beaming Dempsey emerged from the foyer at Celtic Park to face the Press Pack, newspapermen, TV cameras, radio microphones and intrigued supporters, desperate for a snippet of news. 'The rebels have won,' exclaimed Dempsey to an illuminating barrage of popping flashbulbs from photographers' cameras, eager to catch the historic moment. It was the beginning of a new era for Celtic; it was the beginning of the end for Lou Macari. Even before a ball had been kicked in anger, it appeared McCann had already chosen to dispense with Macari and have him replaced. The name of Tommy Burns, then managing Kilmarnock, continually cropped up.

It wasn't an atmosphere conducive to a comfortable rapport between the two most important professionals at the club. Years later, Macari, somewhat ruefully, recalled, 'He saw me as no different from the groundsman or the head chef.' McCann, known as 'The Bunnet' to the fans because of his permanent choice of headgear, had no interest in popularity contests. Without a flicker of emotion, he declared, 'I want people to judge me on what we have achieved after five years. I will go back home to my home in Bermuda, play some golf and live a healthier life.'

Three Celtic managers would attempt to prosper - or merely survive - under his reign. All three - Lou Macari along with Tommy Burns and Wim Jansen - would fail to win the approval of a pragmatic, fastidious, demanding individual inclined towards ruthless tendencies. Jozef Venglos, after seven months of dealing with McCann, would go at the end of 1998/99 season.

Even once-trusted ally Brian Dempsey, the former Celtic director, was forced to walk. He didn't see out 1994 and explained, 'Mr McCann is taking the club in the wrong direction. It's because of this that I have decided I will not be back at Celtic as part of the team for the future.' Dempsey will be forever remembered for delivering his 'the rebels have won' proclamation on the steps of Celtic Park, but McCann later took the credit for the words. 'Brian didn't know what to say,' he claimed. 'I told him what to say and he went out and said it.'

Years later, Dempsey would recall his first clandestine meeting in a London hotel with McCann, eighteen months before they eventually wrested control of Celtic. The Glasgow businessman observed, 'He was a difficult man. He was uncompromising, obdurate, stubborn, implacable and immoveable. I've never come across a character like him and I've met a few in my day.'

All of which may have been music to the ears of McCann. Certainly, the old Celtic board would no doubt have agreed with Dempsey. Right from the start of the campaign for change, the Scots-born Canadian had acted like an unshakeable terrier. When it was obvious the club was in dire financial trouble, McCann headed an underwriting group which offered £13.8million for new shares. The proposal was put to an emergency general meeting in November 1993 and was rejected by the board.

There were those 'in the know' who insisted the Bank of Scotland refused to honour the first installment of his £350,000 transfer fee to Sheffield United for Willie Falconer. There was so much infighting at the time and back-stabbing among the club officials, it was sometimes extremely difficult to separate fact from fiction, information from disinformation. One scribe put it this way, 'Celtic are a family club. This is supposed to sound cosy, but it is, in fact, a dark truth. Here is a family like the Macbeths or the Lears.' At this stage, the overdraft limit of £5million had been exceeded and the bank told the board they were preparing to call in the receivers on Thursday March 3.

Chris White and Michael Kelly were prepared to sell their shares to retail businessman Gerald Weisfeld, whose guarantee to pay off £3million of the overdraft was acceptable to the bank. Tom Grant and Kevin Kelly, however, were not prepared to sell their shares to Weisfeld and, eventually, the proposed deal fell through. Four directors - Kevin Kelly, Jack McGinn, James Farrell and Grant - notified the bank they favoured McCann in the takeover bid. By then, Michael Kelly, Chris White and David Smith were ready to cash in their shares.

On March 4, at the Bank of Scotland in Glasgow's Trongate, Fergus McCann assumed control of Celtic Football Club. It was revealed Celtic had been eight minutes away from being declared bankrupt. Later, McCann told a gathering of fans at the steps at Celtic Park, 'We have new people, a new plan, a new vision and the strength to go forward. And I can tell you we have every intention of reaching the objective that you want, which is Celtic at the very top.'

Celtic drew 0-0 with Hibs at Easter Road in the second game under the new regime, but McCann was not in place in the directors' box for the start of the match against Motherwell at Parkhead on March 26 when 36,199 fans materialised in mass salutation for the enormous role he had played in overthrowing the old board, despised by many. Dempsey remembered, 'He didn't appear until well after the kick-off because one of the turnstiles wasn't working fast enough in taking in the fans' money. He was driven purely by money, nothing else. But he would tell you that himself.'

Situations may have been in the process of being sorted in the boardroom, but there were still rumblings of the dressing room being fractured. Lou Macari recalled how a senior figure among the playing staff had sought him out only weeks into his new job. He informed Liam Brady's successor that 'three or four' players weren't pulling their weight. 'You have to get them out of here,' Macari was told. 'They're a nightmare.' Naturally, the manager did his best to keep a lid on the unrest among the playing staff. It is a testimony to his acting skills that Macari could face the Press at least once a week with his usual bubbly outlook and make all the right noises. 'Difficult season on and off the field...we're still pulling things together...we'll be better prepared for the next campaign.'

The sought-after new era under McCann didn't get off to the desired winning start at Parkhead. Celtic lost 1-0 to Motherwell after yet another calamitous mistake from an error-strewn defence. A simple through ball decimated the back four, goalkeeper Carl Muggleton slid out to collect the pass, fumbled at the feet of the nippy Dougie Arnott and, with Tony Mowbray slow to react, the Fir Park striker rolled the ball into the empty net. Outside the two Old Firm confrontations, this was by the far the biggest attendance at Celtic Park all season. They sighed in unison as the team performed abysmally. Emphasising the lack of understanding among the players, Tommy Coyne should have scored an embarrassingly simple goal in the second-half. Goalkeeper

Sieb Dykstra launched a huge punt downfield, not a Celt was in sight as Coyne raced onto the ball to lob Muggleton, but his effort drifted just wide of the target.

Four days later, only 14,140 fans were in place to witness Simon Donnelly score his first goals for Celtic in a 2-0 win over Raith Rovers. Once again, though, it was hardly an inspiring showing. Celtic were forced to squeeze seven league games into the month of April and Macari managed to guide his team to two wins while settling for four draws and suffering one defeat; eight points from a possible fourteen would never win a championship.

Almost 20,000 fans disappeared off the radar eleven days after the spirited turn-out against Motherwell when Dundee provided the opposition at Parkhead. It ended 1-1 with Donnelly, signed by Liam Brady for zilch from Queen's Park, scoring again. The previous week, Willie Falconer scored his first goal for the club in a solid 3-1 triumph over Dundee United at Tannadice. On April 9, Hearts left Glasgow with a point after a 2-2 draw, Rudi Vata and John Collins scoring for Celtic. On April 16, the team performed abominably in a 2-0 defeat against a distinctly-average Kilmarnock side at Rugby Park. I was accompanied by Peter Grant, sidelined through injury, to Ayrshire that gloomy afternoon. It wouldn't be fair to quote the midfielder, whose dedication to the Celtic cause could never be doubted. Suffice to say, he wasn't too impressed with what he had witnessed, either.

Probably the most interesting part of the day was the journey back to Glasgow when our car was stopped at red lights. A coachload of Rangers fans, returning after watching their team beat Raith Rovers 4-0 at Ibrox, was heading in the opposite direction. It rolled to a halt, just a few feet from us. Sure enough, one eagle-eyed, blue-red-and-white-bedecked individual spotted the Celtic player. The antics after that from a fair percentage of so-called sports fans was a fairly compelling argument for birth control. Pat McGinlay hit two the following week as Celtic won 2-0 over Dundee at Dens Park and Donnelly scored his fourth goal for the Hoops in a dire 1-1 draw with St Johnstone in the east end of Glasgow watched by 10,602 hardy souls. Then came the most bizarre meeting in history between Scottish football's juggernauts in Govan on Saturday April 27.

Macari recalled, 'Not long after McCann took over, we went back to Ibrox with no Celtic supporters in the stadium. It was the first time that had ever happened at an Old Firm game and it will probably never happen again. I was sent with thirteen players and a security officer. If any trouble had broken out, we would have been looking after him. McCann had fallen out with Rangers because they had refused to pay for damage done to seats at Celtic Park. For the return, by way of protest, he chose not to accept any tickets for fans or directors. There was no-one representing Celtic other than the backroom team, those thirteen players and a security officer.'

There is another side of the tit-for-tat story, of course. Rangers owner David Murray claimed there had been a total of £20,000 worth of damage inflicted on his team's stadium on the last six occasions the Celtic supporters had visited Ibrox. McCann, while insisting there had been a certain amount of vandalism on occasions Rangers supporters had been at Parkhead in recent times, also countered by saying he would pay a sum of money, but only if Celtic could arrange for their own stewarding at Rangers' ground in the future. Murray rejected that proposal and, while the Celtic players faced their counterparts on the field and 47,108 in the stands, McCann was at Parkhead that afternoon along with 12,000 fans to watch the reserves beat the Ibrox side 3-1.

Macari added, 'It was a hell of a day. We picked up Tony Mowbray en route. Tony had been looking after his wife, who was seriously ill with cancer. Even on the way to the ground I wasn't sure if he was going to be in the right frame of mind to play against Rangers. Had he turned round and said to me, "I'm not up for it, boss," I would have fully accepted that. He didn't. "Are you ready for a battle, Tony?" I asked. He answered, "No problem, boss. Let's get ripped into them." He was our best player by a mile. We were winning 1-0 after a fantastic free-kick by John Collins, but they equalised with about six minutes to go. That match, for me, as a player and a manager, was my greatest experience at Ibrox. When we scored you could hear a pin drop, save for one lone voice in the crowd shouting for Celtic. I don't think anyone has seen him since.'

There was a humorous interlude when a plane flew overhead trailing a banner proclaiming, 'Hail! Hail! The Celts Are Here.' John Collins said, 'That was genius. Celtic supporters have a great ability to come up with different, fun ways of supporting the team and the guy who hired that plane carried on an admirable tradition.'

Coincidentally, Celtic completed the campaign with two 1-1 stalemates against Partick Thistle and Aberdeen, four identical scorelines in succession. Pat McGinlay netted his tenth goal of the campaign in the deadlock with the Firhill side with only 16,827 fans inside Celtic Park to witness the curtain coming down. Liam Brady's signing completed the programme as the club's top goalscorer, the only performer in green and white hoops to get into double figures for the entire league season. Celtic's legendary defender Tommy Gemmell, in his heyday, wouldn't have been satisfied with that total.

The forty-four-game Premier League season limped to a halt with a draw against Aberdeen at Pittodrie, where a fresh-faced, flaxen-haired Simon Donnelly scored again. The point meant precious little to Celtic as the club were anchored in fourth place on fifty points, dismally four adrift of Motherwell. The Dons were runners-up to Rangers on fifty-five points, three short of their Ibrox rivals. It was the Govan outfit's sixth successive title and they were already making noises about overtaking Celtic's proud nine-in-a-row achievement, which, under the leadership of the incomparable Jock Stein, had come to life in 1966 and stretched into the seventies. It could be added that Big Jock had performed the feat without the assistance of a blank book and that Stein won the European Cup, reached another final and participated in four semi-finals. Rangers failed to get anywhere near Stein's record.

Celtic had agreed to play Manchester United in Mark Hughes' Testimonial Match at Old Trafford on May 16 and the youthful exuberance of the rapidly-emerging Simon Donnelly helped him to two fine goals in the 3-1 win. Willie Falconer got the other with future

Celt Dion Dublin heading in a consolation. There was an odd twist to this game. Chic Charnley, a well-known admirer of all things Celtic, was given special dispensation by his Partick Thistle manager John Lambie to turn out in the green and white hoops as a guest player. By all accounts, the cultured left-sided midfielder performed well against Alex Ferguson's team and had set up Donnelly for his second goal with a deft flick into his path. However, after returning to Glasgow, he heard nothing about the possibility of making the one-off arrangement permanent.

Then, six days later, it was off to Canada to participate in a tournament called the Scottish Football Festival in Ontario along with Hearts and Aberdeen in the Hamilton Cup. A full-strength Celtic beat the Tynecastle outfit 4-2 on penalties after a 1-1 draw and five days afterwards they turned over the Dons 1-0 to win the trophy.

The season, which had kicked off with a different manager and a different board of directors, was over at long last, but the drama was just beginning for Lou Macari.

CHAPTER SIX
A BITTER PARTING

Lou Macari's sacking by Celtic was as brutal as it was abrupt. It was the morning of June 14 and Macari was at Manchester Airport as he prepared to mix business with pleasure; a family holiday in the States where he could also take in some of the games in the 1994 World Cup Finals. Relations with Fergus McCann had become stretched and the breaking point arrived during a terse telephone conversation between the manager and the managing director.

According to Macari, he had booked tickets for the World Cup long before McCann arrived at Celtic. He said, 'I was going to spend my summer months watching the world's best players. That's the way I had operated all my life. That's the way you get a decent team on the pitch. You watch matches. You watch players. McCann thought otherwise. "Yes, you can go," he said, "but only on my terms. After the first match in New York, you fly back to Glasgow to work at Celtic Park on the Monday and Tuesday. You can then fly to America for the next game. Then back to Glasgow for two days, then out to the States again." He had me flying over the Atlantic more often than a pilot. I told him he was being ludicrous.'

The day before Macari was fired, he left a letter on McCann's desk at Parkhead. He had sought the advice of the League Managers Association in England and had asked their lawyer, on his behalf, to respond in writing to his perception of the behaviour of the Celtic supremo. Macari showed the letter to his assistants Peter Henderson and Ashley Grimes and they agreed it was the way ahead. It turned out to be a fast-track to the Parkhead exit. McCann would later state the contents of the letter accused him of interfering in Macari's role as manager and he believed that to be a 'bare-faced insult' to him personally and to the club.

Macari had telephoned McCann to provide him with forwarding addresses and telephone numbers of his whereabouts in America. McCann, once again, said he expected the manager to be back in Glasgow to catch up with club matters. 'I told him he was being ridiculous,' admitted Macari. According to the team boss, McCann responded, 'Can I just get this right? What you are telling me is that you are not going to obey my orders, is that right?' Macari agreed that was, in fact, the position. McCann came back with, 'Well, if that's the case, I'm sacking you.'

By the time Macari arrived in America, he had been officially removed as manager of Celtic. McCann had sent dismissal notices to his digs in Glasgow, his home in Stoke and to a PO Box in America at Hilton Head, South Carolina. In a quandary about his next move, Macari decided to carry on with his World Cup plans. Ironically, he turned up at his first game to discover he was sitting beside Walter Smith, the Rangers manager. The news of Macari parting company with Celtic had yet to hit the newspapers. Smith asked if everything was okay at Parkhead. Macari replied, 'I haven't got a problem any more, Walter. I've just been sacked.'

Macari's lasting regret is that he never got the extended opportunity he required to turn things around on the football pitch. 'There was a massive job to do, but I couldn't even make a start,' he said. 'Even more frustrating was the fact the fans never really knew what was happening behind the scenes.' Macari, with the instinct of a gambler, backed himself to sort out the myriad of problems that awaited him at Parkhead. He couldn't have guessed the extent of the mess that awaited him. It was never a marriage made in heaven and the separation was messy while it was dragged through the courts. After only eight months of a three-year contract, Macari was demanding £431,000 in compensation for his dismissal while he, in turn, was charged with negligence in his duties at the club. Celtic claimed he had breached his contract and were counter-claiming for £250,000, the compensation fee they paid to Stoke City to free the manager from his contract.

In his evidence, McCann complained of long spells when the manager was away from Celtic Park. He had failed to set up a permanent home in Glasgow and often went to Stoke to visit his family. 'I think Mr Macari felt a manager was a kind of freelance operator that could go from football match to football match without taking charge of the actual operation within a club,' asserted McCann. 'I was trying very hard for him to get the message - he had to do the job he was being paid to do.'

Macari hit back saying a permanent move to Scotland had been planned, but until such times as everything was put in place, he believed he could handle the situation while his family continued to live in England. In a rare moment of humour, he added, 'I don't actually believe my wife could have any input into me helping Celtic be a top-class football club again.'

As the mud flew, Macari accused the managing director of having a total lack of knowledge and understanding of the role of a football team manager. The letter stated, 'I suggest that you let me get on with the job I was employed to do. Perhaps a period of reflection whilst I am away (at the World Cup) will assist you in seeing matters in a clearer perspective so that on my return you will see fit to allow me to get on with my task of rebuilding the team and coaching it to success without placing obstacles in my way.'

McCann thought it was an unacceptable attitude. He said, 'The idea of being a free spirit that could come and go occasionally is not, by any definition, the role of a football manager of a major football club. It had become quite clear from the letter and the behaviour he was exhibiting that he was not interested in taking instructions or following directions from me. I am paying this man £150,000-a-year to do a job and expecting him to do it well and part of that job is to follow directions.'

Without meeting any prior disapproval from other board members, McCann sacked Macari during the phone call. He said, 'We basically had reached an impossible stage. There was obviously nowhere to go. He was making no attempt to say, "Let's sit down and see if we can work together." He really put me in a position of having to take action.' McCann said that, although Celtic had failed to qualify for Europe for the first time in twenty years, the team's performance and Macari's dismissal were not connected. He added, 'I knew quite well that a lot of improvements had to be made and it was not an overnight task.'

The Celtic Managing Director also said he was dismayed about the way Macari had given free transfers to fans' favourites Charlie Nicholas and Pat Bonner. He claimed their departure wasn't handled 'in a proper and honourable fashion' and said it reflected badly on the club that their roles weren't properly recognised. McCann also insisted that senior players had complained that they had little confidence in Macari. He told a court he could not remember who, but he thought they were Paul McStay, Pat Bonner, Charlie Nicholas and Peter Grant.

After a courtroom battle that lasted two months, Macari faced a massive legal bill after failing to convince a judge he was wrongly sacked. The 'amiable, but not particularly astute' Macari was ruled by the presiding judge, Lady Cosgrove, to have been in breach of his contract with the club and his claim for more than £431,000 damages was rejected. But she also dismissed Celtic's counter-claim of £250,000. Her eighty-page judgement followed eight weeks of courtroom evidence at the Court of Session in Edinburgh and placed both Macari and McCann in an unfavourable light.

Macari was said to have failed to appreciate the change to the regime brought about when McCann became managing director in 1994. However, Lady Cosgrove also found McCann was an 'uncompromising and somewhat arrogant employer who expected unquestioning compliance'. The former manager said, 'Obviously, I am hugely disappointed at the outcome. I will be meeting my legal representatives to study the findings to see if there are any grounds for an appeal. To be honest, I can't believe it. Celtic didn't win their case against me and I didn't win my case against them. It sounds good to say it's a draw, but to me, of course, it's not a draw.' In a brief statement, the club said, 'Celtic is very pleased with the judgement which was as expected.'

The verdict hit Macari severely in the pocket. His lawyer's fees were over half the £431,000 he had demanded for wrongful dismissal. Celtic, too, had to pay a similar amount to their legal team. It was obvious McCann knew employment law and Macari didn't. No-one came out of it smelling of roses. Several years afterwards, Macari, who also lost a subsequent appeal against the decision, said, 'At the time, you're upset because you know the way it's been manoeuvred and what is being said is untrue. And it leaves a nasty taste in your mouth. Years later, when you see others in the hot seat - Tommy Burns, God rest him, Wim Jansen - it wasn't a personal thing against me. It was the way he (McCann) was.'

Even today, Macari is often been asked if it is a source of disappointment that was not a successful manager at the club he still loves. He answers, 'It was never on the cards. It was never meant to be. People have said Fergus saved Celtic and I understand why they say it. But if Fergus hadn't come in, someone else would have because the job was there to do. In fairness to Fergus, that's where he was smart. He realised what Celtic Football Club had going for it, not just at that time, but what it has always got going for it - a massive worldwide support.'

Fergus McCann and Celtic were back in court after appointing Tommy Burns as Macari's replacement. The Ayrshire club appointed the popular Celt as their player/manager in 1992 and he led them to promotion to the Premier League a year later. They refused to allow Celtic to talk to their boss about the vacant post at Parkhead. After Burns was announced as Celtic's new manager, the Scottish Football Association fined them £100,000 for illegally 'tapping' or speaking to the individual without the Rugby Park outfit's permission. Kilmarnock were also permitted to retain his playing registration, effectively ending his professional career as a player at the age of thirty-seven.

Once again, the wheel of fortune was preparing to spin at Celtic Park as a new season dawned. No-one dared to mention a new era.

CHAPTER SEVEN
TOMMY BURNS: WELCOME BACK TO PARADISE

CELTIC'S league form during Tommy Burns' first season in charge was nothing short of an embarrassment. The team careered wildly from catastrophe to calamity. Chaos lurked in every fixture, despair was a weekly condition. Mishap followed setback; grief piled upon misery.

Admittedly, the team would not have been aided by the fact they did not play a game at Celtic Park while the stadium was being totally rebuilt and Hampden Park became 'home' for the campaign. Nevertheless, the final Premier Division table was x-certificate material as far as the downcast support was concerned.

Reconstruction had trimmed the league from twelve teams to ten and three points would now be awarded for a win. Burns' team hobbled into fourth place with fifty-one points from thirty-six games, shedding an alarming fifty-seven points in the painful process. Rangers collected the crown for the seventh successive campaign, eighteen points ahead of their fiercest rivals. Motherwell and Hibs also had the luxury of looking down on Celtic.

Unbelievably, Burns saw his players fail to win a solitary match in the months of October and November. The shambolic run was only halted on December 18 when, mercifully, goals from Peter Grant and Andy Walker defeated Falkirk 2-0 in Glasgow. The club had set an all-time appalling record by failing to register a victory in a woeful sequence of eleven games - three lost and eight drawn - as they were summarily and disdainfully dismissed as genuine title contenders long before the turn of the year. It was grim stuff for despondent, weary followers brought up on flair and adventure.

Celtic failed to score a solitary goal on ten occasions and their highest total was three which they managed in one game, the 3-0 triumph over Rangers at Hampden in the third last outing of the campaign when it was far too late and the trophy was already destined for Ibrox. The team claimed two strikes in eleven other outings and one on fourteen occasions. In total, Celtic notched thirty-nine goals, just a decimal point better than one a game. The top league marksman was John Collins with eight strikes. Jimmy McGrory once scored eight goals in one game against Dunfermline in 1928. Between them, Pat Bonner and Gordon Marshall combined to concede thirty-three. The League Cup - masquerading under its latest guise as the Coca-Cola Cup - proved to be another disaster area ultimately providing one of the most shocking outcomes in Celtic's history.

And, yet, when the final whistle shrilled on the last day of the season, Paul McStay and Peter Grant, unashamedly, wept tears of happiness as they led the merry band who cavorted around Hampden Park in the midst of the most joyous scenes the national stadium had ever witnessed following a nail biting Scottish Cup Final success against an Airdrie team well up for the occasion and the challenge. However, there was a fairly harrowing season to endure before Celtic reached that wonderful stage of exultation.

There was expectation in the air when Celtic kicked off their League Cup campaign against Ayr United at quaint Somerset Park on Tuesday August 16. I spoke to the First Division side's manager Simon Stainrod before the tie and he was quite happy to reveal he would be keeping his tactics simple; the Celtic defence could expect a sustained aerial bombardment throughout the ninety minutes. Stainrod, who was quite a classy middle-of-the-park performer with Queens Park Rangers and Aston Villa, among others, during his playing days, abandoned his previous values and had transformed a tiny part of Ayrshire into the 'Land of the Giants'. He had assembled a fearsome line-up of six-footers with his burly striker Ian Gilzean, son of former Scotland international Alan, as his squadron leader. Stainrod promised that 'Celtic will know they've been in a game'. He didn't need to draw any pictures.

I attended the game along with Pat McGinlay, sidelined through injury, and Stevie Archibald, my old mate who knew a thing or two about the more scientific approach to the beautiful game after playing for Scotland, Spurs, Barcelona and Aberdeen under the guidance of Jock Stein, Alex Ferguson, Terry Venables and Johan Cruyff. We wondered what to expect that balmy evening. Peter Grant scored early on and, despite frantic and monotonous high balls thrown haphazardly into the visitors' penalty area, Tony Mowbray, Mike Galloway and Mark McNally held firm. It wasn't pretty to watch, but it was progress.

Next up, was the altogether more intriguing encounter against Dundee at Dens Park just over a fortnight later. Paul McStay has a reason to remember a towsy, rough-and-tumble affair on Tayside - he was sent off for the first time in his career. Thankfully, it didn't impact on the final outcome of 2-1 in favour of Burns' side. Before the game, there had been intense media speculation about Arsenal pondering a £3million bid for John Collins, a hefty fee in 1994. Fergus McCann earned more kudos with the Celtic support by ordering the club to take the unusual step of issuing an official denial. In short, Collins was staying put.

Certainly, the rumours, informed or otherwise, didn't blur the focus of the elegant midfielder and he emphasised that point with the opening goal in the eighth minute, a magnificently-struck left-foot angled drive from twenty-five yards that hurtled into the top corner with French keeper Michel Pagaeud a spectator. However, some slack defensive play allowed Ray Farningham to nullify that effort with a glancing header from a Neil McCann cross in the nineteenth minute. It was stalemated until twelve minutes from time when Andy Walker, who had just returned to the Scotland international set-up, provided a virtuoso reason why he was back in favour. The dapper little attacker collected the ball in the middle of the park and embarked on a slalom-like run through the retreating Dundee defence before sliding in the winner.

Referee Jim McCluskey had the distinction of flashing an unwanted debut red card at Celtic skipper Paul McStay who was banished along with Dundee's Czechoslovakian tough guy Dusan Vrto. A newspaper report put it thus, 'The defender held back McStay as he bore down on goal and, as both players got to their feet, McStay made contact with his opponent.' I suppose we could read between the lines. There was no appeal from Celtic and McStay served his punishment. Equally, there were no complaints from manager Tommy Burns.

Celtic were given the opportunity of completing a Tayside double knock-out when they were paired with Dundee United on September 21, this time the tie being played at the national stadium in Glasgow. Ivan Golac, who had lost out to Liam Brady for the manager's job in the summer of 1991, was now in charge at the Tannadice outfit with Jim McLean, at last, gravitating from dug-out to boardroom as chairman. Golac had succeeded in bringing the Scottish Cup to the club in his first year, beating favourites Rangers 1-0 with a Craig Brewster goal. McLean had failed in six previous attempts to annex the silverware.

A solitary goal four minutes from time by John Collins in a quarter-final tie watched by 28,859 fans made certain Golac wouldn't be adding the League Cup to the national trophy on his CV. The Yugoslav, in fact, was sacked in March the following year and never returned to Scotland with his managerial travels taking him to Iceland, Serbia and Ukraine. It had been a strange year for United as they were relegated for the first time since the inception of the Premier League in 1975.

Aberdeen had managed a goalless draw against Celtic in Glasgow on league business on October 8 before they returned for the League Cup semi-final later in the month. The game was played at neutral Ibrox and it was a nerve-shredding head-to-head. Pittodrie gaffer Willie Miller was under pressure to deliver in his third year in charge and the League Cup looked his best bet for silverware. The former Dons favourite had seen the club knocked out of Europe at the first stage by the Latvians of Skonto Riga and the mood of the support was turning against him. How quickly in football heroes can become zeroes. The last-four encounter plodded its way to a goalless ninety minutes with both teams failing to ignite. It was obvious one goal was going to settle such a finely-balanced confrontation. With the clock ticking down, Brian O'Neil threw himself at a high cross, outjumped startled defender David Winnie, and flashed an unstoppable header high past the flailing Theo Snelders.

Celtic were in the Final where they would meet First Division side Raith Rovers at Ibrox on November 27. The Kirkcaldy outfit had struggled against Airdrie in their semi-final at McDiarmid Park and had to rely on penalty-kicks to advance on a 5-4 shoot-out victory. Tommy Burns was now ninety minutes from Celtic's first trophy success in five years. Despite indifferent form in the league, the Parkhead men were massive favourites to stop the rot against Jimmy Nicholl's mixture of journeymen and eager youngsters.

I was among a few of the Press gang who were invited for a chat with the Celtic manager a few days before the game. It was a fairly informal meeting in a Glasgow hotel and Burns took it in turn to sit in with the scribes at a couple of the tables to discuss the game. I realise it is all too easy to be wise after the event and, yes, hindsight does offer you twenty/twenty vision. But I got the distinct impression Burns was dwelling a little too much on the prospect of failure. As you would expect from a worthy sportsman, he refused to write off his opponents, but I detected more than just a hint of good manners. Burns was never the bombastic sort, in any case, but, over lunch that afternoon, I saw him fret more than I would have anticipated. It looked as though he was distinctly uncomfortable at the sheer weight of responsibility that had been heaped upon his slender shoulders.

Remember, this was going to be only his nineteenth competitive game in charge of the club. Maybe, just maybe, he was TOO close to the man on the terracing. He didn't have to imagine the despair and the disgrace a defeat against Raith Rovers would bring to Celtic. He would feel the hurt more than most. Being a deep-thinker, he couldn't have helped but stray towards the worst-case scenario. In normal circumstances, the Celtic manager would throw in a joke or two, an off-the-wall observation. Not on this occasion, though. He was deadly serious throughout our conversation. Unusually, it was a mirthless interlude. Burns realised, also, he could not betray even an iota of his innermost feelings to his players. He had to appear upbeat as he led the team towards Ibrox that grey, bleak Sunday afternoon.

It was Celtic's first appearance in a showpiece occasion since they lost 9-8 on penalty-kicks in the Scottish Cup Final against Aberdeen in 1990. Lightning couldn't strike twice, could it?

A sell-out crowd of 45,384 welcomed both teams onto the field and Burns went with this line-up: Gordon Marshall; Mike Galloway, Mark McNally, Tony Mowbray, Tommy Boyd; Simon Donnelly, Paul McStay, Brian O'Neil, John Collins; Charlie Nicholas and Andy Walker. On the substitutes' bench were Pat Bonner, Paul Byrne and Willie Falconer. Raith manager Jimmy Nicholl had no such riches of talent at his disposal and was attempting to get the best out of the thirty-eight-year-old legs of veteran defender David Narey after his twenty-one years of sterling service at Dundee United. The ever-busy Colin Cameron was in midfield and a youthful Stephen Crawford was making a name for himself as a regular goalscorer in the First Division.

And it was the future Scotland international who gave Celtic a rude awakening in the nineteenth minute after a strangely tentative start from Burns' men. The defence, after failing to clear a routine left-wing corner-kick, allowed the Raith striker far too much time and space to get the ball under control on the edge of the penalty area. He took aim and fired. His low drive might have lacked pace, but there was nothing wrong with the precision as it escaped Gordon Marshall's dive at his right-hand post.

It took Celtic only thirteen minutes to shake themselves from their disturbing lethargy and make it all-square again. Boyd hit an accurate cross from the right, Galloway knocked it back into the mix and Walker dived to head solidly behind Scott Thomson. Strangely, Celtic didn't go for the jugular. Half-time came and went without any additional scoring and the game rolled through the second-half. Thomson was hardly being overworked in the Raith goal and the same could be said for Marshall at the other end. Celtic pushed forward, but there was precious little inspiration. McStay and Collins struggled for a pocket of room in which to work as enthusiastic opponents went about their jobs with a hungry zeal.

With six minutes to go, Tommy Burns clenched both fists, raised his gaze to the heavens and yelled, 'Yes!' He had just watched Celtic take the lead. After neat lead-up play from Collins, Walker swivelled and slammed a ferocious effort against the left-hand post and Nicholas, still retaining that opportunistic penalty-box awareness, was first to react to lash the ball over the line. Ibrox was awash with green and white as the fans partied, so close to bringing a delightful and noisy halt to the so-called 'barren years'. Two minutes later, they were silenced when the Kirkcaldy outfit equalised. Jason Dair swept in a low left foot shot from twenty yards and it looked a simple catch for Marshall. Distressingly, the keeper allowed the ball to escape his frantic grasp and it hit Gordon Dalziel before bouncing into the net.

I have yet to see evidence the Raith forward was onside when Dair hit his shot. To me, he looked at least a yard ahead of Galloway and McNally. Referee Jim McCluskey, Paul McStay's acquaintance from the earlier round at Dens Park, didn't hesitate, neither did his linesman and I believe the Celtic players were simply too shell-shocked to even protest. The goal was given. A few days later, I was with a couple of friends in the office pub on the Broomielaw and Davie Cooper, of Rangers and Scotland fame, was in the vicinity. Don Morrison, my old Sunday Mail colleague, had since moved to the Sunday Mirror and 'ghosted' Cooper's column. They would meet once a week and Don would jot down the thoughts of the player, who was at Motherwell at the time. Cooper overheard my remarks about Dalziel's goal being illegal. 'You're the first guy I've heard say that,' chipped in Cooper, who was, as everyone realised, Rangers through and through. There was a pause before he added, 'You're spot on, he was miles offside.'

Celtic made no headway in the extra half-an-hour while Narey, almost unbelievably, and Shaun Dennis provided an unassailable double barrier. The ball was hoofed skywards time and again and it was impossible for Celtic to find any kind of rhythm in those thirty minutes. I was in the Press Box that afternoon and Stuart Gray, son of former Scotland and Leeds United star Eddie, caught my eye. He was seen as a promising youngster at Parkhead and had already made a few first team appearances. We looked at each and grimaced. Somehow, we just knew what was coming next.

The first five penalty-kicks were taken and scored. Marshall went the wrong way as Raith's sixth successive attempt was thumped behind him. All eyes were now on skipper Paul McStay as the shoot-out went to sudden death. 'It's unthinkable, surely, for the skipper to miss,' said the TV commentator. The captain struck the ball firmly enough, but it lacked accuracy. Thomson threw himself across his goal to his right, got his hands to the effort and beat it away. McStay looked devastated as the Fifers wildly celebrated the upset.

Narey deservedly won the sponsors' Man of the Match award and another defensive stalwart that afternoon was Stephen McAnespie. Afterwards, he revealed, 'When we got to our dressing room, two guys came in behind us. It was John Greig and Ally McCoist and they presented us with a case of Rangers champagne.' Strange, that. In all my years of reporting, I have to admit I hadn't realised either Greig or McCoist had any sort of affinity with the club from Stark's Park, Kirkcaldy. At the Press Conference afterwards, manager Jimmy Nicholl, a former Rangers player, had the good grace to look absolutely stunned at the outcome. Scott Thomson was also invited to meet the media. Someone asked him, 'Is that the best penalty save you've ever made, Scott?' The keeper didn't have to ponder too long with his reply. 'It's the ONLY penalty save I've ever made,' he answered. No-one could have faulted his timing. Gordon Dalziel was asked about his goal. He, too, was candid. 'I think it came off my nose,' he said.

Tommy Burns' worst nightmare had materialised at the home of the club's bitterest rivals. Football can be a cruel game and there were the expected recriminations afterwards. Some of the criticism was merited, of course, but some of it was way over the top. No-one escaped the blanket scorn as the disappointment hit home that an ideal opportunity to put some silverware in the Parkhead trophy cabinet after an absence of five years had been carelessly dismissed.

The league had already been blown. It took Celtic four attempts to win another game after the Raith Rovers debacle. There were draws against Hibs (1-1), Motherwell (2-2) and Aberdeen (0-0) before a 2-0 triumph over Falkirk in Glasgow. Somewhere in that run, Burns had taken his team to Liverpool for Ian Rush's Testimonial Match. The final scoreline of 6-0 did not flatter the Anfield men. Old Hoops favourite Kenny Dalglish came on as a substitute at the interval and played the entire second-half without breaking sweat. In fact, he set up the last two goals. Dalglish was forty-three years old at the time. Burns lamented, 'We're in a different world entirely. We have a long way back to get into that league.'

Only the Scottish Cup remained as a viable target. Did Tommy Burns - and Celtic - dare to dream?

CHAPTER EIGHT
THE CUP THAT CHEERS

Fergus McCann was swiftly earning the mantle of Frugal McCann. As far as enticing new players to Celtic was concerned, his focus appeared to be on matters off the field, a perceived one-eyed approach which was more than a little exasperating and disconcerting for Tommy Burns.

Davie Hay, former player and manager, was brought back to the club by Burns as chief scout and proved to be an astute judge of quality and ability. He kept a steady stream of names for the manager to peruse and Hay also knew there was little point in checking out a player rated upwards of £2million. McCann made it abundantly clear that sort of figure didn't equate with his vision of the fiscal future for the club.

However, even McCann was stirred to loosen the purse strings after the inadequacies he had witnessed in the Ian Rush Testimonial Match at Anfield before the turn of the year. The team may have been shorn of the talents of injured midfield trio Paul McStay, John Collins and Phil O'Donnell, but a selection that boasted players such as Tommy Boyd, Tony Mowbray, Peter Grant and Charlie Nicholas wasn't expected to fold so alarmingly and so meekly. Goalkeeper Gordon Marshall was the lucky one - he missed out after being dropped to make way for Pat Bonner. Marshall hadn't impressed in the League Cup Final fiasco against Raith Rovers and, after a 2-2 draw with Motherwell on December 3, he was axed to make way for the thirty-four-year-old Irishman who kept the position for the remainder of the campaign.

Even McCann, who never professed to being a football aficionado, was left in no doubt that his manager needed quality within his ranks. The team were performing in a perpetual state of bewilderment and a angry Burns spent almost an hour with his team in the dressing room after the humiliation on Merseyside. 'Celtic don't play friendlies,' he reminded a set of players dismissed far too easily. He urgently sought a meeting with the chairman. Burns had added Andy Walker, a second-time around Celt from Bolton for £300,000 in July, while Phil O'Donnell cost £2million from Motherwell at the start of September. In the main, though, he had soldiered on with the squad he had inherited while some critics savagely insisted he should have shown at least half of them the door only weeks after arriving as Lou Macari's successor.

The upshot was that a 6ft 5in Dutch striker in the shape of Pierre van Hooijdonk was introduced to the Celtic fans on a bitterly cold evening of January 11 at Hampden Park in a league game against Hearts. Davie Hay recommended the beanpole frontman and McCann wrote a cheque for £1.3million to FC Rhoda. Van Hooijdonk may not have been an instantly recogniseable name, but he did have exciting credentials. He had netted twenty-five times in thirty-one games for his Dutch side the previous season and, in doing so, had beaten a long-standing Dennis Bergkamp record by claiming goals in eleven successive games. Hay recalled, 'I had travelled to Holland a few times around that period because Dutch football was at a good standard and there were players who could be bought for reasonable fees. Wages, too, were manageable.

'I took in an NAC Breda game one afternoon and Pierre was outstanding. You couldn't possibly miss him because of his height, but he was very skilful on the ground when the ball arrived at his feet. Normally, extremely tall guys are like a giraffe on ice when they are asked to do anything on the deck, but Van Hooidonk ticked all the boxes. I was looking at another striker at Twente Enschede at the time. His name? Michael Mols, who, of course, did eventually come to Glasgow - to sign for Rangers. At that time, though, Celtic had the choice between these players.

'I made another trip to see Pierre in action against Heerenveen and that helped me make up my mind. I had noted in previous games that he never wasted a direct free-kick. He may not always have scored, but he always hit the target. It was an extra in his weaponry and I was impressed. I advised Tommy Burns to sign him and we duly did.'

And, so, Van Hooijdonk stepped onto the frosty Hampden surface in front of 26,491 fans - almost 5,000 up on Celtic's previous Hampden attendance - obviously intrigued as to what to expect from the new boy. They were given a response in only twelve minutes when the giant Dutchman pulled down a clearance out of defence from Mike Galloway, lobbed the ball over defender Neil Berry with a degree of nonchalance, held off another challenge from Willie Jamieson, drifted across the edge of the penalty area and appeared to have been too extravagant with his execution. Then he caught the ball perfectly and his pulverising drive blasted high into the net over the outstretched arms of keeper Craig Nelson.

His manager confided afterwards. 'I thought he had lost his opportunity. You won't get too many big guys who will pull the ball down, beat two men on the edge of the box and score. He is more than just a front player who will run on to balls thrown into the middle, because he links well and has a good touch.'

On this particular evening, all was not happiness and radiance with Burns after witnessing the team's thirteenth league draw of the campaign, the shedding of twenty-six points. He was adamant his side would have won comfortably had it not been for a decision by referee Hugh Dallas. The match official silenced the Hampden crowd when he awarded a fifty-seventh-minute penalty-kick after Gary Mackay had gone down theatrically following a challenge by Stuart Gray. Jim Bett ambled forward to send Pat Bonner the wrong way from twelve yards. Burns observed, 'I am very disappointed about the goal we lost, but I can't say any more about it, though, in case I am accused of being paranoid.'

The Scottish Cup was looming into view and two-and-a-half weeks after Van Hooijdonk's introduction, he lined up alongside Willie Falconer in attack for the Third Round encounter against First Division St Mirren at the national stadium. Campbell Money, sturdy and reliable without being showy, decided to turn in the sort of display every goalkeeper dreams about. With admirable athleticism, he twisted and turned throughout his full repertoire and Tommy Burns and Co must have wondered if a breakthrough goal was ever going to arrive.

It duly did in the sixty-eighth minute when Falconer materialised at the edge of the six-yard box to flash a ferocious header past the heroic Money, the ball zipping in just under the crossbar. Tommy Boyd provided the ammunition with a finely-judged cross from the right. Four minutes later, the keeper conceded again and the Celtic fans could breathe a little more easily. John Collins launched over a diagonal cross from the right, Falconer again proved to be unbeatable in the air as he climbed at the back post to head across the six-yard line. Van Hooijdonk waded through a posse of Saints defenders to bundle the ball over the line.

Burns observed, 'Our patience paid off. Big Pierre scored the type of simple goal that we haven't netted enough of this term. We've been crying out for someone who can just stick tap-ins away. At the start of the season, we said we wanted to get to a Cup Final and we have achieved that already, although ultimately the Final of the League Cup was a major disappointment. So, after losing one Cup, we will just have to go and get ourselves another one.'

On February 18, the Dutchman, swiftly becoming a favourite among the Celtic following, went one better in the 3-0 win over Meadowbank Thistle at the next stage of the competition. It was a breeze for the Bhoys who scored their goals in the first-half. The first from Big Pierre was worthy of winning any trophy as he combined pace, power and precision in one breathtaking moment of splendour. Falconer flicked the ball into his path and the confident striker, racing in at the edge of the penalty area, caught it sweetly with his right boot and his effort whipped high past the keeper into the roof of the net. Van Hooijdonk then rattled the face of the crossbar with a header and Falconer followed up to push the rebound over the line for the second. And it was Pierre who netted the third when he galloped onto a pass on the left-hand side of the box and calmly slotted the ball across the stranded Steve Ellison into the far corner. Remarkably, it was the first time Celtic had won by three clear goals since beating Partick Thistle in a league game on November 6 1993.

Pat Bonner, in particular, was excited when Celtic drew Kilmarnock at the quarter-final stage. Ironically, the popular shotstopper could have been lining up in the opposite goal at Hampden. Bonner's sixteen-year sojourn at Parkhead had apparently come to a halt the previous summer when he was told the news he was being released by Lou Macari. Celtic had just returned from a 1-1 draw against Aberdeen at Pittodrie on the last day of the season when Macari made his announcement. Charlie Nicholas, too, was on the way out. Bonner didn't waste any time in getting fixed up with a new club as he agreed to join former Parkhead team-mate Tommy Burns at Kilmarnock.

But within weeks, Burns and his assistant Billy Stark walked out of the Ayrshire club to return to Celtic. Bonner quickly followed and admitted, 'I had spoken to Tommy and the Kilmarnock chairman about going to Rugby Park. It would have been a wrench to leave Celtic after all those years, but there was a new challenge for me there. Then Tommy took over at Celtic and invited me to join him. Suddenly, I found I had a new challenge back at Parkhead.'

Looking at the forthcoming tie, Bonner said, 'It's a big game for us. We've been in one Cup Final this season and we still wonder how we lost it. We have an opportunity to get to another one. We are one step from the semi-finals and if we can get to two Finals that will be a big improvement on the past few years. The fans have done well to stick it out. Now they seem to want success quicker than ever because of the changes that have been made at the club. But a few changes don't necessarily mean it is going to come rapidly. We are working on a three-year plan. We are trying to build a team which can get back to winning titles, playing in Europe, and, hopefully, one day qualifying for the Champions' League. Those are the goals.'

Hampden was plunged into darkness for twenty-three minutes when the floodlights failed, but there was a shaft of light before the interval when Paul McStay illuminated proceedings. The Celtic captain checked inside past a frantic challenge and threaded a superb pass into the tracks of Brian McLaughlin who was crudely tugged back by panicking defender Tom Black. It was a stonewaller and John Collins tucked the award away from Dragoje Lekovic low down at the keeper's right-hand post. In the second-half, Falconer was out of luck as he tried to soothe the jangling nerve-ends of the home support when he turned swiftly to fire in a low shot that thumped against the base of the post. However, Celtic held on for the one-goal win and Burns was ninety minutes away from a second Cup Final appearance in his first year in charge.

'I'm absolutely delighted,' he said afterwards. 'It was a big effort from all the fans and the players put together. It was a fantastic result. Every one of my players ran themselves into the ground. I couldn't have asked for more and I'm happy for them and the supporters.'

Celtic went into the semi-final draw alongside Edinburgh duo Hibs and Hearts while Airdrie represented the First Division. The Tynecastle side had knocked out Rangers at the second hurdle, hammering them 4-2 in Edinburgh. Like the Parkhead side, though, their league form was erratic. The ballot paired Celtic with Hibs, the game taking place on Friday night, April 7, at Ibrox for the benefit of the TV cameras. Hearts would play Airdrie at Hampden the following afternoon.

The Battle of the Greens, so often a classic fixture in the past, didn't live up to its billing. It became a slog with the defences and midfields dominating. Chances were few and far between, but Celtic had the perfect opportunity to book their place in the Cup Final when they were awarded a penalty-kick in the seventy-third minute. Referee John Rowbotham pointed to the spot after Pat McGinlay, who had rejoined the Easter Road side after being discarded by Burns, brought down Paul McStay. It was a touch-and-go decision by the match official with the initial challenge taking place around the edge of the box.

John Collins and Andy Walker both elected to take the award as the experienced Jim Leighton steadied himself on his line. Walker won the squabble, placed the ball on the spot and looked horrified as his shot, hit with power, was anticipated by the Hibs keeper who fisted the ball to safety. Ironically, it was the same goal where McStay had failed against Raith Rovers. Burns, though, remained upbeat after the bizarre incident. He said, 'There were two of our players fighting to take the kick and that's not a bad thing. We leave it to the players in form to decide who takes the penalty-kicks. Walker wanted to take it and, while John Collins was also ready, it would have taken a blow torch to get the ball off Andy.'

The following day Airdrie shocked Hearts 1-0 with a Steve Cooper strike on the half-hour mark to make sure of their place at Hampden on May 27. Celtic and Hibs had to do it all again four nights after the original stalemate and this time there was no mistake from the Parkhead men. Falconer got the show on the road when he raced onto a superbly disguised pass from McStay and finished with an unstoppable angled drive that saw Leighton clutching air as it sped past him at the far post. And the keeper was stranded again when Collins doubled Celtic's advantage with as sweet a goal as he ever scored at Ibrox - and the midfielder was racking up a few memorable efforts at the Govan ground.

Collins was twenty-five yards out when he dragged the ball onto his left foot and, uncannily, without looking up to monitor Leighton's positioning, arced the ball high into the top right hand corner. The goalie didn't move a muscle; he knew it was a goal as soon as it left Collins' gifted left foot. It was a delightful piece of invention from the midfielder. Keith Wright gave the Hoops a fright by pulling one back, but it was all over when Phil O'Donnell bravely launched himself at a right-wing free-kick from Rudi Vata to send a header soaring past Leighton at his left hand side. 'You'll Never Walk Alone' bellowed out around Ibrox as the Celtic players celebrated at the final whistle. Burns summed up, 'I know what will be said. Here we have Airdrie, another First Division team, and back in November we lost to Raith Rovers in the League Cup Final. Believe me, we have learned from the experience of losing in that game and we don't intend for it to happen again. This was a victory which pleased me. It was something the players deserved and something the support deserved for the way they have backed us.'

Airdrie had already put down a marker by dismissing Hearts in the semi-final, but it is also worth noting their result against Raith Rovers in the quarter-final. They travelled to Stark's Park and inflicted an impressive 4-1 battering on Jimmy Nicholl's team. They had already beaten Stirling Albion (2-1) and Dunfermline (2-0) to make it through to the last eight. Their style of play may not have been easy on the eye, but manager Alex MacDonald, a 'bite-your-ankles' type of midfielder in his playing days at St.Johnstone, Rangers and Hearts, had fashioned an outfit that undoubtedly realised its limitations and played to its strengths. Up front, they had two old-fashioned frontmen who weren't afraid to mix it with rival defences. Andy Smith and Steve Cooper threw themselves at every high ball whether they had the slightest hope of making contact or not. In Alan Lawrence, the Broomfield side had a slight, evasive winger who liked to come inside and support the front two. They were dangerous opponents.

The days ticking down to the Scottish Cup Final must have been agonising for Peter Grant. The grim reality was that he would be unlikely to be fit to take his place in Tommy Burns' selection. However, no-one who knew Peter Grant would ever write him off. Burns was aware of the player's single-minded determination, but, with just under two weeks to go to the grand finale, he confided in friends, 'Peter's got no chance.'

It may have been a surprise to many, then, when the Celtic manager read out the eleven players entrusted with bringing the first piece of silverware to Parkhead after six years entrenched in football's wasteland. Grant, somehow, had magically reached a level of fitness that persuaded Burns that he could play his part at Hampden. He got the nod and it was a decision the Celtic boss would never regret.

He went with this line-up: Pat Bonner; Rudi Vata, Tommy Boyd, Mark McNally, Tosh McKinlay; Peter Grant, Paul McStay, John Collins; Brian McLaughlin, Pierre van Hooijdonk and Simon Donnelly. It showed four changes from the formation which had kicked off the competition with the win over St Mirren at the same venue back in January. Brian O'Neil, Stuart Gray, Phil O'Donnell and Willie Falconer were out. O'Neil would almost certainly have played, but, unlike Grant, his leg injury didn't respond to treatment and he was in the stand that eventful afternoon. McStay returned after being suspended for the opening tie while Vata, Donnelly and McKinlay, signed from Hearts for £350,000 the previous November, also came into the reckoning. Tony

Mowbray had missed the St Mirren match while on compassionate leave following the tragic death of his wife Bernadette and, although he had returned to playing, he was serving a ban by the time the Cup Final arrived.

With O'Neil out, Burns brought Boyd in from the flank to partner McNally, who had last started a game back in February against Hearts in a 1-1 draw at Tynecastle. Vata was given the right-back role. McStay was the most experienced Cup Final exponent on the day, making his sixth appearance on the campaign's most glittering occasion. He had been successful in 1985, 88 and 89, but a loser in 1984 and 89. McStay was also well aware of the fact that the club hadn't won a trophy in his five years as captain.

It was a day for those performers who possessed a backbone to stand up and be counted and no-one wore the badge of courage more resolutely than Grant, an absolute colossus in midfield and defence. And his qualities were required during what turned out to be a difficult, nervy afternoon for Celtic. It was a bright, windless day at Hampden when Donnelly tapped the ball to Van Hooijdonk to get proceedings underway. Celtic actually began the encounter with a praiseworthy verve and gusto. In the opening minutes, McKinlay curled in a right-wing corner-kick with his cultured left foot. McNally was totally unguarded as he got on the end of it, but wastefully headed wide of the post from ten yards. Billy McNeill, once again adopting his match summariser's role for TV, could only utter, 'McNally's not got an awful lot to do to meet the ball. He should have hit the target.'

McKinlay also supplied an inviting left wing cross which was hastily cleared by Kenny Black from six yards while McStay lurked with intent. The Broomfield outfit were under pressure and McKinlay was invited to take another right-wing corner-kick. Once again, the danger was cleared, but it was evident the left-back was finding his range. Tommy Burns and Billy Stark stood side-by-side at the dug-out and surely must have been satisfied with that they were witnessing. Bonner, at this stage, was a virtual spectator; nothing had been seen of the twin threat of Cooper and Smith. Early on, the keeper had come off his line in confident fashion to swallow up a long hanging cross as Cooper clattered into him. Bonner kept his concentration, crashed to the ground, but still held onto the ball.

Burns had urged his players to get an early goal and they obliged in the ninth minute. Unsurprisingly, the wholehearted Grant played a significant role in the lead-up. A ball was hoofed up the park deep into Airdrie defensive territory on Celtic's left wing. Jimmy Sandison, believing he had all the time in the world, practically jogged over to retrieve the misplaced pass. However, Grant embarked on a lung-bursting fifty-yard sprint to put pressure on the defender. Sandison was slow to react and his hasty clearance was picked up by Collins who immediately switched play across to the right with Vata running into space and he toe-poked the ball to McLaughlin.

Black was forced to push the ball out for a throw-in which the Albanian defender took swiftly, lobbing the ball to McLaughlin. His cross into the box was watched by the hesitant keeper John Martin and was scrambled clear by back-four operator Jimmy Boyle who must have thought he had taken care of the immediate threat as his clearance soared out of the danger zone. However, it fell at the feet of McKinlay, who took a touch before angling over an exquisite left-wing cross. Van Hooijdonk seemed to hover in the air as he climbed above the defence to meet the cross with absolute perfection. The ball smacked off his forehead and the effort was directed down and away from the sprawling Martin. As the net swished behind the goalie, Hampden erupted into pure and unbridled green-and-white joy; scarves and banners swaying in glorious technicolour. It was another 'Oh-Hampden-in-the-sun' moment and it had been a long time coming.

The trick now was to prevent Airdrie sourcing an equaliser. Bonner helped considerably when the nippy Lawrence got clear of Boyd in the box to thump a right-foot drive at goal, but the irishman got down well to block the effort. The fans groaned when it became obvious Van Hooijdonk would play no further part in the contest as he limped off before the interval with Falconer sprinting on to take his place.

It can come as no surprise that palpitations were in evidence throughout the Celtic team in the second-half. McStay and Collins did their best to bring a veneer to the play, but it was all far too hectic and frantic with Airdrie, admittedly, forcing the pace. MacDonald's team chased every ball, harried their opponents and rarely stopped for a breather. Boyd and McNally didn't look comfortable against Cooper and Smith. Grant noted the situation and dropped back to play in front of them, mopping up threats before they reached the penalty area.

Collins underlined why he did his best work with the ball at his feet when he squandered a glorious opportunity to deflate Airdrie's spirit. Falconer caught out his opponents with a superb left-foot cross from the right wing and Boyle failed to pick up Collins as he sprinted into acres of space. The midfielder threw himself at the ball only ten yards out and sent a careless header wide of Martin's right-hand post.

Burns attempted to seal the midfield when he took off Donnelly and replaced him with Phil O'Donnell. There was an ugly moment when Black caught Grant from behind with the ball long gone. The Celt went down writhing in agony and the Airdrie man could count himself lucky he found referee Les Mottram in a lenient mood. It was nasty and Grant needed treatment to his right knee before he could unsteadily get back to his feet. There is no way you can keep a good man down, though, and the moment that epitomised Grant's desire to bring success to Celtic that afternoon was perfectly caught in a split-second of raw courage when he thwarted Lawrence and the genuine threat of an equalising goal.

McNally was eliminated when he misjudged a high kick-out from Martin and the ball bounced to Lawrence, running clear in the penalty box. He was about to pull the trigger when Grant took off on a do-or-die mission. He blocked the shot with his right boot and the danger was snuffed out in an instant. Once again, though, he thrashed around in obvious distress and it looked as though he might not be on the pitch to savour the final whistle and the spontaneous eruption of happiness at the national stadium. A wounded warrior, he got to his feet and a minute or so later there came the tannoy announcement that he had been named the sponsor's Man of the Match. It could have gone to no-one else.

Grant burst into tears at the end as did his skipper McStay. Burns hugged Stark and then went in search of rival manager MacDonald to offer his hand in condolence. And then the party got into full swing. Burns looked around the bouncing, singing supporters, waved an expansive arm in their direction, and said, 'This is what Celtic Football Club is all about. We're only here to do a job. They're the guys who pay the money, they pay the wages. We're their servants and I'm absolutely delighted for them. I'm now going to give Peter Grant a big kiss. I thought he was unbelievable today. I don't know what we would have done without him. He was magnificent. I'm happy, too, for Paul McStay. The captain has had a hard time of it and I'm so proud of him.'

Burns looked at the actual game and said, 'Airdrie competed well and they did the things they're good at. I don't think we played well at all. But, to be fair, we were under a helluva lot more pressure than them.' Later on, at the celebrations at Celtic Park, Tommy Burns reflected, 'I know the players we want to bring to this club and we'll do business in the summer to get them here. Now we have won a trophy and we are going back to our own home to play our football.'

He smiled and added, 'It's a new start for Celtic Football Club.'

CHAPTER NINE
THREE AND OUT

Tommy Burns emulated the legendary Jock Stein in season 1995/96 – and won nothing for his exceptional efforts. Extraordinarily, Burns, in his second campaign in charge of Celtic, suffered one solitary league loss in thirty-six examinations just as Big Jock had managed in 1967/68 during a thirty-four game league season.

There was one major difference, though. Burns saw his team finish four points adrift of Rangers while Stein picked up his third successive crown, two points ahead of the Ibrox outfit.

In total, Burns conceded defeat in only three domestic games in three different competitions to the same opponents and that was enough to wreck a complete season. A rare header from McCoist ended Celtic's interest in the League Cup at the quarter-final stage at Parkhead on September 19 and Walter Smith's team returned eleven days later to administer another setback, this time 2-0 in the league. The Ibrox side edged the Scottish Cup semi-final encounter at Hampden in April by 2-1 to complete a horrendous hat-trick for the Parkhead side.

Burns had transformed Celtic from the previous season, earned accolades for the way he had got the team playing, all neat passing and fluent movement, rapturous applause avalanched in his direction for bringing colour back to the grey east end of Glasgow, but the trophy cabinet wasn't exactly groaning under the weight of silverware while the Scottish Cup was bereft of company. And, in a results-driven business, that was all that mattered to the Celtic manager.

Burns realised there had to be a dramatic improvement within the playing ranks. Brian McLaughlin, Brian O'Neil and Simon Donnelly had settled into the first team squad, but other fringe players such as Stuart Gray and Chris Hay weren't quite ready for the step up on a permanent basis. Old favourite Charlie Nicholas had been freed to play out the remainder of his career with Clyde while Tony Mowbray moved to Ipswich Town in a £300,000 deal. As the Celtic boss had promised in the aftermath of the Hampden success over Airdrie, players had been identified and he was anxious to get business done in the close season.

The previous term he had brought in Pierre van Hooijdonk, Phil O'Donnell, Andy Walker and Tosh McKinlay for a total outlay of £3.9million which was a reasonable sum of money. Contrast that, though, with Walter Smith's financial muscle across the Clyde. He was allowed to splash almost £6million in welcoming Brian Laudrup (Fiorentina), Basile Boli (Marseille), Alex Cleland and Garry Bollan (both Dundee United) and Billy Thomson (Motherwell). He also swapped Dave McPherson for Hearts' Scottish international centre-half Alan McLaren.

As Burns plotted for the new campaign, he admitted, 'I was only too aware of Rangers sources being quoted almost on a daily basis that they were now going for eight successive titles, then nine would be the target to equal Celtic and then into double figures. We couldn't stand back and let that happen. I knew the players I wanted, the quality of the individual who would wear the green and white hoops. We had all worked hard throughout the summer because we knew we had to turn the corner once and for all.'

Andreas Thom was the surprise close season signing when he arrived from Bayer Leverkusen on August 4. The former East German international attacking midfielder was once rated as one of the very best by none other than the iconic Franz Beckenbauer, who conceded Thom might have been worthy of a place in West Germany's World Cup-winning team of 1974. Fanciful figures were bandied about concerning the exact amount of the transfer fee with many insisting it was £4million, just £300,000 short of the reported figure paid by Rangers for Paul Gascoigne from Lazio the previous month. The truth is it was almost half Gascoigne's valuation with the deal being concluded and the Bundesliga outfit picking up £2.2million. There was no way Fergus McCann would sanction a £4million move for a player who would be thirty on his next birthday with little or no sell-on value.

Three days after the razzmatazz of Thom's arrival, there was barely a ripple when John Hughes, a rugged, no-nonsense centre-half, arrived from Falkirk in exchange for £350,000. Burns had identified central defence as a problem area, as it had been for predecessors Liam Brady and Lou Macari. Over the course of the first half of the season, versatile Jackie McNamara, son of the former Celtic favourite of the same name, joined in October in a £600,000 shift from Dunfermline and Danish midfielder Morten Wieghorst would cost an identical fee from Dundee in December. Portuguese attacker Jorge Cadete turned up in March the following year in a convoluted and protracted transfer after falling out with his club, Sporting Lisbon.

So, during the entire programme, Burns had spent exactly £4.15million. That, too, was dwarfed with what was happening over at Ibrox. Including the temperamentally-fragile Gascoigne, Smith had taken his spending to a whopping £11.65million by introducing Russian striker Oleg Salenko at £2.5million from Valencia, Danish frontman Erik Bo Andersen (£1.5million, Aalborg), right-back Stephen Wright (£1.5million, Aberdeen), central defender Gordan Petric (£1.5million, Dundee United) and midfielder Derek McInnes (£350,000, Morton). It was hardly a level financial playing field.

David Ginola, the maverick French winger, was within minutes of joining the Hoops revolution and was actually discussing terms with Burns and the money men when Newcastle manager Kevin Keegan placed a phone call to Celtic Park. He was making a last minute move for the Paris Saint Germain star with the matinee looks. Incredibly, the phone was handed to Ginola and Celtic's bid was dead in the water when he picked up the receiver and heard what Keegan had to offer. It doesn't always pay to have good manners.

Davie Hay also makes an astonishing revelation about the identity of another player he was asked to scout. 'A schoolteacher in England, a bloke called John Murphy, was a Celtic fan and got in touch to say we could do worse than have a look at a young midfielder in the lower league levels. I travelled down and that was the first time I ever saw Neil Lennon play. He was with Crewe at the time. I liked the look of him, but, at the time, Tommy needed players who could go straight into the first team and we had Paul McStay and John Collins in there. So, I noted the name, but Martin O'Neill signed him for Leicester City in 1996 and the Celtic fans had to wait another four years before they saw him in the green and white hoops.'

Thom took his bow at Celtic Park on August 8 when Keegan brought his exciting Newcastle United team, including Ginola, across the border for an intriguing friendly. The travelling Geordie fans were as anxious to see their latest signing, £6.5million striker Les Ferdinand, from Queens Park Rangers, as the Celtic supporters were to witness Thom after a fairly spectacular build-up. The £17million new stand loomed large while work was still being done on the stadium and it was strange to see the ground minus what had become known over the many years as the 'Celtic End' behind one of the goals. The East German impressed with his clever play, zestful, darting runs and his eagerness to get into attacking positions. He lasted seventy-one minutes before making way, amid rapturous and appreciative applause, for substitute Andy Walker.

The game ended 1-1 with John Collins sinking a penalty-kick following a foul by Darren Peacock on Thom. Ferdinand levelled when he almost took the net away behind Gordon Marshall with a ferocious header. It must be said Ginola did not receive much of a welcome. So much for the 'Auld alliance'. Keegan had an interesting comment to make about Celtic at the end. 'It is fantastic to see a great club re-born,' he said with genuine enthusiasm. 'It's particularly good to see them starting to get players here. That is the important thing.'

A midweek goalless draw with Liverpool followed - no six-goal walloping on this occasion, just a brisk work-out - and the real action got underway when the League Cup ballot once again pointed Burns and his men in the direction of Ayr United at Somerset Park just as it had done the previous season. Unlike twelve months earlier, this was a saunter for Celtic with new signing Andreas Thom knocking in his first goal for the club as a satisfied manager watched his side notch up a 3-0 victory. It had taken the club five months to win by three clear goals in the previous campaign, now they had achieved the feat in ninety minutes. Pierre van Hooijdonk netted the second with John Collins slotting in the third via the penalty spot.

Van Hooijdonk heaped the praise on his new team-mate. 'Having someone of Thom's ability in the side means the other players will play even better. That's what happened with Rangers and Laudrup - he made them better players. It's much easier to play when there's someone with the ability of Thom or Laudrup looking for the ball. All the lads are enjoying having Andreas around. I am not saying Andreas and I will win Celtic the league. It's all about the team and what kind of lift everybody gets from him.'

An injured captain Paul McStay watched from the stand and said, 'The bonus of winning in the style we did really is a great boost. That's why Tommy Burns paid the money for Thom. You can see the quality of the guy and the way he takes a goal. His movement can rip teams apart. If they are going to be playing like this, it's going to be tough for me to get back in.'

Burns, too, was more than merely delighted. 'After the goal, we settled in well and made a lot more chances,' he noted. 'Another great thing is that our three main goal threats - Thom, Van Hooijdonk and Collins - all scored. From here, we will set our own standards.'

Opposition manager Simon Stainrod still believed Rangers would win the league although he admitted, 'Celtic are a much better team than they were last year, but Rangers have too strong a squad. I feel Celtic will come up against a Motherwell or a Falkirk and not take three points. Rangers won't let that happen when they face these teams.'

The Ayr United gaffer's words proved to be chillingly accurate. Celtic dropped four points in two draws against Motherwell - 1-1 in Glasgow in September and 0-0 away in March - and two more in a goalless draw against Falkirk at Brockville in February. Six points discarded by a team who lost out on the championship by four points. If those draws had been turned into wins, Rangers' title run would have been halted, there would have been no eight-in-a-row. The Ibrox side, on the other hand, took twenty-two from a possible twenty-four points from the same teams, their only blip being a scoreless stalemate at Motherwell in December. That's the wonder of football, though. How many sentences begin with, 'What if...?'

Celtic didn't exactly come sprinting out of the blocks when the league season kicked off on August 26. They had to rely on a headed goal from Van Hooijdonk eleven minutes from time to give them a 1-0 win over League Cup tormentors Raith Rovers at Stark's Park. The League Cup draw had paired last season's finalists for the next round and echoes of a November afternoon at Ibrox were beginning to reverberate around Celtic Park with the game tied at 1-1 in extra-time and heading for penalty-kicks. Van Hooijdonk had put Celtic ahead, but Tony Rougier smashed a free-kick past Gordon Marshall for the equaliser. With the minutes ticking down, Van Hooijdonk turned provider when he curled over a right-wing cross, substitute Andy walker, on for the limping Thom on the hour mark, headed goalwards. Scott Thomson touched the ball away, but Simon Donnelly pounced to fire the winner into the inviting net.

Tommy Burns sighed wearily, 'I am delighted to get through, but it's difficult to understand how we can make life so hard for ourselves.'

On the tenth anniversary of the death of Jock Stein, Burns may have repeated those very words. Celtic were two goals down after ten minutes against Aberdeen at Pittodrie, had John Hughes sent off and came back to triumph 3-2. Big Jock no doubt would have approved of the fighting spirit displayed by his old team that afternoon. Tommy Boyd put through his own goal in the seventh minute and Eoin Jess walloped in a second. Celtic, though, underwent a startling transformation in response to the double setback.

John Collins hauled one back with a spectacular left-foot effort in the twenty-first minute and Andreas Thom equalised twelve minutes later with an angled shot that completely bamboozled Dons keeper Theo Snelders. And, as half-time approached, Thom zipped in a low drive that was fumbled by the Dutch No.1 and in swept Collins for what turned out to be the winner. Hughes saw red in the seventy-second minute after two bookings, but Celtic, battling heroically, held out for a crucial away victory and three points from Roy Aitken's side.

Burns was enthusiastic on this occasion. He said, 'My players performed in a manner for which Celtic are renowned. To be 2-0 down after ten minutes was daunting, but the way we came back was simply fantastic. John Collins' first goal was sensational and Andreas Thom also scored a great goal. He produced skill that you just can't coach into a player. He was a joy to watch, but there is better to come from him with more games.' Opposite number and former team-mate Aitken took nothing away from his old team and added sportingly, 'Everyone saw a classic.'

Frustratingly, Celtic surrendered two points at home to Motherwell in a 1-1 draw the following week, as soothsayer Stanrod had foreseen. In the countdown to the league game, Burns had piloted the team to a 3-2 Cup-Winners' Cup first leg win over Dinamo Batusi in Georgia, the club's first success on their European travels since a Murdo MacLeod goal gave them a 1-0 victory over Shamrock Rovers in Dublin nine years earlier. However, it came at a cost and Thom, who scored twice against the Georgians, and Van Hooijdonk both sustained injuries and were in the Celtic Park stand by the time the match against the Fir Park side got underway. Their attacking presence and guile were missed in a largely nondescript ninety minutes. Phil O'Donnell thumped Celtic into the lead against his former team and Dougie Arnott levelled midway through the second-half after being set up by ex-Celt Tommy Coyne.

Now Burns could prepare for the crucial first meeting of the season against Rangers, due at Parkhead on Tuesday, September 19, to contest an intriguing League Cup quarter-final tie. Tosh McKinlay crystalised the feelings of the Celtic dressing room perfectly, 'A win against Rangers could set us up for the season. We also know that a defeat would knock us back down.'

Unfortunately, Van Hooijdonk wasn't considered fit enough to start the game and had to settle for a place on the substitutes' bench. He came on for Andy Walker on the hour mark. Thom got the green light to start, but struggled to make any sort of impact on his Old Firm debut and was eventually replaced by Brian McLaughlin in the seventy-first minute. Right from the kick-off, Paul Gascoigne had a full head of steam and was charging around recklessly laying down markers, mainly on Paul McStay and John Collins. He clattered into the Celtic captain in only seventeen seconds, but escaped a booking from referee Jim McCluskey.

The English international, a strange mixture of the wild and the wonderful, calmed down after the interval and concentrated on actually playing football. Alas, a piece of individual composure from Scottish football's record signing undid Celtic with only fifteen minutes remaining. He picked up a Charlie Miller pass in the old inside-right channel and strode forward purposefully. Given far too much time and room in which to work, he had the opportunity to gaze up, locate McCoist lurking at the back post and his delicate lob eliminated Tommy Boyd and John Hughes as it arrowed towards its target. McCoist, totally unchallenged, rose to knock the ball past Gordon Marshall who also looked slow to move his feet to counter-act the initial danger posed by Gascoigne.

Goram, at the other end, had defied Celtic throughout the evening and he capped a memorable performance right at the end with a gravity-defying save from a McStay piledriver. A right-wing cross from Rudi Vata was knocked clear by Gough and the ball fell sweetly for the Celtic skipper to hit first-time full on the volley from twenty-five yards. His effort was screaming towards the top left-hand corner until the Rangers keeper, with bewildering reflexes, got across his goal and pushed it away with his left hand. Tommy Burns said, 'Goram broke my heart at that moment.' Walter Smith added, 'That save proved that our keeper is a winner and his influence gets through to the team.'

There was an interesting turnaround in fortunes four days later when Celtic went to the top of the Premier League with an outstanding 4-0 thumping of Hearts at Tynecastle while Rangers collapsed 1-0 at home to Hibs. After failing to score four goals in one game the previous season, Burns saw his team rack up another four-goal triumph on the Thursday against Dinamo Batusi in the second leg of their Cup-Winners' Cup confrontation. Thom notched another two to take his tally to four in the satisfying 7-2 aggregate romp. Unfortunately, the European excursion came to a halt in the next round when Burns' team were mercilessly picked off by Paris Saint Germain. After losing only 1-0 in Paris, Burns was reasonably confident as he prepared for the return leg. Alas, it turned in to a 3-0 massacre with the French aces destroying the Scots with their pace on the break.

Once again, Rangers made a quickfire return to Celtic Park on league business. Tommy Burns got his tactics absolutely spot on for forty-four of the first forty-five minutes before witnessing his team lose a goal just on half-time to go in trailing at the interval. Goram was defiant again and made excellent saves from Paul McStay and John Collins while Celtic dominated. With match official John Rowbotham looking at his watch, the Ibrox side sneaked upfield in a rare foray into the Celtic half and Salenko clipped a high ball to the back post. Left-back Cleland, who wouldn't score another goal all season, chose that moment for maximum impact. Unhampered by any sort of challenge, he rose to head down and across Gordon Marshall. The keeper dived to his left, but the trajectory was accurate enough to escape his outstretched left hand.

Gascoigne, as he had done in the opening forty-five minutes of the League Cup-tie, had been charging around like a wounded rhino and had been booked for one swipe too many. But, remarkably, what was said in the dressing room at the break once more seemed to do the trick. Richard Gough put it this way, 'I told Paul to make sure he stayed on the park because if he got sent off he would be letting the other ten players down. You shouldn't really have to tell an experienced player that, but you can get carried away in these games.'

It was the Englishman who netted the second goal to wipe out Celtic resistance three minutes from the hour mark. Burns' troops were storming the Rangers penalty area in gung-ho fashion when a ball was hacked downfield in the direction of McCoist, running clear with the freedom of the east end of Glasgow. His Geordie team-mate kept pace with him and, with the defence in total disarray, McCoist rolled a pass across the penalty area and Gascoigne deftly lifted it over the outrushing Marshall and the ball bobbled into the empty net. It was a killer blow.

Unusually, Tommy Burns fired a verbal volley at some of his players afterwards, such was his obvious disappointment. He said, 'I felt we were looking for our young players to turn it round in the second-half yet they should have been getting help. They've been doing well, but you can't expect them to take all the responsibility when things are going against us. Mind you, I couldn't believe we were a goal down at half-time, although it was a shocker to lose. After that, it was disappointing and we could use Thursday's European tie against Dinamo Batusi as an excuse, but we won't.'

Celtic would remain undefeated in their remaining thirty-one league games, a record for the Premier League, and still fail to win their first crown in nine arduous, agonising years. There can be no argument they did have their opportunities. Worryingly, when they were presented, Celtic consistently failed to respond to the openings. It became the recurring and unwelcome theme in a distinctly strange season in the club's history.

It's difficult to be too harsh on Burns. He did, after all, sprinkle some stardust on an ailing team and actually delivered a trophy, but there can be little doubt the players did not perform on occasions when they were gifted with favourable occasions to derail Rangers. It wasn't quite a case of style without substance, but, for whatever reason whenever it was really required, the team fell short.

Celtic went into 1996 with their first game against Rangers at Parkhead on January 3. Walter Smith's men arrived on top of the league, took a merciless pounding for a massive percentage of a blood-and-thunder confrontation and left with a goalless draw and their position intact. The Herald reporter observed, 'Rangers are still eight points clear at the top of the Premier Division this morning and that is something Celtic must find hard to believe. Last night saw the fourth Old Firm clash of the season and this was one which was totally dominated by the Parkhead men - and yet they still failed to beat the New Year jinx which has haunted them now for eight long years. It was in 1988 that they last won this fixture and yet, last night, it should have been so different. This was a match they could have won - this was a match they should have won. For most of the game, they were in command and, in the second-half in particular, they dominated as their fans urged them on for the single goal which surely would have settled it. The closing forty-five minutes began with a Phil O'Donnell shot which struck the base of Andy Goram's right-hand post and then ended with a diving header from substitute Andy Walker which went just off target.'

The report concluded, 'Few would argue that Celtic deserved three points. But the reality today is that once again they have failed to get them against their age-old rivals.'

Goram withstood the barrage and, startlingly, might have picked up a win bonus when Paul Gascoigne left a leaden-footed Gordon Marshall stranded with a twenty-yard free-kick which cannoned off the bar with only three minutes to play. Captain Richard Gough, with a fair degree of honesty, admitted, 'I thought it was going to be a case of Celtic pressure and us sneaking it near the end.'

Tommy Burns lamented, 'When I pass away, they will put that on my tombstone - Goram broke his heart. He's probably the best keeper I've ever seen.' The international No.1 had kept Celtic at bay in three consecutive games at Parkhead and Burns still found the ability to lighten the mood when he added, 'I've got a contract out on him.'

Celtic were playing catch-up with Rangers and were compelled to play five more league fixtures in January - four in succession away from home. Remarkably, by the time they played Kilmarnock at Rugby Park on the twentieth of the month they could have taken over pole position. Not for the first time, the players fluffed their lines. The sprint for points began with a meeting against Motherwell in Glasgow and it was a tight 1-0 win with Pierre van Hooijdonk settling the issue. Burns claimed skipper McStay's performance as 'colossal', but there was still the nagging worry that the midfielder, accomplished and astute in his midfield role, wasn't scoring enough goals. HIs last strike had come against Rangers at Ibrox in August 1994 and critics were calling it his 'Achilles Heel'.

The skipper wasn't on the scoresheet, either, three days later as his team won 3-1 over Raith Rovers at Starks Park; O'Donnell, Collins and Van Hooijdonk netting as the Parkhead men extended their unbeaten league run to sixteen games while edging to within five points of Rangers. For the second successive occasion, Celtic gave Aberdeen a goal of a start at Pittodrie and came back to beat them. Billy Dodds fired the Dons ahead early on, but, inside five second-half minutes, Collins had levelled matters and Van Hooijdonk, scoring for the third consecutive outing, hit the winner.

The Dutchman was on a roll and he was on target once more in a hard-earned 2-1 success over Hearts at Tynecastle on January 17. Substitute Andy Walker got the other and Burns said, 'We were relentless. The game was there to be won and we went for it.' Three days later, saw Celtic presented with the ideal opportunity to clamber back to the top spot they occupied all too briefly back in September before Rangers won at Parkhead.

Walter Smith's men had played only two games since their scoreless 'success' in the New Year fixture - and had won them fairly comfortably by the same scoreline - 4-0 - against Falkirk and Raith Rovers. There were few indications they would source a banana skin when they squared up to Hearts at Ibrox on January 20. Allan Johnston managed to do what Celtic couldn't do in four-and-a-half hours' of football at Parkhead that season and that was to stick the ball past Goram. And the Tynecastle striker - nicknamed 'Magic' - enjoyed the sensation so much he repeated it two more times. An agitated Walter Smith, squirming in his seat in the stand, could hardly believe his eyes as his team caved in after losing the opening goal in the sixth minute. Former Celtic winger John Colquhoun set it up with a nice ball across from the left and Johnston tucked it in at Goram's right-hand post with the keeper anticipating a shot across goal to the opposite corner.

Rangers huffed and puffed, but were devastated just after the hour mark when Johnston was allowed to saunter through the middle of their defence, lure Goram from his line and then coolly lob the ball over his frantically-waving gloved right hand into the net. Only seven minutes remained when the Ibrox back lot were posted missing once again. A simple ball sliced them open right down the middle and Johnston sped onto it, drew a shell-shocked Goram, sidestepped him with ease and rolled the ball over the line. That was the cue for the disgruntled home fans to head for the exits.

Undoubtedly, Burns would have been aware of what was happening in Govan, but, implausibly, the invite to take over at the pinnacle was scorned in a wanton goalless draw against Kilmarnock at Rugby Park. The summit was snubbed, but the Celtic manager clearly wasn't too disturbed that his side was still a point adrift of Rangers when they should have held a point advantage with precisely a third of the season left to go. He said, 'Four games ago, we were eight points behind and now it's only one. Over the piece, it's very positive for us and we have to be pleased. It was a hell of a good game. Very few sides come here and dominate in the way we did. We made, and missed, a lot of chances, but we got a point and it is a significant one. There were so many good things to come out of the match. We're well pleased.'

After a 2-1 win home win over Hibs, Celtic threw away another two points against Falkirk, already doomed to relegation, at Brockville. It was disturbing that a team, with so much to play for, could falter so miserably against a mediocre side that would win only six of its thirty-six league games during a campaign to forget. In fact, they could only manage six draws during that run and one came against a strong Celtic team with McStay, Collins, Van Hooijdonk and Thom among its number. The stalemate left the Parkhead men trailing Rangers by three points with ten games still to be played. The draws at Rugby Park and Brockville would come back to haunt Burns and Celtic.

Celtic took time off from chasing Rangers and collecting league points to continue the defence of last season's prized silverware against perennial Cup opponents Raith Rovers at Parkhead on February 17. The Hoops, 3-0 winners over non-league Whitehill Welfare at Hibs' Easter Road in the opening round, had already exacted revenge on the Fifers for the previous season's League Cup Final penalty-kick shoot-out failure by relieving their grasp on the trophy after dumping them

THE WINDS OF CHANGE

back on the last day of August at Parkhead. The Kirkcaldy side, once again proving to be stubborn opponents, came with a blanket defensive formation which was breached twice by Donnelly and Thom without reply. Never again would the words 'Raith Rovers' and 'Cup jinx' be used in connection with the Kirkcaldy side and Celtic.

There were remarkable scenes at Parkhead the following Saturday when Jorge Cadete was introduced to the Celtic fans in the 37,017 crowd before the league match against Partick Thistle. The frizzy-haired Portuguese international was still wrapped in red tape while wrangling went on with club side Sporting Lisbon to come to an agreement about his transfer. Celtic would eventually discover that very little was straightforward as far as this individual was concerned. The rain was spiralling from the ominous, angry clouds above the east end of Glasgow as Cadete took to the pitch, waving and smiling radiantly at his new set of soon-to-be beguiled followers. Celtic won 4-0, but the loudest cheer of the afternoon rang around the ground when the player kneeled to pick up some blades of grass and kiss them. Without kicking a ball, Cadete became an instant hero with the fans.

As far as the actual football went that day, Morten Wieghorst, recently purchased from Dundee, made his debut as a second-half substitute for John Collins and signed in with a flourish by netting his first goal for the club five minutes from time. Pierre van Hooijdonk, with two, and Peter Grant had Celtic coasting at the time. The rousing form continued into the next confrontation, coincidentally another 4-0 triumph, this time against Hearts in Glasgow. The fans were still desperate to get a glimpse of Cadete in action, but the protracted deal was turning into a fiasco. Burns, though, reassured everyone the situation would be resolved and he would be playing for Celtic 'some time soon'.

In his absence, Celtic were continuing to run amok and the Tynecastle outfit were down and out before the half-time whistle with Burns' team coasting three goals ahead. The much-maligned Paul McStay, criticised for his lack of goals, silenced his critics with a whizzbang twenty-five yarder that exploded behind the helpless Craig Nelson for the opener. Pierre van Hooijdonk sent a header whistling past the Hearts keeper for

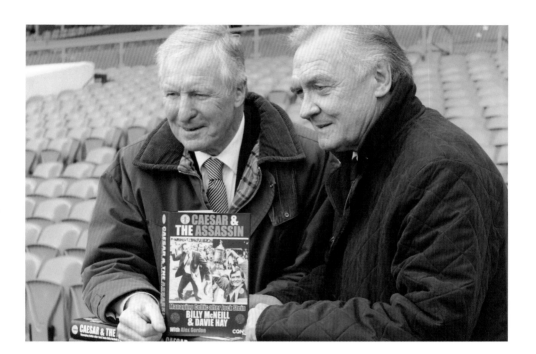

TENNENTS SCOTTISH CUP
WINNERS 1995

the second and Brian McLaughlin, so highly thought of by his manager, scored the goal of the day with a mesmerising left-wing solo run before tucking his shot away with the ease expected of a veteran. Simon Donnelly sent the supporters home happy with a fourth near the end.

Eight days later, two devastating goals in the space of ninety seconds completely turned around the Scottish Cup quarter-final against Dundee United. It was one of the most thrilling climaxes witnessed at Parkhead in years. The Tannadice side were leading 1-0 until the eighty-eighth minute and it looked as though Celtic's grip on the club's only trophy in six years was being prised open.

The Tannadice side led 1-0 at the interval and there could be no complaints from the holders. In fact, they might have been down to ten men if referee Andrew Waddell had sent off keeper Gordon Marshall after he hauled Craig Brewster to the ground to give away a penalty-kick. Waddell thought long and hard while he was given 'helpful advice' from some United players about how to deal with the incident. He decided a penalty-kick award was sufficient punishment and didn't even show a yellow card to Marshall. Owen Coyle took the award and practically hit the keeper with his venomous drive right down the middle of the goal. The ball bounced to Gary McSwegan and his miscontrol allowed it to run back to Coyle and this time there was no mistake.

And that's the way it remained with the clock ticking down and Celtic failing to find a route past Ally Maxwell, the former Rangers shotstopper who was having a superb afternoon. With ninety seconds to go, Jackie McNamara swung a right-wing free-kick into a congested penalty area and Pierre van Hooijdonk's timing couldn't have been bettered. He utilised the full 6ft 5in of his frame to rise above everyone and his twelve-yard header ripped high into the net. Maxwell's effort to stop that one was futile. United, at least, could console themselves with the thought of a replay at Tannadice. Their disappointment turned to despair when McNamara, snapping into a challenge on Coyle in the middle of the park, managed to prod the ball forward into the path of Andreas Thom. The German took off at blistering pace, pushed the ball ahead of him as he raced towards the penalty area and then blasted an unstoppable drive away from Maxwell's left hand. There was barely time for United to recentre the ball.

Van Hooijdonk, with masterly understatement, said, 'We knew it was late and we were running out of time, but, with this team, we always believe we can score.' Matchwinner Thom grinned, 'When I received the pass I just thought about making a goal. That was the only thing in my mind.' Celtic were now about to be paired with Rangers in the semi-final while Hearts would meet Aberdeen. But the league came back into Burns' focus and the opportunity to overthrow the Ibrox side at the fifth time of asking. Their earlier league meeting in Govan in November had rained goals with the clubs settling for 3-3 in one of the most spectacular Glasgow derbies in recent history.

Thom took centre stage in the opening minutes when he instantly controlled a flick from Simon Donnelly and hit a right-foot screamer past Goram from all of thirty yards. Laudrup swept in the equaliser just before the interval, but Collins restored Celtic's advantage with an unerring penalty-kick after Gough had flattened John Hughes. McCoist headed the equaliser after a right-wing Gascoigne free-kick and worse was to follow. A rare Boyd slip in the seventieth minute let in Salenko on the left and the Russian's low cross was missed by Marshall and McKinlay, trying to clear in front of McCoist, bundled the ball into his own net. Two minutes later, it was all-square again when McKinlay swiftly atoned with a superb cross on the run down the left and Van Hooijdonk got in front of Gough to glance a header in off the far post.

There was no way the players could replicate such a feast of football and this time it ended 1-1. There were moments of high drama, though. Jackie McNamara was sent off in the seventy-eighth minute after picking up two bookings by which time Rangers were leading after taking the initiative four minutes from the break. Gascoigne floated in another accurate deadball effort from the left and McLaren, with his back to goal, gave it the merest of touches off his head to send the ball cascading away from Marshall. An incredible reflex save from the Celtic keeper prevented Durie doubling his side's advantage when he managed to paw a header onto the post and to safety. Shortly afterwards, Durie turned defender to hack a McLaughlin effort off the line. Four minutes from the end, Celtic got the goal and the point their efforts merited. Peter Grant sent in a free-kick and Hughes was first to react with a snapping header from twelve yards. When the dust settled, Rangers were still leading the race for the crown by three points.

Tommy Burns said, 'The most important thing for us today was not to lose. Obviously, we were delighted to score a goal late on, but I thought we fully deserved it. We did well in the second-half and we would have been deeply disappointed to get nothing from the game. We had a great deal of possession after the interval and that is when Rangers can be dangerous. Our players could not have given more and no-one was more outstanding than Tommy Boyd. When we looked at the fans in the Broomloan Road stand it was impossible not to keep trying for them. They stayed there right to the end and we couldn't throw in the towel, even with ten men. We had to chase goals for their sake as well as our own.'

Last-gasp hero Hughes saw it this way, 'Scoring the goal was tremendous for me, especially as I was picking up McLaren when he scored their goal. That was my responsibility, but you're only human, after all. We seem to leave things late these days. After our two goals against Dundee United last week, it just shows we never count ourselves out. That is the Celtic style. My goal keeps us in it and it would have been a real shame if we had got nothing out of it. We would have really been up against it if we had lost. These Old Firm games are emotionally up and down affairs, but we keep digging out results this season and we get the feeling there must be something in it for us at the end. If Rangers win all their games from now on, all credit to them. All we can do is keep our ship in order.'

The thinking of the Guardian reporter at the game wasn't quite in tandem with Burns or Hughes. He wrote, 'If the result proved anything, it is that Celtic do not yet possess the surge of nerve and will to carry them to victory over their greatest rivals in matches of utter importance. Their three draws and one defeat from their series in this dramatic championship campaign are likely to be the most decisive factor when the trophy is won seven games from now. The three-point difference in the derby matches is precisely the lead that Rangers retain at the top of the league.'

The scribe concluded, 'If a draw satisfied both parties, it was the Celtic supporters who left with the gnawing worry that their team have yet to prove themselves capable of passing the most stringent test of all.'

The following Saturday, March 23, Celtic dropped two points in a goalless draw against Motherwell at Parkhead and title hopes were sagging, even among the most optimistic among the Hoops' support. There was to be no late-goal bail-out on this occasion. On the same afternoon across Glasgow, Rangers just edged rock-bottom Falkirk 3-2 at Ibrox where Erik Bo Anderson got their winning goal eleven minutes from time. Walter Smith's side struggled the following week, too, at Stark's Park where they trailed 2-1 to Raith Rovers with only seven minutes to go. Celtic, with a day off as they prepared to meet Aberdeen on the Monday night, thought their luck might be in. Ally McCoist, who had scored earlier with a penalty-kick, levelled in eighty-three minutes and snatched the winner sixty seconds from time. The fates were conspiring against Celtic, it seemed.

On April 1, though, the Parkhead fans were in raptures after Jorge Cadete, following a delay of five weeks waiting for his clearance, finally made his debut. Tommy Burns was hoping the late introduction of the prolific marksman might just give Celtic the impetus to get over the finishing line. The Portuguese striker came on for Andreas Thom in the seventy-third minute and two minutes later scored with practically his first touch of the ball. The Dons had already taken a battering and were trailing by four goals, two apiece from Pierre van Hooijdonk and Simon Donnelly. Peter Grant created the opportunity with a raking pass through the already-exhausted defence and Cadete swept onto it, carried it on and whacked the ball past the advancing Michael Watt. You only get one chance to make a first impression and the Portuguese striker didn't pass up the opportunity.

Now there was the little matter of a Scottish Cup semi-final meeting with Rangers at Hampden on Sunday. And there was drama even before the kick-off.

Celtic were informed by Jim Farry, the Scottish Football Association Chief Executive, they would not be allowed to field Cadete. Apparently, he had not been registered in time for the national competition although the Scottish League had already been satisfied that everything was in order to allow him to play against Aberdeen. Fergus McCann was not convinced and immediately sought legal advice. It was a courtroom saga that would be drawn out over almost three years. The stubborn Celtic Managing Director refused to accept any of the explanations put forward by Farry, who was known as an infuriatingly bumptious and punctilious powerbroker within Scottish football's HQ.

The case revolved around the wording of an International Transfer Certificate for Cadete. Celtic forwarded the ITC to the SFA on March 7 1996, with all the other relevant paperwork arriving a fortnight earlier. Initially, the club believed the player was a free agent. He wasn't, but that should have had absolutely no bearing on Farry registering Cadete. Celtic could not convince him of this because of a 'conditionality clause' within the ITC. Under law, this was an irrelevance, as a fax from the world's governing football body, FIFA, explained. Yet, it was not until Celtic lodged a third application to register the player at the end of March that Farry was eventually persuaded of the fact. Under the SFA's 14-day clearance rule, that was too late for Cadete to face Rangers. On March 8 1999 Farry was sacked for gross misconduct. McCann had won his argument, but it was too late to help Celtic's Scottish Cup cause three years earlier.

Before the Hampden tie, goalkeeper Gordon Marshall and striker Simon Donnelly both publicly proclaimed that defeat would deem all the hard work during the season as a waste of time. How ironic, then, that both should play significant roles in the downfall of Celtic in the sixth Old Firm meeting of the campaign.

Two minutes from the interval, the keeper presented Ally McCoist with the breakthrough goal after making a hash of trying to deal with a low shot from David Robertson. The left-back, running on the blindside of Jackie McNamara, tried to pass the ball into the far corner and Marshall appeared to collapse instead of diving to his left to deal with the danger. He looked awkward as he spreadeagled on the ground and could only half-heardedly push the ball in front of the unguarded McCoist a mere six yards out. He couldn't possibly pass up such a gift. The keeper appeared incapable of going through ninety minutes of the most important games without a heart-in-your-mouth moment.

There's no way he could be blamed, though, for the Ibrox side's second goal in the sixty-eighth minute. Celtic were laying siege to Andy Goram's goal when Walter Smith's men were awarded a throw-in halfway in their own half on the right. Alex Cleland threw the ball to Paul Gascoigne who, with one touch, knocked it onto Brian Laudrup who nudged it wide right to Gordon Durie. Without hesitation, he flicked it into the open space behind the Celtic back lot and Laudrup chased after it with the burly John Hughes in pursuit. Unfortunately, it looked as though the centre-half was running on treacle and the Rangers winger had time to head it down and then casually lob an effort over the stranded Marshall, who had strayed to the edge of the box. It was the absolute epitome of a perfect breakaway goal and Celtic must have wondered what had hit them.

There was a naivety about Burns' teams sometimes, but you could never fault their battling qualities. They came back at Rangers who were by now content to filter into deep defence and look for another four-touch movement that could provide a third goal. They were rocked, though, when Celtic pulled one back eight minutes from time when Jackie McNamara, suddenly finding space to venture forward with his immediate opponent, Laudrup, visibly tiring, sent in angled cross. Pierre van Hooijdonk's timing was impeccable as he raced in front of the hesitating Alan McLaren to glide a header low past Goram.

The Celtic fans were in a frenzy and three minutes later they could have been celebrating an equaliser. McNamara again hit the touchline before swinging over a cross and Donnelly had to stretch to get his head to the ball. Alas, his effort from four yards, went over the bar with Goram isolated at his near post. With three minutes to go, Donnelly missed a sitter. He raced clear of the ponderous McLaren, drew Goram from his line and then, lacking in composure at the crucial moment, blazed the ball off target. You just knew a guy called Jorge Cadete might have scored with one, if not both, of those opportunities.

A worrying feature of the semi-final was Andreas Thom's obvious reluctance to mix it with John Brown and Co when the boots were flying in a packed penalty area. Too often he was found wandering in areas where he couldn't possibly hurt Rangers and even popped up in the left-back position at one stage with Celtic two goals adrift and desperately looking for some firepower at the other end of the pitch. The opposition, apparently, could 'persuade' the gifted German to operate away from the danger zone and he was rarely a threat in this encounter.

Facts showed afterwards that Celtic had sixty per cent of possession, had forced ten corner-kicks to Rangers' two and had ten attempts at goal to the opposition's six. At the end of the day, though, the only statistic that really mattered was the one that read, Rangers 2 Celtic 1. Burns, predictably, didn't agree with the pre-match observations of his players Marshall and Donnelly and talked about the progress that had been made since he took over the job. Alas, that advancement would not be measured in trophies.

In the midweek game after relinquishing the Scottish Cup, Celtic were handed another invitation to close the gap at the top and once again they displayed a distressing reluctance to accept. A last-minute goal from Van Hooijdonk gave them a 1-1 draw with Kilmarnock at Parkhead after trailing at half-time to a Jim McIntyre goal. Carelessly chucking away two precious points was difficult enough to accept for the fans leaving the ground that night, but their mood darkened further with the tannoy announcement that informed them Rangers had lost 2-0 to Hearts at Tynecastle. Tommy Burns may have had many qualities, but you would have to argue against one of them being his sense of timing.

With four games to go, Rangers, despite the loss in Edinburgh, knew they could wrap up their eighth successive league championship with a match to spare. On April 13, they beat Partick Thistle 5-0 while, a day later, two goals from Van Hooijdonk gave Celtic a 2-1 win over Hibs at Easter Road after Pat McGinlay had opened the scoring. A week later, Burns' men eased to a 4-0 triumph at home over Falkirk with Thom

(2), Cadete and Donnelly on the scoresheet. At Fir Park, Rangers made no mistake with a 3-1 victory over Motherwell.

Now it was down to the weekend of April 27/28 with Celtic playing Partick Thistle at Firhill while, twenty-four hours later, the Ibrox side were due to face Aberdeen in Glasgow. Burns winced as his players made it extremely difficult for themselves against less-than-average opponents who were sitting second bottom of the league. Celtic had to come from behind twice before two goals from Van Hooijdonk and singles from Cadete and Malky Mackay, the young centre-half getting a rare top team outing, gave them a 4-2 triumph. However, a runners-up place was the best the Parkhead men could hope for if the Dons failed to win in Govan. Brian Irvine gave the visitors the advantage in the nineteenth minute, but Gascoigne levelled and then scored two goals - one a penalty-kick - in the last nine minutes and the race was over.

On the last day, a crowd of 37,318 turned out at Celtic Park to serenade Tommy Burns and his players with a chest-thumping version of 'You'll Never Walk Alone'. The football was almost immaterial as the supporters threw a party for a team, which had won zilch. It was evident, despite the lack of tangible rewards, the fans had enjoyed what they had witnessed and there was now reason for extreme optimism.

As for the actual game, Jorge Cadete scored in the first minute as the team romped to a 4-1 triumph over Raith Rovers. Stuart Gray and Peter Grant added two more by half-time. Peter Duffield pulled one back before Cadete scored his fifth goal in six games on the hour mark. At the end, the players, bedecked in green and white scarves, flags and tammies, linked hands in the middle of the pitch and took a collective bow. It was a rousing send off to a barren season which bordered on the surreal.

On the same afternoon, Rangers beat Kilmarnock 3-0 at Rugby Park and completed the campaign on eighty-seven points with Celtic four behind. The Ibrox side were also eleven goals better off than their rivals. They had lost three times - twice to Hearts and once to Hibs - but had drawn only six of their games as opposed to the Parkhead side's eleven stalemates. It was a statistic that damned Celtic to failure.

The initiative for Tommy Burns in the new season was clear. The manager was required to put together a Celtic team that was better than Rangers and would earn the silverware to prove its superiority. Praise was good; points were a necessity.

CHAPTER TEN
TROUBLE LOOMING

A passionate, emotional and proud human being, Tommy Burns was conspicuously fired up as season 1996/97 loomed into view. Rangers were embarking on another sensational spending spree that would peak at almost £11million as they attempted to equal Celtic's nine successive league titles. Burns was charged with the task of making certain such a dreaded prospect was beyond the scope of his club's fiercest rivals.

As a Celtic man, he heaped awesome pressure upon himself. He was under no illusion and there was no blurred focus; Rangers had to be stopped.

Even in the most trying of circumstances, Burns often remarked that managing Celtic was 'a labour of love'. His affection must have been strained during John Collins' interminable contract extension negotiations with the club throughout the summer. Fergus McCann refused to budge on his final offer to the midfielder and Burns realised it wasn't a bluff from the managing director. So, too, did Collins. Celtic risked losing their first £1million player for nothing under the new Bosman Ruling. Collins was spirited out of Parkhead on Freedom of Contract and signed a lucrative three-year deal with AS Monaco.

McCann, as anyone with a single digit IQ would have anticipated, fought vigorously through the courts to obtain a transfer fee for the midfielder, who would have been at least rated in the £4million bracket. The new FIFA ruling left McCann frustrated and Celtic without a penny in exchange for a key player. McCann argued the Bosman Ruling did not did not apply to this case because AS Monaco were based in a principality and outside European Union jurisdiction. It was a good try, but no cigar. The compensation claim collapsed and the court's decision would rebound big-style on Burns with dire consequences during the forthcoming campaign. McCann would not be caught twice.

On the plus side, Burns had added more flair to his already-adventurous line-up by bringing in £1.5million Paolo di Canio, from AC Milan. The twenty-eight-old extrovert, who had also played for Lazio, Napoli and Juventus, would prove to be something of a mercurial Italian genius who, more often than was comfortable, veered towards eccentricity. Life was never dull with Paolo around. Jorge Cadete was virtually a new signing after making only six appearances due to his transfer saga the previous season that would, ultimately and justifiably, topple Jim Farry from his SFA seat of power. Burns, too, had no hesitation in obliterating Celtic's transfer record by shelling out £3.5million for Bolton's ball-playing centre-half Alan Stubbs. Jobbing defender and honest toiler John Hughes' days at Parkhead were numbered.

However, one who escaped Burns at the time will no doubt surprise Celtic followers. It certainly made me sit up me when I received a phone call from an acquaintance, who, I knew, was a close confidante of the manager. He was giving me the nod in the right direction of the club's interest in a young forward. I was sworn to secrecy until the time was right. My version of 'Deep Throat' was very enthusiastic about the ability of the player on Burns' radar. 'The lad's got everything,' I was assured. 'He's big, strong, can hold the ball up, good in the air and can score goals. And he can run like a gazelle.' The name of the rookie centre-forward? None other than Emile Heskey, at that time only eighteen years old with just one full season behind him at Martin O'Neill's Leicester City.

Davie Hay confirmed, 'Yes, I watched Heskey a couple of times and gave him the seal of approval. He looked a Celtic player to me.' Of course, nothing came of the club's initial interest and that certainly would have come down to finances. The future England international later joined Liverpool for £11million in March 2000.

Burns realised Celtic had relied far too much on the goals from Pierre van Hooijdonk, who completed the season as the Premier League's top scorer with twenty-six strikes. Contrast that with the eight collected by Collins the previous year or the ten from Pat McGinlay during the campaign before that. The manager was confident Jorge Cadete would also supply goals, but he still wanted to add firepower and Heskey, even at that tender age, was the one he had in mind. A three-pronged attack of Van Hooijdonk, Cadete and Heskey would have been a terrifying proposition for any defence to even attempt nullifying.

Burns, eagerly anticipating the opening day of the campaign, must have wondered if Paradise was about to be regained. The Celtic manager would have looked around the away dressing room at Pittodrie on August 10 and would have seen the quality in his squad ranging from captain Paul McStay to his signings Andreas Thom, Phil O'Donnell, Van Hooijdonk, Cadete and Stubbs and the unsung stalwarts such as Tommy Boyd, Jackie McNamara and Tosh McKinlay. He must have believed he was on a solid foundation as he prepared to take his team forward.

Instead, the Celtic manager was destined for quicksand.

Inside nine months, Burns' reign as Celtic boss was over. He was relieved of his managerial duties by Fergus McCann with three league games still to play; assistant Billy Stark reluctantly stepping in. Burns was offered a post in charge of youth development, but his self-esteem would never have allowed him to accept the position. Technically, on May 2 1997, he resigned. To all intents and purposes, though, he had been sacked. His vision of an exciting, attractive Celtic had been buried under the rubble of a disastrous campaign that saw Rangers achieve their target of nine consecutive championships.

Even worse was the curiously tentative resistance of Celtic to block their bid. Burns watched in anguish as his team lost all four of the Old Firm league games, the first such occurrence in the twenty-two years of the Premier League. The club went out of the League Cup, beaten 1-0 in extra-time by Hearts at Tynecastle in September. First Division Falkirk triumphed 1-0 in the Scottish Cup semi-final replay at Ibrox on April 23, Burns' last game in charge. The UEFA Cup adventure didn't get beyond the First Round, beaten soundly home and away by SV Hamburg for an emphatic and embarrassing 4-0 aggregate. Celtic had struggled against little-known Kosice, of Slovakia, in the qualifying round, drawing 0-0 away from home and eventually winning against ten men with a goal two minutes from time by Cadete. Four European games and a solitary goal to show for it. Burns and Celtic, in truth, were falling well short of expectation levels.

Possibly, the warning lights were flashing as early as the opening league fixture against Aberdeen. Celtic were leading 1-0 with only sixteen minutes to go, then Alan Stubbs was sent off after gifting a penalty-kick and had to rely on a last-kick equaliser to snatch a point. After the final whistle, Tosh McKinlay was involved in a violent scuffle with a Dons player, had a verbal spat with the referee and, like Stubbs, was banned from the next game. As far as omens went, this was not the most reassuring.

And, yet, it could have been a vastly different tale after Celtic had deservedly taken the lead following twenty-eight minutes of sparring with Roy Aitken's team. Pierre van Hooijdonk curled an unstoppable twenty-five yard free-kick over Michael Watt's right shoulder for the opener and the travelling fans sat back in anticipation of a festival of football. It unravelled, though, in the seventy-fourth minute when Stubbs allowed a pass from the plodding Dean Windass to slip under his boot to the equally-cumbersome Duncan Shearer. The big-money signing compounded the error by hauling Shearer to the ground. Referee Hugh Dallas had little option but to point to the penalty spot and administer a red card to the debutant. Windass blasted the award into the net to Gordon Marshall's left. Six minutes later, the Dons went ahead when Shearer tucked another behind the Celtic keeper. A complete horror story was averted when Jackie McNamara slung over a cross from the right and Andreas Thom thumped in a last-gasp leveller.

McKinlay got involved with David Rowson as the teams made their way to the tunnel and then, foolishly, turned his attention to the match official. His actions were noted, forwarded to the SFA and an automatic suspension kept him out of the League Cup-tie against Clyde the following midweek. Stubbs would have company in the Broadwood stand as Celtic beat their part-time opponents 3-1. Stubbs moaned,

'If we had lost, I would have sent the fans a public apology.' He added, 'My debut dream went out the window.' It would be followed by many others within the next nine months.

With aspirations of progress in the UEFA Cup and the League Cup already decimated, all eyes were on their first Glasgow derby of the season on September 28 at Ibrox. Burns could have been better prepared for the occasion. A contract row with Van Hooijdonk had been simmering in the background before it blazed into the public domain. The Dutchman had been offered £7,000-per-week, but reckoned that sort of payment was merely acceptable 'for homeless people'. The quote didn't go down well with many of the populace, including Big Issue sellers everywhere. There was obvious friction among the three main protagonists, the player, the team boss and the managing director. Burns decided to drop Van Hooijdonk from his squad for Ibrox and, with Jorge Cadete also out with an injury, Rangers, at a stroke, realised they would not have to face the menace of two players who had already collected seventeen goals between them so early in the season.

Walter Smith's side were two points ahead after six games by the time Celtic arrived in Govan. Tommy Burns' team were also protecting a thirty-seven game undefeated league record. The last side to beat them had been the Ibrox outfit a year earlier. There was a catalogue of calamity for the Celtic boss before kick-off. Van Hooijdonk, of course, had been dumped and crocked duo Paul McStay and Phil O'Donnell joined Cadete on the sidelines. Burns took a risk on the fitness of Andreas Thom who had been nursing a rib injury. The gamble was destined to fail and the forward was forced off after only twenty-three minutes to be replaced by Morten Wieghorst, a move which hardly helped the balance or structure of the line-up. Alan Stubbs was deployed in midfield with John Hughes in central defence.

In only ten minutes, Burns could have been forgiven for believing it wasn't going to be Celtic's day. Paolo di Canio tricked and teased his way into a glorious shooting position, but Goram managed to get a hand to the ball to divert it to Simon Donnelly. The Celtic support reckoned joy had merely been postponed for a second or two, but the youngster's goalbound effort was frantically scrambled off the line by Petric. Gascoigne, unsurprisingly, became the game's first booking in the nineteenth minute for kicking Brian O'Neil as the Celt lay on the ground. He would later be joined by team-mates Gough and van Vossen while Celtic left-back Tosh McKinlay saw red after two yellow cards in the first-half. Colleagues Tommy Boyd, Di Canio and Hughes joined him in the book.

One Sunday newspaper reporter observed, 'Referee Willie Young scattered yellow cards around like confetti and McKinlay should have been joined by Jorg Albertz after the German midfielder astonishingly escaped punishment for a most cynical piece of violent play, stamping on Brian O'Neil under the gaze of linesman Joe Kelly, who failed to notify the unsighted Young.'

Rangers took the lead against the ten men six minutes after the interval when Gough blitzed a header past Gordon Marshall following a corner-kick from Albertz, the Ibrox club's £4million summer signing from SV Hamburg. However, Peter Grant - and every last one of the 50,124 spectators - thought he had levelled nine minutes from time when he scorched a low drive beyond Goram. The ball smashed against the inside of the left-hand post and ran tantalisingly along the goal-line before being hacked clear. Worse was to follow a minute from the end. Hughes also left the Rangers keeper stranded with a bullet-like header. This time it whacked off the face of the bar and, within seconds with the frame of the goal still trembling, Gascoigne broke upfield to score a second for the home team. The pass that released the Englishman was despatched by Albertz, who, by rights, shouldn't even have been on the pitch at that stage.

Afterwards, Burns was defiant. He said, 'You can write us off at your peril. We'll see who is top of the table at the end of the season. Remember, there are still twenty-nine games to play.' All stirring stuff and it had been obvious to all who had witnessed the ninety minutes that Celtic hadn't received a shred of good luck against their ancient foes, but the league table now showed Rangers, who capitalised on Dame Fortune's radiant smile, five points clear. Also, they had now remained undefeated in their last seven games against the Parkhead side.

Celtic returned to action on October 12 after an international break and still the Van Hooijdonk/Burns/McCann row rumbled on. The Dutchman had been ordered to train on his own, but, because of the chronic number of call-offs, he was given a reprieve and led the attack against Motherwell at Parkhead. Burns was without Paul McStay, Phil O'Donnell, Tosh McKinlay, Andreas Thom and Jorge Cadete for a variety of reasons as Alex McLeish brought his Fir Park outfit to the east end of Glasgow. Once again, a Celtic player didn't last the ninety minutes and this time it was Gordon Marshall who was invited to leave proceedings with only seven minutes to go and the game balanced finely at 0-0. The keeper never quite mastered footwork and he emphasised that weakness once more with a ridiculous fresh-air swipe at a simple passback from Tommy Boyd. He then hauled down Lee McCulloch outside the box and awaited the inevitable conclusion from referee Bobby Orr. Off he trudged and on came young Stewart Kerr, with Brian McLaughlin being sacrificed, for his Celtic debut.

Van Hooijdonk had the final say when he snatched the winner in the fading moments. Celtic Park erupted in joy and a couple of minutes later there was another surge of uncontrollable bonhomie throughout the ground when it was announced Rangers had lost 2-1 to Hibs at Easter Road. Van Hooijdonk clenched a defiant fist and positively snarled in the direction of the directors' box as he came off the field. Fergus McCann, no doubt, wouldn't have received any mixed signals from the team's unhappy marksman.

A week later against Hearts at Tynecastle, the towering striker scored two excellent goals, but the team dropped two points in a 2-2 draw, conceding the equaliser deep in injury time. Tommy Burns sighed, 'We did not have the composure when we needed it most.' Celtic were leading courtesy of Van Hooijdonk's double when Colin Cameron pulled one back in the fifty-second minute. 'We were sleeping,' said Burns. Davie McPherson forced in the leveller in the fading seconds. 'We were defending far too deep,' observed the manager. At least, the goals from Van Hooijdonk provoked a response from the managing director who made a revised offer of an enhanced four-year contract. The player promised to get back to him.

Celtic returned to Edinburgh six days later to swamp Hibs 4-0 at Easter Road with Van Hooijdonk again getting on the scoresheet. Burns had ordered Thom to be more greedy around the penalty box and the German gave his reply in the shape of two fine goals. Simon Donnelly chipped in with the fourth. There was a surprise before the kick-off, though, when it was revealed Peter Grant would no longer be team skipper. Alan Stubbs led the team out against Hibs and Burns explained, 'The responsibility was dragging Peter down. It's a big thing for him to be captain of this club, but his play was being affected and that is why the switch of captaincy to Alan Stubbs is permanent until Paul McStay returns.'

At the beginning of November, Fergus McCann put yet another offer on the table to Van Hooijdonk. The Dutchman would be the third highest-earning player at the club behind Thom and Di Canio. Van Hooijdonk, clearly, had no intention of being third in the salary stakes to anyone. Fresh talks didn't even get off the ground. And the frontman was missing, too, when Celtic prepared to take on Aberdeen at Parkhead. Apparently, he was injured. Italian Di Canio earned his crust by hitting the only goal of the game to send Burns' team to the top of the Premier League for the first time in the season, albeit on goal difference. Against all expectations, Rangers had struggled in Kirkcaldy on the same afternoon and shed two points after sharing four goals with Raith Rovers.

Tommy Burns said, 'We have had opportunities in the past to go above Rangers and blown every one of them. It showed character and perseverance to do what we have now accomplished. I asked Di Canio to be the side's father figure because, with so many young players, they needed someone who could slow the game down. He is a passionate man who has quickly developed a strong feeling for this club.'

On Thursday, November 14, Celtic were presented with the ideal opportunity to go three points clear at the top when Walter Smith's side arrived at Parkhead for another thunderous tussle. Yet again, it was a powderkeg confrontation that carved out ninety pulsating minutes and Burns, fuming at some strange decisions from referee Hugh Dallas, was ordered from the dug-out after a particularly vehement disagreement with the fourth official, Eric Martindale. It was that sort of fiery encounter. Rangers won 1-0 with a simple goal from Laudrup in the seventh minute which was crafted out of nowhere and was due to an unfortunate slip by Brian O'Neil. The defender lost his footing with no-one near him and the Dane seized on the loose ball and carried on before sweeping his effort wide of the exposed Stewart Kerr.

The keeper, who only celebrated his twenty-second birthday the previous day, kept Celtic in the game when he made a magnificent penalty save from Gascoigne in the sixty-eighth minute. Parkhead was in uproar when Dallas pointed to the spot after the rookie keeper had gone down at the feet of Laudrup. It looked like a fifty/fifty challenge with neither combatant showing any inclination of pulling out. The match official waved away all protests and justice was done when Kerr dived to his left to hold the spot-kick effort.

With five minutes to go, and the ground still throbbing, Celtic threw away the chance to draw level and remain at the Premier League pinnacle. Gough's challenge on Simon Donnelly was more of an assault than a tackle and the only reasonable conclusion was another penalty-kick. Hush descended on the packed stadium as Van Hooijdonk sized up the situation. He stepped forward, aimed for the right-hand corner and was left open-mouthed in astonishment as Goram dived full-length to push the ball round the post for a corner-kick. Laudrup's early strike was enough to take the points to Ibrox and restore Smith's side back to pole position.

Burns had calmed down considerably by the time he attended the aftermatch press conference. He said, 'I will pay my fine, bite my tongue and learn from the experience. We all get carried away sometimes. It's disappointing to lose in the fashion we did, but that is not an excuse. There is only so much you can ask of a team and I thought we did well, in spite of the result. Great things are built from perseverance and we will not change our style of play. It will one day get us to where we want to be.'

The manager refused to point the finger of blame at penalty-kick culprit Van Hooijdonk. 'When there are five minutes left of an Old Firm match, there are not many players who will volunteer to take an award such as that one. Pierre has scored many great goals for us and he will do so again. At least, he had the courage to put himself in the firing line.'

When asked about the poor run of recent results against his team's oldest foes, Burns replied, 'I was lucky enough to play for Celtic when we went ten years without losing to Rangers at Parkhead. So, we won't get our knickers in a twist because of the last eight games. We haven't had much luck, but we won't change our philosophy, which is to entertain, pass the ball and play at pace.'

It was all very admirable and, Burns, undoubtedly, meant every syllable of every word at the time. But Celtic fans were growing more concerned and more vocal as another campaign of impending doom was beginning to materialise, pre-season promises toppling into the void of darkness. Burns, too, was having second thoughts about his footballing philosophy. Before the turn of the year, after a 1-0 victory over Dundee United in Glasgow, he admitted, 'It wasn't nice to watch, but winning is the name of the game, particularly for us.'

The Arctic conditions meant it would be more than a fortnight before Celtic were in action again. What transpired on November 30 in a 2-2 stalemate with Hearts at Parkhead will still be scorched into the memory banks of the 50,034 fans who were there to witness it and the watching millions on television. It was an act of sheer folly that had a fuming Tommy Burns questioning the sanity of one his own players.

Paolo di Canio, who, on occasion, possessed the ability to make an agitating fanatic look sane, reasonable and rational, took centre stage in the seventy-sixth minute after scoring the penalty-kick that would give his side a point. Before the Edinburgh side had the opportunity to kick off again, Di Canio, arms waving and looking heavenwards for some divine intervention, was heading for the dressing room after picking up a red card from referee Stuart Dougal following an extraordinary flashpoint incident. The Italian had been brought down by Neil Pointon to earn the spot-kick which he despatched unerringly beyond Gilles Rousset. So far, so good, but what happened next went way beyond acceptable.

Di Canio raced into the net, groped for the ball in the rigging, got into a tangle with the keeper, emerged with the required item under his arm, bawled at anyone wearing a maroon jersey, stopped and looked as though he was going to have a good old-fashioned square-go with ex-Celt Stevie Fulton. Some venom spewed the match official's way and Dougal produced a yellow card to match the one the volatile individual had received earlier and banished him from the field. Di Canio gesticulated in his best Latin manner, pleading with the referee to change his mind. Eventually, he was persuaded to utilise the dressing room facilities, but not before more hand gestures and grabbing his shirt and kissing the badge. Burns, clearly annoyed, grabbed the player and angrily propelled him in the direction of the tunnel.

One report referred to Di Canio's actions as 'lunacy'. It went on, 'He was pumped up at the start, then obnoxious, then increasingly downright inflammatory, until his behaviour grew so demented he was required to depart the playing field. If we required irony, his leaving occurred within seconds of his equalising goal for Celtic.'

A frustrated Burns said, 'Di Canio was stupid. That's all it was; sheer stupidity. If he had stayed on, I think we would have won and I've told him that. For an experienced player like him, it was very disappointing. He will definitely be disciplined. We've spoken to him before about his behaviour. He earned the penalty-kick and we would have had three points if he had stayed on. There's no defence. The players have been told any semblance of dissent from now on will cost them heavily. We understand their frustrations, but the job is difficult enough without people being suspended.'

Amidst the furore and controversy, it seemed to be overlooked that Celtic had now dropped five out of a possible six points at home. Colin Cameron gave the visitors the advantage just after the half-hour mark, but Brian O'Neil nullified that effort with a splendid header two minutes from the break. Neil McCann restored Hearts' lead in the sixty-fourth minute before Di Canio made his indelible mark upon the encounter.

Burns, looking at the overall picture, added, 'Two-and-a-half years ago, this club had nothing and were going nowhere. The way in which we lose crunch games when they come along tells me that it might be time to invest in a better quality of player.'

Celtic went into December with a game against Motherwell at Fir Park to address. Genuine championship aspirations took a severe jolt that chilly afternoon in Lanarkshire; Alex McLeish's team winning 2-1 with a last-minute goal. Burns was left in the knowledge they could now thrash Rangers in their two remaining Old Firm fixtures and it would no longer be enough. Celtic were now eight points adrift and the bleak conditions mirrored the thoughts of the manager afterwards. He snapped, 'It's difficult to find something good to say.' There was no need for him to elaborate.

It was distressing to watch a team of players displaying a collective lack of mental strength. The points were there to be won, but there was little cohesion or eagerness or fire about this line-up. Billy Davies put Motherwell ahead five minutes before the interval and it took Celtic until ten minutes from the end to force a leveller through young Chris Hay, netting his first goal for the club. It would have been bad enough to settle for a draw, but in the last minute Stewart Kerr pushed a shot from Andy Roddie straight to substitute Ian Ross and he bundled the rebound into the net from close range. The only thing Burns could add was, 'We really should have had enough to beat this Motherwell team.'

Pressure was building on Burns and the strain was showing. He watched his team scramble a 1-0 win over Dundee United two weeks later in front of 46,483 spectators at Parkhead with Phil O'Donnell, returning after his long-term thigh problem, scoring the winner before the break. It was a nervy showing from the home team and the last twenty or so minutes were played out in slow motion as far as the Celtic followers were concerned. Astonishingly, Burns turned on the club's support afterwards. 'The attitude of the fans has disappointed me,' he bristled. 'Being a Celtic supporter myself, I know that we are one hell of a group for arguing among ourselves. It can be a healthy thing sometimes, but when it becomes abusive, then it de-motivates people. We're doing everything we possibly can to win this league, but if it's not meant to be, then it's not meant to be. The players have been low in confidence and, really, I would like a bit more help and for people to show a bit more optimism than they have been doing in recent weeks.'

Paolo di Canio hit the headlines again on Boxing Day - this time for all the right reasons after scoring a late winner against Aberdeen at Pittodrie to rescue three points. Once again, Celtic made it an uphill struggle by allowing the Dons to take the lead in the fourteenth minute through Billy Dodds. However, Jorge Cadete wiped that out with a typical effort in the fortieth minute and then came Di Canio's magic moment seven minutes from the end. Tosh McKinlay launched a long free-kick into enemy territory and the Italian, wearing eye-catching gold boots, brought the ball down with sublime ease, lobbed it over stranded keeper Nicky Walker and nudged it over the goal-line. Thankfully, the Italian's histrionics were confined to running to the fans and blowing kisses to everyone in the vicinity.

Pierre van Hooijdonk, still locked in a very messy public dispute with the club, passed a fitness test, but the nearest he came to the pitch that evening was the substitutes' bench. On the game, Burns observed, 'We have to get away from the theory that it is Celtic who always have to play the pretty football - and the players are now beginning to realise that.'

On the Van Hooijdonk situation, he reported, 'The Celtic supporters will make up their own minds about Pierre. They can't be kidded and they see through things and understand the game. But I would hope that when Pierre is playing for us they would support him - he is still a Celtic player, after all. One thing I didn't want this season was obstacles like this being put in our way. The time to talk about contract and wage rises should be at the end of the season.'

Burns had plenty of time to reflect on the previous four months of the campaign as the Celtic team coach headed for Glasgow that cold, stark night. One inescapable fact remained, though, and that was Celtic were now fourteen points adrift of Rangers. Certainly, they had three games in hand, but even allowing for three straight wins, it still left a little matter of a five-point canyon between the Glasgow rivals.

Paul McStay, after missing fifteen consecutive games with his troublesome ankle injury, was given a hero's welcome by 45,818 fans as he returned to first team action against Dunfermline three days before the end of 1996. The midfielder might have wondered what he had let himself in for when former Celtic player Gerry Britton put the Fifers ahead in only six minutes. And there was a scare moments later when Britton got through again, but trundled a shot wide of the target with only Stewart Kerr to beat. It was a let-off and Celtic realised it. Two quickfire efforts turned the game around before half-time.

Jorge Cadete, displaying excellent predatory instincts, equalised in the thirty-fifth minute and a restored Pierre van Hoiijdonk grabbed a second three minutes later. The Portuguese raider got No.3 in the fifty-second minute and Simon Donnelly had overworked keeper Ian Westwater fishing the ball out of the back of his net for a fourth time just before the hour mark. Britton got a second for Bert Paton's side.

Burns was all smiles at the end, particularly with the return of his skipper McStay. He enthused, 'We've really missed him while he has been out. It's only when you try to buy someone as a replacement you realise that no-one is quite as good. The important thing Paul brings is composure. You want to try to put passes together and perform as a team unit and Paul helps that happen. He has got the experience to make up for what he is lacking in match fitness and he is absolutely thrilled to return to the team, though both he and I knew he would make it back.'

He added, 'Over the last few games, the players have given everything in the knowledge we can't afford to drop a single point. Sometimes the silky stuff has to go and you've got to be prepared to sweat and we have shown we can do that.'

Celtic were now due to travel across Glasgow for the New Year head-to-head with Rangers at Ibrox on January 2 to usher in 1997 in the traditional tribal manner. There could be no settling for a point by Celtic on this occasion which Burns was more than aware played perfectly into the hands of Walter Smith and their ancient adversaries. All too often, the Parkhead men had been picked off by a set of opportunists more than content to sit back, absorb pressure and hit on the break when the opening arose. Celtic had exposed their back more than was comfortable in recent years and had the scars to show for it.

Burns, of course, had another problem - could he afford to take a chance on Paul McStay, his onfield leader? The savage heat of an Old Firm confrontation is not an occasion designed to accommodate anyone other than those in peak condition. McStay, with only one game since August, couldn't possibly have been completely match-fit for the ninety-minute rigours required of such an encounter. The Celtic manager, though, had supreme faith and the utmost belief in his midfielder and McStay's name was one of the first on his team sheet for a vitally important set-to where only the most resolute would emerge victorious.

Unfortunately, McStay, awarded an MBE in the New Year Honours' List, had nothing to celebrate after a high-octane, controversial Glasgow derby that scorched through ninety minutes of contentious issues. Rangers won 3-1, but the story behind the scoreline made for interesting reading and, possibly, also made for huge embarrassment for referee Jim McCluskey and his farside linesman Gordon McBride. Neither could have been remotely satisfied with what they had contributed to another evening where Burns and his Celtic players must have wondered about the fickleness of fate. Even Walter Smith had the good grace to admit, 'The first-half was pretty even, but in the second-half Celtic had much more pressure. They looked the team more likely to score and even go on and win. I had a feeling they would cause us much more problems in the second forty-five and that was the case.'

On this particular occasion, there was a lot about the treatment of Paolo di Canio that was reprehensible, on and off the pitch. The Italian's vulnerable, brittle temperament became a shameful target throughout the confrontation and it is to his credit he did not respond to the merciless goading and inexcusable taunts. In only ten minutes, Di Canio was completely taken out of play by a blatant bodycheck from centre-half McLaren. The match official adjudged it to be a yellow card offence and the Rangers defender could count himself extremely lucky.

Twenty minutes later, the Celtic forward was, rightly, halted in his tracks as he sped onto a Jorge Cadete pass. He was offside by at least three yards and didn't bother complaining as he turned away and started to jog back upfield as the ball ran through to Goram. The keeper, for no apparent reason, didn't wait for the ball to be placed for the free-kick. Instead, he blasted the object off Di Canio's exposed back.

Of course, the volatile forward reacted and, within minutes McStay, Ally McCoist and, inevitably, Paul Gascoigne were involved in a squabble. Referee McCluskey, astoundingly, took no action against the goalie, who triggered the aggro. The Rangers fans chanted Goram's name for the next few minutes in appreciation of his actions and also his accuracy with his right foot. And so it went on, but Di Canio held his feelings in check and, thankfully, refused to retaliate.

Rangers took the lead in nine minutes with an unstoppable free-kick from midfielder Albertz, known as 'The Hammer' as testimony to his awesome shooting power. Jackie McNamara, who would perform better in future games at Ibrox, gave away a free-kick thirty yards out after a trip on raiding left-back Robertson. The German took a full fifteen-yard run-up to the ball before hitting a pulverising left-foot strike through the wall and low past Stewart Kerr. McNamara, last man in the wall, turned away just as Albertz made contact. The shot was later timed at a shade under eighty-miles-per-hour. The Celtic goalie didn't stand a chance.

Di Canio gave nemesis Goram a fright with a cunning free-kick that skipped up off the damp surface. The keeper fumbled the ball and it was booted clear. Goram was involved again shortly afterwards when he was unhappy after a mid-air challenge from Alan Stubbs at a left-wing corner-kick. Defender Petric had to grab his colleague, drag him away and attempt to calm him down before play resumed. Little had been seen of the much-vaunted Gascoigne, now a preposterous peroxide blond, as the game ebbed and flowed at a frantic pace. Burns introduced Pierre van Hooijdonk for Simon Donnelly seven minutes after the turnaround and the Dutchman responded with a flying header, which was pushed away by Goram at his right-hand post.

Moments later a Di Canio effort was frenziedly booted off the line by a desperate Goram.

A goal just had to come and Celtic got the equaliser they so richly deserved in the sixty-sixth minute. Tommy Boyd started the move by carrying the ball towards the penalty box, it was shuttled speedily between Pierre van Hooijdonk and Cadete and fell perfectly for Di Canio to rifle a low shot under the Rangers goalkeeper. Burns' men stepped up the pressure as they went in search of a second goal and Smith pulled off the ineffective Peter van Vossen in the seventy-fifth minute and replaced him with Erik Bo Andersen, a young striker bought from Danish outfit Aalborg for £1.2million the previous season. It was to prove a pivotal substitution.

With seven minutes remaining, McNamara and Brian O'Neil got involved in some suicidal head-tennis on the edge of their penalty area. To be fair to the right-back, he was blameless when he nodded the ball inside to the centre-half to cut off an intended pass to Albertz. O'Neil must have taken a rush of blood to the head as he decided to knock the ball back to his team-mate. The ball took a bounce and completely eliminated the surprised McNamara. Albertz gathered the gift, fired it low across the six-yard box to the unguarded Andersen and he toe-poked it past Kerr. It was an act of utter recklessness by O'Neil and, once more, Celtic were forced to pay the most severe of penalties.

However, four minutes later, Burns and Billy Stark were hugging on the touchline in delight as the ecstatic occupants of the Broomloan Road stand got a great view of Cadete's swivel and shot that zoomed high into the net past a static Goram. McNamara's right wing cross had been knocked down by Phil O'Donnell into the Portuguese attacker's path and his touch and turn completely flummoxed his marker, Petric. However, the Celtic grins quickly became groans when the farside linesman raised his flag and signalled for offside. In fairness, referee McCluskey, on this occasion, couldn't be faulted and had to go on the say-so of his assistant, McBride. He got it terribly wrong and there can be no plausible explanation for his faulty call because TV evidence proved he was right in line with the incident. He had the best view in the ground. Cadete was at least a yard onside when O'Donnell first made contact with the ball to head it on. Clearly, it was a travesty of justice.

Two minutes later, Rangers were 3-1 ahead. Alas, a tiring McStay, who had been well off target with two shots earlier, fluffed a pass inside. It was smuggled through to Andersen who flicked it out to Albertz on the left. The Dane took off in a direct line for the Celtic goal as McNamara tried to keep pace. However, the fresh legs of Andersen gave him the advantage and he was in the clear by the time the midfielder slid the ball in front of him. He took time to check Kerr's positioning before clipping his effort wide of the keeper's outstretched right leg and in at the far post. Forlornly, McNamara could only follow the ball into the net.

Celtic had now gone nine consecutive games without beating their arch rivals. There were many hard luck stories in the midst of the confrontations, but statistics tend to be cold and uncaring of circumstances. And those were the heartless facts only two days into a new year with Rangers fourteen points clear at the top of the Premier League.

Burns observed, 'Football can be a very cruel game. The boys put in a tremendous fight and, as far as the goals go, there is nothing you can do to allow for individual mistakes. Those sort of things have happened in football for more than a 100 years, but you just have to live with it. It was more difficult to take because Rangers had so few chances against us.

'The good thing is that the boys applied themselves after going behind so early. They showed intelligence and endeavour and my disappointment is for them – especially after putting so much into the game – and I don't feel that the scoreline reflected the run of play. I thought we were going to go on and win the game. In the second-half, we were getting better and better. And I don't think Jorge's strike was offside. Di Canio, Van Hooijdonk and Cadete did very well, but Andy Goram was Andy Goram, though it wasn't him who beat us this time.

'We still have eighteen games to go and we will try to win every one of them, as was the case before this match even if we had won. We are certainly up for that and we will not be throwing in the towel.'

Celtic's lowest home crowd of the season - 45,374 - watched the team take on Motherwell only two days later in the punishing schedule that would see Burns' men play a total of six league games in January. It couldn't have been a surprise to anyone that Paul McStay was missing from the line-up. Alan Stubbs was out, too, and Tommy Boyd took over as captain. The fans who stayed away missed a scintillating five-goal performance from Celtic with Fir Park keeper Steve Woods the busiest man in the east end of Glasgow that crisp, biting afternoon. Woods, of course, would return to Parkhead as an excellent and influential goalkeeping coach once his playing days were over. However, he must have been relieved to get as far away from the ground as possible that afternoon after being put through ninety minutes of sheer misery.

Paolo di Canio stroked home a smooth penalty-kick in the twenty-eighth minute to get things started and Pierre van Hooijdonk, now being linked with a move to West Ham almost on a daily basis, knocked in a second just before the break. Jorge Cadete got in on the act in the seventy-fifth minute with the third and Woods was left exhausted and helpless after conceding two goals in the space of two minutes near the end. The Portuguese striker hit No.4 and Morten Wieghorst made it five.

Tommy Burns observed, 'This result showed the mettle of the team. It was always going to be a difficult game coming so soon after the bitter disappointment of losing at Ibrox, despite playing so well. There's always a worry that there might be a reaction, but we were very positive from the off and the result was good for the goals for column and good, too, for the fans who were certainly entertained. We've always said we wouldn't give up the title chase at any stage.'

Four days later at the same venue, a hat-trick from Cadete helped Celtic to go one better against Kilmarnock with three goals in the last ten minutes putting a gloss on the 6-0 scoreline. McNamara, Wieghorst and Hay got the others in a performance that left Burns' team eleven points behind their Ibrox rivals with a game in hand. The quote of the day belonged to Cadete who revealed, 'I believe it is still possible to catch Rangers in the championship. If I did not have that belief, I would ask the manager if I could go on holiday.'

Thankfully, he was still around on a cold, wet and blustery Tuesday evening on January 14 at Stark's Park where Celtic were seventeen minutes away from a dreadful result. Danish striker Soren Andersen shot the Fifers into the lead in the thirteenth minute and after that it was all about Raith Rovers' resistance against opponents who were finding it difficult to cope with the appalling conditions. However, Cadete managed an equaliser in the seventy-third minute and Hay, a late substitute for Donnelly, snatched the winner with two minutes remaining. A relieved Burns said, 'We gave the players a bit of stick at half-time and told them we needed courage to win. Rovers' pitch doesn't lend itself to good football, but our will-to-win spirit was the most pleasing thing for me.'

The following Saturday at Parkhead, Celtic breezed through a 4-1 victory over Hibs with Van Hooijdonk (2), McLaughlin and Cadete on target while Kevin Harper hit a late consolation effort for the men from the east. The Portuguese attack leader had now claimed nine goals from his past five outings and, overall, an extremely-laudable twenty-two in twenty-four games. He was on the scoresheet yet again on the final Wednesday of the month, the twenty-ninth, as Celtic overcame Dunfermline 2-0 at East End Park with a lot more ease than the tight scoreline would suggest. Paul McStay claimed his only league goal of the campaign to open the scoring in the thirty-eighth minute and Cadete doubled the advantage two minutes later.

'When we fell fourteen points behind Rangers after the Old Firm game, everyone said it was the end of the world,' reflected Burns. 'But the players deserve great credit for what they have achieved since then. They have hung in there and shown they are prepared to battle and scrap.'

So, Celtic's sprint through January after the setback in Govan read: Played five, won five, goals for nineteen, goals against two and points fifteen. It had been a faultless reply to 1997's disappointing entrance. Interestingly, Rangers had four games over the same period and won three - Hibs (2-1), Aberdeen (4-0) and Motherwell (3-1) - but dropped two points in a 1-1 draw with Kilmarnock at Rugby Park.

On February 1, Rangers shed two more points in a goalless home draw against Hearts, but there was little by way of celebration in the east end of the city; Celtic had been turned over 1-0 by Dundee United at Tannadice, losing out to a goal two minutes from time. It didn't ease the despair that the winner had been scored by a player rejected by Walter Smith. The Parkhead men travelled back from Tayside fully in the realisation they had shot themselves in the foot. Paolo di Canio, on two occasions, Jorge Cadete, normally so deadly, and Paul McStay all missed chances and, right on cue, in the eighty-third minute Gary McSwegan, not rated by Rangers, replaced Robbie Winters. The substitute took five minutes to catch up with the tempo before seizing onto a long pass, twisting beyond Jackie McNamara and lobbing the ball over Stewart Kerr. And, with awesome simplicity, Celtic were undone.

Burns remained remarkably philosophical in the circumstances, saying, 'It is not a question of us and Rangers winning every match between now and the end of the season. Footballers are only human and people should remember that. We have had a good run of games and the law of averages dictates that we must lose sometime. Indeed, we haven't had many games to rue in the last twenty months. There is a long way to go and the race moves on to another stage. We didn't deserve to lose. Our players worked very hard against a much improved United side, although we conceded a bad goal. There won't be many teams that come to Tannadice and make the number of chances we did. Over the piece, our players gave their all.'

On February 6, Celtic beat Raith Rovers 2-0 in Glasgow to reduce Rangers' lead to four points, although the Ibrox side had a game in hand. Once again, there was controversy; once again Jorge Cadete was involved. At 0-0, it looked as though the Portuguese striker, who favoured playing on the shoulder of the last defender, had scored a perfectly good goal in the thirty-fifth minute, but it was ruled out by referee Cammy Melville. Afterwards, a clearly agitated Cadete said, 'I'm becoming frustrated with this. It has happened four times to me now this season - against Alloa, Kilmarnock, Rangers and now Raith Rovers. LInesmen are not machines - just as I am not a machine and I suppose they are bound to make errors. Maybe not so many.'

Cadete managed to get on the scoresheet twelve minutes from time to add to Paolo di Canio's effort shortly after the turnaround. It brought the player's total to an impressive thirty-two goals from thirty-three games. The encounter was played in swirling wind and rain and Tommy Burns added, 'That was a difficult fixture for us, but, although I am pleased we got the victory, I reckon we should have scored more goals. We've played ten games in the last four-and-a half weeks and I think the players are looking a bit tired. I was a little concerned at 1-0 as there is always a danger that if you are not clinical there will be a price to pay. But the result was the most important thing.'

The last league game in February was played out at Fir Park as Celtic conquered Motherwell 1-0 with a tenth minute strike by Jorge Cadete. Two days before the game, Burns had rushed through the £300,000 signing of defender Enrico Annoni from AS Roma. The travelling supporters were anxious to get their first glimpse of the menacing-looking, shaven-headed Italian, but he remained on the substitutes' bench throughout the ninety minutes. Ironically, he was called upon by the authorities for a random drug test after the game. Welcome to Scottish football, Enrico.

The wind howled and shrieked around the trim Lanarkshire ground on a day when it was a challenge for the players to remain vertical. The ball took on a life of its own when it was in the air - which was far too often for a purist's liking. UFO-seeking enthusiasts were served up a feast. Paradoxically, though, the only goal of the game didn't just overcome the Motherwell back lot, but also the elements. Simon Donnelly and Paolo di Canio were involved in a slick, swift movement before the ball was switched to the feet of Jorge Cadete who adroitly sidestepped the flailing arms of keeper Scott Howie before angling the ball in with elegant grace. Pierre van Hooijdonk sat beside Annoni on the bench for ninety minutes and looked far from happy with his lot. He had gone public to say the club had reneged on a contractual promise when he signed.

Fergus McCann, in withering tones, often referred to Van Hooijdonk, Cadete and Di Canio as 'The Three Amigos'. The managing director was experiencing turbulence from the Dutchman, the Portuguese and the Italian, admittedly a supremely-talented trio, but a threesome who could also be troublesome, especially where filthy lucre was concerned. McCann, after being stung by John Collins' Bosman move to AS Monaco, vowed never to be placed in the same uncomfortable position again. While a player was agitating and still under contract, the managing director would cash in to the maximum. As far as 'The Three Amigos' were concerned, it would be a case of 'Sell! Sell! Sell!' To the detriment of the team and the manager.

Of the game, Burns observed, 'We decided to opt for Di Canio playing up front with Cadete as Paolo can hold the ball up and Jorge is always on the last defender. He had two or three other chances to score, but I'm very pleased overall with the players' approach to the game. Paul McStay was tremendous in the middle of the park as we played some good football in stages. It was always going to be a difficult game for us and latterly we were aware that Motherwell could be in with a chance of sneaking something from the game.'

Van Hooijdonk was asked how he felt about spending the game on the subs' bench. 'How do you think I felt?' he grumbled. On March 10, he was sold to Nottingham Forest for £4.2million, the club were relegated from the English top flight at the end of the season and, in the summer, the Dutchman demanded a transfer.

Tommy Burns would follow him out of Celtic Park fifty-three days and ten games later.

CHAPTER ELEVEN
THE GRIMMEST NIGHTMARE

It was becoming increasingly obvious a solitary dark cloud would always find Tommy Burns on a sunny day.

The 1996/97 Scottish Cup expedition brought with it a coruscating high to be followed by an agonising, steep descent, a disturbing plummet from grace that ultimately cost Burns his job as Celtic manager.

The first step on the quest for triumph in the national competition was watched by 16,102 fans against Clydebank on January 26 1997. The Third Round tie had been switched to Firhill, home of Partick Thistle, for crowd safety reasons. The Scottish League's mid-season breakdown confirmed Celtic's status as the major box-office attraction in the country, emphasising the fact they were attracting, on average, over 1,000 more followers than Rangers, a team aiming for its ninth title in succession.

Burns' side displayed the flamboyance the thrill-seekers craved as they hammered their opponents 5-0 with Jorge Cadete scoring the opener in only sixty-five seconds. He added a second in the tenth minute and Malky Mackay fizzed in a header from a Paolo di Canio free-kick for the third just before the half-hour mark. Pierre van Hooijdonk added a fourth after the interval and there was a comical interlude nine minutes from time when Celtic were awarded a penalty-kick. Cadete would have been in the position of claiming a hat-trick and a £500 bonus from the tournament sponsors, Tennent's. It would also have afforded him the opportunity of scoring his thirty-first goal in his thirty-first game for the club. Paolo, proving he was far removed from a sentimental Italian, took the kick and scored.

The Cup bandwagon rolled onto Easter Road on February 17 for a confrontation with a Hibs side that had already been vanquished three times in the league, with Celtic claiming thirteen goals and conceding one. It appeared the Edinburgh outfit were continuing to read from a well-worn script when Van Hooijdonk set up Phil O'Donnell for the first goal in sixteen minutes. However, Hibs clawed their way back into the contest, showing a zest for the Cup tournament so puzzlingly absent from their league intentions. The troublesome wind played its part in their deserved equaliser, though. Keeper Stewart Kerr left his line in an attempt to secure a high ball when he would have been better advised to stay put. With the ball seemingly caught in mid-air, Kerr was out of position as it dropped to Darren Jackson. Alan Stubbs compounded the error by whipping the feet from his future team-mate and Jackson accepted the responsibility for taking the penalty-kick and sent it whistling past Kerr with seven minutes to play.

Sportingly, Burns said, 'We had a lucky escape, so all credit to Hibs. They could have won it in the second-half. Now we just have to put things right in the replay.'

Nine days later, with 46,424 fans in attendance at Parkhead, Celtic followed their manager's orders and won 2-0 in a largely one-sided affair. The draw had been made for the quarter-final prior to this game and the winners knew that a prize would be a home tie against Rangers. After almost three seasons of missed opportunities, Celtic couldn't let this one get away. They dominated straight from the kick off and Peter Grant sliced open the Hibs rearguard with a measured pass to O'Donnell who slashed a drive wide of the diving Jim Leighton and in off the left-hand upright for the opener in the thirty-fifth minute. Di Canio sealed Hibs' fate nine minutes after the break when he hit an exquisite drive from the edge of the box that soared beyond the struggling keeper. As soon as the ball smashed against the rigging, the Celtic fans knew they would be back on March 6 for another Old Firm battle.

'I am very happy with our commitment to the game and the way we played,' said Burns. 'We should have scored more, but I was pleased with the quality of the goals. Phil's was fabulous and Paolo's was sublime.'

Sandwiched in between the Cup-ties was a league meeting against Hearts in Glasgow on March 1. It was a breeze for the Hoops, winning 2-0 with a goal in each half. Cadete registered the first in the twenty-eighth minute and Di Canio cemented the points with the second just after the hour mark. Thankfully, the Italian restricted himself to kissing the club crest on this occasion and remained on the field until he was replaced by Van Hooijdonk with three minutes to go.

The 49,729 spectators didn't realise it, but they were witnessing the Dutchman's last appearance for the club. The player who had heralded his somewhat truncated, but always interesting, career at Celtic with a sensational goal against Hearts, didn't quite manage such a rousing send-off against the same opponents. Enrico Annoni made his debut and marked it with a solid and dependable ninety minutes while picking up his first booking in Scottish football courtesy of referee Willie Young.

Burns, after hearing Rangers had drawn 2-2 with Aberdeen at Pittodrie, was all smiles afterwards. He said, 'That's as well as we have played in recent months. The most pleasing thing was we looked a tasty side. There is no doubt that the influence of the foreigners makes us a more special team. Back in January, we were basically beating sides because of our superior fitness, but over the past few weeks we have shown greater patience and that has paid off.' He had time, too, for a word about his latest Italian import. 'Enrico looked every inch the complete defender. There is nothing flash about him. He is strong, experienced and knows the job inside out.'

After that ringing endorsement from his manager, it was no surprise Annoni kept his place for the visit of Rangers on Scottish Cup business the following Tuesday. In the days counting down to the tie, Tommy Burns was to be found situated in that extremely uncomfortable place between a rock and hard place. The manager, deservedly, had received credit for making the team a highly watchable entity again, as attendance figures proved on a weekly basis. But - and it was a massive but - Celtic had failed to beat Walter Smith's team on their previous nine meetings, irrespective of how the final results were achieved. It was a record that hardly enhanced Burns' CV.

On a grey, gusty March evening of high tension in the east end of Glasgow, Celtic set about dismantling the liability that had engulfed them for far too long. A crowd of 49,519 filtered into Parkhead to witness a spectacular role reversal. Malky Mackay and Paulo di Canio physically lifted the two-year-old monkey - some said gorilla - off Celtic's back and, at the same time, eliminated the holders from the competition. As the players took their positions for combat, Tommy Burns was incarcerated in the directors' box, starting a six-month ban from the touchline for misconduct after the spat with fourth official Eric Martindale during the previous provocative Old Firm confrontation. The manager was also hit with a £2,000 fine for good measure.

Inside four minutes the tone of a fiercely-contested game was set. Rangers' tough Australian defender Craig Moore lost possession in midfield before launching a furious assault on Tosh McKinlay. His boot was high and the studs were showing as it thudded into the left-back's right ankle. Referee Jim McCluskey, six yards from the incident, awarded a free-kick, but Moore went unpunished. It could have been worse only three minutes later when Laudrup, racing onto a Albertz pass, eluded Annoni to set up a shot at goal, but keeper Stewart Kerr reacted in an instant to race from his line, narrow the angle and beat away the Dane's low drive. Moments later, Phil O'Donnell, completely unmarked, put the ball over the bar from eight yards. It had to be placed in the 'Miss of the Season' category.

In the tenth minute, Goram was required to do something that was becoming alien to the Rangers qoalkeeper; pick the ball from the back of his net in the east end of Glasgow. Goram had gone four games at the home of Celtic without being asked to undertake the deed, but, on this occasion, he could have no room for complaint. Di Canio, who launched into the confrontation like a man possessed, swung in a corner-kick from the left and centre-half Mackay was surprisingly unmarked inside the six yards box. He rose in front of the frantically grasping Goram to nod in the simplest of goals. Afterwards, he said, 'Only my dad would have bet on me to score. I was 50/1 for the first goal and nobody but him would have had a bit of those odds. It shocked me to get a free header, but I wasn't complaining.'

Eight minutes later, the Rangers custodian was wrestling with the rigging behind him again to retrieve the ball after a superb Di Canio penalty-kick. McKinlay angled in a dangerous ball from the left, Jorge Cadete's turn and run caught Swedish defender Bjorklund, a £2.7million summer buy from Vicenza, totally on his heels and he halted the progress of the dashing attacker with an awkward tackle with his right foot across Cadete's left leg and McCluskey pointed to the spot while waving away some half-hearted attempts at a protest from a Rangers contingent. Di Canio snatched the ball, placed it strategically on the spot, meandered forward and sold Goram a glorious dummy. The Italian shaped to put it to the keeper's left, but at the last possible moment of impact, turned his right foot and rolled the ball in at the opposite corner. Goram looked flummoxed.

There were two other legitimate calls for penalty-kicks in a testosterone-charged first-half, but the match official denied both claims. One was a stick-on and the other was in the 'I-have-seen-them-given' category. The first, was an assault on Di Canio by a panicking McLaren as the Celtic tormentor took him on for pace and was getting away from his opponent before he was bulldozed to the turf. McCluskey, amazingly, indicated it was a fair shoulder charge. That would certainly have been true if Di Canio's right shoulder had been situated somewhere near the centre of his chest. David Robertson then caught Peter Grant as he stormed into the box. It looked a good call, but the referee clearly believed the midfielder had taken a dive. Having been awarded one spot-kick, it was obviously absurd to believe another would be forthcoming from the match official without someone actually losing a limb in the penalty box.

As the half wore on, it looked a case of how many Celtic would score. Di Canio was immense, but Rangers' indiscipline transformed into an epidemic as they tried to curtail him. Iain Ferguson cynically cut down the waltzing matador and was booked for his actions. Just before the interval, Gordan Petric launched into a challenge on the Italian from behind. It was reckless and dangerous, but he escaped a booking. On another evening with another referee, it could very well have been game over for the Serbian defender. Tragically, from Celtic's point of view, anyway, it was the last that would be seen of Di Canio. He grimaced as he held his left ankle and it was no surprise when he didn't reappear for the second forty-five minutes with Andreas Thom taking his place.

There was the surreal sight of two Celtic players writhing in obvious pain only yards from each other minutes into the second-half. Robertson clattered into Jackie McNamara off the ball and then collided with Thom, leaving both flattened. McCluskey brandished the yellow card as the encounter entered its untidiest phase. McLaren was booked for a late challenge on Alan Stubbs and then Stubbs and Annoni, almost inevitably, joined him in the growing list of miscreants. It had been a boisterous, frenzied encounter that was laced with a hint of nastiness, but, when McCluskey blew for full-time, the shrieking peep of his whistle also signalled the end of an awful run for Burns against Walter Smith.

It had been two years in the making and how the Celtic supporters lapped it up. 'When the Celts go up to lift the Scottish Cup, we'll be there' was the joyous acclamation from the green-and-white bedecked followers. No-one bothered to point out that Celtic had knocked Rangers out of the national competition twelve times in the past before the Cup Final and had failed to lift the silverware.

Burns said, 'I'm thrilled for our fans - they can now go to work with a smile on their face. The players gave all they could and we had the breaks we needed at the right time. The team followed my instructions perfectly. We've shown we can play more than one way against Rangers. But it is only one win. The fact that it came against Rangers makes it a bit more special because it's a first for a lot of our players. We now need to get ourselves ready for our most important game of the season - not a week on Sunday against Rangers, but against Kilmarnock on Tuesday.'

His oppositie number Smith, still unhappy at the award of a penalty-kick against his team, said, 'Celtic claim they never get any decisions, but they got this one. Tonight shows Celtic can win if they play well enough. Celtic competed better than we did and deserved the victory. Strangely, they probably created fewer chances than in recent games against us when they've come away with nothing. Losing the first goal from a setpiece was poor from our point of view and it was always going to be an uphill climb after that.'

Skipper Paul McStay chipped in, 'We had the self-belief we needed. Beating Rangers was a hurdle we had to overcome. We've now got to believe we can go on to win the Scottish Cup AND the Championship. The pressure was on us to turn this thing around. We put in a lot of effort and our attitude was bang on. We went ahead early on and contained them well after that. It was a double hurdle - to get into the semis and also to get rid of that jinx.'

Celtic landed back to earth with a resounding thud four days later, toppling to a 2-0 defeat against Kilmarnock at Rugby Park. Twenty-four hours later, for the benefit of television, Rangers took centre stage and went down by the identical scoreline at home to Dundee United. It was another opportunity carelessly scorned in the pursuit of the league flag and it tells you everything you need to know when the goalkeeper was Celtic's outstanding performer.

Burns lamented, 'It is difficult to understand why our performance should have been as bad as it was. Most of our players seemed to forget that the match which was sandwiched in between two Old Firm games was just as important as playing Rangers. The only success we had was Stewart Kerr and I am deeply disappointed about that. The rest never played at all. It was a desperately disappointing result, especially for our supporters. They were up for it and gave us every encouragement, but there was simply no response. We have to live with what has happened, though, and dust ourselves down for Sunday and Rangers at our place. It is the perfect game to come back in after a result like this one.'

As a battle cry, it didn't rank with any chest-thumping, bombastic directives from the past, but it was the one the Celtic manager chose as he readied his troops for what had turned out to be a win-or-bust confrontation with Rangers on Sunday, March 16. 'It's time to look out the big nappies,' remarked Burns, a rallying call no-one could ever remember being voiced by Jock Stein. However, in its basic fashion, it got the message across.

Burns' team went into the encounter five points behind with six games to play. Clearly, it was a now-or-never situation and it looked as though the advantage had swung decisively in Celtic's way. Walter Smith was lumbered with a massive dilemma when Andy Goram was forced onto the sidelines with a rib injury. The Ibrox gaffer sent out football's equivalent of an SOS and it was answered by Manchester City reserve Andy Dibble, who was only a few days short of his thirty-fourth birthday. He had no future with City and had been loaned out to Aberdeen, Middlesbrough, Bolton, West Brom and Sheffield United over an eight-year period. Smith enquired originally about a temporary transfer, but the English side obliged by granting the veteran a free transfer. Dibble probably didn't know the names of most of his team-mates as he was rushed straight into an Old Firm confrontation.

Smith was also struggling for forwards and astounded everyone by bringing back Hateley for £400,000 after selling the player to Queens Park Rangers for £1.5million in November 1995. These were desperate days for the Rangers manager as he scrambled to assemble a team for a game that could propel them to within touching distance of Celtic's historic feat of nine successive championships. Ironic, really, when you consider the money splurged on new players earlier in the campaign.

Tommy Burns, on the other hand, had no such problems. Captain Paul McStay was passed fit to play and the charismatic double-act of Jorge Cadete and Paolo di Canio were also in the starting line-up. Celtic had lost the three previous Glasgow league derbies and history was against the men from Govan achieving a whitewash. However, with 49,929 watching, a depleted Rangers did just that as they scrambled to a 1-0 win after an ugly, snarling, bad-tempered affair that flared from the first minute to last and would see Malky Mackay and Hateley red-carded, eight players - four from each team - booked while Di Canio was called to referee Hugh Dallas' room at the end to be shown a second yellow card which amounted to a sending-off offence. The Italian and Rangers' Iain Ferguson were caught up in the general mayhem as the game descended towards the gutter.

Stewart Kerr, Enrico Annoni, Malky Mackay and Peter Grant were the Celts cautioned while Gough, Moore, Charlie Miller and Durrant were yellow-carded for the opponents. Mackay and Grant earned three-game suspensions after crashing the penalty points barrier. An unseemly episode in the history of two of football's bitterest rivals was topped off by the Rangers players indulging in a provocative mock huddle near the tunnel, supporters from both sides piling onto the pitch and the police reporting almost forty arrests in the immediate aftermath.

Celtic, it must be admitted, did not rise to the occasion. There was a distinct fear of failure about the team and they appeared to afford Hateley the biggest of compliments with Mackay and Stubbs watching his every move. This, remember, was a player who had performed so poorly at Loftus Road - three goals in twenty-seven appearances - that he was loaned to Leeds United where he drew a total blank in six games. The play from both sides was as untidy as the wind-swept, litter-strewn pitch. However, there was an instant of wonderful invention in the fortieth minute when Grant lifted a free-kick into the air and Di Canio, from twenty-five yards, struck the ball sweetly with his right foot on the volley. It skudded off the crossbar and flew over with Dibble a spectator.

On the brink of half-time, some dreadful defending from the home side gifted Rangers the lead and the psychological advantage. The Ibrox side had negotiated eight successive league games over four years without losing at Parkhead and bouts of overwhelming generosity from their hosts had often contributed to the Rangers cause. Stubbs was the opponents' unwilling benefactor on this occasion. The club's record signing made a hash of an attempted clearance from an Albertz free-kick and let Durrant squeeze in behind him to lob the ball over the head of the advancing Kerr. Laudrup reacted with a lot more haste and urgency than Mackay as the ball breezed towards goal. The Celtic man hesitated while the Dane eagerly pursued the opening and knocked the opportunity into the net from virtually under the crossbar. It was a wretched goal to concede and, sadly, it didn't look out of place during this disagreeable rumpus.

Ibrox skipper Gough limped off just after the hour mark to be replaced by midfielder Miller as Smith was forced into another reshuffle. And he had something else to contend with when Hateley was banished from the field after ludicrously headbutting Kerr during a sixty-sixth minute melee as players from both sides piled in during another explosive disagreement. Mackay had hauled down Laudrup to give away a free-kick and tensions overflowed as players got involved. Mackay was booked and Kerr came out of his penalty box to throw in his tuppence worth. Hateley took exception, motioned his head into the keeper's face and Dallas flashed red. Kerr was booked for his part. Mackay was living on borrowed time and it was ten versus ten shortly afterwards when he was invited to leave proceedings following an awkward challenge on Laudrup.

The game limped to a sorry conclusion with Celtic bereft of the spark of ingenuity that might have furnished an opening to put pressure on a mediocre goalkeeper, who would play only six more games for Rangers. The opportunity to stop their age-old rivals in their tracks had been blown. It was a grim-faced and somewhat defensive Burns who said afterwards, 'If I'm to be judged. I'll be judged on what I've done here and not all the excess baggage we had to inherit. We're not prepared to accept blame for what happened to this club seven years ago. I'm not prepared to forget the great progress we've made, especially in the last twenty months. We've won something like forty-five games out of sixty-five and lost around seven. We've set levels of consistency this club hasn't had for many years.

'Unfortunately, in that time, Rangers got seven titles, so I don't think it's fair for people to say that the current players are to blame. It's unfair to give someone six championships of a start and then we're the ones who have to defend the nine. I don't think anyone in their right mind can look at what we've done and then say that. Ultimately, if I am to blame, I'll certainly take that responsibility. I won't walk away from it.'

Somehow, those words came across as though they had been only too well rehearsed.

Burns ended the postmatch interview with a verbal assault on his critics. Adopting a scattergun approach, he fired out, 'Some people, who should know better, take the short-sighted view. You're judged by people who know nothing about football, nothing about management and nothing about coaching, whether it's TV, radio or writers.'

The pressure on the Celtic manager was incessant and, twenty-four hours later, Burns was again making headlines as he reacted to a fresh storm of criticism, especially the actions of Di Canio towards Ferguson near the end of the game and after the full-time whistle. Burns insisted his player was goaded into reacting by 'trouble- makers' in Walter Smith's side.

He said, 'There are people who are involved in Old Firm games who know the damage that can be done around the country by not behaving properly. Those who are new to it will get caught up - not that I'm condoning them - but they don't understand what is going on. Ultimately, I would defend Paolo's actions. He is a very passionate man about his football, who let himself be wound up by certain people who should know better. I have spoken to him and that's enough. I have found out the reasons why he got involved and after what he told me he was perfectly entitled to get involved.'

Di Canio claimed Ferguson, in the foulest of language, had questioned his parentage and, foolishly, he had reacted. Burns then revealed Ferguson had phoned him to insist he had not sworn at Di Canio. The Celtic boss added, 'I appreciate the fact that he has contacted me to put his side of things. At least, that shows there is a willingness to try and calm the situation. There are times we need to remember it's only a game. For some wee boy who's had his head split open, for any woman that's been attacked or any man who's been stabbed ... it's not worth it. We've had fans killed leaving this ground and people's sense of reality has been lost when that happens. There's too much hype.'

There may have been hype, but there was precious little hope for Celtic in the league run-in. They had just surrendered six points in back-to-back defeats against Kilmarnock and Rangers and they would throw away another two when they visited East End Park and shared four goals with Dunfermline on March 22. The flaws of the team on the field were more obvious than the inner turmoil that threatened to tear the club apart. Paolo di Canio was making noises about preferring to play elsewhere while Jorge Cadete's wife and child had returned to Portugal and the player was known to be unhappy about earning less than half as much as Andreas Thom. He would later claim, 'I was treated like a dog.' As a gesture, he threw his shirt into the crowd after the stalemate in Fife.

And, in the midst of the carnage and chaos enveloping the dressing room, the offer of a new contract for Tommy Burns had been put on hold by Fergus McCann. The craziest and most implausible of soap operas seemed to being played out at Parkhead.

Celtic, in fact, were fortunate to escape East End Park with a point after trailing by two goals inside half-an-hour. Gerry Britton claimed the opener in the sixteenth minute and Harry Curran added a second. Burns watched his team toil until Phil O'Donnell pulled one back just after the hour mark and Simon Donnelly rattled in the equaliser in the seventy-second minute. On the same afternoon, Rangers crashed 2-1 to Kilmarnock at Ibrox in this bizarre league campaign. The Ibrox side were now on seventy-one points with the Hoops seven adrift. Burns declared, 'This result keeps us hanging in there and we'll keep going. A hell of a lot can happen in five games.'

One reporter thought the words had a distinctly hollow ring to them. On the possibility of Celtic claiming the title, the unimpressed scribe wrote, 'The odds on that happening are on a par with the Loch Ness Monster making a personal appearance to present the championship to Paul McStay.'

Celtic, by now, were more insipid than inspired and that was underlined in the next game, a spiritless 1-1 draw with Raith Rovers at Stark's Park. It was goalless until the eighty-ninth minute when Di Canio snatched the breakthrough goal. The team, lamentably, couldn't hold the lead for sixty seconds and David Craig equalised in the fading moments. Alas, the result was in keeping with Celtic's patchy, nervy performance, beginning to look more like a team going through the motions in the league with an eye on their only hope for a trophy, the Scottish Cup. The draw meant they had dropped ten points in four games since beating Rangers in the national competition. The Ibrox men comfortably strolled to a 4-0 triumph over Dunfermline in Glasgow on the same day. Tommy Johnson, signed by Burns from Aston Villa for £2.3million to bolster his attacking options during the run-in, made his debut against the Fifers in the second-half as a substitute for Simon Donnelly. His initial enthusiasm was stifled by the general apathy of the afternoon.

Paul McStay deserved a greater farewell to football than a nondescript ten-minute outing in Kirkcaldy with only a paltry 7,914 fans in the ground to witness the sad departure of a true Celtic legend. However, the ankle injury that had plagued him throughout the season finally persuaded the skipper to call it a day, although no-one knew it at the time. As he hobbled off, the club was swept closer to the rocks of desolation.

Burns' attitude at the end of the game was somewhat surprising, verging on the mystifying. He admitted, 'I don't think we deserved to win the game.' Asked about the evident lack of desire and spirit within the side, he replied, 'It's up to you to decide.' The answer was delivered with a sigh and a shrug of the shoulders, a demeanour that appeared to reflect the ills that were being inflicted upon the very heart and soul of the club.

He warmed to the prospects of the Scottish Cup semi-final, which was due at Rangers' stadium with Hampden under reconstruction. With a hint of candour, he said, 'I think people are wondering about the possibility of a shock at Ibrox and will be sitting back and hoping to get it. Since we lost to Rangers in the league, there has been nothing much for anyone at the club to smile about and this Saturday the onus is on us to make the supporters smile again. We must beat Falkirk, keep our season alive and put ourselves in a position to lift silverware. The importance of a Cup win should not be underestimated. Claiming the Scottish Cup would mean that the season was successful. We still have a ghost of a chance of winning the title with four games left to play and, as long as that is the case, we will concede nothing.'

Burns was eight minutes away from leading Celtic to their second Scottish Cup Final appearance in three years when fate stepped in. Tommy Johnson scored his first goal for the club after a strangely-subdued sixty-six minutes on a perfect afternoon for football. Craig Nelson, the Falkirk keeper, could count himself unlucky when, after blocking efforts from Di Canio and Cadete, the ball eventually broke to Johnson who casually swept it home. Later on, the Englishman had the opportunity to make certain when he bore down on Nelson, but his effort was repelled and, with bewildering speed, the Brockville side had switched play to the other half of the pitch and equalised.

Falkirk manager Alex Totten urged his 6ft 7in centre-half Kevin James to move up front and the gamble paid off handsomely. After Nelson's save, the ball was delivered down the right wing to Jamie McGowan who arced a cross into the box from close to the bye-line. Stewart Kerr, eyes firmly on the ball, was about to spring and cut out the danger when he lost his footing. Falling backwards, the keeper tried frantically to paw the ball away, but James leapt with conviction to bury a header into the empty net. A replay on April 23 would be required at the same venue.

Burns kept it brief afterwards. 'We'll be back on Wednesday week and we'll get the job done then.' The words were delivered through clenched teeth.

The manager was a bit more forthcoming after watching his team beat Aberdeen 3-0 with goals from Cadete (2) and Donnelly at Parkhead on the Saturday prior to the Cup semi-final replay. He said, 'I'm very pleased with the performance, but, most of all, I'm pleased for the supporters. They have been very encouraging although we have disappointed them over the last few weeks. We want to thank them by giving them something tangible between now and the end of the season.'

Tommy Burns' grimmest nightmare was just around the corner.

Swollen, dark clouds hovered menacingly over the south side of Glasgow for most of the day and threatened a downpour on the evening of Wednesday, April 23. As the Celtic team coach turned into the Ibrox car park, the arrival of the manager, staff and players was greeted by a deluge from the heavens. The torrential rain still hammered down long after the full-time whistle and the last of the drenched 35,879 fans had escaped to the refuge of shelter elsewhere. Somehow, the drab, grey, unappealing setting seemed so fitting for what had just unfolded on a soaking, greasy Ibrox playing surface with a restless wind also creating chaos.

Celtic were removed from the Scottish Cup. And the manager was days away from being out of a job.

The team that had destroyed Rangers in the quarter-finals never got out of the starting blocks. Certainly, they could insist the monsoon conditions played a part in their downfall, but Falkirk, with more aggression and gumption, harnessed their energy and focused their attention of a place in the Cup Final the following month. They scored in the nineteenth minute and Celtic did little in the remaining seventy-one minutes to conjure up a suitable reply.

Paul McGrillen took advantage of a moment of hesitancy from Stewart Kerr to get the goal. Falkirk, quite rightly in the dire conditions, had adopted a shoot-on-sight policy and the keeper had already fumbled a long-range shot and misjudged a wind-assisted cross. On this occasion, McGowan, provider of the equaliser in the first game, sent a long, diagonal ball into the penalty area. David Hagen swung a foot at the half-chance, but, in his haste, merely scooped the ball up for the unmarked McGrillen six yards out and he looped a header over the motionless and stranded Kerr.

It was a bleak evening when too many Celtic players became anonymous and disappeared in the drizzle. Celtic left the field to a prolonged storm of boos while green-and-white scarves were hurled onto the track. This was not the way it was supposed to be.

No criticism could be levelled at Paolo di Canio, captain of the team on a night of rampant derision and vehement discourse. He became so irate with the performance of Willie Young that he suggested the referee might want to be manager of Rangers the next time he returned to Ibrox. The match official wasn't amused, reported the Italian to the SFA and they slapped a two-game ban on him.

The rapport the Celtic boss once had with the media had been withering in recent weeks. He believed a lot of the criticism was over the top and, naturally, he took some of it personally. He would not have enjoyed reading this excerpt from a daily newspaper the morning after the Ibrox defeat. It stated, 'Tommy Burns' time as Celtic manager looks to be at an end after his team lost this Scottish Cup semi-final replay to Falkirk and completed a second consecutive season without a trophy.

'It was the second time in three years that Celtic had lost a Cup-tie to First Division opposition at Ibrox and now the numbers no longer stack up in Burns' favour. Three years in, the job has seen the manager spend £15million on new players and win only one trophy, the Scottish Cup, against Airdrie, another First Division side, in 1995. Six months earlier, Celtic had lost the League Cup Final to Raith Rovers. Rangers, meanwhile, have this season equalled Celtic's cherished record of nine league championships in a row and have done so while winning all four Old Firm derbies for the first time in the twenty-two history of the Premier Division.'

The report continued, 'The question of Burns' future always presents a dilemma of the heart versus the head for the Celtic support. A much-loved player with the club, Burns' departure would be the cause of sorrow among sentimentalists. The heads of the Celtic supporters, though, tell them that results like the one against Falkirk only confirm the manager's position as being untenable. Once again, the team's level of motivation was called seriously into question. Being taken to a replay by a side who are mid-table in the First Division was bad enough. Losing to Falkirk was unforgiveable.'

Burns said, 'There is nothing to describe my disappointment - nothing. My greatest fear as a player was being involved in something like this. I was fortunate that, in fifteen years as a Celtic player, nothing like this ever happened to me. That is what makes this result all the harder to take. It is very difficult.'

He was asked if the result might sway Fergus McCann's decision in the delicate matter of renewing his contract. Candidly, he admitted, 'That's possibly right. We live or die by success in this job and players are the same. People know my feelings for Celtic, they will know how deeply hurt and embarrassed I am. I have never been frightened to accept my responsibilities. It was my team who lost the game. My responsibility.

No excuses. I spent fifteen years as a player at Celtic Park. I can handle pressure. But I have to admit that we have too many players who can't take the strain. It's at a time like this that you find out about players. I was never afraid of a challenge, but that challenge has to be accepted by players as well as management. We have been hanging on to Paolo Di Canio's coat-tails and need someone to help him shoulder responsibility. There was a desperate lack of leadership against Falkirk. It was disappointing and embarrassing.'

Di Canio, too, refused to hide when he was asked for his thoughts. He said, 'Before the game, I didn't think it would be possible for this to happen. The manager spoke to us, but we played differently to what he wanted. So it was the players' fault, not the manager and not the fans. We put thirty-five balls into the box, but no-one was there. The fans need more passion from us.'

The excitable Italian added, 'Now there is confusion in my head because the one trophy we had left is now finished. There is also a debt in my head to the fans and the manager. I think Tommy Burns merits from Fergus McCann to stay here for a long time. Tommy is good for me, he is a good manager and a good person. I came here from Italy where I played with five or six teams with different managers. They were all different tactically and as people, but Burns is a good man, as well. When he said the team lacked leadership, he spoke the truth and we have to roll up our sleeves for him.'

Stirring and gallant sentiments from Di Canio, but all too late to rescue Tommy Burns. The blood was already in the water and the sharks were beginning to circle.

Davie Hay recalled, 'I was at Old Trafford that night watching a Champions league tie between Manchester United and Borussia Dortmund. I wasn't looking at any specific player, but it was always handy to have a clue about someone's ability if they suddenly became available and they were within our price range. At the end of the game, which United lost 1-0, a Glasgow businessman I knew well and who was big friend of Alex Ferguson, shouted over to me. "Davie, have you heard the score at Ibrox?" I told him I hadn't and my heart sank when he replied, "You're never going to believe it, Falkirk won 1-0." I didn't see that one coming, that's for sure. And, of course, I immediately thought about Tommy. I realised he would be devastated. And then, of course, you wonder about what comes next.'

Fergus McCann made the decision to ultimately sack Tommy Burns on May 2. The friction between two strong-willed characters, with Celtic as their dominant interest, but with vastly different views of how to progress, had been there from the first weeks of working together. Burns would later admit, 'My relationship with Fergus deteriorated to the point there was no returning, basically after weeks in the job. So, it was a difficult three years in trying to build a relationship because we didn't really have one. I just basically didn't like him, but I'm open-minded enough to think being in his position he probably didn't like this wee guy's who's come from the Gallowgate and played for Celtic.'

On the fateful day of Burns' last day as Celtic manager, McCann asked the head of security to escort the newly-unemployed boss to the back door. Tommy stood proud and said, 'I came in through the front door and, sure as God, I've not done anything to make me want to walk out the back door.'

'There was a story going around that Tommy had decided to quit as manager immediately after the Falkirk defeat,' remembered Hay. 'It went along the lines that he was prepared to hand in his resignation the following morning, but was talked out of it by a Celtic supporter he met on his way to the ground after parking his car. Fanciful story and I just don't believe a word of it. Anyone who ever knew Tommy Burns would have realised it would have been impossible for him to walk away from that job, no matter the circumstances. Yes, he would have been deeply hurt, but to my mind that would just have made him all the more determined to turn things around. Tommy Burns was never a quitter.'

Amid the tumult, Billy Stark, Burns' closest confidante at the club, agreed to take charge of the team for the three remaining league games against Hibs, Kilmarnock and Dundee United, but he stressed he had no intention whatsoever of remaining at the club once that obligation was fulfilled. Two days after his friend's dismissal, Stark was in the Easter Road dug-out to watch Celtic win 3-1 with Jorge Cadete (2) and Paolo di Canio on target.

Afterwards, he said, 'I came to Celtic with Tommy and leaving is not a difficult decision to make. I will speak to Mr McCann regarding when I will go in the next few days. I was asked to look after the team and I was mindful of Tommy and I always had the fans' interests in mind, so I thought it was the right thing to do. The events had an effect on everyone, but the players knew they had to stand up and be counted after the semi-final result and Tommy leaving. They have taken some stick in recent weeks, some of it deserved, but after this game they deserve credit. I was delighted with the way the players were committed to the game. Hibs had a lot to play for, but we fought well and it took a little bit of magic from Paolo at a crucial time to send us on our way. The defence played well and we threatened going forward.'

The game was televised live and Di Canio, a born showman, stepped into the spotlight on and off the pitch. He was mesmerising against a bemused Edinburgh side who couldn't get near him as he pirouetted and sashayed his way through a fabulous solo performance. To cap it, he scored with a typically cheeky delivery when, with his back to goal on the edge of the box and with defender Michael Renwick practically wearing the same shirt, shimmied one way, then the other, spotted a tiny exposed spot between Jim Leighton and his near post and promptly banged the ball through the vulnerable space for a memorable effort. It turned out to be his last goal in Scottish football. To mark the occasion he threw his jersey into the crowd.

He showboated, too, on live national television in the interview afterwards. 'I have a little problem with my contract,' he revealed, emphasising the word 'leettle' while holding up the forefinger and the thumb of his right hand to indicate just how 'leetle'. He then launched into some uncensored diatribe that must have rendered the club's managing director apoplectic. 'Fergus McCann has made a mistake and I am very unhappy that my gaffer, Tommy Burns, was not on the bench today. Now I don't know about my future. I don't know if I will be back in the summer. I was very happy with Tommy Burns. I liked him very much. I've been very unhappy for days. I don't know if I will stay here now. Tommy was a good manager.' The coup de grace was the 'leetle problem with my contract and I don't know if I'll be back.'

While the Celtic support took time to digest this stunning revelation, there was more to follow quickly. Cadete, another fans' favourite, admitted, 'My agent has had eight meetings with Fergus McCann in Glasgow and not much progress has been made. I have been loyal to this club, but some things about the contract are not good.' Doom and gloom merchants had a field day; Celtic were, indeed, falling apart.

Di Canio, of course, was missing through suspension when Celtic played out a goalless draw against Kilmarnock three days later at Parkhead. The memory of this game would fade as swiftly as the club's championship challenge. Inertia was setting in and the nearest a crowd of 42,994 came to a Celtic goal was a header from Tommy Johnson that snapped against the crossbar. On the same evening, Rangers cemented their ninth consecutive title with a header from Brian Laudrup giving them a 1-0 win over Dundee United at Tannadice. Billy Stark didn't waste his words afterwards. 'We looked like a team which didn't have anything to play for,' he remarked. 'I can't explain why we were so flat. All we can do is try to atone for that performance when we play in front of our fans for the last time this season on Saturday.'

A remarkable crowd of 46,758 turned out at Parkhead on May 10 for a meaningless game to watch a team that had won nothing and didn't even have a manager. The scoreline mattered not a jot, but, for the record books, Celtic beat Dundee United 3-0 with goals from Jorge Cadete, Chris Hay and Tommy Johnson. Cadete was substituted eight minutes from time and he went through the entire grand theatrical gestures, including kissing the turf transporting memories back to a day in February 1996 when he first made his appearance in Glasgow. He hugged Billy Stark, waved once more to the fans, disappeared up the tunnel and was never seen again in a Celtic strip.

Billy Stark said, 'Obviously, I won't be here next season, but I'm doing everything in my power to make sure Rangers don't go beyond nine-in-a-row. The players are naturally disappointed about not winning the title, but over the past few days I've been trying to lift them. I've told them once they come back from their summer holidays, they'll be fresh and full of optimism about the season ahead. I'm sure they'll be fighting for every trophy that's available to them. Hopefully, it won't be long before they win the league. When we beat Rangers in the Cup, things looked good and we had the chance of the Double. But then we lost to them in the league match shortly afterwards and many thought their world had caved in - and I suppose for some of us it did.

'We were very, very near to stopping Rangers - a lot closer than some would have you believe. Injuries and suspensions cost us dear throughout the season and that is a factor, not an excuse, for us not being able to get the success we wanted. But for some people to claim we lost to Rangers because were outplayed tactically is very naive. It was individual errors that cost us against them and not even the best coach could legislate for that.'

So, the competitive season that kicked off with so much hope and ambition had come to a shambolic and inglorious conclusion. The drama, though, was far from over. Six days after the Dundee United game, Paul McStay was forced to announce his retirement, sixteen years as a loyal one-club man coming to a premature end at the age of thirty-two. The ankle problem that had bedevilled him from day one of the season finally had the last word.

There would be no sign of the inspirational midfielder, acknowledged as 'The Maestro', and, increasingly, it looked as though there would be no sightings of Jorge Cadete or Paolo di Canio who would join the lead of the Third Amigo, Pierre van Hooijdonk, and vamoose Paradise. Cadete claimed he was owed £400,000 as a personal fee for joining the club and, of course, this was vehemently denied by Fergus McCann. Di Canio's demand was somewhat less dramatic; a £900 'private' hotel bill when he first arrived in Scotland. Once again, the club insisted it was his bill and refused to pay it. Di Canio went public with his complaints which brought about a fine of a fortnight's wages while being suspended over the same period.

Celtic had agreed to play a Republic of Ireland XI in a testimonial game for Pat Bonner at Lansdowne Road on May 18 and Di Canio was ordered to stay away from the match. Instead, he was expected in Glasgow for a meeting with McCann. The Italian might have got a 'leetle' confused; he turned up in Dublin, watched the action from the stand, and gave the club's MD a body-swerve. For the record, Celtic lost the game 3-2 with Tony Cascarino, of all people, getting the winner six minutes from time.

After the encounter, watched by over 21,000 fans, Bonner returned immediately to Scotland for talks with McCann about extending his player/coaching role at the club. The goalkeeper was Jock Stein's last signing for the club in 1978. At that stage, the legendary manager was only Celtic's fourth boss in ninety years. Bonner's contract wasn't renewed and, in the wake of this decision, the club severed its last link with their most celebrated incumbent of the dug-out.

Tommy Burns attended Pat Bonner's farewell in Dublin that afternoon. With Burns' departure, Celtic were now seeking their fifth manager in seven years.

CHAPTER TWELVE
WIM JANSEN: A DUTCH OF CLASS

Johan Cruyff, Terry Venables, Kevin Keegan, John Toshack. It was a roll call of soccer royalty and the illustrious names were appearing daily on the front and back pages of the national press as everyone played 'The Great Celtic Guessing Game'. Who was going to succeed Tommy Burns as the new manager of a world famous football club that had lifted only one trophy - the 1995 Scottish Cup - in the past eight years?

The speculators could have added another name to the bulging list of which notoriously extravagant Hollywood movie director Cecil B de Mille would have been envious - Bobby Robson.

The man who had spent eight years as the England international manager from 1982 until guiding his country to the last four of the 1990 World Cup Finals in Italy had just led Barcelona to the European Cup-Winners' Cup the previous season. It may have seemed far-fetched to some, but I was well aware Robson had been discussed at Celtic boardroom level and the wily and astute tactician, then sixty-four years old, had a huge supporter in Fergus McCann.

In fact, three years earlier, McCann had made a surreptitious move to bring Robson AND Tommy Burns to the east end of Glasgow as his dream managerial double-act. The Celtic Managing Director, who made no pretence of being a football know-all, believed veteran Robson's experience would gel with rookie Burns' exuberance to the benefit of the playing side of the club. At that stage, I was reliably informed, an offer had been made to the amiable Robson, then a plain 'mister' before being knighted in 2002.

Robson would be dismissed by Portuguese side Sporting Lisbon in December 1994 when they were top of the league. He made the mistake of describing club president Sousa Cintra as a 'loose cannon' who would frequently sign players without the manager's knowledge or consent during his often-stormy nineteen-month reign in the Portuguese capital. The well-informed among Europe's upper echelons realised Robson could be persuaded to leave Sporting Lisbon in the summer of 1994 - six months before his sacking - such was the friction between team boss and club owner.

McCann, through a circuitous route, made his pitch and at one stage it looked as though Robson might take him up on his offer to return to the UK. Of course, it never materialised, but McCann had been impressed by the Englishman's conduct during the secretive machinations through football's many clandestine channels. Robson wasn't out of work long after being put on the dole; Porto snapped him up and a year later he led them to the national league and Cup double.

Three years down the line, Robson's name came to the fore for a second time. Once again, to those in the know, it wouldn't have been too impractical to make a move to entice the well-travelled manager to Parkhead. Despite his success in Europe and also bringing the Spanish Cup and SuperCup to the Nou Camp stadium, Robson, remarkably, was about to lose his job with the Spanish giants. The board desired a fresh approach and were directed towards a Dutchman who would be coming out of contract at Ajax Amsterdam that summer; a brash individual by the name of Louis van Gaal. He would arrive with impeccable credentials after six years with Holland's most successful club. Robson was informed he was being relieved of his managerial duties while being moved 'upstairs' to the role of General Manager.

Robson, a football man, was far from happy and once again the grapevine was buzzing about his next job. McCann, never a fan of accepting rejection, got word to his target of his intentions. I know the name of the intermediary - not on Celtic's pay-roll - who was given the task to make contact to sound out the County Durham-born sportsman who had been involved in the game since making his debut as a precocious seventeen-year-old inside-forward for Fulham in 1950. Once more, it was given considerable and careful deliberation by this well-mannered character. Once more, it was rejected. Robson did, in fact, remain at Barcelona for one more season and detested a job that had nothing to do with actual football. He had no intention of becoming the world's highest-paid paperclip-counter. Robson was back in the dug-out in 1998 when he was named manager of Dutch side PSV Eindhoven.

Fergus McCann was naturally disappointed as Robson perfectly fitted his identikit of his vision for his new-look backroom team. He had been impressed by the Continental model of a Head Coach whose sole duties would be to the first team, training, supervising, tactics and selection. The new Celtic man would not be burdened with dealing with agents, settling contractual disputes or wage discrepancies. His sole and complete attention was to be focused on putting together a team of individuals, who would be able to go out on the park and win games consistently and, in doing so, bring trophies back to Parkhead.

McCann also wanted the complete implementation of a new system to back up his Head Coach. He would search for a General Manager who had more knowledge of law and contracts than football, a reserve team coach to follow the lead of the first team manager and a Head of Youth Development to oversee the introduction of a continental-style Academy and training facilities. Winds of change? This was a full-blown hurricane.

Jock Brown, brother of Scotland team manager Craig, was better known to football followers as a BBC match commentator, but he was also a lawyer, mainly dealing in sporting issues. Another thing in his favour, according to those who knew McCann, Brown did not have a history with former Celtic board members.

Davie Hay, who had acted as Interim General Manager, looked to be favourite for the post. He said, 'I had an interview for the top job. Apparently, I was found by my interviewers to be "unsuitable". Now, I know a lot of people in the game believed the job was as good as mine and any interview would be a mere formality. Fergus McCann obviously didn't agree with those views. He felt the position should go to someone with a professional background. Jock Brown, who I had once employed as my lawyer, had no previous Celtic connections and, of course, he got the nod. I was massively disappointed, to say the least. So, there was a degree of friction between us right from the start. The Celtic support seemed to be dumbfounded that a bloke who doubled as a lawyer and match commentator could get such an important post. Despite any animosity, Jock and I knew we had to work together for the good of the club in an extremely important campaign.'

Willie McStay, brother of the more acclaimed Paul, was an impeccable fit for the Head of Youth Development role as the McCann jigsaw came together.

But there was still the somewhat urgent requirement of a Head Coach.

McCann had an inordinate distrust of the media and abhorred leaks from his inner sanctum being splashed on the pages of the daily press. Part of Jock Brown's duties would be to act as a buffer to keep the exclusive-seeking snoopers at bay. McCann would allow his new team boss to talk to the media before a game for preview purposes and after one to give his views. Brown was told he would be the club's mouthpiece on every other matter. One misguided hack was fed information of the identity of the man Celtic were about to unveil as their new Head Coach at Celtic Park on Tuesday, July 1 1997. The journalist, eager to steal a march on his rivals on the newstands, couldn't have followed the time-honoured adage of 'check and check again' as he wrote his yarn.

'ARTUR JORGE IS NEW CELTIC BOSS' was the bold headline adorning the covers of his paper on the morning of the announcement. Jorge, as a matter of fact, was looking for new employment after leaving his post as manager of the Portuguese international team. He may have been surprised to learn he was heading for Glasgow when the groundwork had already been done to take him to altogether sunnier climes at Tenerife in the Spanish top flight. That wayward 'scoop' would no doubt have appealed to McCann's wicked sense of the ridiculous.

Wilhemus Marinus Anthonius - better known as Wim - Jansen was introduced to the nation's press later that day. One Celtic official, blessed with misplaced humour, asked the assembled corps, 'Do you know the identity of this man?' The hapless scribe, still refusing to believe his sensational 'exclusive' was slightly wide of the mark, stepped forward to proclaim, with great pride in his triumphal tones, the individual being presented to the media was, in fact, Artur Jorge.

Evidently, the newspaperman had no inkling that Jorge's most famous trademark was his walrus-like moustache, which dominated his features. Jansen, on the other hand, was clean-shaven as had been witnessed by millions in his many appearances for Feyenoord as a ball-winning, industrious midfielder and also his two World Cup Final outings with Holland against host nations West Germany in 1974 and Argentina four years later.

His most distinguishing feature was his explosion of unruly curls that gave him the look of a bumbling, confused Chief Librarian forever looking for a long-lost pen. The national scribes were eager to discover more about the new and, to more than a few, 'anonymous' Celtic Head Coach. Investigations would determine he had a first-class playing pedigree with Feyenoord - where he won a European Cup medal in 1970 against Celtic - two spells at Ajax and a fifty-six game sojourn with Washington Diplomats. He had also won sixty-five caps for an excellent Holland side while his management travels took him back to his Rotterdam roots with Feyenoord, Belgium with SK Lokeren, Saudi Arabia as assistant coach to fellow-Dutchman Wim van Hanagem at the international team and Japan as manager of Sanfrecce Hiroshima for a one-season stint in 1995/96.

It also emerged that Johan Cruyff had taken the trouble to contact Celtic to congratulate them on their choice of Head Coach. Holland's greatest-ever player once admitted Jansen was one of only four people in the world it was worth listening to while discussing football. Jansen did not strike an imposing figure and it was clear during interviews he was far removed from a braggart and had no intention of unduly enhancing his qualities as a coach by talking himself up to exalted levels. He was there to do a job to the best of his ability and be judged where it mattered most - on the football pitch.

However, he hardly had time to take his first training session when a national newspaper dug out a story about his time in Japan. The headline was less than complimentary. It read, 'THE WORST THING TO HIT HIROSHIMA SINCE THE ATOM BOMB!'

Davie Hay, who was now combining the role as Assistant General Manager with the duties of Chief Scout, recalled, 'Of course, the article was offensive and, clearly, wasn't designed to do Wim any favours in a new job in a new country. However, if it bothered him, I failed to detect it. He simply got on with the task of putting together a football team. And I use the word 'team' accurately. We weren't talking about reshaping a squad. Celtic needed tried-and-tested professionals who could go straight into the top side and hit the ground running. Nothing was going to deflect Wim from that and I have to say I admired his single-minded attitude. In fact, I liked him as a person, too, and that always helps when you are dealing with people on a daily basis.'

Murdo MacLeod, the powerful midfielder who spent nine years at the club, had recently returned as reserve team coach, but was quickly appointed as Jansen's assistant. The Dutchman insisted on his No.2 being someone with knowledge of the Scottish game. MacLeod had managed Dumbarton and Partick Thistle and, with the exception of three years at Borussia Dortmund after leaving Parkhead in 1987, had spent his entire career in Scotland. He was in the right age group - thirty-eight years old - and ambitious to make his mark on the coaching side of the game. He ideally suited Fergus McCann's model. Two months later, Eric Black quit his job with the Scottish Football Association to become Football Development Manager, signing a five-year deal.

'Celtic had a new team off the park while assembling a new one on it,' said Hay. 'A fresh campaign was coming up fast and we all realised it was such an important one with Rangers the bookies' favourites to win their tenth successive title. That was unthinkable. So, we wasted no time in the transfer market. Wim, of course, wanted Henrik Larsson and, thankfully, we got him from Feyenoord eventually. However, it must be admitted that a lot of that team which was so hastily put together was down to Tommy Burns. He had identified players the previous season, so we knew who we were looking for. I had scouted them, knew the transfer prices and wages required, so, thanks to Tommy, we had a head start. And, in saying that, I am not taking anything away from Wim who then had to find a system and gel their talents together.'

Celtic received £750,000 from Aberdeen for Brian O'Neil, doubled that fee and bought Darren Jackson from Hibs. The fans weren't exactly overly-enthusiastic about the first signing of the Jansen era.; the ungainly, flailing-elbows approach from the striker hadn't endeared him to the supporters as he made a nuisance of himself with Dundee United and then the Easter Road side. He was more Frank McGarvey than Charlie Nicholas, but Tommy Burns and Davie Hay had reasoned that what he did to ruffle a few of Celtic's feathers, he could also achieve while adorning the green and white hoops and annoying the hell out of the opposition.

Next to arrive was midfielder Craig Burley in a £2.5million deal from Chelsea. He was already a Scotland international and it was more than obvious the team would need someone in that role to replace the retired Paul McStay. And, like McStay, Burley had the added threat of scoring goals from in and around the box. Left-back Stephane Mahe was next in, a solid £500,000 buy from French outfit Rennes. 'I watched him quite a few times,' recalled Hay, 'and I liked what I saw. Of course, I had played full-back as well as midfield in my career and I knew what was required in that position. Stephane ticked all the boxes, as far as I was concerned.

'Interestingly, I also took notice of his team-mate Stephane Guivarc'h, a forward with a superb goalscoring rate. In fact, he won the French league's Golden Boot for top striker at the end of the 1996/97 season. A year later he played for France in their 3-0 World Cup Final win over Brazil and my old mate Kenny Dalglish paid something like £4.5million to take him to Newcastle United. He didn't last long on Tyneside and had a year at Rangers before returning to France with Auxerre.'

Paolo di Canio, in the midst of all the team rebuilding, was making noises about wanting to leave to join 'a big English club'. Jock Brown insisted he would not be sold. The Italian returned to his homeland and claimed he could not come back to join pre-season training because he was suffering from stress. It was a disruption Celtic did not need. A couple of weeks later, the volatile individual joined Sheffield Wednesday in a deal valued at £4million with Dutch winger Regi Blinker arriving at Parkhead in part exchange. Sheffield Wednesday? A big English club? Possibly, 'stress' had disturbed Di Canio's selection process. Brown came under fire from the media after reassuring them the player would not be sold. The new General Manager replied, 'He wasn't sold - he was traded.' The season hadn't kicked off and the snipers were already fixing their sights on Brown.

Hay remembered, 'Wim really wanted to keep Paolo. He had seen what he could do, he was an exciting forward and brought something different to any team. So, it would be fair to say Wim was disappointed when he was allowed to leave. Maybe he thought the club should have done more to hold onto him. That wasn't the case with Jorge Cadete, though. I don't think he was ever in Wim's plans and he wasn't too perturbed when Jorge was sold to Celta Vigo.'

Of course, the one player Jansen was utterly determined to see at Celtic in the new season was Henrik Larsson and Hay added, 'It was obvious Wim wasn't going to accept no for an answer on this one. Wim was well aware there was a buy-out clause of £650,000 in Henrik's Feyenoord contract and that's exactly what we paid for him. No transfer is ever as easy as that, of course, and there was the usual wrangling with agents involved, but the main thing was that Henrik liked Wim and wanted to play for him again. Originally, Wim had spotted him at his Swedish club Helsingborgs and took him to Feyenoord. They both rated each other and that helped push the deal over the finishing line. Thank goodness.'

Jonathan Gould was plucked from the obscurity of Bradford City reserves to bolster the goalkeeping options. Jansen knew nothing of the player who had been handed a free transfer from Coventry City the previous year. Hay, once again, fills in the blanks. 'Craig Brown was the Scotland international manager at the time and he was tipped off about Gould who was eligible to play for the Scots despite being born in London. Apparently, one of his grandparents hailed from Blantyre.

He didn't seem to have much of a footballing pedigree, but Craig must have seen some quality when he watched him. His brother Jock mentioned Celtic were looking for a back-up keeper and that's how Gould arrived at Celtic. He cost £20,000 and missed only one league game all season.'

Gordon Marshall was the man in possession of the goalkeeper's jersey when Jansen, only twenty-two days after being announced as Tommy Burns' successor, took the team to Ninian Park, Cardiff, for the UEFA Cup first leg qualifying tie against the Welsh part-timers of Inter Cable-Tel. Goals from Andreas Thom, with a penalty-kick, Tommy Johnson and Morten Wieghorst gave the visitors a comfortable 3-0 advantage. Logically, the new Celtic manager observed, 'We should have played more up front - you don't make chances at the back.'

A week later, a 41,537 crowd, intrigued as to what might be on offer, turned out to see a 5-0 romp in the second leg with Darren Jackson scoring his first goal for the club. Thom, with another spot-kick, Johnson, David Hannah and Chris Hay got the others. Once again, no-one debated Jansen's summing-up of the action. 'Goals always make games easier,' he said, adding, 'There were good and bad points. When we played the ball quickly after one or two touches, things went well for us. But too often we gave the ball away too easily. We need to show more adaptability in our play. Craig Burley and Henrik Larsson will make the team stronger.'

The real challenge for Jansen and his hastily-pieced together team would arrive at Easter Road on Sunday, August 3, when the 1997/98 Premier League campaign got underway against Hibs. Burley made his debut while Larsson, not completely matchfit, had to be content with a place on the substitutes' bench. The Swede, though, would play a decisive role in the outcome of the encounter and the destination of the points.

In front of a live TV audience, the flaws of a line-up still trying to come to grips with each other's style and preferences, were exposed. The Edinburgh outfit, with veteran midfielder Chic Charnley running the show, won 2-1 and Jansen realised neither he nor his players had reason for complaint at the outcome. Gordon Marshall, who had been signed by Liam Brady and had also played for Lou Macari and Tommy Burns, made his one and only league appearance for the Dutchman. In truth, Jansen had tried to sign a top-class keeper since accepting the job and was content to offer a one-year contract to Jonathan Gould. But he did not see him as the long-term answer. Marshall paid a heavy price for another nervy, jittery, unconvincing display.

He was culpable when Hibs opened the scoring in the twenty-third minute after allowing a Tony Rougier cross to elude him and Lee Power scored from close range. Five minutes later, Malky Mackay powered in the equaliser with a ferocious header from a Simon Donnelly corner-kick. But Marshall was living dangerously when he allowed a Charnley thirty-five yard drive to fly over his head before slamming against the crossbar and being booted clear. Stephen Crawford also hit the woodwork with a crisp shot and Jansen decided to introduce Henrik Larsson to the action in the fifty-seventh minute for the toiling Andreas Thom. Eight minutes later, Charnley flashed in a first-time twenty-yard low drive for the winner after being set up by a wayward pass out of defence from, of all people, Larsson.

Charnley, a huge Celtic fan, recalled, 'To be fair to Henrik, he was back helping out in defence with the ball deep in left-back territory. A defender would simply have belted the ball out for a shy, but I had the feeling Henrik would try to keep the ball in play. I was trying to cut down space in case he attempted to play it inside. Instead, he wanted to put his laces through the clearance and didn't quite make a proper contact. The ball fell straight at my feet and I simply let fly. It was a goal the moment it left my foot. As a Celtic supporter, I'm delighted to say Henrik gave me lots of other reasons to be cheerful in his seven years at the club.'

Jansen said, 'We lost the ball too much, especially in midfield. They fought for everything and deserved to win the game. The pace of the match did not surprise me, but I tried to get my players to slow it down and not play at the same speed as their opponents because when they did that, they lost the ball and that was not good. As a team, we have to work at making chances and, while you don't like to lose, you can learn from this for the next game.'

The manager refused point-blank to lay the blame on Larsson. Instead, he added emphatically, 'What happened with Henrik is just part of football. He wishes he could change it, but he will get over it.'

Six days later, Celtic returned to Edinburgh for a League Cup-tie against Berwick Rangers, which had been switched to Hearts' Tynecastle ground. Amazingly, Jansen had been in charge of Celtic for four competitive games and had played in three different competitions. Henrik Larsson scored his first goal for the club in the twenty-first minute in a whirlwind first-half that saw the Glasgow outfit rattle in five goals and add another two after the turnaround. Regi Blinker got in on the act, too, in the twenty-eighth minute and Darren Jackson, Morten Wieghorst and Andreas Thom also netted in the landslide opening forty-five minutes. Substitute Simon Donnelly was introduced for the second period and scored twice. Jonathan Gould replaced Marshall and it was evident he was there to stay. He signed a three-year extension in December and Marshall joined Kilmarnock a month later. Jansen declared, 'We made a good, concentrated effort in the first-half and scored some good goals. In particular, I thought Regi Blinker and Stephane Mahe played well.'

It wasn't quite so one-sided when Celtic travelled to Austria to face Tirol Innsbruck in the UEFA Cup second round qualifier. There were problems when the team was delayed at Glasgow Airport for almost seven hours while they waited for a replacement aircraft. And, unfortunately, they found their opponents flying during the tie in the Tivoli Stadium when the action got underway. Two goals in seven first-half minutes from Christian Mayrieb piled on the pressure, but Jansen's men were thrown a lifeline six minutes from time when Alan Stubbs pulled one back with a hurtling free-kick. The defender, still trying to live up to the £3.5million transfer fee paid by Tommy Burns, said, 'I used to take most of the deadball efforts for Bolton, but with Pierre van Hooijdonk around, my opportunities at Celtic were few and far between. So, I took the opportunity to show what I could do with this one and, thankfully, it found the net.'

Celtic's top performer, though, was unquestionably goalkeeper Gould, who made several top-notch saves with the club on the ropes. He had no chance when Mayrieb, who had been a menace with his pace right from the start, scored with two fine, well-placed drives. Jansen wasn't too downhearted at the end. He said, 'At 2-0, we only had a slim chance of getting through, but, at 2-1, we have every hope. I am delighted with the way my players responded to what I told them to do at half-time and I think we came out a much better side.'

Sandwiched in between the European ties, Jansen had to take his home league bow in front 45,120 fans before the game against Dunfermline at sun-drenched Celtic Park on August 16. Gould, Burley, Larsson, Jackson and Blinker were also on parade, but injury kept out Stubbs, Wieghorst, Johnson and Mahe. Celtic, once more toppled to a 2-1 defeat, and had nothing to show for three hours' worth of football in a campaign where it was imperative Rangers had to be stopped from going into double figures in their succession of title triumphs. At the kick-off, the home support sat back to enjoy the adventure and were cheering in the fortieth minute when Hamish French bundled over Larsson in the box, referee Martin Clark immediately pointed to the spot and Thom whipped his effort wide of Ian Westwater.

Disastrously, though, the East End Park side were level within sixty seconds of the turnaround when Allan Moore raced down the right wing virtually unchallenged, picked out the unmarked David Bingham and he controlled the ball, spun and left Gould helpless with a precise finish. It got worse fourteen minutes from time. Malky Mackay got involved in a tangle of legs with Moore who took to the floor with relish. Another penalty-kick and French, the first-half sinner, became the second-half winner when he placed the ball behind Gould. A newspaper reporter described Jansen as 'looking slightly bemused by it all' as he stood on the touchline.

Afterwards, the Celtic boss said, 'I was very disappointed with the result as we could have been two or three up going in at half-time. But we came out the dressing room and it was 1-1 right away and a lack of communication hampered us after that. We lost our shape and, just as in the previous game against Tirol, that became our biggest problem. And we only have ourselves to blame for losing the two goals as we gave the ball away for each of them.'

Rangers, after only two games, were already six points ahead after back-to-back home wins against Hearts (3-1) and Dundee United (5-1). Marco Negri, bought from Serie A outfit Perugia for £3.5million in the close season, netted seven goals in the two games, including all five in the rout of the Tannadice side. Astonishingly, the Italian striker netted twenty-three goals in his first ten league games and looked unstoppable. Negri was one of three players newly-plundered from Italy's top division by Walter Smith; centre-half Lorenzo Amoruso arrived in a £5million move from Fiorentina and right-back Sergio Porrini joined in £3million deal from Juventus. Rino Gattuso, a tenacious teenage midfielder, also came in on a free from Salernitana. It was clear money was no option as the Ibrox side chased a decade of championship domination.

It was around this time the Rangers chairman David Murray made his crass and ill-advised statement along the lines of 'for every five pounds Celtic spend, we'll spend ten pounds.' Such vulgar and doltish remarks have a habit of coming back to haunt an individual and, of course, that was the case as time and justice caught of with such reckless spending and the club collapsed and died when it went into liquidation in June 2012. However, that wasn't on the agenda in 1997 as Jansen continued to plot the rebirth of a club that appeared to have lost its way.

Three days after the Dunfermline defeat, Celtic were due to play St Johnstone in the League Cup Third Round and then make a quickfire return to Perth for their third Premier League game of the campaign on the Saturday. Jansen went into the Cup-tie demanding his players accept the challenge in front of them and display the leadership qualities he believed had so far been absent in previous games.

Celtic won 1-0 in extra-time through a Simon Donnelly penalty-kick against a newly-promoted Saints side who lost their composure after the regulation ninety minutes and had John O'Neil and Roddy Grant sent off. It was an unconvincing performance from the Parkhead side and one newspaper reporter noted, 'The most serious effect of Celtic's poor form in these early days of the season is that it convinces prospective opponents they are not to be feared. The erosion of their credibility and authority is almost as damaging as their own ineffectiveness in most areas of the field.'

Matchwinner Donnelly said, 'We've been guilty of not battling enough in recent games, but tonight we've proved we can fight as well as play. Now I hope this result will help get us going.' Jansen observed, 'We came here to get through to the next round of the Cup. We did and I am happy about that. We worked very hard for this result.'

Henrik Larsson displayed the shape of things to come when he scored a sublime goal when Celtic, at the third time of asking, won three points. They returned to McDiarmid Park and upped their game considerably in a 2-0 victory. Larsson started and finished the move that gave Jansen's team the lead five minutes from the interval. The Swede, beginning to get into his stride, accepted a Craig Burley pass in the centre circle and immediately switched it wide to Simon Donnelly. Larsson left a vapour trail behind him as he raced full-pelt for forty yards before Donnelly slung the ball into the danger area. The striker took off on a majestic leap, made perfect contact with the ball and goalkeeper Alan Main hardly had time to move before there was a net rustling behind him. Larsson had arrived! Darren Jackson made certain in the sixty-fourth minute with another excellent strike as he drifted across the eighteen-yard line before curling a spectacular effort high past Main. This time it was an impressive showing from the team from the east end of Glasgow and the scoreline would have been more emphatic if attempts from Malky Mackay, Regi Blinker and Burley had been rewarded with goals rather than woodwork intervening.

Larsson, clearly delighted, said, 'Players have to take their own responsibility and always have to fight for the team, no matter how badly they are playing. I think we did that. There is still more to come and we will get better now we have got rid of the hesitancy we had.' Jansen was content to add, 'We scored two beautiful goals and you could see the confidence these gave the players. The second-half was the best we have played since I came here and that was very pleasing.'

European football was seen merely as a bonus, but Celtic had no intention of exiting the UEFA Cup before the first round proper when Tirol Innsbruck came to Glasgow on August 26 to attempt to protect their 2-1 first leg advantage in the second qualifying tie. And the Austrians were within three minutes of achieving a place in the next round with Celtic winning 4-3 on the night, the tie stalemated at 5-5 and goals away favouring the visitors. One of those goals had actually been put in his own net by Henrik Larsson, his first European strike in the green and white hoops on another memorable and boisterous occasion under the lights at Parkhead.

Simon Donnelly led the goal parade when he flashed in the opener in the thirty-fourth minute. The Austrians were back in control when Christian Mayrieb, who scored twice in the first leg, levelled five minutes later. Andreas Thom restored the lead in the forty-fourth minute, but, within sixty seconds, Larsson diverted a wicked low cross from Myrieb past Jonathan Gould. Donnelly drilled in a penalty-kick for No.3 in the sixty-ninth minute and Craig Burley claimed the fourth a minute later. The fans in the 47,017 crowd were now working out the maths. Celtic were 4-2 ahead on the night and 5-4 overall. As the clock ticked down, Innsbruck sent on substitute Gernot Krinner in the eighty-second minute. Within a few seconds, he materialised at the back post to head in his team's third. It was all getting a bit bewildering. Only three minutes remained when Morten Wieghorst expertly controlled a knockdown from Donnelly and clipped the ball beyond Heinz Weber. Deep in stoppage time, Larsson took off on a mesmerising solo run before setting up Burley to club the ball in to bring down the curtain on a pulsating encounter.

Wim Jansen, normally stoic and reserved, warmly hugged his players as they came off the field. It was an outward pouring of emotion that hadn't been witnessed before by the Celtic faithful. He drew breath, composed himself and said, 'What I take from the victory was the great attitude of the players. They simply never gave up and, willed on by our supporters, continued to believe they could win the tie even when it looked like it might be beyond them. When it was 2-2 at half-time it wasn't so easy for us, but I kept telling them we could still do it if we pressed for two goals from the first minute of the second period.

'That is what they did, showing great energy when we went 3-2 up and refusing to accept we were out even when Tirol made it 4-3. All our players gave it more than one hundred per cent and there was not one failure in our side simply because of the way they kept going right to the end. When it was 4-4 on aggregate we had lots of problems, but I didn't have much time to think about what was happening because one minute we were in, the next we were out and, suddenly, we were in the competition again.

'Of course, we know that we cannot expect to score six goals each time we play and normally if you score four in a European tie you have done enough to go through. That wasn't the case against Tirol and, therefore, being more solid at the back is something we know we must work on. We still need to do more talking on the pitch. Our communication is getting better, but the players must help one another more and make it easier for themselves. As the game swayed one way then the other, I kept urging the players to push on and squeeze the game up. But I have to say a big thank you to our fans. They were right behind us from the first minute. They helped us and the people behind the dug-out just continued to shout encouragement and kept believing the tie could go our way. With these fans backing us, we can achieve things. I'm sure of that.'

Larsson was equally effusive. He said, 'My own goal was unbelievable and, after making Chic Charnley such a big man in Scotland because of my mistake which let him win the first league match for Hibs, I didn't want to go out of the UEFA Cup because of my assist. I saw the large headlines saying, "LARSSON KNOCKS CELTIC OUT OF EUROPE!" I didn't want that.'

Jonathan Gould, beaten five times in his first two appearances in Europe, actually made a handful of breathtaking saves over both legs. He reflected, 'I'm losing my hair as it is, so I can do without any more games like that. I've never experienced a night like it. It was quite incredible and the atmosphere was astonishing. I think that was what got us through. When we were 4-2 up, I remember thinking that there was still another twist to come. Even after Morten Wieghorst made it 5-3, I knew the Austrians would still come at us and, sure enough, they had a couple of decent attempts. I made a save just after that and I knew if I spilled it the way I had an earlier one, striker Christian Mayrleb might score. However, the ball stuck to me and there was a mixture of satisfaction and relief when it did.'

There had been behind-the-scenes drama even before the kick-off when Darren Jackson complained of severe headaches. He was whisked off to hospital and, after overnight tests, he was diagnosed with Hydrocephalus. He underwent surgery to relieve the build up of pressure. Thankfully, the striker was given the all-clear, but Jansen was told to expect him to be unavailable for at least three months while he recuperated.

Celtic nudged closer to elusive silverware on September 10 when a first-half goal from Henrik Larsson earned a 1-0 win over Motherwell in the League Cup quarter-final at Parkhead. Stevie Woods' goal enjoyed a charmed life throughout the evening and Simon Donnelly, with a little luck, could have claimed a hat-trick. The lack of a killer instinct obviously concerned Wim Jansen. He summed up, 'We caused ourselves problems by not scoring a second or third goal that would have made the game easier. But it's nice to know we are in the last four and we will do everything to reach the Final. However, you never know what can happen in Cup games - just look at Rangers.' The Head Coach was referring to events at Ibrox the previous evening when an extra-time goal from Gary McSwegan dumped the holders and earned a place in the next stage for Dundee United.

Coincidentally, as with St Johnstone in the previous round, Celtic now found themselves squaring up to the same opponents in league business on the Saturday - this time at Fir Park. Centre-half Marc Rieper was signed from West Ham for £1.8million on Friday evening and went straight into the team to face Alex McLeish's outfit. The towering Dane hardly had time to introduce himself when his new team were a goal down. Alan Stubbs' passback in the third minute was snapped up by Tommy Coyne and neatly tucked under Jonathan Gould. Henrik Larsson set up the fifty-sixth minute equaliser with a swift run down the touchline and precision cross which was knocked in by Craig Burley for his first Premier League goal.

Two minutes later, Coyne, who was making a habit of scoring against his old side, restored 'Well's advantage. Greig Dernham was then sent off after an altercation with Larsson, who was paid the compliment of being targeted by his opponents, and Burley levelled after a superb pass from Stubbs, atoning for his earlier aberration. With nine minutes remaining, Simon Donnelly, with an acrobatic header, claimed the winner.

Jansen observed, 'That was very exciting. Even though we were behind twice, we were creating numerous chances in front of goal. The players showed their character and it was important for them to keep playing with quality ball circulating and we had to keep Motherwell running. We kept going right to the end which was very pleasing.'

Stealthily, and apparently on the blind side, the Dutchman was quietly and effectively putting together a Celtic line-up that was aware there were several ways to win a ninety-minute game of football. They were coming together as a passing team, but they also knew how to battle and grind out victories. After the horrendous start to the campaign, the new philosophy led to eight successive league wins and a place at the top of the Premier League for the first time in almost a year.

Henrik Larsson, instantly recognisable with his Alice band and flowing dreadlocks, was beginning to make his presence felt as he took centre stage. The Swede may have looked slight, but defenders were beginning to realise he possessed the strength of a middleweight boxer. And he wasn't afraid to mix it with the more bruising of opponents whose intimidatory tactics would often backfire. He was on target twice as Aberdeen were vanquished 2-0 in front of 49,017 fans at Parkhead on September 20. The first goal came in the twenty-seventh minute when Larsson hared onto a Donnelly through pass and eliminated Jim Leighton's dive with a calm, low finish. Twelve minutes later, Larsson, from twenty yards, curled an exquisite free-kick into vacant space at the keeper's right and the game was as good as over. Jansen smiled and opined, 'Henrik showed why we bought him.'

Davie Hay added, 'Henrik was a dream player for Wim. I quickly discovered one of Wim's great hates was a footballer standing still. He demanded that they should be on the move throughout the ninety minutes - and that applied more to the front players than the guys at the back. His reasoning was sound, of course. If someone is playing centre-forward and rarely shifts from the middle of the attack, the defence won't have far to look for him at any time during a game. So, Wim wanted the frontmen to be continually on the go and, in doing so, they could have two or three defenders wondering what they were up to. Henrik, of course, was perpetual motion and you never saw him simply standing around with his hands on his hips waiting for the ball to fall at his feet.'

A week after the win over the Dons, the Celtic Head Coach had the first opportunity of the season to single out his defence for special mention after a 2-1 triumph over Dundee United at Tannadice. Marc Rieper was beginning to dovetail superbly with Alan Stubbs in the heart of the rearguard and Jansen said, 'Our defence looked solid. All four players at the back stuck to their tasks and, whether on the ground or in the air, they dealt convincingly with what came their way.' David Hannah played right-back as Tommy Boyd switched to the left with Stephane Mahe sidelined through injury.

Rieper set the move in motion that brought the opening goal in the twenty-eighth minute when he wasn't too fussy about a high clearance out of defence. Future Celt Steven Pressley misjudged the bounce of the ball, Larsson outjumped him to head it onto Donnelly and he displayed some nifty headwork, too, by nodding over the stranded Sieb Dykstra. Phil O'Donnell came on for the limping Andreas Thom in the forty-second minute and, with practically his first touch of the ball, doubled the lead when he first-timed a left-foot volley high into the net. As expected, United carried more threat after the interval when they threw caution to the wind as they piled forward, but their only reward was a consolation effort from Kjell Olofsson on the hour mark. After that, the defence went shoulder to shoulder to put a smile on Jansen's face.

Celtic were beginning to establish their title credentials and the supporters were also daring to believe again. A crowd of 48,165 turned out to see a devastating four-goals-inside-seventeen-minutes burst demolish Kilmarnock in a sparkling first-half. Before the game, Wim Jansen and Henrik Larsson were presented with their respective Manager and Player of the Month awards and the Swede demonstrated why he had amassed most of the votes by knocking in two while Simon Donnelly and the ever-improving Morten Wieghorst added the others in a runaway 4-0 win.

'I was very pleased with the performance,' said Jansen while observing in a very simplistic fashion, 'If we couldn't get down one side, then we would switch the play to the other and open the game up. It wasn't about concentrating on one channel and we are now playing better week by week.' Bobby Williamson, the well-beaten Killie gaffer, added, 'When you have the type of player Celtic have, you will always score goals.'

Tynecastle was the next testing ground for Jansen and his Celtic warriors and goals from Rieper and Larsson inside the first twenty-one minutes had Hearts struggling. Colin Cameron got one back in the sixty-fifth minute, but a resolute back lot locked out the eager Edinburgh forwards and three more points were heading back to Paradise. Jansen once again praised his stalwarts at the back. 'Stubbs and Rieper understand each other and that contributes to the good play the defence has shown. The whole team is working well together. We were physical when we needed to be and I knew that was a requirement after my first game in Scotland.'

On Saturday October 25, Celtic went to the top of the table for the first time since achieving the feat under Tommy Burns on November 2 the previous year. Over 48,500 spectators watched as two goals in four first-half minutes from Larsson and Donnelly, with a penalty-kick, pointed the side in the direction of a 2-0 victory over St Johnstone. Asked by a journalist if it was a good feeling being in pole position, Jansen, in his thick gutteral Dutch accent, replied, 'Yesh.' Later, he expanded. 'It is important for us to keep this confidence. It's good to be top of the league, but, of course, there is a long way to go. We had a bad start, but you have to play thirty-six games and during that time you go up and down. The most important thing is we continue to play well together.'

Dunfermline, still the only side to inflict a defeat on Celtic in Glasgow, provided the opposition a week later and, as predicted by many, it was far from pretty at East End Park. The Fifers ignored anything remotely scientific about the beautiful game and favoured cloud-bursting clouts from one end of the pitch to the other. As someone remarked rather tritely about their mode of play, 'The ball spends so much time in the sky it qualifies for air miles.'

It was going to be a long and punishing ninety minutes in Fife and it took until the sixty-seventh minute until the visitors got the breakthrough goal. Regi Blinker fired in a happy-go-lucky attempt that took a wicked deflection off Greg Shields' outstretched leg and looped high over the head of the helpless Ian Westwater. With three minute to go, Larsson went on a one-man sortie, skipped past three challenges and rattled the rigging behind Westwater for the killer second. Words of wisdom from Jansen did the trick during the interval. He said, 'We didn't play well in the first-half and could not control the game because we started to play like Dunfermline. They play high balls, but we prefer to play more on the ground. That's what I told the players at half-time. It was important to get a good result before facing Rangers on Saturday.'

On the rundown to the first Old Firm encounter of the season at Ibrox, Celtic had gone out of Europe in the First Round without losing to Liverpool and had also booked a place in the League Cup Final where they would meet Dundee United at Ibrox - with Hampden still undergoing a revamp - on November 30.

The UEFA Cup exit was particularly difficult to accept after outplaying the much-vaunted Anfield side before conceding a goal with virtually the last kick of the ball to make it 2-2 in Glasgow. That was the goal that made the difference when the tie was stalemated after a goalless ninety minutes on Merseyside. Celtic Park was throbbing when Liverpool arrived on September 16 and the stirring rendition of 'You'll Never Walk Alone', bellowed lustily by everyone in the 48,526 crowd, almost lifted the roof off the ground. Unfortunately, it was the 3,000 travelling support who were still in good voice in the fifth minute when Michael Owen, a seventeen-year-old box of tricks, finished off a fine three-man move down the left by beating Jonathan Gould from close range. It remained that way until eight minutes after the break when Jackie McNamara netted with an explosive effort. Henrik Larsson had just struck the upright moments earlier when McNamara played a swift one-two with Craig Burley on the edge of the box and hit a left-foot volley on the run and the ball screamed high past David James.

The England international goalkeeper was beaten again when a vicious drive from Simon Donnelly walloped against the underside of the crossbar, bounced on the line and was cleared. Celtic were buzzing around the Liverpool area and it was no surprise when a flapping James brought down Henrik Larsson and a penalty-kick was awarded in the seventy-fourth minute. Donnelly made no mistake. Wim Jansen's men were in control right up until the fading moments when Steve McManaman was allowed to go on a startling sixty-yard run. Morten Wieghorst raced alongside him, but resisted the temptation to knock him out of his stride. The gangly attacker took full advantage of the Dane's sense of sportsmanship by arcing an eighteen-yard shot wide of Gould to silence Celtic Park. It was a dreadful goal to concede.

Wim Jansen said defiantly, 'It will not be easy for us, but we still have a chance and we know we can cause Liverpool problems.' Roy Evans, the Anfield manager, conceded, 'We were under the cosh for a long time in the second-half. With our goal coming so late, to say it was a bit of a let-off would be a fair comment.'

A fortnight later, 3,000 Celtic fans remained in place long after the final whistle to hail their heroes after a goalless second leg on Merseyside. They were out, but hardly disgraced. Alas, the best chance of the evening fell to Donnelly in the twentieth minute and the young striker completely fluffed the opportunity. Goalkeeper James collided with defender Stig Bjornebye and spilled the ball at the feet of the Celt, who was following up. It looked a certain goal, but he snatched at the opportunity and lifted the ball over the bar from close range. Jansen said, 'Tonight you saw that we can play, but the two goals Liverpool scored in Glasgow were the difference. We had more chances and should have scored, particularly Simon Donnelly's in the first-half. However, it wasn't to be.' His opposite number Evans blew a sigh of relief and admitted, 'I think Celtic are a far better team than a lot of people down here think.'

The disappointment was partly balanced with a 1-0 win over Dunfermline in the League Cup semi-final at Ibrox on October 15. As in the disastrous Scottish Cup semi-final against Falkirk at the same venue the previous season, the rain lashed down all day to turn the pitch into a quagmire. It was not an evening for silky soccer and in the end Celtic had to rely on a whizzbang effort from Craig Burley in the sixty-ninth minute. The midfielder had come close on a couple of occasions just before the barrier-breaking strike. McNamara hit a pass inside from the right, Larsson touched it onto Burley and he sent a twenty-yard piledriver low past Ian Westwater.

Jansen said, 'We had to show a lot of patience and we got our reward. We knew it would not be an easy game and in the first-half we had problems with high balls. In the second-half, we played better, more in our own style. When you come to a club such as Celtic, you come to win Cups and it's important for the club and the fans to be in a Cup Final.'

Celtic had at last broken the Ibrox jinx. Could they succeed on the same pitch in the first Glasgow head-to-head confrontation of the season in November? The support could hardly wait.

CHAPTER THIRTEEN
GLORY POSTPONED

Over the many decades, Celtic supporters making their way to Ibrox had long since come to terms with the fact Dame Fortune possessed a sadistic streak. On November 8 1997, they embarked once again on the well-worn trail of hope and aspiration with the home of their fiercest rivals as their destination. And this time they made the trek with genuine optimism.

The fans had witnessed their favourites winning eight league games on the bounce, forcing their greatest foes to look up at them for the first time in almost a year. Rangers may have spent lavishly during the summer months, but their extravagant use of the chequebook did not guarantee success. As well as their Italian entourage, Walter Smith had brought in Swedish midfielder Jonas Thern from AS Roma on a free transfer while adding squad members such as Staale Stensaas (Rosenborg), Tony Vidmar (NAC Breda), Antti Niemi (FC Copenhagen) and Jonatan Johansson (Flora Tallin). Critically, on October 14, they persuaded ex-skipper Richard Gough to rejoin them from Kansas City Wizards.

In total, Rangers spent a stupendous £14.5million in bringing in ten new players and their only notable sale during the season was Paul Gascoigne to Middlesbrough for £3.45million in March 1998. The Champions League excursion didn't get beyond the second qualifier as they were derailed 4-1 on aggregate by IFK Gothenburg before August was out. They dropped into the UEFA Cup, but that was embarrassingly short-lived, too, when they lost home and away to RFC Strasbourg to go out on a 4-2 aggregate. A goal from their former player Gary McSwegan stopped the League Cup journey at the quarter-final stage with Dundee United winning 1-0 at Ibrox. The Tayside outfit triumphed 2-1 to hand them their first league defeat two weeks before the visit of Celtic while Aberdeen (3-3) and Motherwell (2-2) also held them to stalemates. In short, Rangers were there for the taking.

Celtic's cause had gathered further impetus with the £2million signing of Champions League winner Paul Lambert from Borussia Dortmund. Wim Jansen had been searching for the sort of holding midfielder he had been used to in Dutch football. The coach was delighted with the dovetailing of Craig Burley and Morten Wieghorst in the middle of the park, but he realised an important component was missing. Lambert, an unfussy, controlled professional, would provide the answer.

The player had quit Motherwell at the end of his contract just over a year beforehand to join Borussia Dortmund on a Bosman deal. Against all the odds, he forced his way into the star-studded first team and played a key role in their 3-1 Champions League Final triumph over Juventus, snuffing out the considerable threat of Zinidine Zidane. However, Lambert's wife Monica, pregnant with their second child, couldn't settle in a foreign country and a story was related to me that brought the uncomfortable situation to a swift conclusion. There was a panic one evening over a health scare concerning three-year-old son Christopher. The Lamberts simply did not know how to cope with the predicament. In Scotland, they were one phone call away from a resolution. With their lack of fluent German, it was far from that simple in Dortmund. It brought the matter to a head and any doubts about the wisdom of a return home were expelled that evening. Celtic were alerted to the player's availability, made their move and, a few weeks later, he was on the substitutes' bench at Ibrox.

The first Old Firm encounter of the campaign had been scheduled for August, but had been postponed in the wake of Princess Diana's death. So, supporters of both clubs were forced to wait until November for their first taste of the rarefied Old Firm atmosphere. Wim Jansen went with Jackie McNamara, Craig Burley and Morten Wieghorst as his midfield three with Henrik Larsson and Simon Donnelly leading the attack. It looked a well-balanced formation, but he was forced into a change as early as the sixteenth minute when Alan Stubbs was forced to come off and Enrico Annoni was introduced to the action, taking his place alongside Marc Rieper in the heart of the rearguard. It still looked a strong enough ensemble to win against opponents who had been far from intimidating in the games leading up to the fixture.

Inexplicably, a strangely-lethargic Celtic appeared to take stage fright in front of just over 50,000 fans. A twenty-ninth minute goal from the returning Gough separated the teams at the end of a frustrating, puzzling afternoon in Govan. Paul Gascoigne was given the freedom of the midfield, roaming around while randomly materialising where he thought he would create most menace. Tommy Boyd and Stephane Mahe toiled in the full-back areas and it was a particularly forgettable event for the Frenchman who was culpable at the only goal and didn't last the entire game after being ordered to leave proceedings by referee Kenny Clark with nine minutes still remaining following two yellow card offences.

Jonathan Gould prevented Gascoigne from giving Rangers the lead with a spectacular high-flying save to his left as he tipped away a screaming twenty-yarder after the English international skipped past a couple of half-hearted challenges. Gough hit the outside of the left-hand post with a header from the resultant corner-kick. The alarm bells among the visiting support were already ringing.

Larsson gave them hope with two whiplash headers from left-wing crosses, but Goram was equal to them and scooped both away from the goal-line at his right hand side. Then a rush of blood to the head from Mahe unlocked the back door for the home side. His timing was awful as he attempted to cut out a Stuart McCall measured pass to Laudrup. As the left-back slid out of play, the Dane galloped into the box and picked out the unmarked Gough who hit a first-time drive across Gould and in at the far corner. Lambert came on in the seventy-third minute for Boyd for his first taste of the Glasgow derby, but it was not to be a happy homecoming.

Jansen, clearly disappointed, made no excuses. 'We weren't really in the game, especially in the first-half,' he observed. 'We couldn't play as we wanted to, gave the ball away too often and failed to get it to the forward players and move up in support. The second-half was a little better, but too late. Chances were there, but we didn't really play. In great games like this, all eleven have to perform and we had too many who didn't. On these occasions, players have to stand up and it was our disappointment that too many didn't. It was our plan to play the same way as normal, but Rangers were far more aggressive and pushed us back.'

Goalkeeper Gould, a rare success alongside Rieper, Annoni and Larsson, said, 'The manager let us know in no uncertain terms at half-time that things were going badly wrong. He told us that if we continued playing the same way we would lose heavily. We sorted things out in the second-half, but it still wasn't good enough. We didn't do ourselves justice and I just can't explain that.'

It was just as difficult to offer any sort of reasonable explanation for the next game, a 2-0 home defeat against a toiling Motherwell team who arrived in Glasgow anchored at the foot of the Premier League. Stephane Mahe, of course, was banned after his Ibrox indiscretions, but strong-willed Wim Jansen refused to even consider Tosh McKinlay as a replacement at left-back. The international defender had been involved in a training ground fracas with Henrik Larsson prior to the meeting with Rangers. The Swede was left with a bloodied nose and a black eye. Jansen had no doubt who was to blame and McKinlay was told he was no longer in the coach's plans. He didn't even make the 16-man squad for the visit of Motherwell and right-sided David Hannah was pitched into the No.3 position.

Celtic may have been bereft of a little confidence after their Ibrox setback, but there was no evidence of a lack of conviction as they started in whirlwind fashion against Alex McLeish's Fir Park strugglers. Inside the first ten minutes, Larsson headed a cross against the bar, had an effort ruled out for offside by referee Willie Young and Alan Stubbs had a header cleared off the line. The game turned in the space of seven first-half minutes. Poor Gould was left utterly flummoxed in the twenty-eighth minute when the visitors took the lead with a bizarre goal. Owen Coyle had a go and his drive from the edge of the box struck Hannah and then Stubbs before bouncing over the line. The double rebound completely wrong-footed the keeper. Shortly afterwards, Regi Blinker got involved in a shoving match with Kevin Christie that saw the Motherwell player go down as though he had been hit by a train. Match official Young produced a red card and indicated the winger was walking because of the use of his elbow. A grim-faced Jansen glowered at Blinker as he trudged past him and up the tunnel.

After the break, Celtic piled forward. Young ruled out a Craig Burley 'goal' and the ball refused to find a passage beyond Steve Woods. Jansen took off Paul Lambert, put Enrico Annoni on at centre-back and pushed Marc Rieper up front as a makeshift battering ram. All to no avail. Motherwell, practically hemmed in for the entire second-half, broke forward in the last minute, Dougie Arnott set Mickey Weir scampering clear and he rolled No.2 past Gould. It was Motherwell's third shot on target all afternoon. It didn't help the mood of the fans at the end when they discovered Rangers had dropped two points in a 1-1 draw with Aberdeen at Pittodrie. They had heard it all before during the Tommy Burns era.

Jansen once again refused to offer up lame excuses. He said, 'In the first twenty minutes we should have scored enough goals to make the game safe. We then lost a silly goal and had a man sent off which forced us to re-organise. We tried absolutely everything to score in the second-half, but nothing came of our efforts. In soccer, there are no easy opponents and we have found that to our cost today.'

Four days later, Rangers provided the opposition again for the second time inside a fortnight in the reorganised confrontation at Parkhead. The Ibrox side crossed the Clyde satisfied in the knowledge they hadn't lost to their age-old rivals in nine successive league games. It was a run that had to end some time, but it wasn't to be on this particular evening of high drama. They went home with a point from a 1-1 draw, but Walter Smith was far removed from the happy individual he was with only a minute to go of an absorbing contest. Rangers were leading 1-0 despite having Paul Gascoigne ordered off just before the hour mark. The suspect temperament of the excitable midfielder snapped as he was challenged by Morten Wieghorst. There was a bit of tit-for-tat tugging until Gascoigne suddenly flung a windmill arm in the Dane's face. Referee John Rowbotham, only yards from the incident, immediately flashed the red card. Without hanging around to debate his punishment, the erratic England international headed for the tunnel.

Gascoigne, it must be said, had been playing exceptionally well on the night and Wieghorst, who was never far from his side, was having an uneasy evening trying to curtail his opponent's clever sorties as he probed for weaknesses in the Celtic defence. Negri passed up two reasonable opportunities during that period, but Wim Jansen's men, too, had chances to put Goram under pressure. However, with the removal of Gascoigne, there was a renewed vigour about the home team. There were only 3,000 Rangers fans in the 49,509 crowd, but they made their voices heard in the seventy-first minute when, against the run of play, Negri, with his twenty-seventh goal of the campaign, gave them the lead. Durie threaded a pass into the stride of the onrushing Italian and he swept a low drive between Gould and his near post.

And it remained that way until a matter of seconds from time. Celtic forced a corner-kick on the right which was swung in by Jackie McNamara. Goram pawed fresh air, but it was scrambled away and found its way back out to McNamara. Displaying the skill of a natural winger, the right-back stunned the ball, looked up and flighted in a cross to the back post. Alan Stubbs rose above a pyramid of players and thumped a solid header back across the motionless Goram and into the far corner of the net. There appeared to be a moment's hesitation among the crowd before the place erupted in a wall of noise. Rangers kicked off and referee Rowbotham blew for full-time. Durie was so agitated at the loss of the late goal that he continued to argue with the match official and picked up a straight red card for his trouble.

Jansen looked relieved at the end. 'The way they defended made it very difficult for us to score a goal,' he said. 'Richard Gough was particularly outstanding. But I thought the character of our side was excellent, especially in the final twenty minutes. My players tried everything and eventually got the equaliser.' Smith, whose sidekick Archie Knox was cautioned for remarks in the tunnel, moaned, 'This feels like a defeat.'

Celtic were now due to play Dundee United in back-to-back encounters over an eight-day period, starting with a Premier League meeting at Parkhead on November 22 and then a week on Sunday in the League Cup Final - still in its guise as the Coca-Cola Cup - at a sell-out Ibrox. Jansen, quite correctly, ordered his players to forget any thoughts of winning only the club's second piece of silverware in the nineties to concentrate completely on the first game.

A solitary penalty-kick from Andreas Thom was the difference between the teams at half-time, but three goals in fifteen minutes made certain the points would remain in Glasgow. Henrik Larsson helped to put Celtic in the comfort zone in the sixty-fourth minute and Thom added a third. The Swede notched No.4 to put the 48,581 supporters - or most of them, at least - in party mode as they prepared for Ibrox. Jansen remained level-headed under his wayward curls and said, 'This win will have no bearing on the Cup Final, but what we will have taken from it is that we have the ability to score goals against Dundee United.'

On November 30 at the ground of their venerable adversaries, Celtic did indeed lift their second trophy of the decade following the 1995 Scottish Cup success during Tommy Burns' reign. Remarkably, only one player - Tommy Boyd - was involved against Dundee United who had been in the starting line-up two years earlier that had beaten Airdrie 1-0. Simon Donnelly made it two when he came on as a second-half substitute for Andreas Thom. Wim Jansen went with this team: Jonathan Gould; Tommy Boyd, Marc Rieper, Alan Stubbs, Stephane Mahe; Jackie McNamara, Craig Burley, Morten Weighorst; Henrik Larsson, Andreas Thom and Regi Blinker. Enrico Annoni and Paul Lambert also made appearances as second-half substitutes for McNamara and Blinker respectively.

The atmosphere was tense with anticipation as a crowd of 49,305 applauded both sides onto the pitch. Two goals inside three frantic first-half minutes had the organisers already looking out the green-and-white ribbons for the trophy. In the twenty-first minute any trace of nerves within the Celtic ranks began to dissipate. Thom sent Wieghorst racing clear on the right wing and the elegant Dane sent in a peach of a cross. Rieper knocked everyone around him out of the way as he stormed forward, leapt to an extraordinary height and pummelled a colossus of a thumping header high into the roof of the net with Sieb Dykstra saving himself the bother of getting his knees dirty in any vain attempt he instantly realised would have been doomed to failure.

Moments later and Larsson struck with the second to send the Celtic fans' joy soaring to a wonderful place. United defender Mark Perry attempted a crossfield pass, which was seized upon by the lurking Swede. He carried the ball forward, drew back his right boot and unleashed a drive at goal from just outside the penalty box. It took a nick off the challenging Maurice Malpas as it looped up and over the head of Dykstra, again a mere spectator as his net bulged behind him. Just before the hour mark it was all over. Larsson, busy as ever, sought out Blinker on the left with a cute ball to switch wings. The elastic-limbed Dutchman eluded two tackles before pitching over a delightful cross. Burley's timing couldn't have been bettered as he raced between two defenders and, from six yards, threw himself full-length to get his head to the ball and bullet it towards its inevitable destination. It finished 3-0 and Gould, after only four months in Scottish soccer, found himself collecting his first winners' medal. He achieved the feat without conceding a solitary goal in the competition.

Wim Jansen, typically, refused to get carried away. 'Of course, it was good to win and to score three goals,' he said. 'We wanted to get a goal and build on it and it worked out that way. I am delighted for the supporters who deserve this day. There is still much work to be done and we cannot rest.' Larsson added, 'Everybody is so happy. The fans have been waiting for this for a long time. We hope we'll feel the benefit of this win in the championship. We've got a lot to do, but we will do well if we keep playing like this.'

There was one massive fundamental difference between Jansen's League Cup triumph and Burns' Scottish Cup win. The Dutchman and the players could draw confidence and impetus from such an important victory with over four months of the season to play and two trophies still up for grabs. His predecessor's success came at the end of a campaign and there was the summer break before they attempted to pick up the thread again. Jansen's team had momentum on their side. They went into the Cup Final having lost four league games to Hibs, Dunfermline, Rangers and Motherwell. After overwhelming Dundee United, they would lose only two more league games in the race for their first championship in a decade.

Disturbingly, though, they were involved in seven draws - and the loss of fourteen points - in those twenty-two matches. And the first of those deadlocks came six days after the League Cup celebrations in a goalless encounter against Kilmarnock at Rugby Park. Jansen explained, 'After the elation of the Cup win over Dundee United, I was a bit wary. I was disappointed we could not carry it on. Today there was no sharpness and I was concerned about our lack of creativity.'

With four games to go before the arrival of 1998, Jansen ordered his players to maintain their focus. Darren Jackson, in his first full game since August following his return from brain surgery, celebrated with the vital second goal in a 2-0 win over Aberdeen at Pittodrie. He pounced on a slip by former Hibs team-mate Jim Leighton when the Dons keeper spilled an effort from Regi Blinker in the seventy-third minute. He had every right to be ecstatic at the finish. 'That goal was the old Darren Jackson,' he said. Henrik Larsson had knocked in the opener just before the break for his fourteenth strike of the season. Jansen, as ever, was good for an unusual sound bite. 'I like it when everybody plays well because, although it's harder for me to decide who should play in the team, it makes the actual game easier.'

After months of speculation, Harald Brattbakk made his first appearance as a Celtic player at Parkhead on December 13 in front of a frenzied crowd of 50,035 against Hearts, who were leading the league at the time. Brattbakk sealed his £2.2million move after his Norwegian club, Rosenborg, had their interest in the Champions League extinguished. With his trademark candour, Jansen admitted he had never seen the striker play. Davie Hay admitted, 'I watched Brattbakk a couple of times and I must have caught him on good days. He was a bit different from what we had and I reckoned he would be a good addition to the squad. We thought about Leeds United's Tony Yeboah around this time, too. He was the scorer of spectacular goals and two, in particular - against Liverpool and Wimbledon - still pop up on TV today. In the end, though, we opted for Brattbakk.'

The Norwegian came on just after an hour for Regi Blinker with the game against the Edinburgh outfit still scoreless. However, with ten minutes left, Larsson, thrusting and exploring as ever, turned centre-half Alan McManus twice before crossing to Craig Burley. The midfielder chested the ball down, took aim and drilled a low drive under Gilles Rousset for the game's only goal.

Jansen revealed that Larsson had played through the pain barrier to go out for the second-half. He said, 'Henrik did very well to get that cross in for the goal because he was playing with the hint of a pulled muscle. I said to him at half-time we should wait and see how it progressed. He wanted to stay on and he played his part. It was a psychological lift for us, but we know we have to keep on winning every game.'

There was still no sign of the much-vaunted Brattbakk in the starting line-up for the visit of Hibs in the next game although he did come on as a sixty-sixth minute substitute for Wieghorst with Celtic already four goals ahead as they cruised to a 5-0 success against the team who had inflicted defeat upon Larsson on his debut at the start of the term. Craig Burley (2), Wieghorst, McNamamra and Larsson shared the goals.

Four days before the turn of the year, Larsson's worth to the team was highlighted. Injury had caught up with the inspirational Swede and Jansen was forced to leave him on the sidelines for the trip to Perth. It was a dire display and a seventy-second minute goal from George O'Boyle settled the argument. Jansen lamented, 'St.Johnstone were aggressive and we knew we would have to match and get on top of that, but we simply didn't do it. You can't score goals when you don't make chances.'

Rangers, four points ahead in the league, were due to bring in the new year on January 2 at Celtic Park. The occasion manifested into a monumental meeting of the Glasgow giants and, for Celtic, a genuine turning point in a delicately-balanced campaign. There was a genuine dread of losing and drifting seven points behind Rangers - Wim Jansen admitted to the fact afterwards - and Celtic's last league win against the Ibrox side had been as far back as May 1995. They hadn't celebrated success in the NewYear fixture since 1988 when Billy McNeill delivered the Centenary Double. Three managers since then - Liam Brady, Lou Macari and Tommy Burns - had tried and failed. Wim Jansen had no intention of attaching his name to the collection of catastrophe.

In his meticulous manner, he studied tapes of the previous two Old Firm games of the season. Before the kick-off on this occasion, he was convinced he knew how Walter Smith would set out his team. He was an acknowledged admirer of his fellow-Dutchman Regi Blinker - some fans believed he had blinkers as far as Blinker was concerned - but he had no qualms about ditching the winger and giving Harald Brattbakk his first start. Brian Laudrup had largely enjoyed uninterrupted forays against the team from the east end of Glasgow, but Jansen ordered Enrico Annoni to shadow him everywhere. It was a remit that was accepted with relish by the Italian tough guy.

The Celtic players who raced down the tunnel that typically chilly and frosty afternoon had no doubt what was required on this occasion. There was a grim determination about the men hand-picked for the challenge by their Head Coach. Defeat was not an option. The two best chances of the first-half fell to Brattbakk, bought to score goals, but who had yet to register after three appearances. Morten Wieghorst found him in space in the penalty box, but he rushed his shot and it cannoned off the relieved Andy Goram. And the Rangers keeper was thanking his lucky stars shortly afterwards when the Norwegian staged an action replay with another effort that lacked conviction and accuracy.

In the dressing room at half-time, Jansen reminded his players he was not interested in a draw that would keep Rangers four points ahead. He insisted Celtic could finish them off within the next forty-five minutes. Frustratingly, another opportunity came Brattbakk's way and, once again, his finishing effort was too close to the outrushing Goram. The ball rebounded to Jackie McNamara who found Henrik Larsson at the far post, but his first-time volley flicked off Alex Clelland, guarding the line, onto the woodwork and away to safety. On this day, though, Celtic would not be denied. In the sixty-sixth minute, they made the breakthrough with a delightful goal.

Paul Lambert nudged a pass in front of McNamara who took a touch before sliding an impeccable reverse ball into the path of Craig Burley, unmarked inside the area. The midfielder left Goram stretching full-length to his right, but there was no stopping the well-drilled drive as the ball whipped low into the net at the far corner. Celtic Park erupted. The obvious joy of the players matched that of the fans in the stands. Jansen was right and their opponents, without the luxury of their favourite out-ball towards the shackled Laudrup, were rocking and lacking alternatives. One observer made the point, 'Rangers were playing as though stricken by fear.'

For fifteen minutes or so, the midfield trio of Lambert, Burley and Wieghorst ran riot against leaden-footed rivals. Jansen urged his team to keep taking the game to Rangers; the match was now being played almost exclusively in the visitors' half. The goal that sealed a memorable and long-overdue 2-0 triumph came with only four minutes to go. It was a thing of beauty, too. Darren Jackson, who had just replaced Brattbakk, swivelled on the edge of the area to thump a vicious right-foot drive that was superbly punched away by Goram, leaping to his right. The inevitable was merely delayed a few seconds. The ball was knocked back into the packed penalty area, Gough couldn't get distance in his attempted headed clearance and Ian Ferguson's hasty swipe simply set it up for Lambert, about thirty yards from goal.

The midfielder battered the ball with an almighty whack and it is was a blur as it zoomed high into the net. The Rangers keeper threw himself to his left, but an army of Andy Gorams would have surrendered to that unstoppable effort. The raging drive just about tore a hole in the rigging as the Celtic fans rose once again in unison. The title race was back on.

Burley, who, quite rightly, won the Man of the Match award, revealed afterwards that some stern words from Jansen after the 1-0 defeat from St Johnstone stirred the team to greater lengths. He said, 'After last weekend's game, we did have a bit of a ding-dong in the dressing room. During the week, there were also a few harsh things said. We knew exactly what we had to do in this one. Wim is one of the quietest men I have ever worked with. Very rarely do you see him shouting, but last week he was as angry as I have ever seen him. Everybody got it off their chest. There would have been no excuses for failure this week.'

Jansen admitted, 'We know the system they like to play, so we wanted to play pretty much the same way with an extra man up front. I'm delighted with the way we played, especially in the second-half when we put them under pressure from the first minute. I feel the way we played today can give us confidence. I reckon we played better as the match progressed and dominated after the break. After a shaky first twenty minutes we just got better and better and increased the pressure on them as time went on and scored two excellent goals. We passed the ball to feet at all times and defended very well. And we stayed firm when they attempted to get back into it.'

Ominously, the Dutchman conceded, 'It was such an important game for us because I think if we had gone seven points behind, it would have been too far away.'

Eight days later at Fir Park, Darren Jackson was wasteful with a late penalty-kick and Celtic had to be content with a 1-1 draw against Motherwell. If Wim Jansen's men were going to win the club's first title in a decade, they seemed dedicated to achieving the feat the hard way. They forced fourteen corner-kicks - ten in the first-half alone - and didn't make a dent on the home side's rearguard. Motherwell won four in ninety minutes - and scored their goal from one of them. Former Celtic striker Willie Falconer found a pocket of freedom in front of Jonathan Gould and couldn't miss with a powerful header ten minutes after the turnaround. Paul Lambert equalised six minutes later with a pulverising drive that bettered his effort against Rangers. This time the midfielder was thirty-five yards out when he decided to have a blast and the ball hurtled into the net. Jackson had the opportunity to seal the comeback five minutes from the end, but weakly sent his spot-kick wide of the target.

Wim Jansen was far from satisfied. 'This is a bad habit we will have to get rid of. We play well in one game and then fail in the next. However, I know we have it in us to win these kind of games.'

Celtic were asked another question in the next league game when they travelled to Tannadice for an evening meeting with Dundee United on January 27. They were in trouble as they trailed 1-0 at half-time with Kjell Olafsson on target for the Taysiders. However, things turned after the interval and two goals in the last thirteen minutes sent the points Glasgow-bound. Simon Donnelly, on as a substitute for Jackie McNamara, levelled in the seventy-seventh minute and Craig Burley lashed in the winner with three minutes still to play. The win enabled Celtic to leapfrog Hearts into second place, three points behind Rangers. Wim Jansen said, 'My players showed a winning mentality and that's what we needed.'

There were leaks in the press that all was not well behind the scenes at Parkhead as Celtic awaited the visit of Aberdeen on February 2. Reports insisted there was friction between Jansen and General Manager Jock Brown and there can be no argument the Dutchman was very unhappy at the abrupt dismissal of Davie Hay, a professional he trusted and admired. There had also been talk of bust-ups between Hay and Brown and the former manager admitted, 'Let me admit right away there were faults on both sides. As time progressed, I thought Jock was veering away from the actual football side of his role and becoming more involved in the finances.

'I tried to get it across to him that the supporters were more interested in watching a good football team than pouring over a balance sheet. I said so forcibly at times. I also realised Wim and Jock didn't gel and a division was becoming obvious. In addition, I thought I deserve an enhanced contract from the club, but I never got any support from Jock. Something had to give. It came to a head and Fergus had to make a choice. Once more, I found I was expendable.'

Away from the off-the-field bickering, David Rowson gave the Dons a shock eighth minute advantage, but, after Alan Stubbs and Jackie McNamara had hit woodwork, Morten Wieghorst equalised in the twenty-first minute, Henrik Larsson netted the second before the break and Darren Jackson settled the outcome with five minutes remaining. They were now level at the top, a shade behind on goal difference. The Head Coach was content to say, 'We deserved to win.'

However, there was a scowl back on the face of Jansen six days later and no-one could blame him for his black mood. Celtic had outplayed Hearts at Tynecastle and were leading with a Jackie McNamara goal just before half-time. The confrontation was deep in injury time when Jose Quitongo emerged in the penalty area to force a leveller beyond Jonathan Gould. It was daylight robbery. Jansen said, 'I am angered we did not finish it off. The game went on a few seconds too long for my liking. If we had scored a second goal the game would have been over.'

The Celtic support had now watched Harald Brattbakk on eight occasions and were still awaiting to cheer his first goal. Off the pitch, the Norwegian wore black-rimmed spectacles and grey suits. He also sported a 'sensible' hairstyle. A fair percentage of fans thought he resembled an accountant. Unfortunately, they were beginning to get the notion he played like an accountant, too. That was until the meeting with Kilmarnock in Glasgow on February 21 when the home side triumphed 4-0 and Brattbakk helped himself to all four goals. Jansen said, 'If you score four goals, you have had a pretty good game. It was important for him to score and he did well. He was always in the right place and was unlucky not to score more than he did.'

Four days later, Brattbakk continued the transformation from pen-pushing accountant to penalty-box assassin with two goals in the 5-1 victory over Dunfermline at Parkhead. Henrik Larsson, Phil O'Donnell and Morten Wieghorst added the others while Andy Tod collected a consolation for the Fifers. Celtic were now the Premier League pacesetters and Jansen said, 'It's nice to be on top, but staying there is more difficult and there are a lot of games still to go. But we will do everything we can to keep going. So far the players have handled the pressure well.'

A Marc Rieper goal in the twenty-fifth minute was enough to separate Celtic from Hibs at Easter Road in the next game. Jim Duffy, the architect of Jansen's debut nightmare, had been sacked and replaced by

Alex McLeish as the Edinburgh outfit teetered on the verge of relegation. On the same evening, Rangers and Hearts dropped points in a 2-2 draw in Glasgow. The Dutchman observed, 'We used to lose this kind of game. Now we don't. It's in our hands now and it's going to be very hard, but we mustn't look to others. It's up to us to finish the job.'

A goal fifteen minutes from time by Dundee United dangerman Kjell Olofsson handed the visitors a 1-1 draw at Parkhead on March 15. Simon Donnelly had scored in the twenty-seventh minute, but again the club couldn't apply the killer touch. 'The result was very disappointing and we missed so many chances,' said Jansen. 'I didn't think our second-half had anything to do with tension. Sometimes these things happen.' Celtic were two points ahead of the lurking Hearts and four ahead of Rangers, but still seemed hell bent on seeking out banana skins on their way to the championship.

Jansen replaced flair with fire and favoured power over poise for the March 21 trip to take on an Aberdeen side that hadn't beaten Celtic since 1995. He had told his players this would be an occasion to grind out a result and so it proved when Craig Burley scored the only goal with a penalty-kick on the stroke of half-time after Stephane Mahe had been clattered by David Rowson. Jansen may have forsaken some of his beliefs to achieve the victory, but he was satisfied at full-time. 'Every game is now like a Cup Final for us and this was no different. We knew before the game we would have to battle for the points and we did that very well. At 1-0 ahead, we remained compact to protect our lead.'

Before the Hearts game at Parkhead on March 28, Wim Jansen was annoyed to discover another boardroom leak had found its way into the national newspapers. Although he had signed a three-year deal in the summer, there were reports insisting he had a get-out clause after twelve months. Whether or not the timing was deliberate in an attempt to derail Celtic, it was an irritation for the Head Coach who insisted he wanted solely to concentrate on his team. A crowd of 50,038 watched a goalless encounter against the Tynecastle side and Jansen, while batting away queries about his contract, said, 'Our passing game was missing, but I can't complain about the input from the players. They gave everything, but we have to accept there were tired legs out there. Maybe a draw was a fair result.'

Jansen still faced fierce interrogation from the media eager to discover about the release clause in his contract. Fergus McCann, Jock Brown and the Head Coach got together to put out a statement that all contractual talk would be put on hold until the end of the season. The Dutchman was allowed to focus on the April 8 trip to face Kilmarnock at Rugby Park, a ground where Celtic had claimed a mere two wins in eight previous visits. Thankfully, they made it three out of nine when strikes from Henrik Larsson - his first goal since February 21 - and Simon Donnelly in either half gave them a 2-1 win on a treacherous, rain-sodden pitch. The conditions made it practically impossible for the team to indulge in their rhythmic fluency and passing combinations, but, despite the equalising goal from Alex Burke before the interval, they did enough to remain three points ahead of Rangers.

Jansen said, 'The problem has not been with the way the team has played, but only in their final touch around goal. As for the tiredness, that comes from chasing goals. There are times when you have to be patient, to allow goals to come, rather than using up too much power and energy going after them. It's when players are on top and the goals don't come that they press harder. The longer it takes to score, the more energy you use looking for that goal. If you look at Henrik Larsson and Harald Brattbakk, there's not much wrong with their general form - they are just having problems with that last touch around the goalmouth. That is something you can practice all day, but in the competitive environment, it's a different thing entirely. When players do not score early then they can lose patience. We cannot afford to do that in any of the games we have left. Overall, though, I was very happy with the result.'

Smiles were not in abundance, though, in the next game against Rangers at Ibrox on April 12. Celtic fell into Walter Smith's time-honoured trap, enjoyed most of the play and were hit twice by sucker-punches as they collapsed to a dismal 2-0 defeat. A crowd of 50,042 watched the home side take the lead in the twenty-fourth minute when a header from

Marc Rieper fell straight to the unmarked Jonas Thern about twenty-five yards out and the Swede smacked an unsaveable effort high over Jonathan Gould's right shoulder. One newspaper reporter noted, 'The most shocking aspect of Thern's goal was that it should arrive at a time when Celtic were so clearly in control of the game that it was difficult to imagine how Rangers could make any impact.'

Celtic, with Harald Brattbakk replacing the limping Darren Jackson in the first-half, bombarded Andy Goram's goal in search of the equaliser. Their best opportunity arrived early in the second-half when Paul Lambert tricked and teased his way into the box, skillfully manoeuvred his way past Lorenzo Amouso and, with just the keeper to beat, swept the ball yards wide of the upright. It was a terrible miss and it cost Jansen's men dearly when Jorg Albertz scored a second in the sixty-sixth minute courtesy of some kamikaze defending, particularly from Alan Stubbs. The German midfielder was allowed to pick up the ball on the halfway line and head in the general direction of Gould. Craig Burley slipped as he raced to catch up and, suddenly, Albertz was left with only Stubbs as an immediate opponent. Unbelievably, the defender allowed the Rangers player to shift the ball to his favoured left foot about twenty yards out and he crashed a low shot past Gould at his left hand post. It was a remarkably naive piece of defending from the Englishman.

Wim Jansen, clearly disappointed, would merely say at the end, 'We know that we now need to win the remaining four games if we are to win the league. We also have to remember it could go to goal difference, so we will have to score a lot of goals. Every game coming up is nothing short of a Cup Final.'

Brattbakk, who wore the cloak of anonymity after replacing Jackson at Ibrox, was ditched from the squad for the next game, a home encounter against Motherwell. Celtic, in their customary fashion, gifted Steve McMillan an opening for a twelfth-minute strike for the visitors before coming back to win 4-1 through two goals apiece from Craig Burley and Simon Donnelly. Jansen was asked about the non-appearance of Brattbakk and, unusually for the normally laidback Dutchman, he snapped back, 'It was my decision to drop him and I don't need to explain it. Harald is a professional and he understands the situation.' On his thoughts on the title, he responded, 'I am not a betting man and I only believe in reality and not the dream. But even after the Rangers result, we were still confident. It is more important the players are confident of winning the league than me.'

Celtic were stumbling rather than strutting with the finishing line in view. That was illustrated again in a goalless draw against Hibs at Parkhead where 50,034 fans - with ex-boss Liam Brady making a fleeting visit to Glasgow in the stand to lend his support - expected three points to be posted against a team that was heading assuredly for relegation. It was a tension-laden afternoon and it spilled off the pitch onto the touchline where Jansen's assistant Murdo MacLeod and Hibs manager Alex McLeish, former Scotland international team-mates, got involved in a squabble and were sent to the stand by referee George Simpson.

Jansen, after hearing Rangers had won at Hearts to cut their lead at the top to a solitary point, said, 'You could see from the first minute we were not as sharp as usual. Some of our players once again looked a little tired. However, we do remain in the lead and we know that, in this moment, we have to win our last two games to win the league.'

It wasn't just Celtic who were experiencing the pressure and unease of a long title crusade. Rangers, too, were beginning to wilt and, incredibly, dropped three points in their second last game against Kilmarnock at Ibrox on Saturday May 2. Ally Mitchell netted, incredibly in the ninth minute of injury time, in Glasgow to secure a shock 1-0 victory for the Ayrshire men. This left the stage clear for Wim Jansen's men to win their first title in a decade against Dunfermline at East End Park twenty-four hours later.

Agonisingly, Celtic were seven minutes away from Premier League glory when they had the championship prised from their hopeful grasp. It was a fraught, anxious and suspenseful afternoon in Fife, but everything looked as though it was going according to plan when Henrik Larsson slipped a pass into the tracks of Simon Donnelly in the thirty-fifth minute and the underrated, boyish-looking forward finished in clinical style with a low drive wide of Ian Westwater. Larsson was creating mayhem in the Dunfermline ranks any time he got on the ball and he flashed an effort off the woodwork as the Parkhead side dominated proceedings. Edginess was never far away, though, as Celtic sought a second goal to soothe the nerves.

Larsson was flattened by a crude assault by Craig Ireland in the seventy-first minute and it seemed certain referee John Underhill would point to the penalty spot. Instead, he waved play on and Jansen, not an individual who overly indulged in touchline histrionics, was clearly furious with the decision. In the eighty-third minute, Craig Faulconbridge, a striker on loan from Coventry City, managed to get his head to a swirling cross to send it goalwards. Jonathan Gould was helpless as the ball was guided by an unseen hand into the top corner of the net. Apart from the odd cheer from the home fans in attendance, the 12,866 supporters fell silent. Tommy Boyd and Marc Rieper had a heated exchange of words and Gould had to intervene before the situation escalated.

The title had been within touching distance and once more it remained just out of reach. Even then Celtic could have won it in the few remaining minutes. Morten Wieghorst beat Westwater with a cunning attempt and, as the Celtic fans held their collective breath, Scott McCulloch materialised on the goal-line to block the shot and hack it out of play.

Jansen rarely got involved in concerning himself with decisions from match officials, but he couldn't hold back afterwards. 'It looked like a penalty-kick, but the referee didn't give it. You cannot be angry after the game because you cannot turn back time, but it WAS a penalty-kick. We were seven minutes away from winning the title when they scored from nothing. Now we have to pick ourselves up for the last game of the season against St Johnstone next Saturday.'

History would have to wait another week.

CHAPTER FOURTEEN
THE TRIUMPHANT FAREWELL

It began with jitters and ended in jubilation. Ten years of misery, a decade of anguish, an interminable period of suffering in football's version of Purgatory came to a shuddering halt at Celtic Park on Saturday May 9 1998. Wim Jansen had succeeded where the three previous inhabitants of the Parkhead hot seat had proved to be deficient; the Premier league championship would be welcomed back to Paradise for the first time since 1988.

The last day of the season was heading for a nerve-shredding, angst-ridden crescendo and the position was clear - if Celtic, already two points ahead, beat St Johnstone by any margin they would be crowned champions of Scotland. Rangers, who kicked off the campaign with the promise of a world record ten titles in a row, were due to play Dundee United at Tannadice and the outcome would be rendered irrelevant if Jansen's team avoided any horrors against the men from Perth.

Tension smothered the east end of Glasgow where a capacity 50,500 crowd sang a booming version of 'You'll Never Walk Alone', bouncing around the stadium and beyond, long before the kick-off. Even Celtic's King of Cool Henrik Larsson admitted to being 'a little bit nervous' as he waited in the tunnel before racing onto the pitch to a tumultuous welcome.

Inside three minutes, the Swede had presented Celtic with the start they could only have dreamed of on this most crucial of afternoons. A misdirected kick-out from Saints goalie Alan Main dropped to Paul Lambert on the halfway line and he wasted no time in switching the ball to the roaming Larsson on the left. Immediately, he got into his easy-going fluent stride as he took the ball towards right-back John

McQuillan. Larsson shaped to go wide and hit the bye-line, but changed direction to glide inside. The defenders backed off and the graceful frontman took a few touches before he was satisfied there was an opening. Without pausing, Larsson curled a spectacular effort with immaculate precision from twenty-five yards and the ball arced and plunged past the diving Main as it swept in at the keeper's left-hand post. Celtic Park erupted.

The goal should have eased the apprehension in the electrifying atmosphere with so much at stake, but there were still obvious signs among the players the threat of a mistake was an intolerable burden. Celtic still took the game to Saints, though, as Jansen urged them to go forward. Too often he had seen his side dominate and get precious little for their endeavours by not killing off the opposition. Larsson came within a whisker of providing the safety net of a second goal as he again cut in from the left to leave Main stranded with a deft flick. Unfortunately, the ball drifted just over.

There was a fright, too, for Celtic when the Saints made a rare raid up the right wing. McQuillan joined his forwards to hit a swirling cross from the touchline that brought alarm to the home defence when Jonathan Gould, normally so compose and reliable, misjudged the flight of the ball and George O'Boyle, completely unmarked eight yards out, headed over the crossbar. It was a heartstopping moment as the Celtic defenders looked guiltily at each other. The incident served to remind them of the fickleness of the situation. News filtered through that Rangers had taken the lead on Tayside through Laudrup and that added to jangling nerve-ends of the players on the pitch and the supporters in the stands, both united in anxiety.

On the hour mark, with Rangers now 2-0 ahead following an Albertz penalty-kick, Jansen took the courageous decision to remove the industrious Phil O'Donnell and throw on Harald Brattbakk in an ambitious move designed to help the side in the pursuit of a second goal. The Norwegian was undoubtedly a curiosity whose style mystified the fans and probably his Head Coach, too. He had the ability to seek out good positions in even the most crowded of penalty boxes, but his finishing touch was often lacking. Before the Saints match, statistics showed he had scored in only two league games out of seventeen appearances - the four goals against Kilmarnock and the double against Dunfermline. Jansen, by his own admission, was not a betting man, but he was willing to gamble big-style on this occasion.

Twelve minutes after his throw of the dice, Brattbakk scored to push Celtic towards the thirty-sixth title triumph in their history. And the £2.2million man tucked the ball away with the accomplished artistry of a performer who gave the impression he rarely missed. Tommy Boyd got the ball rolling by picking up a stray pass deep in his half before launching on an adventurous thrust down the right wing. He played the ball in front of Jackie McNamara who maintained the pace of the move as he sped away from Allan Preston. Brattbakk's timing in entering the danger zone was excellent as was McNamara's low ball across. The puzzling striker didn't have to break stride as he met the ball sweetly with his right foot and his effort zipped low past Main. There were still eighteen minutes to play, but there was no way Celtic were going to fail to win the glittering prize that had eluded them for what felt like an eternity among the support.

Skipper Boyd was shaping to take a free-kick wide on the right when referee Kenny Clark stepped forward, picked up the ball while simultaneously blowing for full-time. The defender turned towards the fans, yelled and raised his arms in salute. The wait was over. The title was coming home to Paradise. Larsson, who scored nineteen goals in his debut season in Scotland, couldn't stop grinning when the TV interviewer grabbed him just minutes after the final whistle. Swiftly, he paid tribute to Wim Jansen. 'He is the main reason we have won the Championship. He has built a tremendous side and we'll be even better next season,' smiled Larsson as he waved his arm towards the celebrating supporters. 'Look at those fans - magnificent! I love it...I love it.' He calmed down sufficiently to add, 'I reckon that was my most important goal and, to be honest, I think we deserved today's success and to win the title.'

Of course, there was the little matter of the so-called get-out clause in Jansen's contract. Live on air, the Dutchman was asked to clarify the situation. Clearly, he had no intention of doing so although he did admit the decision had already been made and only his wife was aware of his intentions. He said, 'I have made up my mind what I will be doing next season, but I will not be explaining it here. I will talk to Fergus McCann. This game has not affected the way I've been thinking about my future. But it's not important to talk about that today.'

After exhausting 'You'll Never Walk Alone' and the 'Celtic Song', the fans then exercised their tonsils with an energetic rendition of 'Cheerio To Ten-In-A-Row'. As the Celtic supporters celebrated well into the night there was one nagging doubt, 'Would Wim Jansen be in charge for the new season?' The man who could have walked the length of Sauchiehall Street and not be recognised by anyone a year earlier had been taken to the hearts of the fans.

Not only had he delivered the Premier League title and the League Cup, but he came within 90 minutes of leading Celtic to a place in the Scottish Cup Final. That march faltered, unfortunately against Rangers on another occasion where Jansen's team enjoyed much of the possession, had the bulk of the pressure - and lost two goals to breakaways. It was a deja vu x-certificate tale for the Celtic players and fans. Particularly, as the breakthrough goal in the seventy-fifth minute was claimed by old adversary Ally McCoist who had only regained first team recognition after Marco Negri had been sidelined following an accident while playing squash with team-mate Sergio Porrini when he was struck on an eye with a ball. McCoist, like manager Walter Smith and a handful of his team-mates including Brian Laudrup, Andy Goram, Richard Gough and Stuart McCall, realised the end was nigh at Ibrox. The story had already leaked that Dutchman Dick Advocaat would be the new Rangers manager once his contract at PSV Eindhoven expired in the summer. And that would signal the last curtain call for McCoist and Co.

But there was still time for one last hurrah at Celtic's expense on April 5 in the Scottish Cup semi-final, which was played at Parkhead after a ballot. Hampden was still undergoing its much-needed refurb and the semi-final would be played at either Celtic Park or Ibrox. Celtic won the draw and were allowed 26,000 tickets with their opponents receiving 22,000. That was the only piece of good fortune to come the way of Wim Jansen's side regarding another tense Old Firm encounter. Celtic controlled the opening forty-five minutes and Goram twice denied Larsson. However, the home team appeared to run out of steam after the hour mark with Paul Lambert, in particular, struggling. The midfielder, who had been dominant at the start, had been battling a flu virus right up to kick-off, but reassured his manager he was prepared for the challenge ahead.

However, with fifteen minutes to go, Celtic's defence simply fell asleep when a cross came in from Albertz on the left. McCoist was only two yards out and unmarked as he stooped to head past the startled Jonathan Gould. Five minutes later, the German, who had been switched to left-back as an emergency defender, made certain there would be no comeback. Extraordinarily, he picked up the ball in his own half and was allowed to carry it forward without a worthwhile challenge being offered. Unhindered, Albertz simply kept rolling forward until, unforgiveably, he was allowed to bring the ball to his left foot and he struck a low drive away from Gould from the edge of the box. Craig Burley netted in the last minute, but Celtic, once again, paid a heavy price for their errors in this fixture.

Jansen said, 'We played well in the first-half, but, of course, didn't score a goal. As soon as they scored, it was not easy for us. And, yes, we know the quality of McCoist - there was one split-second and he scored. It was our final touch that let us down. People might think this defeat increases the pressure on us, but I don't think so. We are out of the Cup and must concentrate on the league.'

Harald Brattbakk, who had struggled to make an impact in the championship, netted in the three Cup-ties leading up to the semi-final. The Norwegian got the opener in the 2-0 home victory over Morton in January, hit the winner in the 2-1 triumph over Dunfermline at East End Park a month later and claimed another vital strike in the 3-2 success over Dundee United at Tannadice in the quarter-final. However, his goal touch deserted him against Rangers and he was withdrawn in the seventy-first minute with Darren Jackson entering the fray.

In the recent past, a defeat in the semi-final of the national competition would have been accepted as a disaster by the Celtic community. All too often, the league was blown before January or February was out to leave the Scottish Cup as the only realistic hope of silverware. On this occasion, though, there was no mass weeping or wailing. This time around, Celtic's eyes were on the bigger prize.

With the championship safely delivered, Celtic were due to play Sporting Lisbon two days later in a friendly in the Portuguese capital as part of the original Jorge Cadete transfer contract. Ironically, it was at the luxurious Hotel Palacio - the same HQ utilised by the team during their 1967 European Cup Final triumph - that Jansen broke the news he would be leaving the club. It was clear he had been unhappy for some considerable time and there were leaked tales of constant friction between the Head Coach and General Manager Jock Brown. Jansen was frustrated, among other things, with Brown's refusal to set a limit on transfer funds that could be made available for the new season.

He was told he would have to identify the players first before Brown decided if Celtic could afford the targets. In frustration, Jansen named three Manchester United players - Ryan Giggs among them - he wouldn't mind seeing in Celtic's colours.

So, no-one was unduly surprised at the Dutchman's decision to walk, but he did raise a few eyebrows when he revealed he had contemplated quitting Celtic after only a fortnight in the job. He admitted, 'My relationship with Jock Brown was bad from the beginning to the end. I cannot work with him and our relationship was getting worse and worse. There was no base to work with. This is the reason I am going because the important thing is you have to work together. How can I plan for next season when I don't know if I have £1million or £20million to spend on players?'

While the Celtic support was digesting this information, Fergus McCann retorted in kind that he was going to sack Jansen in any case. The Managing Director said, 'You can't have one man saying, "I am Celtic Football Club." This is a team effort and everyone is part of it. The league title was not won in one year and by one man.'

Jansen fulfilled his contractual agreement and was in the dug-out at the Jose de Alvalade stadium to witness the team losing 2-1 to Sporting Lisbon in a non-event encounter. Afterwards, he said, 'The players were a joy to work with and I will miss these boys because they were such a good group. I will go back to Parkhead, stay in Scotland for a couple of days and then I will go home to Holland. Going back to Parkhead will not be a problem. Parkhead did not do it.' The Dutchman sighed and added, 'It will not be necessary for me to speak to Jock Brown after this.'

Celtic had gone from triumph to turmoil in the space of forty-eight hours. It was time now to look for their third manager in three years.

CHAPTER FIFTEEN
JOE VENGLOS: CZECH MATE

Fergus McCann fully expected to unveil Gerard Houllier as the new Celtic Head Coach in time for the kick-off to the 1998/99 season. The Frenchman, who had been out of club football since leaving the manager's job at Paris Saint Germain in 1988, had been contacted by Jock Brown while working as a technical director with the French World Cup-winning team during that eventful summer.

The Celtic General Manager was convinced Houllier would accept the post to become Wim Jansen's successor. As far as the deal was concerned, Brown believed, it was just a question of when - and not if - everything would be signed, sealed and delivered. Alas, football, as an occupation, rarely conforms to the basics which are the norm elsewhere.

There appeared to be every indication from Houllier that he would accept the invite to move to Scotland to take over the team with worldwide appeal that had just been crowned the champions of their country. He told friends that summer, 'I have two options for my future. I can stay with the French Football Federation or I can become manager of Celtic. The offers are on the table.'

Liverpool, though, were alerted to the situation. The Merseyside outfit weren't entirely satisfied with the efforts of Roy Evans. They were loathe to sack a committed club servant and someone in the boardroom hatched the plan to have joint managers in place for the upcoming campaign. Hindsight was not a required commodity to realise that such a two-man structure would be a completely unworkable situation. Who would buy the players? Who would pick the team? Who would set out the tactics? And so on.

Coincidentally, Houllier, who never played football at top professional level, had spent a year in Liverpool in 1969/70 as part of his degree as he trained to become a schoolteacher. He became an assistant at Alsop's Comprehensive School and was a regular visitor to Anfield. He returned to France to become Deputy Headmaster of the Ecole Normale d'Arras until the age of twenty-six when he began his full-time managerial career at Le Toquet in 1973. Nine years later he was in charge of Paris Saint Germain. Celtic were favourites to entice him back to club football - until Liverpool made their move in July. Houllier was left in sole charge of team matters when Evans 'resigned' in November.

Fergus McCann and Jock Brown would have to think again. Very quickly. The Champions League first round qualifier against St Patrick's Athletic was due in Glasgow on July 22 and, a mere week before the tie, Celtic were without a Head Coach. Eric Black, in his role as assistant, had been taking care of first team matters, but he was never considered for the post on a permanent basis. Murdo MacLeod, Wim Jansen's No.2, had also parted company with the club during the end-of-season upheaval.

There was some frantic, feverish behind-the-scenes activity before July 17 - five days away from the visit of the Irish part-timers to Parkhead - when Celtic announced Dr Jozef Venglos as Jansen's replacement. The Czech was sixty-two years old and had come on Celtic's radar due to his participation during the World Cup Finals in France as a member of the FIFA technical committee. He was sounded out by Brown. Venglos admitted, 'We spoke about the possibility to go to Celtic. I didn't know the full situation at the club, but the chance to be manager was very nice. It would be a demanding job and an honour for any coach. I told him I would think about it. Then we spoke once more and I said it would be a privilege to come. We had another meeting in Vienna and then one in Amsterdam.'

Fergus McCann offered Venglos a one-year contract. It was hardly a ringing endorsement in the faith placed in the new Head Coach by the Managing Director, but McCann explained his five-year plan for Celtic would reach its conclusion in March 1999 and his successor could then take on future decision-making. Venglos agreed it sounded fair and logical. He signed the twelve-month contract and would take his chances. Celtic had failed to appoint a Deputy Headmaster, but had managed to lure an individual with a Doctorate in Physical Education and an expert in Psychology. Despite his footballing pedigree - most notably managing Czechoslovakia for four years from 1978 to 1982 and then again for one season 1989/90 - not a lot was known about the good doctor. Typically, most tabloid newspapers ran with the banner headline, 'DOCTOR WHO?'.

He had been manager of Aston Villa for one campaign in 1990/91, taking over from England-bound Graham Taylor who had led the Midlands club to runners-up spot in league. One of the first things Venglos attempted to do at Villa was change the dietary habits of his players. One of them complained, 'Steak and chips before a game went out the window.' Remember, this was twenty-four years before Ronny Deila implemented such guidelines at Celtic's Lennoxtown Training Centre. The fans, though, were only interested in results and not the eating habits of their stars and when the club limped into seventeenth place at the end of a decidedly dodgy season, Villa chairman Doug Ellis, known as 'Deadly Doug' when it came to dispensing with managers in quickfire fashion, sacked the Czech.

Now, though, Venglos was back in the UK and this time at Celtic. He had little time to be introduced to his players before he had to select a team to face St Patrick's Athletic on the evening of July 22. By a remarkable coincidence, he had already featured in the dug-out in a European encounter at the home of his new club. It wasn't a particularly happy occasion for the Czech as Celtic, managed by Davie Hay, hammered Venglos' Sporting Lisbon 5-0 in a UEFA Cup-tie in November 1983. As he took his seat alongside Eric Black, he must have hoped lightning wouldn't strike twice.

A crowd of 56,864 turned out to witness their favourites' return to Europe's top tournament after a ten-year absence. The new stadium had been completed during the summer. I was there, too, and couldn't have asked for a better view of Venglos' debut. I was invited to the Celtic

Directors' Box and found it quite absorbing, mainly for events off the field. Given the full VIP treatment before, during and after the tie, I got the distinct impression the Parkhead hierarchy didn't really know quite what to expect from their managerial appointment. The fans left the ground that evening fairly mystified, as well. The game, played in a downpour, ended goalless and had the feel of a pre-season friendly. Afterwards, Venglos said, 'There have been better results, but, then, you have games like that. We have to now prepare ourselves for a different game next week. I have not changed my opinion about my players and I have total confidence in them.'

Seven days later in Dublin, Harald Brattbakk, who had been substituted at half-time in Glasgow, scored in twelve minutes and Henrik Larsson, who had been unusually subdued, hit the second eighteen minutes from time. Celtic were now 180 minutes away from being involved in the cash-rich Champions League group stages with Croatia Zagreb barring their progress. Venglos said, 'The timing of the first goal was very important. Harald had a chance like that at Celtic Park and failed to score. Tonight was different. Harald got his goal and I'm sure he will score more. Overall, I felt it was a good, disciplined performance.'

A row over the size of the bonuses for European success had been bubbling under since the summer. Venglos must have wondered what he had taken on with the discontentment from last season among the first team squad following on into the new campaign. The squabble sunk to pathetic depths when the players refused to get involved in extraneous functions and no-one turned up for the launch of the club's new strip. Fergus McCann was fuming at the non-appearance of his players and, instead of any bonuses, he immediately donated £50,000 to Yorkhill Hospital. The cash incentives for performing at Europe's pinnacle were no longer an issue when Celtic lost 3-1 on aggregate to Croatia Zagreb in the second qualifier. Darren Jackson got the only goal in Glasgow - where Mark Viduka played for the visitors - but they were overwhelmed 3-0 in the return a fortnight later and dropped into the UEFA Cup.

A clearly disenchanted Venglos was pinned down by the Press afterwards with the players refusing to give interviews. Questions were ignored or answered with 'No comment'. The Head Coach said, 'I am not ready to talk about the situation. I am concerned mainly with what happens on the field. I have to analyse what is going on there.' The only Celtic player who got passmarks from Venglos was goalkeeper Jonathan Gould who prevented a total embarrassment.

My good friend Alex Cameron, of the Daily Record, was the doyen of Scottish sportswriters of the era. In a typical, hard-hitting, forthright editorial, he had this to say about a potentially ruinous situation so early in the season. 'The intense suffering inflicted on the legions of loyal Celtic fans is no longer tolerable. Their view is important. They're putting money into Celtic while the rest, including the team, are taking it out. Grasping players and the mulish Fergus McCann and his board have wrecked hopes for the future. Indeed, the two sides share blame for the worst Celtic shambles in living memory.

'On and off the field, they are wielding the tools of self-destruction, knifing themselves at home in the league and away in Europe. Some of Celtic's best friends say the club has lost its soul. They certainly don't have a leader either feared or respected in the mould of Sir Robert Kelly or Desmond White. Nobody's visible at the tiller. McCann, with his Andy Capp bunnet, is too remote and has a wee guy's fondness for a verbal scrap. Along with Jock Brown, he should consider Oscar Wilde's waspish words, "Men can't be too careful when choosing their enemies."'

He added, 'Thousands of season ticket holders think they've been conned into believing the flag-winning side would be bolstered by at least one important buy. It's obvious the priority is a big, strong striker. Once upon a time, fans would have supported McCann and the championship winning team to take on the world. Now they wouldn't back them with a long start in an egg and spoon race. McCann's failure to spend some of the record ticket money on a new player before the Euro deadline was a serious blunder.

'Something must be done. There are splits in the dressing-room and among the fans as McCann lays down his cards like a poker player with an unbeatable hand. A Kissinger-style go-between is what is needed, but both sides think they're right and won't budge. Even though the bonus row was made obsolete in Croatia, it will be raised again after the UEFA Cup draw.'

While wallets at Celtic were bolted shut, Rangers went into overdrive in the transfer market in an ostentatious attempt to reclaim the Premier League championship. Dick Advocaat displayed an eagerness bordering on the berserk to write massive cheques and it was equally obvious the Rangers owner, David Murray, would indulge the every whim of the Dutchman. History shows that such frenzied transfer activity inevitably led the club to its death, but, back then, it was the promise of football riches that sustained the deluded support.

Advocaat showed the signs of things to come by paying £5million for his PSV Eindhoven left-back and captain Artur Numan. On one day, July 6, he splashed a further £9.2million on two more recruits, midfielder Giovanni van Bronckhorst, £5million from Feyenoord, and striker Gabriel Amato, £4.2million from Real Mallorca. Nine days later he broke the Scottish transfer record when Fiorentina accepted £5.5million for former Manchester United winger Andrei Kanchelskis.

Not content with the financial outlay of £19.7million on four players, Advocaat, who preferred to be known as 'The Little General', brought in goalkeeper Lionel Charbonnier at £1.2million from Auxerre. He also lured free agent Rod Wallace to Ibrox when the striker quit Leeds United on a Bosman. Before the end of the month, he had parted with another £2.2million for defender Daniel Prodan, from Atletico Madrid. That particular transfer was sheer folly. I know for a fact Rangers were warned about the injury problems that had beset the Romanian international at the Spanish club. Advocaat still charged ahead with the open chequebook and it's worth noting that Prodan did not make a single first team appearance for the Ibrox side.

Rangers lost 2-1 to Hearts at Tynecastle in their opening game of the league season on August 2 and that prompted the Dutchman, forty-eight hours later, to pay Blackburn Rovers £4million for Scotland centre-half and skipper Colin Hendry. It was a spending spree the like of which had never been seen in Scottish football. Before the end of the season, he had paid another £9.25million in bringing in striker Stephane Guivarc'h (£3.5million, Newcastle), winger Neil McCann (£2million, Hearts), midfielder Claudio Reyna (£2million, Wolfsburg), central defender Craig Moore (£1million, Crystal Palace) and goalkeeper Stefan Klos (£750,000, Borussia Dortmund). When the exhausted roulette wheel eventually spun to a halt, the new Rangers manager had spent a mindboggling £36.35million.

In stark contrast, over the same period, Jozef Venglos' cash outlay was £6.35million in buying four players - Mark Viduka (£3million, Croatia Zagreb), Lubomir Moravcik (£350,000, MSV Duisburg), Johan Mjallby (£1.5million, AIK Stockholm) and Vidar Riseth (£1.5million, LASK Linz). Pound for pound, who do you think got the better value out of his signings? The prizes may have found their way to Ibrox, but in that quartet the Czech clearly demonstrated his ability to spot a quality player.

Venglos' main problem was an obvious one; he wasn't afforded the time required to get his plans and strategies across to his players. In the opening league months of August and September, Celtic played eight games and won only two, lost two and drew four. The dithering to replace Wim Jansen would have severe consequences. And without a Head Coach to identify targets, the lack of investment in the playing squad would also back-fire. Season 1998/99 is not one that will be fondly remembered by many of the Celtic persuasion.

In the most bizarre of circumstances, the newly-won Premier League Flag was unfurled on August 1 before the first game of the campaign against Dunfermline at Parkhead. A crowd of 59,377 was in attendance as sunshine embraced the shiny new stadium. Venglos stood alongside Jock Brown while Managing Director Fergus McCann, accompanied by captain Tommy Boyd, made his way to the flag pole on the touchline. After ten insufferable years in the championship wilderness, you would have been forgiven for believing the roof would have been raised in total acclaim. You would be wrong. Wim Jansen and Murdo MacLeod had been invited along to the ground and had centre row seats in the stand. Many saw it as a cheap publicity stunt, others believed it was outright mischief-making. Either way, Jansen and MacLeod were rousingly applauded to their seats by fans eternally grateful for what they had achieved at that very ground on May 9 when the title was cemented with the 2-0 triumph over St Johnstone.

There was the curious mixture of cheering and jeering when McCann attempted to address the fans. The supporters who were applauding attempted to drown out the mutinous fans making dissenting noises and the situation developed into a sad, horrible farce. Jock Brown was also singled out for hostile chants from a section of fans and, before a ball had been kicked in anger, it looked like being a season of chaos in Paradise. Clearly, it was an embarrassment for the club and Venglos looked more than slightly perplexed by it all. Afterwards, he said, 'I think the chairman (Fergus McCann) deserves respect and support for what he has done for a great club. It is important for all the directors, supporters and players to be part of the same Celtic family.'

As for the game itself, the champions strolled to a 5-0 triumph with Craig Burley netting the first hat-trick of his career and Simon Donnelly and Malky Mackay chipping in with the others. Burley demonstrated a lack of Nostradamus qualities when he said, 'I think it's going to be more difficult overall this season, but I feel we are going along the right lines.' Celtic lost 3-2 to Aberdeen at Pittodrie in the next encounter in defence of their crown. It was their first defeat to the Dons in three years. Adding to the misery, Burley and Donnelly both missed penalty-kicks, Darren Jackson was sent off and Regi Blinker scored an own goal. The home side were already leading by three goals when Henrik Larsson collected Celtic's consolation efforts, one, remarkably, from their third spot-kick award of the game.

Three nights later, Celtic relinquished their hard-won League Cup of the previous season when they faltered at the first hurdle against Airdrie at their new ground, the grandly-named Shyberry Excelsior Stadium. Before the game, the public address system blared out the Tremeloes' sixties pop song 'Silence is Golden' as an obvious jibe at the Celtic players who were still refusing to talk to the press while continuing their war over bonuses. They might have agreed in the end that silence was, indeed, golden such were the decibel levels reached by the wholehearted booing by frustrated fans after a shamefully tame performance in the 1-0 defeat. The only goal arrived in the fifteenth minute when referee Hugh Dallas awarded Alex MacDonald's team a contentious penalty-kick when Stephane Mahe tangled with Allan Moore, who was running away from goal. Jonathan Gould pushed out Marvyn Wilson's badly-placed attempt, but the ball broke straight back to the same player who made no mistake second time around. Like Liam Brady in 1991, Jozef Venglos suffered a setback against Airdrie in the League Cup.

The Czech said, 'Of course, I am very disappointed with the result. We were not good enough to create chances or score a goal. I am not going to look for excuses. The performance simply was not good enough.'

Venglos' only other success in the opening couple of months came three days later when it looked as though they were heading for a third consecutive defeat. Robbie Winters had given Dundee United a thirty-first minute lead in front of a crowd of 59,738 and it remained that way with only ten minutes remaining. A little piece of magic from Henrik Larsson, who missed the Airdrie debacle while on international duty with Sweden, opened the way for Craig Burley to race through and beat Sieb Dykstra. Three minute later, debutant Mark Burchill, on for the atrocious Harald Brattbakk, got on the end of a Simon Donnelly pass to roll in the winner. 'I've been dreaming about a moment like this ever since I can remember,' exclaimed the teenager breathlessly afterwards. 'And now it's happened. It's just brilliant!'

Unfortunately, Burchill didn't experience the same feeling of elation in his next appearance at Parkhead on September 23. St Johnstone hadn't won in the east end of Glasgow for twenty-seven years, but that was to change when a fifteenth-minute effort from Nick Dasovic was deflected past Jonathan Gould for the only goal of the game. The Perth side leapfrogged Celtic into fourth place in the league. After seven games, the Hoops were three points adrift of joint leaders Rangers and Kilmarnock and two points behind Hearts and St Johnstone.

Venglos, who kept his first signing Vidar Riseth on the substitutes' bench throughout, sighed, 'We played so much of the game in the centre of the park which was crowded. We didn't play out on the flanks so much and it made it easier for them to defend. I have been asked why I did not play Vidar, but I felt he would do better to sit and watch and see how we play before he is involved. It was my decision and I feel it was the right one. The supporters can be a little impatient and I respect them and I am not complaining. But the players do need their support. Expectations are high, I know that, and I am trying to fulfill the spectators' wishes. I know I can't change the result, but I am not afraid to take the responsibility for it.'

Celtic's four stalemates came against Dundee (1-1), Kilmarnock (1-1), Hearts (1-1) and Rangers (0-0). Of course, all eyes were on Ibrox on September 20 when Glasgow's age-old gladiators squared up for their first contest of the campaign. History was made with both clubs being managed by foreigners for the first time in this 110-year-old tussle. Walter Smith, who, unexpectedly, was named Everton boss in the summer, was in the stand among the 50,026 crowd to witness the action. No doubt, after years of frustrating Celtic with his cat-and-mouse tactics, he would have secretly applauded Venglos' set-up which was designed to hit on the break. Darren Jackson played up front with Henrik Larsson roaming in the space behind him. Surprisingly, Simon Donnelly was detailed to watch midfielder Barry Ferguson with Craig Burley, David Hannah and Phil O'Donnell a screen in front of the back four. It worked a treat.

The nearest to a goal in a cagey ninety minutes came in the first-half when Larsson slipped a pass wide to Jackson and then took off at full-pelt into the Rangers penalty area. Jackson picked him out with a curving cross and the Swede made perfect impact. It looked a goal all the way until Lionel Charbonnier frantically thrust up a hand and diverted the ball onto the face of the crossbar. The French keeper defied Celtic right at the death when Tosh McKinlay, who came on for the tiring O'Donnell in the eighty-third minute, swerved in a cunning drive that was pawed to safety. Walter Smith might have come close to acknowledging the hit-and-run tactics deployed by Venglos on his Old Firm baptism.

The Czech said, 'I was pleased with the spirit shown by my players. We played as a unit and worked hard for each other. There was good team spirit and tactical discipline. I thought it was an exciting derby. We had our chances and Rangers had theirs, but we had the opportunities to win at the end of the game.'

Intriguingly, Dick Advocaat admitted, 'Celtic deserved to win in the last five minutes.' However, he swiftly added, 'But we deserved it in the first eighty-five. We played exciting, good football, but failed to score. In the last five minutes it was so difficult because we had used up so much energy. Still, in the end, a draw was a fair result.'

Celtic had been knocked out of the UEFA Cup by the time the second Glasgow derby came around in November. After the dismal display in Zagreb in the Champions League knock-out, no-one gave Venglos' team much hope of advancing too far in the consolation competition. A few may have been revising their thoughts when the club travelled to Portugal to face the dangerous Vittoria Guimaraes on September 15 and were leading 2-0 with only four minutes to play. Henrik Larsson gave them a dream start with the opener inside the first minute. Paul Lambert released Phil O'Donnell, making only his second start of an injury-ravaged season, on the left wing. He flashed over a cross and the Swede, so deadly in the air, buried a header beyond Pedro Espinha. Larsson set up the second goal in the seventieth minute when he broke into the box and measured an effort for the far post. The keeper got to it, but couldn't hold the ball and Simon Donnelly wouldn't be denied from close range. Brazilan Geraldo threw his team-mates a lifeline near the end with a drive Jonathan Gould just couldn't prevent from rolling over the line.

Venglos, his backroom staff and the players missed the club's AGM in Glasgow on the same day. Some 3,500 shareholders were determined to have their voices heard. Fergus McCann was barracked by more than a few, but, in the end, he was afforded a standing ovation. What was consistent, though, were the thoughts from the supporters about General Manager Jock Brown. They were still raging after stories about friction between Brown and Wim Jansen and also Davie Hay, two highly popular individuals in the eyes of the fans. Brown had remained while Jansen and Hay had departed and some were determined to see the General Manager also leave the premises.

A fortnight after the away win, Celtic staged an action replay at Parkhead with another 2-1 triumph. Alan Stubbs got the first-half opener with a neat header, Vittoria's Brazilian attacker Gilmar squandered a sixty-sixth minute penalty-kick by blasting the ball off target, Swede Sven Soderstrom equalised on the night with a dipping effort in the eighty-seventh minute before Henrik Larsson made it 4-2 on aggregate in the fading moments. Venglos summed up, 'The opposition were a clever team with short passing, but our players responded well tactically. There are no easy teams in Europe and we worked hard for our win.'

The second round draw paired Celtic with FC Zurich, the first leg to be played in Glasgow on October 20. A dour confrontation, watched by 44.121 fans, ended 1-1, but the Parkhead outfit knew they had a Swiss alp to climb in the second leg where they would be without the banned duo of Craig Burley and Tommy Boyd. The midfielder picked up a booking to go over the threshhold and the skipper earned a straight red on the verge of half-time when he stopped a certain goal with his hand on the line. Jonathan Gould proved equally as good with his mits and he saved Cesare Santanna's powerful drive. However, the keeper was helpless when a seventy-fifth minute angled cross from Urs Fischer drifted over his head and high into the net. Harald Brattbakk had shot the hosts into the lead in the fifteenth minute with a sweet left-foot volley.

Once again, there were rumblings off the field concerning Jock Brown. Paul Lambert, who was named skipper in place of the suspended Boyd, had hoped to hold a Press Conference at Prestwick airport to publicise his newly-published autobiography before the squad flew out for Zurich for the return a fortnight later. Apparently, he was denied permission and there was no such conference. There had been speculation about an ongoing spat between the pair and it would eventually come to a head. About 1,000 fans made the trip to Switzerland and many took the opportunity to fire a hail of abuse at the General Manager during departure and arrival. The situation threatened to get out of hand on the team's return and Brown required a police escort on his way from the airport.

In the midst of all this, Venglos was attempting to put together a team that might still have a chance of reaching the next stage of the UEFA Cup. As well as the ineligible pair of Burley and Boyd, the Head Coach was also robbed of the defensive qualities of the injured defensive trio of Alan Stubbs, Marc Rieper and Enrico Annoni. He was forced to switch left-back Stephane Mahe to centre-half alongside midfielder David Hannah. On this occasion, it was a mountain too high. Incessant rain poured down throughout the tie as the pitch was transformed into a sea of mud. An astonishing four goals in ten minutes burst in the second-half brought the game to life - unfortunately, three were for the home side. Giorgio del Signore headed the first past Jonathan Gould in the fifty-first minute. Phil O'Donnell responded with a quickfire equaliser before Frederic Chassot claimed a second for the Swiss in the fifty-sixth minute. South African striker Shaun Bartlett added a third and Gould was forced to go off injured shortly afterwards. Stewart Kerr took over in goal. Larsson made it 3-2 in the seventy-second minute, but it was all over when first leg penalty-kick culprit Cesare Santanna had a drive deflected past the stranded stand-in keeper. Celtic were out on a 5-3 aggregate against distinctly mediocre Swiss opposition.

Venglos might not have realised it, but the Parkhead side had now failed to reach the third round of European competition every season since 1984. He said, 'Every time we scored, they scored at the other end to make things difficult. That was disappointing. So, too, are the injuries that just go on and on. You saw our bench tonight. I had to bring in five youngsters, so I am obviously looking for new players, but it is a question of how and when.'

Three of Jozef Venglos' four signings were in the line-up for the second Old Firm game of the season. Vidar Riseth, Lubomir Moravcik and Johan Mjallby were in for a treat when Rangers came visiting in November.

CHAPTER SIXTEEN
THE 'UNKNOWN' GENIUS

The mellifluous tones of U2's 'The Sweetest Thing' swept soothingly over Celtic Park on November 21 1998. The sentiments matched the perfect harmonising among the Celtic players only an hour or so earlier during one of the most extraordinarily one-sided Old Firm confrontations in decades. As the impatient frost on a chilly early evening in the east end of Glasgow began to settle on the field of dreams, the Celtic supporters were in no rush to leave the scene of such a wondrous celebration. The scoreboard told but a mere fraction of the story: CELTIC 5 RANGERS 1.

Dr Jozef Venglos had been vilified in the days leading up to the confrontation. Scorn and ridicule had been heaped upon the Head Coach. He had turned to a thirty-three-year-old fellow-Czechoslovakian by the name of Lubomir Moravcik in his efforts to revive Celtic. Dick Advocaat, across the Clyde, was shelling out millions of pounds on World Cup players and Venglos' answer was to pay £325,000 to MSV Duisburg for a veteran midfielder, largely unknown on these shores, who had been dumped into the reserves after only five first team appearances for the German outfit.

The week before Rangers arrived at Parkhead, Moravcik had played in a Celtic team that toiled and then toppled to a 2-1 loss against St Johnstone in Perth. In fact, the game against Advocaat's team was only the third of Moravcik's embryonic career in Scotland and, as luck would have it, his first went almost unnoticed; a runaway 6-1 victory over Dundee in front of 58,974 euphoric supporters. The performance and the result were enough to make the fans gleeful, but everything seemed to be overshadowed by the fact, only an hour before kick-off on Saturday, November 7, came the news that the club had parted company with General Manager Jock Brown, the No1 hate figure for so many followers.

As reports of Brown's demise hurtled around the stadium, the supporters were already singing and dancing long before the kick-off. There can be little doubt the individual had been left shaken by the sheer vitriol that came his way following the UEFA Cup exit four days earlier at Prestwick Airport. As was normal, the General Manager had a meeting with Fergus McCann on the late morning of a home matchday. On this occasion, though, there was a topic on the agenda that required to be urgently addressed. Without fuss, Brown resigned his post after only eighteen months in office. The Press, who had the former BBC match commentator in their sights almost from his first day in office, were given the information. Very quickly it spread and sparked off a vigorous fanfare in the stands.

Moravcik trotted onto the pitch for the very first time for a kickabout fifteen minutes or so before the start and must have wondered about the gaiety of the fans pre-match. He might have thought, 'What must they be like when they're celebrating a win?' He received his answer some ninety minutes later. Dundee, with future Celt Rab Douglas in goal, had lost only once in their previous five games, but were swamped on this occasion with Celtic 2-0 up inside eighteen minutes; Henrik Larsson leaving his future team-mate helpless with two expertly-taken penalty-kicks. Former Celtic defender Barry Smith was sent off and, although Eddie Annand pulled one back, they were undone when Mark Burchill made it 3-1 before the interval. The teenager netted again shortly after the turnaround, Larsson completed his hat-trick and Simon Donnelly added the sixth. The gleaming smiles from all corners of the ground at the end might have rendered the floodlights redundant.

Jozef Venglos, undoubtedly irritated by the constant barrage of irrelevant questions from persistent sports reporters, refused point-blank to discuss the Jock Brown situation. He implored, 'Please do not ask me about other things which happen off the field. I have been asked these for three months. Ask me about the game. Just let me relax and enjoy this result. I can tell you this was our best performance we have had since I arrived. It was skilful and the team played well as a group. We had good passing, plenty of goal opportunities and good finishing.'

Hardly anyone noticed the little Czech who orchestrated many of the moves and, with a sharp mind and a delicate touch, keenly anticipated the runs of Larsson and Burchill and continually found them with searching passes into vulnerable areas behind the Dundee defence. He proved to be as adept with his right foot as with his left as he sprayed the ball around. Asked once about which foot he considered to be the better, he replied, 'They are both my better foot.' Nothing got lost in the translation; Lubomir Moravcik knew exactly what he meant.

One week later, goalkeeper Tony Warner arrived on loan from Liverpool while a knee injury forced Jonathan Gould onto the sidelines. Deputy Stewart Kerr was also out with a ligament strain. Under-21 star Andy McCondichie played his only game of the season in the rout of Dundee, but Venglos believed he was too inexperienced for some tough games ahead, including the meeting with Rangers. Warner was pitched into the match against a St Johnstone team who had been humiliated 7-0 by Dick Advocaat's side only seven days beforehand on their own ground. It must be admitted that the Celtic Head Coach never had far to seek for his sorrows. On this occasion, central defensive partners Marc Rieper and Alan Stubbs, clearly vital to the team's set-up, were both out with injuries as was Craig Burley and Enrico Annoni. On top of those woes, Paul Lambert was suspended.

The encounter turned out to be a personal disaster for Vidar Riseth, playing his seventh successive game since his £1.5million arrival from LASK Linz. He was penalised by referee Eric Martindale for obstruction on the stroke of half-time as he attempted to usher the ball behind for a goal-kick. Bewilderingly, the match official awarded the Saints a free-kick which was quickly taken by Kieran McAnespie and redirected across goal by Alan Kernaghan to Portuguese striker Miguel Simao who touched it behind Warner from six yards. Henrik Larsson, lively throughout, knocked in a cross from Mark Burchill for the equaliser. The winning goal defied explanation. Riseth, for reasons known only to himself, decided to pitch a high ball across his own goal when he would have been far better served thumping it downfield. McAnespie could hardly believe his good fortune as the ball turned into a perfect pass and he nodded into the empty net with Warner stranded at his near post.

Riseth said, 'It was my fault we lost the game and also that of the referee. He was unbelievable. I have never seen such bad refereeing in my career.' The Norwegian would swiftly learn that the Scottish Football Association did not warmly embrace or encourage such forthright observations of match officials. Venglos added, 'When we were 1-0 down, the response from the players was good for fifteen or twenty minutes and we scored a goal. Then we lost the kind of goal that sometimes happens. It was not a good one. Now the players have to prepare themselves for the game against Rangers.'

As usual, things were happening off the pitch. A story was leaked insisting club legend Kenny Dalglish and Jim Kerr, lead singer with rock band Simple Minds, were fronting a consortium who wanted to wrest control of the club from Fergus McCann. The identities of the takeover group were unknown, but, in the end, the money didn't stack up and the matter disappeared without trace. On the transfer front, Celtic were linked with powerful Swedish international midfielder Johan Mjallby, who was valued at £1.5million by AIK Stockholm. It was also reported Croatia Zagreb had accepted an offer of £3million for striker Mark Viduka, but the deal would be delayed because of red tape as Celtic sought to get the Australian a work permit.

At 3pm on Saturday November 21, the shrill from referee Willie Young's whistle ushered in the fifth and last Old Firm game of 1998. The move for Mjallby had gathered momentum and he had signed a four-year contract just three days earlier. Venglos put him straight into the middle of his defence alongside Alan Stubbs who had overcome his injury problems. Marc Rieper, however, was still out. So, too, was Jonathan Gould and Tony Warner kept his place in goal. Paul Lambert returned after suspension, but the Head Coach provoked criticism by leaving out Mark Burchill and, even more unlikely, replacing him with Lubomir Moravcik as Henrik Larsson's frontline partner. The spluttering of indignation and the questioning of Venglos' ability were muzzled amid tumultuous applause in the twelfth minute. Moravcik had just scored his first goal for Celtic and, in a heartbeat, had wiped away any doubts surrounding his qualities.

Stubbs took the ball off Rod Wallace deep in his own penalty area and strode forward with purpose. He pushed a pass to Phil O'Donnell on the left who transferred it swiftly into the tracks of Simon Donnelly, speeding away from right-back Sergio Porrini. He cut a crisp low ball across and Larsson wrong-footed Colin Hendry with a neat stepover. Moravcik, two yards outside the penalty box, pounced on the opportunity with an exquisite first-time left-foot drive and goalkeeper Antti Niemi hadn't a chance as the ball nestled low to his left hand corner of the net. The wily little midfield mastermind stood back as if admiring his handiwork. He admitted later, 'I didn't know what to do. I didn't know how to celebrate. The stadium was bouncing and I just looked around me. Then my team-mates arrived.'

Not everyone admired Moravcik's grace of movement. Scott Wilson, Rangers' central defensive enforcer, left his beat and followed the Czech ten yards into Celtic's half before launching a high and reckless challenge on his opponent. There is the train of thought that a perpetrator of such violence might escape the harshest of punishments for such a foolhardly tackle if it is done far enough away from his team's own danger zone where it cannot be deemed a goal-denying foul. Willie Young was having none of it. The referee immediately went to the pocket where he kept his red card and the game was over for Wilson in the twenty-second minute.

If Wilson, less than gifted in the fine arts of the sport, thought Moravcik would be intimidated for the remaining sixty-eight minutes by his act of thuggery, he got it badly wrong. Four minutes after the turnaround, a motionless Niemi was beaten for a second time and once more the ball was tucked safely behind him by Venglos' protege. Tommy Boyd joined the attack as he rampaged up the right wing and he picked out Moravcik, standing in isolation in the penalty area. With a leap, an arched back and a swift forward thrust of the side of his head, the

Czech made impeccable contact and his effort whooshed in at the corner. Again, Moravcik showed he hadn't rehearsed a goal celebration in advance as he stood rooted to the spot, looking around in almost childlike wonderment.

Three minutes later, rampant, ruthless Celtic were three goals ahead. Donnelly slipped a pass in front of Larsson who accepted it on the run, dashed past Hendry and deftly flicked the ball over the outrushing Niemi. Sixty seconds after that, Giovanni van Bronkhorst pulled one back with a twenty-five yard free-kick that struck the inside of Warner's right-hand post before finding the net. The whirlwind of goals continued as Larsson got a fourth. Phil O'Donnell whisked over a delightful left-wing cross and Larsson rose with immaculate timing to bullet in a header. Niemi, once again, didn't have time to move a muscle. Astutely, with the points in the bag, Venglos afforded Moravcik the opportunity of a standing ovation when he took him off with eight minutes to play. Celtic supporters rose as one to the hitherto 'unknown' midfielder who couldn't get a game for a second-rate German team. In time, it emerged he had fallen out with the coach and his punishment was to be banished to the second string.

On came Burchill and he joined in the frolics with the fifth goal in the last minute. Larsson set him up with a clever ball inside the struggling Porrini and the youngster took it first time to fire it beyond the flapping Niemi. Dick Advocaat had let everyone know Rangers would have had a thirteen-point advantage over Celtic if his side had won this game, the fifteenth of the league season. If he was trying to out-psyche his opposite number, it failed miserably. The old sage didn't bite. It was the Ibrox team's biggest defeat at Parkhead for thirty-two years when Stevie Chalmers struck a hat-trick in an identical 5-1 success for Jock Stein's men on their way to nine in a row.

Venglos could afford to smile afterwards. 'Do you think I do not know the qualities of Moravcik after seventy-three international caps and his games in World Cups and European Championships under me?' he asked, coming close to chiding the non-believers. 'He is a very good player with lots of skill and awareness.' On this occasion, there were no dissenting voices. He continued, 'I think we have to be happy with a good performance today. Hopefully, we can build on this result because we have had one or two false starts this season. We played with spirit, passion and determination and we will need that in every game from now on.'

Johan Mjallby, still looking wide-eyed after his first game, admitted, 'I thought I knew about it all - then the game started. For the first ten minutes, I was shit-scared. I mean it. I didn't want the ball anywhere near me and when it did come to me I felt my touch was terrible. The noise all around the place was incredible. I've never experienced anything like it. After that start, though, I really began to enjoy it. That game will live with me forever.'

It was inconceivable, then, that Rangers' next visit to Parkhead would result in a 3-0 win for the Ibrox men. And it was just as incomprehensible to accept that the victory on a gloriously sunny Sunday evening on May 2 1999 would see Dick Advocaat's side crowned Premier League champions with three games still to play. In a season of strange twists and turns on and off the field, this was possibly the most exasperating to grasp.

Jozef Venglos had to pick his team up after losing 1-0 to St Johnstone the previous week at McDiarmid Park. Celtic had gone into the encounter in Perth with only one defeat - a 2-1 reverse against Hearts at Tynecastle in December - from a praiseworthy consistent run of seventeen games which had also seen thirteen wins and three draws. One of the stalemates came in the January 3 1999 clash against Rangers at Ibrox where a torrid confrontation with eight bookings - four from each side - finished 2-2. Alan Stubbs gave the visitors the advantage in the thirty-ninth minute when he latched onto a misplaced headed clearance from Lorenzo Amoruso and curled an unstoppable right-foot effort from the edge of the box high past the stranded Stefan Klos. Gabriel Amato headed in the equaliser in first-half injury time.

The game turned in the space of two second-half minutes. Stephane Mahe was clearly sent crashing to the turf after a crazy sliding challenge from Kanchelskis. It had to be a penalty-kick, but, much to Rangers' relief and everyone else's disbelief, referee Jim McCluskey merely awarded a corner-kick. Moments later, a cross from Amato on the right spun off Tommy Boyd into the air and Rod Wallace leapt acrobatically to hook a shot wide of Jonathan Gould. Parity was restored and justice was done when Henrik Larsson headed in the leveller in the sixty-sixth minute after a devilishly dipping twenty-five yard drive from Lubomir Moravcik exploded against the crossbar. Scottish football took its first voluntary winter break with Rangers ten points ahead of Celtic.

Amid the victories was a fabulous four-goal show from Henrik Larsson in a rousing 7-1 thrashing of Motherwell at Fir Park, a 5-0 stroll against Dunfermline and a 3-0 trouncing of Hearts. The good work was undone in Perth against a Saints outfit that was emerging as a bogey team after winning 1-0 in Glasgow in September and 2-1 on their own ground two months later. On this occasion, Keith O'Halloran headed in a left-wing cross from Gary Bollan in the fifty-fifth minute for the game's solitary goal.

Of the side that had routed Rangers 5-1, Venglos would be without five influential players through injury and suspension when Dick Advocaat brought his team to the east end of Glasgow at the beginning of May. Missing were keeper Jonathan Gould, skipper Tommy Boyd and midfielders Craig Burley, Johan Mjallby and Lubomir Moravcik. The Head Coach was strapped for replacements and had to bring in Scott Marshall in an emergency loan deal from Southampton. The right-back, brother of former keeper Gordon, choked in the claustrophobic atmosphere of a bruising Old Firm collision. He contributed next to nothing and, after a substitutes' appearance against Dunfermline, was hastily returned to his parent club. In fact, Venglos was so short of players there was a place on the bench for Tommy Johnson who had started only one league game since the departure of Tommy Burns.

This Glasgow derby never made it to the pantheon of memorable Celtic v Rangers encounters. It never came close to being a classic and would be remembered, alas, as a shameful, spiteful, snarling episode in Old Firm history. The Ibrox side won 3-0 when the ugly face of football was uncovered in ninety minutes of mayhem and indiscipline. Rival fans spat bile at each other and the feud continued well into the night. A crowd of 59,918 was in attendance for the tussle that could see Rangers reclaim their title after a mere year in the grasp of their great rivals. Venglos played Harald Brattbakk up front alongside Mark Viduka, with the £3million deal for the Aussie frontman with Croatia Zagreb finally going through in late February. The delicate Norwegian was taken off after virtually refusing to get involved in a bad-tempered roughhouse and never started another league game for the club. In January 2000, he was sold to FC Copenhagen for a fraction of the £2.2million he cost two years earlier.

It was a patched-up Celtic team that took the field and within twelve minutes they had conceded the first goal. With Marshall nowhere to be seen, Rod Wallace was allowed to race unchallenged down the left, cut into the box and pick out Neil McCann who slotted the ball beyond Stewart Kerr. The bad feeling that had been simmering even before a ball had been kicked was given further impetus when match official Hugh Dallas booked Stephane Mahe after a tussle with Wallace where it was clear the French defender had been elbowed in the chest by his opponent. Rangers, rather oddly, were awarded the free-kick and Mahe vehemently protested. As soon as he opened his mouth, Dallas was fumbling for a yellow card.

Mahe was distraught in the thirty-first minute when Dallas booked him again and then flashed the red card. Any watching neutral would have been hard pushed to explain the actions of the referee. The left-back, raiding on the wing, had his legs taken from underneath him in a deliberate and callous foul from McCann. Mahe immediately leapt to his feet to remonstrate with the Rangers player. There was no hint of a physical assault, but Dallas thought his reaction warranted another yellow card and that led to his banishment from the field. Mahe protested long and loud, but no-one was listening. McCann was merely booked for his part in sparking the uproar.

Celtic fans perceived an injustice had been perpetrated against the team by a referee of whom they had been suspicious for a long time. A fan had already breached the security cordon to ill-advisedly race towards the match official before he was stopped in his tracks. Dallas awarded Rangers a contentious free-kick at the right-wing corner flag five minutes from the interval. Another pitch invader had to be escorted away by stewards. Unfortunately, an object thrown by an irate fan, a totally inexcusable action, hit the referee on the forehead and he went down at the bye-line in front of the Celtic support. Blood was visible from a cut that required two stitches during the interval. He recovered within a couple of minutes to signal for Giovanni van Bronckhurst to take the free-kick. The Dutchman flighted it into the box, there was the usual bumping and jostling and, to everyone's amazement, Dallas blew his whistle and, without the hint of hesitation, pointed to the penalty spot. He ruled Vidar Riseth had fouled Tony Vidmar and, once again, his decision sparked disorder. Vidmar had demonstrated his prowess at the backflip that would have guaranteed his native Australia a gold medal in any Olympics. In truth, it was a nonsensical, unfathomable award. That mattered little to Jorg Albertz. Once the rammy has subsided, the German calmly placed the ball on the spot before thundering it past Kerr, sending him the wrong way.

There was a dark cloud of worrying malevolence hanging over the ground during the interval. A storm was brewing in a corner of Glasgow. In the seventy-sixth minute, it was all over bar the insults. Rangers broke upfield and McCann sped away from a heavy-legged Stubbs, rounded Kerr and poked the ball into the empty net. Astoundingly, McCann then left the field of play to run to the fans behind the goal and complete a circuit before returning to the pitch. On a night like this it could easily have incited more bedlam. And there could be no argument that his momentum had carried him over the line. Clearly, it was is choice to indulge himself in an impromptu mini-lap of honour. The letter of the law requires a yellow card and that would have meant the winger seeing red after his booking for bringing down Mahe in the first-half. Dallas was content to usher the Rangers player back onto the field without a word of censure.

Four minutes from time, Wallace, previously booked, was needlessly banished after getting involved following a spat with Riseth. Seconds from the final whistle, Riseth, with a full head of steam, bludgeoned

Claudio Reyna near the left-wing corner flag. 'I didn't wait for the referee to show me the red card,' said the Norwegian. 'I knew I was being sent off. I just headed for the tunnel.'

The final whistle blew, Rangers had claimed their tenth championship in eleven years and some bright spark within their ranks believed it was a good idea to recreate a mock huddle in front of Celtic fans while the ground was seething with outright hostility. The nauseating gesture was an anathema on such an evening. It was a turbulent, disturbing encounter that deserved to be buried under the rubble of distaste. At the end of the campaign, Dick Advocaat's team succeeded with six more points than their closest rivals. How Jozef Venglos and his players must have cursed shedding nine points to an inferior St Johnstone side, who, despite that hat-trick of victories, still finished fourteen points adrift of the Glasgow side. Later, Celtic were fined £45,000 after the SPL Commission of Enquiry's investigations into the so-called 'shame game' and the same body then cleared Rangers of provocative celebrations.

As luck would have it, the country's juggernauts were on a collision course again only twenty-seven days later. Once again, a massive prize, this time the Scottish Cup, was up for grabs. Once again, Celtic were depleted by injuries. And, once again, Hugh Dallas was the man in charge. Someone from another country might have wondered if Scotland possessed only one referee. The Scottish Football Association, despite the furore that centred on the match official's perplexing decision-making in the pandemonium at Parkhead, elected to give the event to Dallas.

A variety of injuries would deny Jozef Venglos the services of Mark Viduka, Craig Burley and Jackie McNamara while the versatile Vidar Riseth was called up for international duty by Norway. The Head Coach created a stir before the kick-off when he left Mark Burchill off the substitutes' bench and, instead, named Stewart Kerr as reserve goalkeeper. Only three subs' places were available in the national competition and Phil O'Donnell and Tommy Johnson got the other spots. Dick Advocaat, on the other hand, went with three outfield players in Andre Kanchelskis, Scott Wilson and Ian Ferguson. After the loss, Venglos was criticised in some quarters. Hindsight, as they say, is a wonderful thing. And, as I have said far too often in my lifetime, it is also bloody useless.

Henrik Larsson claimed five goals in the three rounds leading to the semi-final. Celtic beat Airdrie 3-1 in the opening game, the Swede netted a hat-trick in the next home tie, a 4-0 romp against Dunfermline and he was on target, too, in the 3-0 quarter-final win against Morton at Cappielow with his new frontline partner, Mark Viduka, contributing two. The talented Aussie got the killer goal as Dundee United were downed 2-0 in the semi-final. Regi Blinker got the opener in the tie at Ibrox which was watched by 43,491. That attendance dwarfed the 20,664 who turned out for Rangers' 4-0 semi-final triumph over St Johnstone at Parkhead.

So, on May 29, it was Celtic v Rangers in the deluxe occasion of the Scottish Cup Final at Hampden Park with 52,670 fans eagerly anticipating the confrontation. And a nation held its breath and prayed for the moment to be remembered only for the football and not the fiasco of the previous league meeting. It was the sort of tight, cagey game where it looked as though it would be settled by a solitary strike and, unfortunately for Venglos and his players, that proved to be the case and it was Rod Wallace who snapped up the winner four minutes after the interval. The nearest to a goal before that was a pulverising twenty-five yard volley from Paul Lambert that zipped past Stefan Klos, his former Borussia Dortmund team-mate, and thudded against the crossbar before whistling out of play. As Phil O'Donnell, playing his last game before joining Sheffield Wednesday on a Bosman along with Simon Donnelly, exclaimed, 'A couple of inches lower and that would have been one of the great Hampden goals.'

The one that separated the teams was an untidy effort, but no-one from the Ibrox contingent was complaining. Left-back Tony Vidmar, charging into the box, squared a pass in front of Neil McCann. Hastily, he struck the ball and it flipped up off the challenging Alan Stubbs and dropped perfectly for Wallace. From close range, the little Englishman couldn't miss and he walloped a shot beyond the helpless Jonathan

Gould. Celtic piled forward throughout the half and there were a few scares for Rangers, but they held out and Dick Advocaat, in his first season in Scottish football, had achieved the Treble.

Jozef Venglos was defiant when he spoke to the press afterwards. He said, 'I do not have to defend myself. We tried to do our best and I think during the season the team tried to give everything. Today I think we were not the worst team. We had our problems, especially with injuries. I have no regrets about not playing Mark Burchill in the Final. If you saw how the game was running, there were so many bodies in front of the penalty area it was not for counter-attacking players or those who run at opponents. It was not his game. There were seven other players left out and I could not speak to all of them. Maybe if we had been allowed more substitutes he would have been on the bench. Maybe the Cup organisers should allow more players on the bench. I am never satisfied, but it was a difficult season. We have a very good team with good players, but nobody can take seven or eight regular players out of a team and hope to win.'

Interestingly, the Head Coach also talked about the new campaign. He added, 'Next season we will be successful. I know that we have quality players and I know we will win. There are two things for us to consider before next season. We need to bring in new players, but also I hope players such as Burley, McNamara, Rieper and Johnson are fully fit. That is very important.'

Celtic, of course, would be going into season 1999/2000 with a new Chief Executive. Fergus McCann's grand five-year plan expired in mid-March and, bang on schedule, the Managing Director prepared to leave the club and return to North America with financial experts reckoning he would be banking something in the region of £40million for his efforts and initial £5million outlay. Although the individual, thought to be far too abrasive by many who dealt with him, had delivered on his promises, he was criticised for not investing more cash in the team. However, he was leaving the club with a strong infrastructure that would allay fears they would ever sail close to the rocks of bankruptcy again.

Davie Hay put it this way, 'You can't take anything away from Fergus. He did exactly as he had promised from day one. I've worked with chairmen and chief executives and some tend to meddle in team affairs. That is not their remit and I have had to remind a few of that over the years. My job was in the dressing room while theirs was in the boardroom. And never the twain. To be fair, Fergus never got involved in issues that did not concern him. I've gone on record as saying I liked Fergus on a personal level, despite him getting rid of me. My only complaint would be that he could have done the job in a more friendly manner. He didn't have to be brusque and offhand all the time.'

As McCann prepared to leave, he had already appointed Frank O'Callaghan as non-executive chairman. McCann and the rest of the plc board then set about the search for a new Chief Executive. Allan MacDonald, a lifelong Celtic supporter who was an executive with British Aerospace, was appointed to the post and took over immediately when McCann left in early April. He agreed an initial two-year deal which would be followed by a rolling one-year contract.

MacDonald would make a monumental decision early in his new career that would have severe repercussions for Celtic.

CHAPTER SEVENTEEN
JOHN BARNES AND KENNY DALGLISH: THE GAMBLE

John Barnes' tenure as Celtic Head Coach lasted exactly eight months. Six years earlier, Lou Macari's occupancy endured a further nine days. Neither record stacked up well when compared with the club's first-ever manager, Willie Maley, who was in proprietorship for forty-two years and four months.

Allan MacDonald, as the club's recently-appointed Chief Executive, was eager to prepare for the new season after the disappointments of the previous campaign. Back in April 1999, he had no intention of parting company with Dr Jozef Venglos as Head Coach. Instead, the Celtic-supporting supremo had plans to financially back the veteran gaffer, whose footballing philosophy was a source of admiration. According to MacDonald, he asked Fergus McCann if Venglos had an opt-out clause in his contract similar to the one utilised by Wim Jansen. Emphatically, he was informed this was not the case and that no condition existed. To MacDonald's surprise, Venglos did indeed have such a specification and evoked it only a few days after the Scottish Cup Final defeat.

MacDonald had already got the ball in motion to bring back club legend Kenny Dalglish in the newly-created role as Director of Football Operations. Originally, the idea was for Dalglish, the Chief Executive's golfing buddy, to work alongside Venglos without any responsibility for day-to-day team matters. That notion was jettisoned when Venglos moved out of the dug-out to accept a post as the club's new European Technical Advisor with scouting responsibilities. No-one was quite clear what the role actually entailed, but it was evident the crafty old Czech, now sixty-three years of age, was not prepared to endure the unique pressures thrust upon a Celtic manager for a second successive term.

Enter John Barnes and the remarkable announcement that originally invited disaster and acute embarrassment, but eventually triggered the ground-breaking move that paved the way for the arrival of Martin O'Neill.

On the day of their joint appointment, Dalglish attempted to clarify the situation. He said, 'John is the first team coach and is responsible for everything connected with the first team. He will pick the team, he will take the training sessions and he will have total control over the pool of players. I won't be interfering with that. When it comes to identifying players he might want to bring into the club, or even players he decides should be leaving, then, again, he will put the names forward and then we shall have talks on how to go into the transfer market. I shall work with him on that aspect and then the negotiations regarding salaries or fees will be worked out by the finance people at the club.'

Barnes added, 'It is good that I have someone with Kenny's experience around and, if I need advice, I know he will be there. But the responsibility for the first team is mine and I shall be talking to Eric Black soon to take on board his assessments of the playing staff. I have seen the team, I watched some of the derby games last season, but I know that have to familiarise myself with all of them. Once I have done that, we shall start to identify areas of the team which might need strengthening and that's when Kenny and I will talk.'

Dalglish was also tasked with setting up a soccer academy and building a training ground. Another role would be to liaise with Venglos. Dalglish added, 'Dr Venglos is a very intelligent man and someone who is very knowledgeable on modern training routines and preparation work and we shall be consulting him once we start the job. He is not being kept at the club simply because he is a gentleman, he is here because he will make a valuable contribution.'

Barnes, like Liam Brady in 1991, had an outstanding footballing pedigree as a player and had made seventy-nine international appearances for England while playing at the highest club level with Liverpool for ten years. He had two seasons at Newcastle United before being released and moving to Charlton. After three months, the London club were relegated from the top flight and Barnes was a free agent once more.

He had never managed a club at any level when MacDonald made his move to team him up again with his old Anfield pal Dalglish, who had championed his cause and claimed he had 'great potential' in a coaching position. The newspapers daubed them 'The Dream Team' and, as usual, there were smiles all round as both waved Celtic scarves outside the front door at Parkhead on June 10. All too quickly, the grins evaporated.

MacDonald admitted, 'Appointing John Barnes is a high risk, but, hopefully, not too high a risk. We have put in place an enormous insurance policy in the shape of Kenny Dalglish. We want this management team to grow with Celtic. What we now have is a team in place for the next five, six, seven years.' Unfortunately, the longevity of the partnership fell well short of the Chief Executive's expectations.

Neither Barnes nor Dalglish would have cause to complain about the so-called 'biscuit tin mentality' of the new man in charge. MacDonald made funds available and Celtic set a new Scottish transfer record fee of £5.75million when they bought cultured Israeli midfielder Eyal Berkovic from West Ham, beating Rangers' cash outlay for Andre Kanchelskis from Fiorentina the previous season by £250,000. Centre-back Olivier Tebily was brought in from Sheffield United with the price tag of £1.2million and Chelsea keeper Dimtri Kharine and Ipswich Town winger Bobby Petta also arrived on Bosman deals. After much red-tape wrangling, a la Viduka, Bulgarian midfielder Stilian Petrov received his work permit and arrived in a £2.2million deal from CSKA Sofia. On the same day, Enrico Annoni was released and the versatile defender returned to Italy. Young French striker Stephane Bonnes, who arrived from bankrupted FC Mulhouse, was offered a four-year contract.

Celtic fans in the 52,715 crowd got their first hint of Barnes' footballing philosophy in a pre-season friendly against Leeds United at Parkhead on July 24. Berkovic, Tebily and Petta all played as the Elland Road side, distressingly, cantered to an all-too-easy 2-0 triumph. Ivory Coast defender Tebily scored a spectacular own goal and was thereafter christened 'Bombscare'. Barnes was far from downhearted at the end and observed, 'That was a typical performance from a team that's been together for two or three years to one that is just beginning.'

I was invited to the Directors' Box for the match against Newcastle United three days later when a staggering crowd of 59,252 turned out on a pleasant, balmy evening. Celtic won 2-0 and this time Tebily put the ball in the opponents' net for the opener while Mark Viduka hit the second. Henrik Larsson, who had missed the previous disappointing display through injury, returned to indulge the support with an irresistible performance. Ruud Gullit, the St James's Park manager, actually applauded the skills of Larsson from the touchline on several occasions.

Allan MacDonald realised Larsson was on the wanted list of several top clubs across the border. Worryingly, he had discovered there were directors who were more than willing to part with the charismatic fans' favourite if the price was right. MacDonald immediately got the current Scottish Player of the Year to agree a four-year extension to his contract with weekly wages believed to be around £25,000. Actually, I have heard of higher figures with all sorts of add-ons, but, thankfully, Larsson was now in the sort of earning bracket that would make Manchester United or anyone else think twice about attempting to lure him from Glasgow.

Barnes was fervently applauded all the way along the Pittodrie trackside to the dug-out opposite the halfway line as Celtic opened the league season - and, apparently, ushered in yet another new era - against Aberdeen on Sunday, August 1 1999 with the TV cameras beaming the match nationwide and beyond. The new Head Coach was very much in focus and an intrigued audience of millions enthusiastically tuned in to see what he could provide as a tactician. Beaming broadly, and as if walking on air, Barnes floated back to the dressing room at the end of the action. Celtic, playing with verve and dash that was easy on the eye, had just pummelled Aberdeen 5-0. Ebbe Skovdhal, the Dons' new Danish coach, had arrived with a huge reputation for his deeds at Brondby, but neither he nor his players had an answer as their aspirations were swept into the North Sea long before the interval.

Barnes' team were coasting at 3-0 as they weaved pretty patterns all over the immaculate playing surface. It was polish aided by power; class with clout. Henrik Larsson knocked in the opener in the fourth minute and Mark Viduka added two more in the space of six sparkling minutes before half-time. The large travelling support in the 16,080 crowd cheered their team off the field and wondered if the second-half would provide something of the same. Only three minutes after the turnaround, the home side were given the opportunity to pull one back when Olivier Tebily hauled down Robbie Winters for an undeniable penalty-kick. Eoin Jess hammered the ball to Jonathan Gould's left and watched in dismay as the keeper threw himself full-length to claw the ball out of the air. Larsson showed Jess how it should be done from the spot four minutes later when he smashed his effort wide of David Preece. Just after the hour mark, Viduka limped off and Barnes introduced Mark Burchill who claimed the fifth goal in the fading moments.

It had been an exhilarating performance by Celtic and Barnes enthused, 'This is the way I have always wanted to play and, fortunately, I have the players to do it.' Forgetting for a moment that football is a results-driven business, the rookie boss added innocently, 'I would even accept the odd defeat during the course of a season as long as we played like that.' Skovdahl, with a measure of honesty, admitted, 'I have to say that if I was not the Aberdeen manager, then I would have enjoyed watching Celtic.'

Six days later, a truly astounding crowd of 60,253 turned out at Parkhead to witness the 3-0 victory over a St Johnstone team that had managed to beat Celtic three times the previous season. Statisticians claimed it was the biggest attendance for a league fixture in a decade. The average football fan's thirst for entertainment was always unquenchable and Barnes' outfit were by far the biggest draw in town. Once more, the game was just about done and dusted in the first half-hour. Johan Mjallby claimed a rare goal in only six minutes and Mark Viduka hit the second. Morten Wieghorst joined in with the third only five minutes after the break.

In the midst of all the joy and gaiety, Lubomir Moravcik was reassuring his new legion of fans that he could function without the aid of mentor Jozef Venglos. In fact, Barnes was already a confirmed admirer of the Czech sorcerer. He singled him out after his display against the Saints and said, 'Am I impressed by Lubo? I am impressed with him even when I see him in training. He is almost as old as me and he is just such a fantastic and gifted all-round footballer.' In fact, Moravcik was thirty-four at the time, one year younger than his new Head Coach.

A week later, on August 15, Barnes unexpectedly witnessed the team's first plunge to defeat of the season when Dundee United won 2-1 at Tannadice. Efforts from Craig Easton and Billy Dodds had the Tayside outfit two goals ahead at half-time. It had been a puzzling performance from Celtic in the opening forty-five minutes. One scribe observed, 'So, Celtic are not invincible, after all. In fact, there is reason to suspect they still might be seriously flawed.'

United asked questions of the central defence, a luxury not afforded to either Aberdeen or St Johnstone who were otherwise engaged at the other end of the pitch. Johan Mjallby and Olivier Tebily formed the partnership in front of Jonathan Gould and, on this viewing, neither looked comfortable in each other's company. Tebily's positional sense alarmingly deserted him on occasions and that was the case when a completely unmarked Dodds lobbed Gould for United's second goal. Barnes had some work to attend to in the dressing room at the interval. It was the first time he had been placed in such an awkward position. Did he have the nous to turn things around? There were no immediate changes, but new boy Stilian Petrov made his league debut when he was introduced to the fray in the sixty-eighth minute as a substitute for Morten Wieghorst with the team still two goals adrift. It probably wasn't the baptism the young Bulgarian had anticipated.

With time running down, it looked obvious to throw on Mark Burchill beside Viduka and allow Larsson to roam around behind the front two. Petrov, though, was the only change that afternoon. With nine minutes to go, Berkovic drilled in a handsome goal from the edge of the box after United failed to clear a Moravcik corner-kick. As the contest edged towards its conclusion, Vidar Riseth passed up the opportunity of a leveller. A troublesome shot from Moravcik was juggled by keeper Alan Combe into the air and hovered perfectly for the Norwegian to head in from close range. Unfortunately, he displayed the attacking instinct of a defender, his timing was a little awry and the chance was lost. The consensus of opinion, though, was that an equaliser would have been unfair on the home team.

Barnes said, 'United made it difficult for us and we gave away two bad goals. We lost in the right way. We tried to do the right things and we created chances. If we had lost 2-1 having not played well and they had peppered our goal, then I might have questioned our system. But that did not happen.'

Fevered brows among the concerned Celtic support were soothed again when Hearts arrived in Glasgow and were sent back to the capital in disarray after a 4-0 thumping. Alan Stubbs was now fully rehabilitated following an operation for the testicular cancer, which had been diagnosed following a random sample at the end of the previous season's Scottish Cup Final. The popular Englishman was welcomed back to the middle of the rearguard alongside Tebily while Mjallby moved into midfield. The home fans in the 59,607 crowd were delighted to witness a swift return to form with Viduka and Larsson combining superbly again. The Aussie and his Swedish frontline sidekick got the first-half goals and Berkovic claimed two midway through the second-half. Barnes, charm restored after the Tannadice hiccup, said, 'I was not surprised with our quality of play. We played some great one-touch football and I've got to be happy with that performance.'

There was no respite for Barnes, especially with Rangers winning all five of their league fixtures in the month of August while Dutch newcomer Michael Mols, a £4million summer signing from Utrecht, hit four goals in a 4-1 win over Motherwell. September was ushered in with a hard-fought 1-0 win over troublesome Kilmarnock at Rugby Park, so often a graveyard for Hoops' hopes. The only goal was notched by nineteen-year-old Mark Burchill who started the game in place of the injured Mark Viduka. The keen youngster bent his run superbly to get on the end of a Craig Burley pass and, with the Kilmarnock defenders desperately claiming offside, he carried on into the box before sizzling a low drive away from Colin Meldrum in the seventy-second minute. The overall performance wasn't pretty, but it was productive.

The same could also be said for the next league game, another away fixture, this time against Hibs at Easter Road. The Edinburgh side's manager Alex McLeish had brought in Marseille's 1993 European Cup winner Franck Sauzee from Montpellier to add midfield finesse to his newly-promoted line-up. After losing three goals in the previous fixture to Kilmarnock, McLeish thought the Frenchman's subtle skills would aid a defence that often lacked composure. That was the theory, anyway. Just before the interval, Sauzee flattened Larsson and was booked by referee Hugh Dallas. Ten minutes after the break, sophistication again deserted the acclaimed international as he clattered into Riseth. Off went Sauzee and, within moments, Celtic were leading. Moravcik swung over the resultant free-kick, Larsson, at the near post, headed down and Viduka applied the killer touch in front of goal. Ten minutes later, the skilful Aussie repeated the feat and it was game over.

Barnes had selected Dmitri Kharine ahead of Jonathan Gould and dropped Craig Burley in favour of Regi Blinker and afterwards explained, 'I was not taking a chance in a Premier League game as this is still our most important objective this season, but I wanted to have a look at them to see what they could give us. There are eighteen to twenty players at the club who have as much right as anyone to a place in the team.'

Celtic were still packing them in and a remarkable 60,033 turned out on Saturday, October 16 which transpired to be an eventful afternoon for the club - they ran riot, scoring seven goals for their highest tally of the campaign and Rangers' run of eight successive victories came to a halt against Kilmarnock at Rugby Park where they had to settle for a 1-1 draw.

Poor David Preece, the Aberdeen goalkeeper. Signed from Darlington in the summer, he conceded five goals on his debut when Celtic hammered them on the opening day of the season. This time Henrik Larsson and Mark Viduka claimed hat-tricks after Eyal Berkovic had opened the scoring. He was taken to hospital following the game for an exploratory test after receiving a knock on the head. The goalie claimed he couldn't remember a thing. Boss Ebbe Skovdahl may have been experiencing the feelings of a condemned man after the humbling, humiliating loss, but he could still summon up a moment of mirth. 'I wish I could say the same,' he smiled ruefully. The brutal taking apart of the Pittodrie side was their biggest hiding since they had capitulated 8-0 on the same ground in 1965 when the Big John Hughes - the original Yogi Bear - ripped them to shreds while enjoying a five-goal spree.

John Barnes wasn't entirely satisfied and complained, 'At times we gave the ball away too sloppily. Better opposition would have made us pay for that.' The Head Coach mentioned no names, but Olivier Tebily was certainly living up to his early nickname of 'Bombscare'. And Barnes was right - superior teams would have helped themselves to a few goals with the opportunities that were being presented haphazardly with lamentably slack passing around the penalty box.

At Rugby Park, it was a seventy-third minute goal from Michael Jeffrey that salvaged a 1-1 draw for Kilmarnock and derailed Rangers who had opened the scoring in the sixteenth minute through Giovanni van Bronckhorst. Dick Advocaat fumed, 'The way we played we were lucky to get a point. There was only one player in my team who did okay and that was Craig Moore. All the others weren't on the park.' Clearly, the Little General didn't react too well to disappointment.

Five days after the mauling of Aberdeen, Celtic lost 1-0 to Lyon in the first leg of their UEFA Cup Second Round tie at the Stade de Gerland. The result was dismissed almost as a mere triviality. The main concern was the fact Henrik Larsson had suffered a horrendous broken left leg and would be out for the remainder of the season. Immediately, Barnes said, 'Whether we had lost 2-0 or won 2-0, it wouldn't have mattered. What is important is that Henrik gets back to health and that's all I'm focusing on at the moment.'

The Swede was carried off on a stretcher in obvious distress after a freak accident in the eleventh minute when he chased back to tackle Serge Blanc. He appeared to catch his studs in the turf and went down writhing in pain. The sheer horror on the faces of team-mates and opponents was a clear indication of how dreadfully his leg had been snapped. There was a silence on the pitch for some minutes. 'You could tell right away that it was serious because of the reaction of the players close to him,' said Barnes. 'We didn't tell the players until after the game how bad it was.'

Paul Lambert was close to the incident and added, 'It's an absolute shocker for Henrik. I saw his leg and it was not a very nice sight. It's such a tragedy for him. He has been a wonderful player all the time I've been here. We just want to see him back as soon as possible.' Mark Burchill, who replaced the Swede, said, 'Henrik is such a great player and I cannot believe what has happened to him. It's a tremendous blow to lose anyone as good as him. I hope we can do the business while he's out.'

Burchill, in fact, was involved in a moment of high controversy when he was sent crashing in the penalty box in the first-half. Viduka released his eager team-mate who raced towards the exposed Gregory Coupet, touched the ball past him and prepared to follow through with the move when he was upended by the keeper. Dutch referee Rene Temmink didn't agree with the penalty shout from the 4,000 travelling fans in the 42,000 crowd. He provoked gasps of disbelief when he produced the yellow card to book Burchill for diving and awarded a free-kick to the French. The Celt insisted, 'It was a definite penalty-kick. I was through on goal and had gone round him. All I had to do was hit the ball into the net. Why would I go down at that point? I couldn't believe it when the referee booked me.'

With a sledgehammer slice of sarcasm, Barnes, who thought TV pictures proved conclusively it was a spot-kick, said acidly, 'Mark has apologised to us for going round their keeper, getting kicked, falling to the ground and getting booked.'

Lyon got the evening's only goal in the sixty-third minute when thoughtful midfielder Vikash Dhorasoo, for once eluding his marker Lambert, pushed a pass into the tracks of Blanc who left Jonathan Gould stranded with a vicious left-foot effort that soared high into the net. It was a gallant show by Celtic, but the sickening injury to Larsson, the country's top scorer with thirteen goals and the club's talisman, made it a depressing journey home. The following day, after surgery at Bon Seccours hospital in Glasgow, it was revealed both bones in the Swede's lower leg were fractured. He wouldn't play again until the last day of the season on May 21 2000.

Before the next game against St Johnstone in Perth, the travelling fans chanted Larsson's name before, during and after the 2-1 success. John Barnes brought wide players Regi Blinker and Bobby Petta back into a midfield with Stilian Petrov and Paul Lambert adding the strength. As expected, Mark Viduka and Mark Burchill were given the main attacking roles. The Aussie and the Scot proved there could be life after Larsson by dovetailing well and sparking off each other. Celtic dominated a fair percentage of the opening half, but, disconcertingly, went in a goal adrift at the interval. On the half-hour mark, Nick Dasovic robbed Lambert, sent George O'Boyle clear and he picked out Nathan Lowndes who slipped the ball wide of Jonathan Gould. And, just like that, the visitors, who could have been three ahead in the opening seventeen minutes, were one down.

Three minutes after the turnaround it was all-square when Burchill snapped onto a Blinker cross, shimmied one way and then the other to take two defenders out of the equation before rattling a drive behind Alan Main. Controversy appeared to enjoy spending time in the young Celt's company and ten minutes from time it looked as though he had scored a second only for it to be ruled out by referee Hugh Dallas. With only a handful of seconds remaining on the clock, the match official was on the verge of nullifying another Celtic effort. Morten Wieghorst's header from a corner-kick was touched onto the post by Main and was then frantically booted clear by Paul Kane. It was a tough call, but linesman Bob Gunn signalled to Dallas the whole of the ball had crossed the line before the intervention of the Saints player. The referee awarded the goal to spark protests from the furious home players.

Barnes gave his surprise verdict afterwards. 'It didn't look as if it was a goal and St Johnstone are entitled to feel hard done by, but these things tend to even out over the course of the season. We have had a spot of good fortune, but I am sure that will be balanced by decisions in the future. St Johnstone have had a fair share of good fortune in the past and will do again.' He added, 'We weren't allowed to play the sort of football we like to, but we chipped away at them and ground out the result. Overall, I thought we were the more progressive side.'

The mood of the Head Coach changed dramatically after the next game, a midweek encounter against Motherwell, which was played throughout in monsoon conditions at Parkhead. Celtic not only conceded their first goal at home, they also carelessly threw away the opportunity to go top of the league by nosediving to a dreadful 1-0 defeat to a side that played for almost an hour with ten men. Little wonder Barnes moaned, 'That was our worst performance of the season.' The team, without the inspirational Larsson, toiled hopelessly, devoid of imagination and bereft of penetration. Kevin Twaddle scored in the fifteenth minute and the resolve of the Celtic players seemed to dissolve in the swirling rain. In the thirty-fourth minute, central defender Shaun Teale, the sort of rugged defender who gave you the impression he shaved with a blow-torch, knocked over Burchill. It was a crude challenge and immediately merited a red card from referee Dougie McDonald.

With the one-man advantage, the Celtic fans in the 58,731 attendance must have expected a spirited revival from their heroes. What they got instead, though, was an inept, bungling display that rarely worried their old foe Andy Goram, now with the Fir Park outfit following his release from Ibrox. He might even have admitted he had to work a lot harder for more than a few of his win bonuses at Parkhead during his days as a Rangers player.

Barnes, looking a little punch drunk afterwards, didn't bother with lame excuses. None would have been accepted, anyway, by anyone who had witnessed the debacle. 'After about twenty-five to thirty minutes of the second-half, we knew we could have been there all night and not scored,' he admitted with some lack of guile. 'We couldn't pass the ball straight. No matter the team system or formation, we should be able to pass the ball. It's the basics and if we do not get them right, then it makes everything else so much more difficult.' There was a hint of desperation when he added, 'I can only hope it was a one-off. I believe it is, because these are international players. I can't accept this is because we missed Henrik Larsson. If that is the case, this would be a one-man team and I don't think I or any of the players in the dressing room would accept that.'

Ian Wright, the thirty-six-year-old former England and Arsenal striker, was hastily signed by Barnes on a deal until the end of the season. It was obvious Celtic lacked cover for Larsson and it was hoped the prolific veteran, who had just been released by West Ham, would provide a quick fix. Certainly, his old international team-mate believed in his ability to come up with the answer. Barnes was asked what would the frontman bring to the team. 'Goals,' he said confidently. 'That's what Ian Wright is all about - goals.'

And three days later, Wright did, indeed, score on his debut as he had previously done at Arsenal, West Ham and during a ten-game loan spell at Nottingham Forest just before turning up in Glasgow. Kilmarnock must have thought they were about to emulate Motherwell in front of 59,720 fans when Christophe Cocard, unmarked smack in front of goal, opened the scoring with a header in the thirty-sixth minute and held the advantage until the interval. Wright, who took Mark Burchill's place in attack, thought he had equalised five minutes from the break when the unconvincing Michael Watt failed to hold a Craig Burley shot. The frontman was in speedily to smash home the rebound, but referee Mike McCurry ruled it out and baffled Wright and just about everyone in the crowd while doing so.

The roof fell in on the Ayrshire side when Viduka got into his majestic stride and Killie centre-back Martin Baker was red-carded after an off-the-ball skirmish with Moravcik, who, admittedly, had gone in late with a slide tackle. It wasn't exactly Muhammad Ali v Joe Frazier stuff at Madison Square Garden, but it was enough for the match official to dismiss the errant Rugby Park player and book the Celtic midfielder. Wright sent Viduka through with a deft head-flick in the fifty-second minute and the frontman powered a lot shot past Watt. Two minutes later Moravcik sent over a cross from the right and Viduka flashed in a header. He completed his quickfire hat-trick in the fifty-sixth minute with another header. The crowd were willing Wright, all action right from the start, to get a goal and he threw himself full-length to nod an effort away from Watt, but the ball struck the bar and flew over. In the seventy-seventh minute, Burchill, on for Viduka, threw over an inviting ball from the left and Wright's timing in the air was first class as he nodded past the bewildered Watt. Burley smashed in the fifth six minutes from time.

Barnes exclaimed, 'Ian Wright lifted everyone, the players and the fans. His coming here is a high-profile situation and I'm sure opponents will try to get to him. But I'm sure he is mature enough to stay out of trouble.' Wright was positively beaming at the end. 'To come to Celtic at my age and play in front of 60,000 fans is just unbelievable, absolutely sensational. It's a one-in-a-million chance and this has been an unforgettable experience.'

Celtic's European dream died in the midst of a strange, deadly hush as they surrendered fairly meekly to Lyon in the return leg of their UEFA Cup-tie on November 4, their third successive 1-0 midweek defeat. As early as the seventeenth minute, after Tony Vairelles had scored in a breakaway, Barnes' men were struggling and most of the 54,291 onlookers seemed to realise that the three goals required to go through would be beyond this team and the brakes were about to be applied on another Continental adventure. Celtic had beaten Welsh minnows Cwmbran Town 10-0 on aggregate and then Happoel Tel Aviv 3-0 - with Henrik Larsson getting the three goals home and away - to set up the meetings with the French side. There was a perfectly-observed one minute's silence before the game in honour of the extremely popular Jimmy Steel, the club masseur, who had passed away. It was just as quiet at the end with the players and the fans seemingly accepting their fate long before the final whistle.

Barnes said, 'Our all-round performance was poor. There was no urgency in our passing or movement and the players and the crowd went a bit flat. Lyon were worthy winners.' The French club's coach Bernard Lacome revealed he had spotted deficiencies in his opponents' formation. He admitted, 'We had identified weaknesses in defence after watching them in three games recently. I felt the gaps between the full-backs and the central defence were too big. I told my team to take advantage and that's what they did.'

The gloss was fading and the new era was beginning to look a little tatty around the edges as the impetus of the Dalglish-Barnes Dream Team clearly started to wilt. However, the Head Coach realised he had the perfect opportunity to turn it around if he could inspire his charges to something his predecessors had been unable to do over the previous five years - beat Rangers at Ibrox. Three days after the tame European exit, Barnes was about to experience his first Old Firm encounter at the home of the club's deadliest foes on Sunday, November 7.

There had already been tales of unrest in the dressing room, disgruntled players being ordered to take on specific roles they didn't have the ability to fulfill. Vidar Riseth was continually selected at full-back which didn't suit the Norwegian, who was brought to the club by Jozef Venglos as a midfield player. Barnes was an admirer of Brazil's flamboyant defender Cafu and demanded Riseth followed his example of bombing down the wing and firing in a stream of crosses. There was little doubt the Celt possessed an engine to cope with the first part of the task, but he admitted candidly, 'I'm probably one of the worst crossers of a ball at the club.'

Stilian Petrov, too, was being asked to do exhaustive work on the right flank and that didn't complement his style, either. Craig Burley insisted his natural game was being marginalised as he was deployed in a more withdrawn role with extra defensive duties which nullified the goal threat that had gone such a long way to helping the club to the Premier League title triumph in Wim Jansen's solitary year. When he scored his late goal against Kilmarnock, he followed the ball over the line and again hammered it viciously into the net. There were no celebrations. As he trotted back up the pitch, Burley looked across to Barnes as if to say, 'There are a lot more like that if you play me in the correct position and give me my freedom.' I doubt if those were his exact thoughts, but you get the drift. However, Barnes persisted. And at Ibrox he paid a heavy price.

Celtic, after leading 2-1 just before the interval, capitulated 4-2 and were bossed around during a clueless second-half. Foolishly, Ian Wright had said pre-match that the rival defenders would be scared of his reputation. If that was the case, no-one noticed. The thirty-six-year-old rarely figured and was fortunate to last all of seventy-five minutes before being withdrawn and replaced with Mark Burchill. Alas, the contest was over by that point. There was to be no stirring fightback on this occasion. Dick Advocaat obviously noticed the same flaw as the Lyon coach because he deployed Jonatan Johansson, a fleet-footed Finnish attacker, to raid in between Jackie McNamara and Alan Stubbs on the right and Riseth and Olivier Tebily on the left. In the early moments it almost paid off with a goal. Johansson spotted the gap between Riseth and Tebily, raced into empty space and collected the ball before driving a vicious angled shot high past Jonathan Gould. His effort smashed against the underside of the crossbar and, such was the ferocity of the shot, it bounced all the way out for a shy on the other wing.

Gould, who had looked cocky and assured under Wim Jansen and Venglos, was struggling to maintain that form with Barnes in the dug-out. That was highlighted when he gifted Rangers the opening goal in the nineteenth minute. The defence couldn't deal with a simple long throw-in from the left by Jorg Albertz and Gabriel Amato outjumped the immobile Riseth to turn a feeble header towards goal. It was a routine pick-up for the keeper, but, horribly, Gould fumbled the ball and, as it came loose, Johansson was in quickly to turn it over the line. It was a howler from the goalie and he knew it. However, Eyal Berkovic spared his blushes only two minutes later when he came in from the right, played a superb one-two with Mark Viduka and slid the ball between Stefan Klos' legs for the equaliser. And the Israeli looked a £5.75million player again three minutes from the break when he pushed Celtic into the lead. Viduka seized upon a calamitous bit of miscontrol from Lorenzo Amoruso and zeroed in on Klos. The ball was blocked and Berkovic, following up, cleverly changed his body shape to sidefoot an effort low to the keeper's right when he expected the shot to go across him towards the other post.

There had been a few stoppages in the first-half with the usual over-zealous tackling from both sets of players and three minutes were added. In the last of these, Albertz drew a challenge from Paul Lambert inside the box. As the midfielder slid in, the German went over his lunge and referee Kenny Clark pointed to the spot. The Ibrox player's knee smashed into the side of Lambert's face and that was the end of the game for the Celt with Johan Mjallby coming on in his place. Albertz kept his composure throughout the three-minute delay before sending Gould the wrong way.

Four minutes after the turnaround, Celtic were trailing and Rangers were given a massive slice of good fortune. Albertz, from twenty-five yards, tapped a free-kick to his right where Amoruso was poised. The Italian hit his shot perfectly towards the defensive wall. Gould went to his right before the effort took a deflection off the thigh of Tebily and spun in the opposite direction. It was all over when the visitors' rearguard was exposed yet again. No-one picked up Amato as he ran through onto a lobbed pass. He drew Gould from his line, touched it round him and, from an exceptionally tight angle, tucked the ball in at the near post. Tebily looked as though he could have got back to guard the post, but he was content to merely move at an ambling pace without the hint of urgency and got there just in time to see the ball crossing the line. Celtic fans in the 50,026 crowd were far from satisfied with a submissive second-half from the players. The pressure was mounting on the Head Coach with the team now four points adrift of Rangers who had a game in hand.

A fair percentage of the spectators with even an iota of a Celtic leaning could hardly believe their ears with the words that followed from Barnes as he gave his verdict. 'I can't fault my players as individuals.' he said with a straight face. 'The effort was there, although the quality could have been better. We didn't do it as a team. We changed to three at the back in the second-half, but formations don't matter - we have to pass the ball better. It's disappointing for me, the players and the fans. They have to face their workmates and the Rangers supporters. Unfortunately, we can't do anything about it now. If they hadn't got that penalty it possibly could have been different, but I don't like to think like that. You can never tell what would have happened if we'd gone in 2-1 up. The fact is we didn't and they went on to win the game. At the time the penalty was awarded I felt aggrieved, but I'll need to see it again on television.'

He added, 'I believe that we can win the majority of our games and keep in contact, but unless Rangers are now going to drop points then the gap will stay the same so, obviously, we're playing catch-up. I'm always looking to strengthen the squad, but the quality of player we're after isn't often available. We can take heart, though not much, from some of our play today. If we can get these players to perform like that consistently for ninety minutes in every game, then fine. Otherwise, we need to bring in more quality.'

As a player, the Liverpool supporters insisted an uber-performing John Barnes could walk on water. As a Head Coach, the Celtic supporters wondered how an under-pressure John Barnes would cope with thin ice.

CHAPTER EIGHTEEN
'ACCIDENT WAITING TO HAPPEN'

There were raucous celebrations amid the chaos, the inharmonious din punctuated with the incessant demanding chants of 'We want four.' The joyous chorus reverberated around the stadium, vibrantly piercing a stubbornly cold February evening in the east end of Glasgow. The euphoric supporters whooped it up as their grandstanding collection of joiners, electricians and plumbers continued to showboat against demoralised opponents, repeatedly outmanoeuvring them in all areas of the pitch. The acclaimed victors were safe in the knowledge their position in the next round of the Scottish Cup competition was secure long before the strident shriek from referee Dougie McDonald's whistle finally, and mercifully, put the hapless home team out of their misery.

John Barnes, staring into the darkness with expressionless eyes, had just presided over the worst result in Celtic's history.

As the players of part-time, second tier Inverness Caley Thistle cavorted and cartwheeled in front of their exultant travelling band in the immediate aftermath of their extraordinary 3-1 success on the Tuesday evening of February 8 2000, the Head Coach admitted he was clueless. In two days' time, he would also be jobless. And virtually unemployable with an unremovable stain on his CV. After two years of soul-searching, from the safety of a location many miles from Kerrydale Street, Barnes eventually declared, 'It had been an accident waiting to happen.'

Celtic had gone into the Scottish Cup-tie on the back of a morale-sapping 3-2 home defeat from Hearts, a result that left them ten points adrift of Rangers. Displaying a refreshing never-say-die spirit, Eyal Berkovic, another costly mistake by Barnes, volunteered his opinion that he believed any chance of winning the league title was already blown with sixteen games still to play. Hardly, the sort of stirring comment from an individual you would welcome in your trench when the going got tough.

The distress flares were already being looked out after the feeble capitulation against a hardly-awesome Tynecastle outfit. Celtic were two ahead inside the opening half-hour after goals from Lubomir Moravcik and Mark Viduka and the bulk of the 59,896 crowd settled back to watch a procession. Instead, Darren Jackson, sold to Hearts in the summer, displayed an adroit touch seldom witnessed during his Celtic days when he set up Colin Cameron for an early response. Ten minutes after the break, Gary Naysmith, who terrorised Vidar Riseth with his sorties up the left wing, hit the equaliser and, with only seven minutes to go, substitute Tommy Johnson gave away a penalty-kick with an awkward challenge on the wily Jackson. Cameron duly sidefooted the award beyond Jonathan Gould. Barnes cut to the chase in his summing-up, 'If we continue to play like this, we'll be lucky to finish second.'

It was clear there was disharmony among the ranks at Parkhead, the initial surge under the so-called 'Dream Team' had all but petered out. And yet no-one in the 34,389 attendance the following Tuesday would have given the visiting Highlanders a ghost of a chance. Barnes didn't realise as he prepared for his first Scottish Cup-tie that it would also be his last. Steve Paterson, the Caley Thistle boss, came with a game plan and his players stuck to it, their willing endeavour putting the home side to shame. The encounter was only sixteen minutes old when the visitors put down their marker. Barry Wilson's header beat a seemingly half-hearted gesture from Gould as the ball soared over the keeper's left shoulder to open the scoring. The goal must have alerted the lacklustre Celtic players they might have to roll up their sleeves to earn a win bonus. Two minutes later, Mark Burchill attempted to play in Mark Viduka, his pass was blocked and rebounded straight back to the young striker and, without hesitation, he slammed it low past Jim Calder. It was time now for Barnes' team to keep their collective foot on the throttle.

Amazingly, though, Caley Thistle were back in front in the twenty-fourth minute and Celtic by now might have been awakening to the fact that this might not be their night. Olivier Tebily, with a few options, needlessly gave away a right-wing corner-kick. Bobby Mann scorched in a header that looked as though it was speeding for the outside of Gould's right-hand post. Unfortunately, Lubomir Moravcik, of all people, lost his bearings and lunged at the ball to deflect it into the opposite corner. The nearest the home fans got to applauding a first-half equaliser came in the twenty-eighth minute when Stephane Mahe blitzed in a ferocious left-foot drive which was turned onto the woodwork by Calder. The half-time whistle was greeted by a cacophony of boos, drowning out the cheers of disbelief from the 3,000 travelling supporters who were only forty-five minutes away from witnessing one of the tournament's most sensational results.

A full-blown mutiny was played out between management and players in the Celtic dressing room at the interval. Barnes, watching helplessly, offered little in the way of taking charge of an explosive situation. If any single moment encapsulated the fact he was in over his head this was it. The experienced Moravcik sat in a corner and watched the madness unfold. Assistant Eric Black had a go at Viduka to provoke a reaction. He certainly achieved his goal - the Aussie, seething with rage, took off his boots, threw them in a bin and told a bewildered Barnes and Black he had absolutely no intention of going out for the second-half. Years later, Ian Wright, who replaced Viduka for the second-half, revealed, 'Mark Viduka came in at half-time, took his boots off and said, "Fuck this". We couldn't believe it. He refused to play and that's the first time I had ever seen that. I thought he was a disgrace. I remember leaving the ground that night and we had to have a police escort because of some of the Celtic fans were going crazy. When Viduka came out, they actually cheered him!'

Celtic had half-a-game in which to galvanise themselves, resuscitate their Cup ambitions, restore some pride and give their fans reason to believe. With no-one to motivate them - either on or off the field - the players, some probably still alarmed over what they had just witnessed, performed dismally. The malaise even got to the usually imperturbable Moravcik. Goal thief Wright had ghosted into a superb position on the left-hand side of the box and a simple square pass would almost certainly have resulted in a goal. However, the Czech, unusually selfish, had a go from an angle and wildly slashed the ball high and wide. Celtic were heading for the exit with more than a third of the contest still to be played. Regi Blinker got in a fankle with Wilson who went down easily. The match official pointed to the spot and it would be churlish, not mention pointless, to debate the award all these years later. Paul Sheerin placed the ball neatly into one corner as Gould went to the other. Thereafter, the Highlanders were content to play keep-ball and a dispirited Celtic team went through the motions to the utter frustration of their disillusioned support.

One of the most damning and revealing insights into the shocker came from Caley boss Paterson when he summed up, 'From what I had seen of Celtic in recent games, they seemed to lack direction and leadership.' He didn't specify if his comments were directed at performers on or off the field. He would have been accurate on both counts.

According to Chief Executive Allan MacDonald, Barnes came to him the midst of the confusion and asked, 'What do I do next?' MacDonald replied, 'I don't know, but I'll let you know.' Stories of the rumpus in the dressing room had reached the ears of the press who wanted to know more. Barnes answered, 'We had a bit of a problem. There was a situation, so there is no real point in hiding that fact. It was a serious situation and there will be meetings about it in the coming days. After that, we'll release a statement.'

Kenny Dalglish had missed the debacle after spending time in La Manga where he had a holiday home. MacDonald made it clear he would have preferred the club's Director of Football Operations to be at Parkhead on the evening of a Scottish Cup-tie. 'I asked him not to go,' admitted the club supremo. Dalglish returned the following day as MacDonald stepped into the breach. He planned to put the club icon in charge of the team. He said, 'That was the solution. That was me saying to the Director of Football Operations, "You run the show because he (Barnes) wasn't managing the dressing room." Kenny comes back and John works for Kenny. But John refused, so he was fired.'

Eric Black and Terry McDermott were also shown the door. Shortly before he was sacked, Barnes was allowed to spend £5million on a Brazilian centre-half by the name of Rafael Scheidt from Gremio. He came with glowing recommendations and three full caps for his nation. No-one had taken into consideration that, back in the nineties, Brazil were sponsored by soft drinks giants Coca-Cola who insisted on the team playing one game practically every month. All sorts of players up and down the country received caps for non-event friendly internationals. Scheidt, who, for obvious reasons, preferred to be known by his Christian name, also claimed he had knocked back AC Milan to join Celtic. He started one first team game at the club - a 4-1 win over St Johnstone in March - and was booted into oblivion when Martin O'Neill took over. Dalglish was quick to distance himself from the Scheidt deal. He said, 'It was John who signed all the players at Celtic. I don't know who was the worst although there were more bad ones than good ones.'

Allan MacDonald admitted there was 'never a prospect' of Dalglish taking over as full-time manager of Celtic. The search for a new Head Coach had already been kicked into motion. Only a seismic shift in his intentions would see Dalglish back in a dug-out in the new season. He would take charge of the team for the remainder of the campaign while also helping to identify a permanent successor to his departed friend. Celtic fans concluded that three continuous days of acrimonious bloodletting were enough. The support, as they had done so considerately and with reaffirming regularity in the past, returned to active duty to back Dalglish and his beleaguered players when they travelled to Dens Park to take on Dundee in the next fixture four days after the Caley calamity. They roared the team on, especially in the second period in which they lifted their side to three late goals and a deserved victory.

Dalglish took charge of a team for the first time since being sacked by Newcastle in September 1998. Six of the previous starting line-up were immediately sacrificed. Jonathan Gould was axed and Dmitri Kharine returned for only the third start of his Hoops career. Regi Blinker got the chop, too, while Eyal Berkovic, Olivier Tebily, Colin Healy and Mark Burchill were relegated to the substitutes' bench. Dalglish, to the astonishment of many, elected to play Mark Viduka up front. The light drift of snow that had swirled around at kick-off time was now suitably thick in the second-half to warrant the introduction of an orange ball. With only twenty-three minutes to go, Johan Mjallby headed in the first following a Lubomir Moravcik corner-kick. Two minutes later, Moravcik played a through ball to Viduka on the left wing, from where he cut inside before gliding a low right-foot shot into the corner of Rab Douglas' net from outside the box. The future Celt was beaten again eight minutes from time when substitute Healy skilfully lofted the ball over him from fully thirty-five yards.

Dalglish said, 'The reception I and the players received from the fans was magnificent. That helped us win the game. What we have to do is to point the players in the right direction and we did that today and they responded well. I could not have asked for any more of a response from them. This was always going to be a difficult game because Dundee are a good side. So, to win by three goals was a good performance from the lads. I have to admit that I never thought I would be walking out of that Dens Park tunnel again. The last time I did it was as a player and, while I have been back often enough, it has been in the boardroom and the directors' box . . . and that is a bit different.'

Almost unheralded in the wake of the Scottish Cup fall-out, Dalglish, the following Wednesday, was only ninety minutes away from leading Celtic to the League Cup Final. John Barnes was in place for the opening 4-0 win over Ayr United at Somerset Park in October and he saw Morten Wieghorst claim the only goal of the game to defeat Dundee at the start of December, but was nowhere to be seen when Kilmarnock provided the opposition in the semi-final at Hampden. A disappointing crowd of 22,926 bothered to attend. Both sets of players responded to the lack of atmosphere and the flatness of the occasion. Once again, snow embroidered the playing surface and offered no assistance to those attempting to raise the entertainment to a higher level.

Lubomir Moravcik got the only goal in the sixty-sixth minute with impeccable reactions after Jackie McNamara had flighted a ball into the box. From about fourteen yards, he met the ball with his forehead and sent a soaring effort over the hands of Colin Meldrum into the net off the underside of the crossbar. A few minutes later, Killie's

READ ABOUT CELTIC HEROES PAST AND PRESENT
EVERY DAY ON **WWW.CELTICQUICKNEWS.CO.UK**

Christophe Cocard was red-carded after a squabble with McNamara who was booked for his part in the dust-up. Celtic were now set to play Aberdeen for the season's first silverware at the national stadium on Sunday, March 19. The Dons, who beat Rangers 1-0 in the quarter-final, booked their place with an identical win over Dundee United in their last-four confrontation.

Dick Advocaat's Ibrox side were due to visit Parkhead for the second time of the season - the first had ended in a 1-1 draw on December 27 where Mark Viduka, who had earlier struck the post with a delightfully cheeky effort, opened the scoring in the eighteenth minute with a flashing low angled drive past Lionel Charbonnier. A few minutes later, Lubomir Moravcik thumped the crossbar with a ferocious right-foot attempt. Billy Dodds equalised in a rare breakaway in the twenty-sixth minute, but there was more agony in the second-half when Moravcik struck the frame of the goal for a second time with an impudent header. Celtic had two games to face before King Kenny squared up to the Little General on March 8.

On the first day of March, there was a special cheer for Tommy Burns who had agreed a short-term contract as Assistant Head Coach to help out Dalglish. Dundee provided the midweek opposition and Burns found himself in sole charge with Dalglish laid low with a stomach bug. And what a return it was for the fans' favourite, so brusquely dismissed by Fergus McCann in 1997. Celtic were 5-0 ahead at the interval and Rab Douglas must have wondered if it was worth his while coming out for the second period. Tommy Johnson returned to the team after a lengthy spell with injury and netted twice while Viduka also claimed two, one a penalty-kick. Stilian Petrov got the other. Johnson completed his hat-trick in the second-half while goals from Hugh Robertson and James Grady made the scoreline a slightly more respectable 6-2. Burns said, 'It was strange to be back. It was an important game for us because the last time Celtic played on their own ground Inverness Caley Thistle won. Of course, that result hurt every Celtic supporter - me included - so we had to go out and entertain the fans, to give them something to enjoy.'

Disappointingly, Hibs brought the mini-revival to a halt with a 2-1 victory at Easter Road four days later. Dalglish was back in the dug-out and he saw Pat McGinlay and Kenny Miller score to put the Edinburgh outfit 2-0 ahead just after the hour mark. Viduka pulled one back in the seventy-third minute after Nick Colgan had mishandled a Mark Burchill shot. The Aussie then had an attempt cleared off the line by Tom Smith, Martin McIntosh sliced a clearance onto his own post, Alan Stubbs smashed a drive against the underside of the bar and Morten Wieghorst passed up a glorious opportunity right at the end. Dalglish said, 'The way we started the game was the biggest contribution to us getting nothing. '

When Rangers arrived at Parkhead on Wednesday March 8, Celtic had the opportunity to cut their lead at the top to six points. A goal four minutes from time by Rod Wallace left the home side twelve points adrift. Kenny Dalglish became the most recent manager to see his team outplay the Ibrox outfit for lengthy periods and complete the ninety minutes with nothing to show for their efforts. There were far too many infuriating, irritating and frustrating Old Firm repeat performances to be good for the blood pressure levels of anyone with a Celtic connection. The green-and-white bedecked fans in the 59,220 attendance must have realised they were about to witness another exasperating lopsided derby as early as the eighth minute when Mark Viduka was left with only Klos to beat from six yards after being brilliantly set up by Stephane Mahe. It looked impossible to miss, but the Aussie managed the feat by striking the heel of the sprawling Rangers keeper and the ball rebounded to safety.

The virtual one-way procession continued throughout a rain-sodden confrontation and Viduka thought he had atoned for his earlier appalling attempt in the sixty-fourth minute when he outjumped Amoruso, raced onto his header and lashed an unstoppable twenty-five yard effort past the helpless Klos. An eagle-eyed linesman waved frantically to signal Viduka had used an arm to bring the ball under control. Television pictures proved the decision to be correct although there could have been the usual ball-to-hand argument. Referee Jim McCluskey took the word of his assistant and the cheers were stilled in a matter of seconds. Viduka had a couple of other opportunities, but was denied by the German keeper, by far the busiest individual on the field. With eight minutes to go, a tired-looking Johan Mjallby hauled back Neil McCann for an obvious penalty-kick for the visitors. McCluskey might have thought about a red card for the Swede, but decide to merely administer a booking, instead. Albertz once again forsook precision for power and this time his thundering effort was too close to Jonathan Gould who dived to his left to save.

Dalglish took a gamble at this stage and removed Mjallby to throw on Mark Burchill. It was a brave move that, unfortunately, backfired. With Celtic forcing on play at the other end, Rangers broke, Giovanni von Bronckhorst sent Wallace clear, he sidestepped the exposed Gould and rolled the ball in at the post. Once again, there was no reward for Celtic after just about dominating proceedings. Dalglish said, 'We get a lot of credit, but no points and that's what counts. It's difficult for us to take, but I didn't see a league championship being handed out there tonight. We put on a striker in Mark Burchill because we wanted to win the game. I could have brought on Rafael, but we decided to go for it.'

Dalglish, after only six games in charge, had the opportunity to achieve something Liam Brady couldn't manage in two-and-a-half seasons and Jozef Venglos couldn't match in a year. It would also put Dalglish on a par with his good mate Tommy Burns who only had one trophy - the 1995 Scottish Cup - to show for three years of toil. He warmed up for the March 19 League Cup Final against Aberdeen at Hampden with a 4-1 triumph over St Johnstone at Parkhead eight days earlier. The game was billed by some as a championship wake after the defeat from Rangers, but an astonishing 59, 530 still turned out to cheer on Celtic. There was a soporific nature to the lacklustre opening forty-five minutes. It was all-square at half-time after Paddy Connolly had nullified Mark Burchill's seventeenth-minute opener. Three goals in six minutes gave the supporters something to cheer with Viduka putting Celtic ahead in the sixty-fifth minute, adding a quickfire third before Burchill claimed his second of the afternoon.

There was an innocuous start for Rafael Scheidt, the outrageously-expensive Brazilian defender, but he didn't reappear for the second-half after sustaining a thigh knock. Olivier Tebily took his place in the middle of the rearguard. Stephen Crainey made his first appearance for the club when he came on in the seventy-seventh minute for Stephane Mahe, who had been booked after a kerfuffle with Keith O'Halloran, who was also the recipient of a yellow card. Dalglish reasoned, 'It seems to be a like a pop-up toaster with the yellow card when Stephane goes near anyone. He can help himself in these situations, but we need to be vigilant, too, and try to protect him because he is an important player for us.'

Eyal Berkovic had played particularly well against the Perth Saints and had been involved in setting up three of the four goals. Dalglish now had a decision to make before the League Cup Final. Mark Burchill had missed out on the previous season's Scottish Cup Final after scoring two goals against Dundee United in the preceding game. Could it happen again? There were also absurd stories going around that Henrik Larsson was about to make his comeback at Hampden, but the Swede, thankfully, put an end to the nonsensical speculation by admitting, 'It would be dangerous for me to play just now.'

Celtic had at least eighteen reasons for being confident as they prepared for the silverware showdown with Aberdeen at the national stadium on a sun-kissed March afternoon with 50,073 in attendance. In their three Premier League head-to-heads with the Pittodrie side they had won 5-0, 7-0 and 6-0 - eighteen goals for and none conceded. Dalglish went with this team: Jonathan Gould; Vidar Riseth, Johan Mjallby, Tommy Boyd, Stephane Mahe; Jackie McNamara, Stilian Petrov, Lubomir Moravcik, Morten Wieghorst; Mark Viduka and Tommy Johnson. Eyal Berkovic was on the bench, Mark Burchill was in the stand. Alan Stubbs was the other outfield player named as a substitute with Stewart Kerr as back-up goalkeeper.

It has to be admitted Hampden Park was not exactly a cauldron of suspense for this particular Cup Final. Celtic took the lead through an unusual source in the fifteenth minute and the sponsors - CIS Insurance, on this occasion - could already have tied the ribbons to the trophy. Wieghorst, who played intelligently throughout, set up Riseth, who went through the entire league campaign without a goal to his name, and the Norwegian defender didn't make a clean contact with his left foot, but it was enough to send the ball spinning away from Jim Leighton. The second goal, in the fifty-eighth minute, was a lot crisper in its execution. Viduka struck a neat pass to Johnson who flashed a right-foot drive across the keeper and in at the far post. It was all too much for Dons defender Thomas Solberg who headed for an early bath two minutes later after a foul on the goalscorer. He had already been booked for a similar obstruction on McNamara and referee Kenny Clark had no option. In the fading moments, Stubbs and Berkovic came on for Moravcik and Johnson respectively.

Tommy Boyd was still waiting to collect the trophy when Dalglish was asked the obvious question, 'Who is going to be Celtic's Head Coach next season?' He was prepared for the grilling. 'Any decision we make on the manager's job, the supporters will play a part in it,' he said. 'Whether it is my position or anyone's position regarding football, they are very much in our mind and so they should be because they are an important part of the club.'

Switching his attention to the game, he added, 'Some people have described this tournament as meaningless and I suppose it is if you're not in it, but we were in it and the supporters showed how much it meant for them. Although the win doesn't cure all the sores and pain they felt with some of the results this season, I'm sure it will soften the blow just a little bit and they got a little bit of pride back by winning the Cup.'

On selecting his line-up, Dalglish explained, 'It's difficult to pick any team for a Cup Final and it's a great disappointment for players when they aren't playing. Being a substitute is no compensation as they all want to play. If they are not disappointed in being left out then we would be disappointed in them. We took a chance with Tommy Johnson and someone had to be left out and, unfortunately, it was Mark Burchill. But he's young enough and good enough to be back here a few more times in the future. I accept, though, it must have been a great disappointment for him.'

A week later, Dalglish set out his team to face Rangers in the fourth and final league meeting of a traumatic campaign. It was another ludicrously one-sided game, but Celtic had no complaints on this occasion. Rangers were a goal up in three minutes courtesy of some incredibly sloppy defending and, just before the end, Jonathan Gould picked the ball from the back of his net for the fourth time. It was an embarrassing 4-0 defeat, but, truth be told, it would have been more distressing if it hadn't been for at least three last-ditch saves from the overworked Celtic custodian. Dalglish, standing at the dug-out with arms folded across his chest, visibly winced when Dick Advocaat bounced onto the touchline beside him to salute his side's opening goal.

Stephane Mahe was forced to give away a corner-kick on the Celtic left as Kanchelskis, the unpredictable Russian winger, decided to have his best game of the season with some direct raiding on the wings and through the middle. Van Bronckhorst swung the corner to the far post where an unchallenged Kanchelskis met the ball to head it back into the mix. With Gould out of position, the keeper might have hoped for some assistance from his fellow-defenders. He got none. Albertz actually had to get in front of team-mate Dodds to nod the ball into the empty net from just about underneath the crossbar. Four minutes from the interval, Kanchelskis, played onside by a dozy Johan Mjallby, skipped onto a Van Bronckhorst through ball and, with only the Govan breeze between him and Gould, thumped in the second with obvious glee. Six minutes from the end, Neil McCann was left unguarded on the left, he sidestepped Gould and flicked the ball across to Albertz and he stuck the third into the vacant net. In the fading moments, with Celtic's defence well and truly in tatters, Van Bronckhorst curled a twenty-yarder past the stretching Gould.

Celtic had rather lamely surrendered eleven points to their deadliest foes after a solitary draw and three defeats. The final Premier League table for a miserable 1999/2000 season made for grim reading. Celtic managed to win only twenty-one of their thirty-six games, while losing nine and drawing six. They finished with sixty-nine points. Rangers, who made certain of the trophy with five games still to play, took pole position with ninety points. It had been a wretched campaign, despite Celtic picking up only their fourth trophy during the reigns of Liam Brady, Lou Macari, Tommy Burns, Wim Jansen, Jozef Venglos, John Barnes and Kenny Dalglish.

One of Dalglish's last acts as interim manager was to tell Henrik Larsson to get ready to go on as a substitute in the last game of the season against Dundee United at Parkhead. There were twenty-five minutes left to play and Celtic were already leading 2-0 with goals from youngsters Simon Lynch and Mark Burchill. The 47,586 fans rose as one as the Swede replaced Lubomir Moravcik. Larsson didn't extend himself, but, even in that brief period, he showed his touch and graceful style had not deserted him through his months out of action. He said, 'I have to admit it was very emotional running back onto the pitch. I was pleased to get as many minutes as I did. It's rewarding to come back in the same season as breaking my leg. I felt strong although it was for only twenty-five minutes. I felt good when I had the ball. Now I can look ahead.'

It was time for what was becoming an annual routine - who would be in the Celtic dug-out for the 2000/01 campaign? As usual, the names tumbled forth hither and yon. One of the first to emerge was that of Co Adriaanse, of Dutch outfit Willem II. The speculation didn't last long, though, as he agreed to join Ajax for the new season. Another Dutch coach reported to be in the mix was Leo Beenhakker, who was on the verge of leaving Feyenoord. Ironically, he went to the Amsterdam giants, too, as Director of Technical Affairs. After a year, he fired Adriaanse and brought in Ronald Koeman. Berti Vogts, who had quit as manager of Germany in 1998, was another to get a mention. The man who would one day became the Scotland international coach put an end to that particular guessing game by joining Bayer Leverkusen.

Luis Fernandez, coach at Athletic Bilbao, stepped onto the managerial merry-go-round, but he was another who was destined for a place elsewhere when he took over at Paris Saint Germain in the summer of 2000. Peter Reid, then manager at Sunderland, threw his hat into the ring, too. John Toshack, linked with Celtic before Wim Jansen got the job, had just resolved a contract wrangle after leaving Real Madrid, but he headed for Saint Etienne. Former centre-half Mick McCarthy, who had played in Billy McNeill's centenary double-winning side, was the Republic of Ireland manager and he, apparently, was interested in returning to Parkhead. Dublin-born Joe Kinnear, who had quit

Wimbledon the previous year, was a personal friend of majority shareholder Dermot Desmond and, thus, was also said to be in the running. Martin O'Neill fell into the same category, but, to all intents and purposes, he was happy in the English top flight with Leicester City. The names were coming thick and fast. One of the most curious was that of Romanian Angel Iordanescu, who was coming out of contract at Saudi Arabian club Al-Hilal.

Clear favourite, though, was Guus Hiddink, who was on the verge of completing his short-term agreement at Real Betis. The former Holland international boss, who had also managed Real Madrid between July 1998 and February 1999, looked a shoo-in at one stage. Allan MacDonald and Chief Executive Frank O'Callaghan flew to Spain to have talks with the fifty-three-year-old Dutchman who would be a free agent in June. Hiddink admitted he had met the Celtic delegation 'out of courtesy and nothing else'. He also had a meeting with Tommy Burns and it was obvious some ground rules were being put in place. Jim Hone, the club's Contracts Manager, also made contact with the highly-rated coach and an annual salary of £1.4million was mentioned in the media. Things were moving apace when the coach's deal with Betis was abruptly terminated in May with the club heading for relegation.

Now, apparently, there was nothing to prevent Guus Hiddink from being appointed as the thirteenth individual to be the full-time manager of Celtic Football Club.

CHAPTER NINETEEN
MARTIN O'NEILL: THE EMERALD ANSWER

Dermot Desmond, suavely dressed in an immaculate grey suit, breezed into the luxurious suite at the exclusive London hotel and announced to the invited guests, 'Gentlemen, meet Celtic Football Club's new manager.' He paused for dramatic effect, ushered the smiling individual into the room and added, 'Mr Martin O'Neill.'

Silence. The audience was made up of Celtic boardroom members and there was little doubt that more than a few expected a Dutchman to be presented to them that day instead of a dapper Irishman. Somewhere along the way, Guus Hiddink had become history, as far as the billionaire major shareholder of the club was concerned. Desmond had remained suspiciously silent as the quest for Celtic's fourth managerial appointment in as many years dominated the daily newspapers.

One intrepid reporter caught up with the financier during one of his rare trips to Glasgow, which were never pre-publicised. The pressman seized the opportunity and asked the inevitable question, 'Who is going to be the Celtic manager?' Without a flicker of hesitation, Desmond looked at the blue skies above and replied, 'It's a lovely morning in Scotland.' And with that observation, he took a backseat in a sleek limousine and was whisked away to another destination. The Fourth Estate would have to wait for the public announcement just like everyone else. The debonair businessman, with the dashing Biggles-style moustache, had been busy in the background. He recognised Celtic urgently required stability and the revolving door policy concerning team bosses was having a chaotic effect on the club and, importantly, the fan base. They needed a manager who could meet the requirements and demands of a job that had convincingly demonstrated it had the ability to overwhelm individuals. Martin O'Neill came into focus. Liam Brady was someone Desmond sought out while looking for advice and background knowledge of the somewhat quirky Leicester City boss. Brady gave O'Neill a more-than-favourable review. From that moment, the job was O'Neill's.

However, before the club could dispense with the news, they had to agree compensation terms with Kenny Dalglish who still had twelve months remaining on his £600,000-a-year contract as Director of Football Operations. There was not the remotest possibility of O'Neill and Dalglish working together. Dalglish would eventually take the club to the Court of Session in Edinburgh accusing them of unfair dismissal. Figures ranging from £750,000 to £1.2million were bandied about before the sorry, messy situation was resolved. Unwaveringly, though, O'Neill was on course to meet his new supporters at the front door at Celtic Park on June 1 2000.

Another problem had to be resolved, too. There was the small matter of O'Neill having already agreed a three-year extension to his Leicester City deal in June 1999, reputedly worth £600,000 a year, matching Dalglish's salary at Celtic. By the summer of 2000, O'Neill had been team boss of the modest West Midlands outfit for five years after beginning his managerial career with non-league Wycombe Wanderers in 1990 and moving on for a brief stint at Norwich City in June 1995. The strong-willed character from the village of Kilrea, in Northern Ireland, had a disagreement with chairman Robert Chase over transfer policy and resigned six months later. He joined Leicester immediately after leaving the East Anglian club. He guided the Filbert Street side - with a ground capacity of 22,000 - to the Premier League in his first season. He also led the team to two League Cup Final successes and it wasn't long before clubs with superior financial resources were looking in his direction. O'Neill, bright and astute, triggered his release from his Leicester City contract after exercising a clause that allowed him, during the close season, to speak to clubs interested in obtaining his services.

And, so, on a particularly wet afternoon in the east end of Glasgow, O'Neill, with a fair degree of confidence, made his way to the front door at Celtic Park and, holding up his left hand to acknowledge the cheers of his new supporters, he had a few words for the gathering throng. O'Neill said, 'First of all, thank you very much for waiting in the rain. I really appreciate it.' He paused, waved again and continued, 'It's an absolute honour for me to be the manager here, I'm telling you that now. It's an absolute honour.' He stepped back as the rapturous applause gathered momentum. He signed off, 'I will do everything I possibly can to bring some success here to the football club. Thank you.' And with that the fourteenth full-time manager in Celtic history disappeared back into the labyrinth of his new football home where he would rule for five extremely interesting years.

O'Neill would be working again with John Robertson, his former Nottingham Forest team-mate who was also his assistant at Wycombe, Norwich and Leicester, and Steve Walford, his Head Coach at Carrow Road and Filbert Street. Once more, Celtic had their very own version of the Three Amigos, although this particular trio would prove to be less troublesome. In fact, you could add a fourth to that list because O'Neill extended Tommy Burns' emergency contract from the previous season to coach alongside Walford. Tommy didn't need any persuasion to agree the deal.

It was important O'Neill got to know the Scottish press with whom he had practically no experience in the past. On a gloriously sunny afternoon only a week after O'Neill's appointment, I was one of the few invited to meet the new manager at the chic Crutherland Hotel, set back in beautiful gardens on the way to East Kilbride. So, along with a handful of other selected journalists, I was given the opportunity to greet the incoming boss for the first time. O'Neill, fashionably about an hour late for the lunch date, was soon addressing a dining room mainly consisting of total strangers.

O'Neill looked around the room and said, 'Just to be absolutely sure about this, I want you all to know that I bear a grudge. No, I'm not joking. Seriously, I do bear grudges. Honestly, I do.' I have to admit it was quite an impressive 'maiden speech'. I sat opposite him for an hour or so that day and swiftly realised he wasn't a massive fan of mirth. He appeared to be solemn and withdrawn and made little effort to indulge in idle chit chat with anyone around about him, including me. However, I did get the distinct impression he was sizing up everyone in the room, making little mental notes and gathering strength.

When it came to coffee and liquors, the man given the task of breathing urgent life into the ailing giant that was Celtic Football Club moved to the top of the table to grab everyone's attention. He went through the usual preamble; 'Big club, big job, big test.' All that sort of stuff. Once he had got the formalities out of the way, the real Martin O'Neill took over and he had no intention of leaving anyone in that room in any shadow of doubt about what he expected in the coming years while he was manager of 'one of the greatest clubs in the world.' He wasn't just talking about his players, either. No member of the press left the Crutherland Hotel that day with any uncertainty about what was around the corner. The feeling was unanimous, 'Cross me and you're in trouble.' It was loud and clear. He came across as a singleminded, fiercely-committed individual who wouldn't lose a wink of sleep on slamming doors on people.

He meant every syllable of his 'bearing grudges' speech, no doubt about it. He was laying down the law, setting the ground rules and everyone was warned what to expect if they didn't toe the line. If he was looking for any favours from the media, I must have missed it. Nope, he was Martin O'Neill and it was his way or the highway. They say you only get one chance to make a first impression. I would say that most certainly is the philosophy of a fairly astute chap from Kilrea.

So, with the press suitably chastised and put in their place, O'Neill could now turn his attention back to more important matters. It was clear Mark Viduka believed his time as a Celtic player had come to a halt. His Australian agent, a character by the name of Bernie Mandic, had been touting him around Europe for almost half-a-season and there was reported interest from Spanish sides, but it was always more likely the striker would take the well-worn path to England. David O'Leary, another good friend of Dermot Desmond, parted with £6million to take the player to Leeds United. O'Neill acknowledged the undoubted skills of the striker, but wasn't keen on an unhappy player in his dressing room. Undoubtedly, he would have been aware of Viduka's antics when he spat out the dummy in the general direction of orbit during the eventful half-time of the Inverness Caley catastrophe, the very game that would eventually open the door to Parkhead for O'Neill. God only knows how the Irishman would have dealt with a mutinous player that evening; it doesn't bear thinking about.

As Viduka headed for the exit, O'Neill went into overdrive in his wheeling and dealing for a replacement. He had his eye on Chris Sutton, who was in the throes of being frozen out at Chelsea following his £10million move from Blackburn Rovers the previous summer. The energetic, powerful attack-leader, for whatever reason, couldn't fit into the London side's style of play and scored only one league goal in twenty-nine appearances. He was aware his miserable twelve-month stint at Stamford Bridge was as good as over when he failed to make Gianluca Vialli's squad for the FA Cup final against Aston Villa at the end of the season. Chelsea were willing to cut their losses and O'Neill was first in with a bid of £6million, the fee he had received from Leeds for Viduka. However, Bryan Robson, the former England international stalwart who was manager at Middlesbrough at the time, matched that figure and the decision rested with Sutton. The player, thankfully, chose Celtic; the persuasive Irish tongue of O'Neill had won the day.

Without kicking a ball, Sutton became an instant hero with the Parkhead faithful. After completing the signing, he said, 'I know the expectations of the Celtic fans. That's to win the league and put Rangers in their place.' Sharp and succinct, the words of a winner.

Unfortunately, the same could not be said for Rafael Scheidt. O'Neill made his mind up about the bungling Brazilian after only a few minutes of seeing him in action in a pre-season game in Ireland, a 3-2 win over

Bray Wanderers. The centre-half, with time and space, elected to shell a ball down the wing and, in doing so, almost decapitated the new Celtic boss who had to swiftly duck as the hurtling object sizzled over his head and into the unfortunate fans behind the dug-out. A loan deal was hastily put in place to take Scheidt back to Brazil with Corinthians for a year. The player had an interesting take on his days in Glasgow. He told South American journalists, 'I have left the hell that has been unbearable for me. I have suffered a massive process of rejection. Football is ping-pong with the ball going back and forward. Martin O'Neill has told me he thinks I am not good enough to play for Celtic. He told me to tackle harder, to fight for every single ball and to elbow my opponents. I told him I couldn't do that and he thought I never followed his instructions. Celtic were trying to send me on loan to an English club, but I refused to go there.'

O'Neill later admitted to being 'completely baffled' at the thought of anyone spending any sort of fee on the only Brazilian player he had ever witnessed who couldn't control and pass the ball. The defender's temporary transfer with Corinithians was extended for a further season and he said he wanted to return to Celtic after that period to show his real qualities. Choosing his words as carefully as he picked his passes, the South American was quoted as saying, 'I want the year to be known as the Scheidt year'. Celtic paid off the remainder of his contract in 2002, he joined Atletico Mineiro and a year later moved to Botafogo. They released him in 2006 and he spent a season in China with Shaanxi Baorong. Without argument, he is the most mystifing transfer deal in Celtic history as well as being the most extravagant waste of money. O'Neill, a keen criminologist from his days as a law student in Ireland, is fixitated with the Lord Lucan mystery. He's got a better chance of solving who shot the nanny than getting to the bottom of the Scheidt riddle.

It's been fairly well-documented that O'Neill never rushed into a transfer decision. As someone once pointed out, 'You would think it was Martin's own money he was parting with.' And Neil Lennon said, 'I think he must have watched me about thirty times before he decided to buy me from Crewe for Leicester City in 1996. Mind you, the fee was £750,000, so that would have been massive money for Martin to shell out at the time.' Lennon would cost considerably more when he was reunited with his manager at Parkhead in December 2000.

The Celtic manager had been impressed by the defensive qualities of Belgian international Joos Valgaeren during his nation's displays in the European Championships in the summer and, on this occasion, decided swiftly he wanted him in Glasgow. Time was not on his side, anyway, with reports Bayern Munich and Ajax were also showing an interest in the versatile back-four performer who could play left-back and centre-half. There was also the fact Marc Rieper had been forced to retire after failing to overcome the toe injury that decimated the previous season. Dutch outfit Roda JC accepted a bid of £3.8million for Valgaeren on July 28 and he made his debut two days later in the Premier League opener against Dundee United at Tannadice.

O'Neill's first Celtic selection for competitive action, in a flexible 3-5-2 formation, was: Jonathan Gould; Tommy Boyd, Alan Stubbs, Joos Valgaeren; Jackie McNamara, Paul Lambert, Eyal Berkovic, Stilian Petrov, Stephane Mahe; Henrik Larsson and Chris Sutton. Tommy Johnson replaced Berkovic in the sixty-fourth minute. After only fifteen minutes, one thing was abundantly clear to any spectator - Larsson was out to make up for lost time after his leg-break misery. The Swede began at a terrifying pace and kept going throughout an awesome performance which left his new team boss breathless and proclaiming afterwards, 'No doubt about, Henrik Larsson is world class.' It was the stylish frontman who scored the opening goal eight minutes from the interval and it was stamped with genuine quality. Sutton found his partner with a forward pass and Larsson, from just outside the penalty box, sized up the situation in a split-second and drilled a first-time drive that swept past Alan Combe at his right-hand post.

News had leaked before the game about O'Neill making a loan move for Mark Bosnich, Manchester United's unpredictable Australian goalkeeper. There was also talk of him fancying Ipswich Town's future England international Richard Wright. Possibly the speculation unsettled Jonathan Gould because the goalie was doing little to convince his new manager he was the man to be entrusted with the job for the remainder of the season. He was flapping at high balls and was bailed out by Valgaeren after completely misjudging a corner-kick from Jim Paterson. Gould had no such luck, however, four minutes after the turnaround when Neil Heaney whipped in a free-kick from the left. Gould's timing was out completely, he appeared to trip as he attempted to cut out the danger and David McCracken was presented with an open goal only six yards out and he thumped a header into the net. Standing on the touchline, O'Neill rubbed his chin and looked far from impressed.

Sutton equalled last season's league haul in England with the winner in the sixty-sixth minute. Larsson had been peppering Combe's goal with a variety of efforts and it looked as though it was only a matter of time before the visitors went ahead. The keeper made a fabulous high-flying save to push away a Jackie McNamara whizzbang effort, but the ball fell right at the feet of Stephane Mahe, enjoying the freedom of the left wing in his new-look role in O'Neill's line-up. The Frenchman zipped the ball straight back in again. It might have hit the net under its own steam as it roared wide of Combe at his left, but Sutton made completely sure by sliding in and, from almost on the goal-line, nudging the ball home. That proved to be the winner in an exciting and entertaining encounter. When Ken Bates, the snooty Chelsea owner who clearly wanted rid of Sutton, heard his former player had just netted the all-important goal on his Celtic debut, he sniffed, 'I'm not surprised - it's easy to score goals in Scotland.' No-one could remember the last time the haughty supremo of the London side had actually watched a Scottish game.

O'Neill was suitably impressed by his team's performance and didn't want to single out an individual, but it was obvious he had been blown away by the eye-popping display from Larsson. He was pleased, too, with debutants Valagaeren and Sutton and declared, 'We've got off to a win and the trick is to win the next one and the one after that and just keep going.'

A crowd of 59,057 took their seats to welcome the new manager to

Parkhead on Saturday, August 5. Motherwell were determined to spoil the party, but it was the gross incompetence of referee Alan Freeland that came closest to denying O'Neill his first win in front of the support who demonstrated they were behind him all the way. Not since the reign of Tommy Burns had the Celtic faithful witnessed a team boss whose animated antics emphasised he, too, was enduring and sharing the same see-sawing emotions as themselves on matchday. Wim Jansen, Jozef Venglos, John Barnes and Kenny Dalglish rarely shifted their positions in the dug-out or on the trackside. O'Neill, however, was just a tad different. There was the studious pose, hand on chin, at the start of the game, the sleeves rolled up to the elbows and the arms folded. Then came the back and forward and sideways movements along the touchline as he peered left and right and appeared to fret over every kick of the ball. If a player dared to drift out of position he would be greeted with the frenzied windmilling of the arms. And, of course, there was the wonderful spontaneity that heralded a goal; the jump into the air, knees bent, fists clenched and arms thrust forward in unbridled celebration. One newspaper tagged him the 'Leaping Leprechaun', but, thankfully, the appeal of that particular moniker didn't stick.

The odd decision-making of the match official had O'Neill going through the full extensive range of his passionate reactions against Billy Davies' side. The contest settled quickly and it was no surprise when Celtic went ahead in the eleventh minute. Paul Lambert and Stilian Petrov were two other players who would enjoy the restructured roles they had to play in O'Neill's plans, in particular the Bulgarian who wasn't asked to run and fetch up and down the wing throughout the ninety minutes. Petrov simply didn't have the legs to carry out the wishes of Barnes or Dalglish and his strengths obviously lay elsewhere. It didn't take his new boss too long to realise this and he was given a dedicated role in the midfield with the green light to get forward when the situation afforded itself. The goal was a masterpiece of simplicity. Lambert caught the Motherwell defence square, lobbed a ball over them to Petrov, who stunned it on his chest before firing low beyond Andy Goram.

The game became a little towsy after that and there was the intriguing 'game within a game' between Chris Sutton and his immediate opponent Greg Strong, two big guys who could dish out the punishment without complaint. Although the Fir Park side were a goal adrift, they did little to shed their cloak of stifling tactics. They had Ged Brannan sitting in front of his back four while it looked as though Benito Kemble had been given free reign to clatter into anyone wearing green and white. Both combatants carried out their manager's orders with relish. John Davies, booked in the fifth minute for flooring Petrov with a reckless challenge, received another yellow card in the thirty-seventh minute for pulling back the Bulgarian, again cleverly attempting to get into space behind him. Kemble was next in Freeland's book for a crude foul on Henrik Larsson.

The confrontation was threatening to descend into a roughhouse and the incompetent match official simply couldn't control the situation. Sutton thought he had doubled Celtic's advantage just after the hour mark when Lambert set him up following a swift free-kick, but the club's record signing could only look on in anguish as his effort beat Goram only to come back off the upright. Amazingly, McNamara was booked after a tackle on Strong in the sixty-sixth minute and, shortly afterwards, the Scotland international tangled with Kemble. That was enough for the referee to flourish another yellow card and McNamara's part in the proceedings came to an abrupt end. It didn't get any better for O'Neill or Celtic when Sutton, previously booked, was ordered to take the same path after a clash with Strong nine minutes from the end. The crowd was still simmering after those decisions when Lee McCulloch, who had also been yellow-carded earlier in the game, kicked out at Stephane Mahe and his actions were ignored. In itself, it warranted a straight red card, but Freeland thought otherwise. In the end, Celtic hung on for the three points.

O'Neill said, 'That was hard work. I know we can play much, much better. We didn't reach the same heights we had against Dundee United and we were probably a bit nervous of the home crowd. I thought when we got the goal it would settle us down, but it never really did. The sendings-off changed the complexion of the game and I was pleased with the players' application, that we had the durability to see it through.' O'Neill was asked about the attention paid to Sutton by Strong. He replied, 'It is a bit early to make assessments on that. Chris is a physical player, but so are the players he is playing against. It is a man's game. I don't know if there is a campaign against him. I thought he reacted well throughout the game and I felt his sending-off was harsh. The second booking was such a 50-50 ball that I thought we were going to get the free-kick.'

Midfielder Lambert, the team's most accomplished player on the day, said, 'Billy Davies has their team well organised. But winning was good because last year we blew it against ten men here and that didn't happen today. They had a bit of a flurry towards the end when they had the extra man, but they did not have any real scoring chances. The spirit is good in the team, but it has always been that way, even last season when things went wrong. Of course, we know what the new manager is thinking. He has told us what he wants and we all know that if we do not play well, we won't be in the team. We all fear for our first team place. He has that fear factor instilled in us now. If we let the team down at all we will be out. He has been quite clear about that and that is the way it has to be at any top club. That fear factor makes you play because you know that there is real competition for first team places.'

Celtic took a breather from domestic competition in midweek to travel to Luxembourg to take on the part-timers Jeunesse Esch in the opening stage of the UEFA Cup. It turned into a 4-0 canter with Lubomir Moravcik (2), Henrik Larsson and Bobby Petta on the scoresheet. O'Neill was suitably impressed by the veteran Czechoslovakian midfielder. He said, 'Lubomir is a wonderful talent. Where has he been for the last fifteen years?' A fortnight later, O'Neill took the opportunity to rest a host of players and the team were still good enough to win 7-0 with Mark Burchill claiming a remarkable hat-trick in three minutes. The youngster had fallen behind in the firing squad pecking order behind Larsson, Sutton and Tommy Johnson and had asked for a transfer. O'Neill said, 'Mark took his goals brilliantly and I'm very pleased for him. I don't know if this changes his plans, but I have made it clear I want him to stay at the club and battle for a place.' The Irishman added, 'Who knows, though? After tonight, someone might make a bid of £6million for him.' Eyal Berkovic (2), Vidar Riseth and Stilian Petrov got the other goals in front of a healthy attendance of 40,282.

Unfortunately, Celtic's European odyssey didn't travel beyond the third stage before they were extremely unluckily dismissed 3-2 on aggregate by Bordeaux in extra-time at Parkhead on September 11. Two weeks earlier at the splendid Stade Lecure in the south western wine-growing region of France, a twenty-fifth penalty-kick by Henrik Larsson nullified an earlier headed effort from Christophe Dugarry following a corner-kick. The stalemate set up Celtic perfectly for the return when 51,242 turned out to witness a controlled display for seventy-eight minutes. Lubomir Moravcik had given O'Neill's men the lead in the fifty-fifth minute with a measured low shot that swept past the impressive Ulrich Rame, who had earlier made quality saves to deny Moravcik, Henrik Larsson, Chris Sutton Sutton and Tommy Boyd. With twelve minutes to go the roof fell in on Celtic. The French equalised through an untidy goal from Lilian Laslandes when the striker bundled the ball past a surprised Jonathan Gould from close range. Incredibly, it was the first effort Bordeaux had on target all night. The same player snatched the winning goal in the second period of extra-time with an angled drive, which flew high over Gould's outstretched arm into the roof of the net.

An incredulous O'Neill said, 'It's galling to think we outplayed a very talented side and didn't win the match. We had them beat. It is very hard to take. I could not have asked for an ounce more effort from the players, but we could not convert the chances we created in a game we should have killed off by half-time. Right now, this is the most disappointed I have felt because it was a match we should have won, there wasn't even a doubt in my mind. Now we are desperate to get into the Champions League and take on the best teams in the Continent.'

In the previous round, two first-half goals from Larsson gave Celtic the initiative over HJK Helsinki in a 2-0 first leg victory in Glasgow. However, the inability to add to the early strikes almost cost them dearly in Finland when Gould, strangely nervous again, was blamed for the loss of two goals, both claimed by Paulus Roiha in each half. However, an extra-time strike from Sutton after service from Moravcik steered the team past a difficult HJK Helsinki outfit. O'Neill said, 'I'm not disappointed with the display because we had a lot of chances, but they just wouldn't go in. Their keeper had a fantastic game.'

With the passports returned to the players, Celtic could now concentrate on the domestic campaign and O'Neill never wavered from his priority target, the league title. On August 13 at Parkhead, O'Neill watched the team maintain its perfect hundred per cent start with a 2-1 win over a stubborn Kilmarnock side who led at half-time through a spectacular curling twenty-five yard effort from Andy McLaren in the eighteenth minute. However, Larsson levelled five minutes after O'Neill's half-time rallying call. Moravcik and Lambert combined on the right to release the Swede and, in a one-on-one situation with Gordon Marshall, there was only going to be one winner. Tommy Johnson, who had replaced the suspended Sutton, then benefited from a thoughtful through pass from Larsson in the seventy-third minute to gallop through, draw Marshall and slot the ball into the corner.

Kilmarnock's central defender Martin Baker, sent off at Parkhead the previous season, replicated the feat with a minute to go when he picked up his second caution for a foul on Moravcik. O'Neill refused to get carried away. He said, 'I'm utterly delighted with the victories we've had, but you can see yourself we've still got loads to do yet. We turned round a goal down and the crowd could have been edgy, but they stayed with us. I really thought they were magnificent.'

A highly intriguing month of August would be complete with a home confrontation against Dick Advocaat's Rangers, but before O'Neill could turn his thoughts to that particular test, he had to take Celtic to Edinburgh for a meeting with Hearts, who were unbeaten, but had failed to win their first three games with draws against Hibs (0-0), St Johnstone (2-2) and Aberdeen (1-1). O'Neill and his players reckoned they were not getting the credit their play deserved, despite a hat-trick of odd-goal wins. Unflatteringly, some observers were labelling the team, 'Leicester City in Celtic tops.' However, after a beguiling, entrancing showing in the capital, everyone was beginning to sit up and take notice as the Irishman's revolution really kicked in. The scoreline was 4-2 in favour of the Glasgow visitors, but the 16,744 fans of both sides had just witnessed a pulsating performance that saw Celtic go in 3-0 ahead at the interval after a whirlwind seventeen-minute spell.

Some critics wondered if Sutton was qualified to hold the mantle as the most expensive player in Scottish football history and, after this encounter, the towering Englishmen gave them every reason to believe the £6million paid to Chelsea for his services was a bargain. Some Hearts fans were heading for the exits before the half-time whistle to the chorus of 'cheerio...cheerio...' from the gleeful Celtic support. Sutton's first, in the twenty-third minute, was set up by Bobby Petta, rejuvenated after the arrival of O'Neill. His left-wing cross was so accurate, Sutton nodded it in from close range and said, 'It was more difficult to miss than score.' Five minutes later, Petta swung in a right-wing corner-kick and Sutton rose at the near post to flick the ball wide of Antti Niemi. Hearts were being shredded by their opponents at this stage and with Petta, Petrov and Lambert dominating proceedings, it seemed only a matter of time before Larsson scored. He struck the post after connecting with a Moravcik effort and, only minutes later, was more fortunate when he turned a Lambert pass beyond Niemi.

The Swede, however, proved he was only human when he squandered a penalty-kick shortly after the turnaround. Sutton was hauled down by Scot Severin and referee Willie Young pointed to the spot. Amazingly, the fans' favourite missed the target with his flawed attempt sailing over the bar. Severin capitalised on the lucky break when he pulled one back in the fifty-sixth minute with a low drive eluding Jonathan Gould. Moravcik had his manager and the travelling fans breathing more easily when he restored the three-goal advantage in the sixty-second minute when he skipped past a couple of insipid challenges and crashed the ball in off the crossbar. Tricky little Spaniard Juanjo claimed the home side's second three minutes later, but there was no chance of a sensational fightback.

A breathless O'Neill said, 'I think Chris Sutton is genuinely a top-class player. He was brilliant for us today, not only with his goals but his whole play. Overall, I think he was immense. At 3-0 up, I was absolutely delighted although I always believed Hearts would get a little motivation, especially after we missed the penalty-kick, which would have put us four ahead. I could see the ball going over the bar and I thought, "Oh, you so-and-so..." But, really, Henrik did well for us. But when he missed, Hearts roared back and it's put years on me! There were some really great signs for us and also some ominously worrying ones. Overall, of course, I have to be pleased with the result. And perhaps we should make allowances for the fact a little tiredness was there. Remember, some of our players had been on international duty in midweek.'

Rangers, like Celtic, also had a one hundred per cent record as they prepared for another titanic Glasgow tussle the following Saturday. They had overcome St Johnstone (2-1), Kilmarnock (4-2), St Mirren (3-1) and Dunfermline (4-1). Martin O'Neill couldn't have failed to notice the defence hadn't kept a clean sheet while Bert Konterman, a £4million buy from Feyenoord in the summer, was attempting to build an understanding in central defence alongside Amoruso. While the Celtic followers were now salivating over the all sorts of possibilities and prospects, O'Neill looked forward to his Old Firm baptism.

CHAPTER TWENTY
DEMOLITION DERBY

'Maybe the result highlighted Rangers aren't quite as good as they think they are. There are still only two teams who can win the league and it is far too early yet to say which of us it will be. But just so long as Celtic don't get carried away by this one result and continue going about things the way we have been so far, I think you could see me celebrating come the end of the season.'

Celtic Park was still rocking and heaving as Martin O'Neill reflected on the remarkable, rampaging 6-2 mauling of Rangers on August 27, 2000, a classic confrontation that would be welcomed to history with the title 'Demolition Derby'. The six-goal haul was as many as the club had bludgeoned into the net of their Ibrox rivals since the equally astonishing 7-1 League Cup Final victory on October 19, 1957. Suddenly, there was belief - genuine, tangible belief - that Celtic had the right man in charge; a grounded individual whose masterful motivational and man-management skills were becoming more obvious with every passing match.

Rangers had been contemptuously knocked aside, wrecked by a green-and-white tornado that left their manager Dick Advocaat ashen-faced while sportingly accepting his team had been beaten by superior opponents. There were no excuses from the Dutch hard-liner who had ruled the roost so comfortably the previous season over John Barnes and Kenny Dalglish and had, in fact, won three of the four Old Firm encounters, the last being the horribly one-sided 4-0 hammering at Ibrox only five months beforehand. That was then and this was now; Barnes and Dalglish were history and O'Neill's strong hands were on the tiller.

There is little doubt the confidence gleaned from this fascinating face-to-face between the Glasgow giants went a long way to breaking Rangers' psychological stranglehold on their opponents that had stretched over a decade of misery, interspersed with a spasmodic moment of joy which passed far too swiftly. The Ibrox men held such a dominion over the team from the east end of Glasgow it was beginning to look as though Celtic were existing to merely make up the numbers. That changed on a gloriously sunny day when such thoughts of inferiority were reversed. In an hour-and-a-half of riveting football, the oppressed had assumed the mantle of oppressors as the landscape transformed so dramatically. Celtic scored six; it could have been eight if they had upped their level of mercilessness.

Billy Dodds, one of the Rangers players engulfed in the storm, was honest enough to admit frankly, 'It was scary. I had been in Old Firm games before, but this was unbelievable. The noise coming out of Parkhead! Bang! Bang! Bang! It got louder and louder and you're thinking, "F****n' hell, this is a whirlwind." The stadium was rocking. Oh, my God, they took the roof off. You're thinking, "This could be a double-figures job if we don't get to grips with it."'

Chris Sutton, bought, by his own admission, 'to put Rangers in their place', terrorised Amoruso and Konterman at the heart of the Ibrox defence. With the Italian given no opportunity to stroll around and adopt the role of a poseur and the disorientated Dutchman clearly in a state of shock, there was the obvious potential for destruction. Sutton, clearly, was up for the job. By the eleventh minute, with Celtic a mesmerising three goals ahead, goalkeeper Stefan Klos must have wondered about the wisdom of getting out of bed that morning. Bobby Petta, rejuvenated in the rebirth of the team, was magisterially strutting around on the left wing, bringing mayhem with his every touch. It would have been an unimaginable scenario only a few months beforehand. Another Advocaat recruit at £4million from AZ Alkmaar, right-back Fernando Ricksen, eyes staring wildly at his very public humiliation, was spared by his thoughtful fellow-Dutchman when he withdrew him in the twenty-first minute to put on another midfielder in the shape of the Turk, Kerimoglu Tugay. The defender, seemingly hypnotised by fear, offered no protest at his early removal.

Henrik Larsson had, of course, missed all four Glasgow derbies the previous season and, immediately from the offset, illuminated the impression he would once again enjoy and thrive in these unique spectacles, none more so in the fiftieth minute, with the score at 3-1, he scored such a beautiful goal of gleeful impertinence that it will be forever seared into the memory banks of anyone who witnessed it. His masterly moment of impudence underlined he was by far the best player in the country by some distance. A panicking Advocaat would shell out a ludicrous £12million for Chelsea's Tore Andre Flo in November, but it would soon become obvious the Norwegian striker possessed only a fraction of the Swede's accomplished skills. With Larsson on the field and O'Neill in the dug-out, Celtic supporters had every reason to believe. The supporting cast wasn't too bad, either.

This most impassioned of Old Firm collisions had an extraordinary start as Sutton scored inside a minute with 59,476 fans looking on in a mixture of bewilderment and delirium. Lubomir Moravcik arced in a treacherous left-wing corner-kick with Sutton challenging Amoruso at the near post. The ball spun clear towards Larsson, who, off balance, didn't connect properly and his mishit effort looked to be going wide until Sutton, lurking with intent, turned sharply to whip a right-foot shot wide of the challenging Amoruso with Klos scrambling across his line. On my watch, it was exactly fifty-three seconds from Sutton kicking off to the Englishman smashing the ball into the rigging. Amoruso appealed for offside, but clearly wasn't aware team-mate Dodds was on the goal-line and also played Sutton on. Referee Stuart Dougal waved away the plea.

And Dodds got a good view of Celtic's second goal in the eighth minute as he stood rooted to the line as Moravcik curled in another devastating right-footed left-wing corner-kick. The Rangers defenders were concentrating on Larsson, Sutton, Alan Stubbs and Joos Valgaeren and, in total disarray, failed to pick up Stilian Petrov. The Bulgarian, with inch-perfect timing, shook off the half-hearted attentions of the hapless Ricksen and, with Klos again caught out, took to the air to send a thumping close-range header into the net. Celtic Park erupted once again as O'Neill did an impromptu jig of delight on the touchline.

Rangers, who arrived for the game in imperious mood after winning the Premier League title by a phenomenal twenty-one points the previous season, were in tatters, their so-called superior attitude obliterated by the eleventh minute when Celtic claimed a third goal. Petta and Moravcik combined on the left and Lubo, with his outstanding ability to think clearly and react quickly in the most frantic of circumstances, saw Paul Lambert racing clear just outside the box. With impeccable timing, Moravcik rolled the ball into the midfielder's stride and he didn't hesitate as he first-timed a vicious drive from sixteen yards wide of Klos, the ball crashing into the net as the goalkeeper valiantly and unsuccessfully threw himself to the left. Euphoria swept down from the stands as the players celebrated in the certain knowledge that, even before the fifteen-minute mark, the game was over. Rangers were rocking; Celtic had no intention of following the script.

O'Neill had to readjust his game plan when Lambert had to go off with an injury in the thirty-sixth minute following a fierce challenge from Neil McCann, who had already been booked early in the game for a reckless tackle on Jackie McNamara on the touchline. The industrious and clever midfield man tried to carry on, but the damage was so severe he collapsed and had to be replaced with Johan Mjallby. While Celtic were getting to grips with the reorganisation, Rangers scored five minutes later when Claudio Reyna got on the end of a left-wing cross from Rod Wallace. He directed his header down towards Jonathan Gould's left-hand post and the keeper did well to get across his line to smother the attempt. However, match official Dougal deemed the ball had crept over the line and awarded a goal, despite no conclusive proof of this being the case. That decision was perhaps balanced, though, when Wallace sent an angled drive wide of Gould, but was flagged offside just before the interval. It was dangerously close.

Any threats of an unexpected comeback from the Ibrox side were dynamited when cool customer Larsson scored with a wonderfully crafted lob five minutes after the turnaround. A clearance from Gould was directed into the Swede's path by the chest of the quick-thinking Sutton. There was still a lot of work to be done with Tugay racing in to challenge and Konterman barring his way to the penalty box. Almost disdainfully, Larsson eliminated the Turk with a burst of pace, the nervous-looking defender was treated with the utmost contempt as the ball was knocked between his legs before the solo move was delightfully completed with a nonchalant flick over the head of the transfixed Klos from eighteen yards. It was simply breathtaking in its artistry and execution.

Rangers were awarded a penalty-kick five minutes later when Wallace went down under a challenge from Stephane Mahe and Dodds rapped it wide of Gould. However, the day belonged to Celtic and, just after the hour mark, Petta floated over a right-wing free-kick, Larsson could barely believe the nearest opponent to him was Barry Ferguson, who was three yards away. The attacker rose, snapped his neck muscles upon impact and his deft flick soared past the motionless Klos. The raucous atmosphere obviously got to Ferguson, yellow-carded earlier for a foul on Petrov, who deliberately handled the ball and was excused duties for the last nine minutes of the game.

In the last minute, Sutton, just about out on his feet after heaping misery on Amoruso and Konterman, summoned one last surge of power as Petta set Mahe clear on the left. The Frenchman's speedy delivery along the ground was met by the striker's lunge at the back post and the sixth goal was tucked into the Rangers net. Sutton had finished what he had started. The startled Rangers players positively raced towards the sanctuary of the tunnel as Dougal blew for full-time, none of them wishing to hang around as the party got into full swing.

O'Neill, once he had recovered his composure, exclaimed, 'We got off to a great start, but there were plenty of uncomfortable moments. It could have been 3-2 after the first seventeen or eighteen minutes of the match, but you can't take anything away from the effort of the players. They were absolutely fantastic. Even at 4-1, I was thinking there is a long, long way to go. They got back to 4-2, and I think the only time I ever really felt comfortable was when Sutton put the sixth one in. But, at the end of it all - and I am not being patronising - Rangers are still the benchmark and are a top-class side.

'We couldn't have dreamed for a better start. We could play for another one hundred years and not get a start like that again. I'm delighted and I thought the players were brilliant. The performance was really, really immense. I would have settled for scoring in the last minute and winning the game 1-0 - but there won't be many 1-0 games here. The players are all delighted, but there is no feeling of euphoria because a few of them have been here a couple of years and they know not to get too carried away with anything. I'll be happy tonight and maybe tomorrow morning, but after that I and the players will concentrate on the next game. Dick Advocaat has said that he has seen Celtic make great starts before and we know that the players have often been in the shadow of Rangers, so I don't think anyone is getting too excited. Most of the players are going away on international duty and I just hope they come back unscathed.'

Opposite number Advocaat, still looking shaken and more than a little aghast, reflected, 'We lost in the first twenty minutes, especially with the goals we gave away. Quite simply, we have to give all the credit to Celtic. The scoreline doesn't lie and they deserved to win. If you give goals like that away at this level, you will get punished, but, at least, we know what we have to change. It seemed like every attack they made was a goal. They had periods when they really had us under the cosh. We have four internationalists at the back - and I don't want to point the finger at certain individuals - but we were very poor today.'

There was little in the way of sympathy from Henrik Larsson. He said, 'We always try to play as a team, but, as individuals, we were really on fire. You could see everyone really wanted to win, as you always do, of course. We went for it and things went our way.'

Paul Lambert gave the credit to O'Neill. 'The manager has installed an unbelievable air of confidence in the players. He has made us play better and made us want to win even more. We now possess a great will to win every game.'

Years later, Tommy Boyd, who replaced Moravcik in the second-half, said, 'There was a sea change that season and there was a wave of optimism because of Martin's appointment. He had rightly said Rangers were the benchmark of Scottish football, but we reached that and matched it. That result was a huge step.'

Chris Sutton, as sharp as ever, said, 'It was a great win. I may be new here, but I am aware of the feeling that exists between these teams. The derby games are vitally important and this is a good start. The main thing for everyone at this club is to win the SPL championship. That is our priority. If we keep winning, they'll have to play catch-up and we'll see how that suits them.'

CHAPTER TWENTY-ONE
STAYING POWER

John Hartson was in Glasgow for signing talks as he prepared to quit Wimbledon following their relegation from the top flight. The Welsh international striker, a robust presence in the frontline, had struggled with injury after becoming the unfashionable club's record signing at £7.5million in January 1999 when he joined from West Ham United where he had scored a creditable thirty-three goals in seventy-three league and Cup appearances.

It was only three days after Rangers had been thrashed 6-2 by Celtic and Ibrox manager Dick Advocaat immediately reached for the chequebook to remedy the situation. As well as his £8million splurge on Dutch double-act Fernando Ricksen and Bert Konterman, he had also brought in Kenny Miller (Hibs), Allan Johnston (Sunderland) and Peter Lovenkrands (AB Copenhagen) during another summer signing spree. Hartson had already agreed personal terms with the club, but owner David Murray insisted the proposed £6million deal would only go through if the burly forward passed his medical. He threatened, 'There is the possibility the medical might not go very well because it is very strict. We have made mistakes in the past and we don't want those things to happen again.' It was already public knowledge Hartson had seen a move to Spurs collapse the previous season because he hadn't reached the required fitness levels.

A few days later, the twenty-five year old was once again given the news the possibility of a transfer had been scuppered and he wouldn't be moving to Glasgow. Martin O'Neill had other ideas about that and resolved to keep tabs on the situation. Advocaat was more successful, though, when he added to his Dutch legion when Barcelona accepted an offer of £4.5million for thirty-year-old midfielder Ronald de Boer, a player he had coached while he was Holland's international manager during the 1994 World Cup qualifying campaign. O'Neill, at the same time, was busy in the transfer market, too, and signed midfielder Alan Thompson for £2.75million from Aston Villa and paid a nominal £50,000 for speedy winger Didier Agathe, who was due to come out of his short-term contract at Hibs in October.

Thompson, who agreed a five-year deal, made his debut in the League Cup-tie against Raith Rovers on September 6 and marked the occasion with a goal in his new club's 4-0 triumph at Parkhead in front of 32,307 fans. Chris Sutton got the opener and Tommy Johnson added two more, one from the penalty spot. Thompson claimed his strike with a cute backheel after being set up by Mark Burchill. Around this period, Allan MacDonald, who had done so much in the summer to attempt to lure Guus Hiddink to the club, unexpectedly resigned from his Chef Executive position. There were reports MacDonald, who had only taken over the previous year, had become increasingly frustrated, both by the cumbersome mechanism of plc board control and major shareholder Dermot Desmond's increased interest in the club's affairs.

On the pitch, though, was where it really mattered to the Celtic fans and the team simply kept on winning and picked up maximum points from their three league games in September. In the first, Martin O'Neill made history by overwhelming Hibs 3-0 in front of a fabulous crowd of 60,091 at Parkhead for the club's ninth successive victory, a post-war feat that not even the legendary Jock Stein could manage. However, displaying an unmatched ambitious streak, the Irishman declared, 'We are playing with confidence, but we're still a million miles away from the finished article.'

Once again, Henrik Larsson and Lubomir Moravcik were inspiring with the Swede scoring two first-half goals - one a penalty-kick - while Mark Burchill claimed the other. Jackie McNamara and Paul Lambert were also performing at the top of their powers and Hibs, unbeaten before this confrontation, were simply outclassed. Alex McLeish, the Edinburgh side's manager, agreed there had been a gulf in quality and said, 'If my players were that good they would be playing for Celtic and I'm not discrediting them.'

Larsson was proving, like the team, to be unstoppable and he got the winner five minutes from time as Celtic had to work hard for their 2-1 win over Dunfermline. Celtic arrived at East End Park having scored thirty-five goals while conceding a miserly six in an unrelenting sequence of ten victories. However, it looked for a moment that the unthinkable might be visited upon O'Neill's men when Stevie Crawford netted with a soft penalty-kick award early in the second-half after referee Willie Young adjudged Chris Sutton had handled the ball. The striker was booked as was keeper Jonathan Gould for delaying the kick. Crawford, though, scored in emphatic fashion. However, Larsson responded and equalised immediately from another spot-kick award after Paul Lambert was downed in the box by Scott Thomson. With time ebbing away, Larsson latched onto an Alan Thompson pass, rounded keeper Marco Ruitenbeek and stroked the ball into the net.

Celtic's late triumph regained their five-point advantage over Rangers and a relieved O'Neill admitted, 'I don't think we played very well at all, but I thought the two lads at the back, Joos Valgaeren and Johan Mjallby, were outstanding and Henrik Larsson's finishing was brilliant. I have to say I thought Dunfermline were excellent and I knew they would be up for the game. We were second to the ball and didn't get our passing movements going. Still, I was delighted that we came from behind because that showed a bit of character.'

Stilian Petrov took over the mantle of matchwinner when Dundee provided the opposition in front of 59,694 fans in Glasgow. The Bulgarian claimed the confrontation's solitary counter just after the hour mark when he headed an astute lobbed pass from the impressive Alan Thompson past the helpless Rab Douglas, who would be a Celtic player the next time he appeared at Celtic Park. Martin O'Neill observed, 'It was a very difficult day and I'm very pleased to have won. We could possibly have scored a second goal because we had a good period after Stilian gave us the lead, but, getting towards the end, you don't want to concede anything. Hence the introduction of Alan

Stubbs. And, of course, Lubo is almost as old as me now (Moravcik was 35), so you have to look after his old legs. We had a lot of possession in the match, without getting to where we wanted to go and, on days like these, you have to be patient. We showed that and, just as important, so did the crowd. Some of the players were just saying in the dressing-room that in similar circumstances last year, the supporters would have been getting a bit restless.'

The Irishman added, 'When I was making assessments of what we had in the summer, apart from watching videos, I wasn't completely sure of what Stilian could do. But I did say that teams with aspirations to high achievement all have midfielders who can contribute goals. I thought he could do that and now he has that role, with Paul Lambert in the holding position. We needed his goal all right, because Dundee made it difficult for us. I think there's no doubt that our being at the top of the league gives opponents more of an incentive. We saw it at Dunfermline, too, when we also had to display patience to get the right result.'

The bandwagon had to slow down at some stage and two points were dropped in a 1-1 draw with Aberdeen at Pittodrie at the start of October. O'Neill, though, was far from disappointed. Celtic had just returned from a punishing trip to Finland to play HJK Helsinki and had annexed a place in the next round courtesy of Sutton's extra-time goal. It had been a gruelling game in stamina-sapping conditions and the manager acknowledged that fact by leaving Moravcik on the bench until the second-half. Sutton played throughout after suffering a broken nose in the UEFA Cup-tie. The Dons, after conceding twenty-five goals in five meetings against the Parkhead side the previous season, were in the mood to take any advantage against a wearisome visiting outfit.

To be fair, Ebbe Skovdahl's team played exceptionally well. Celtic rarely troubled Ryan Esson in the first-half with only two long-range shots from Thompson worthy of note. The Dons opened the scoring on the stroke of half-time when a Derek Young pass sliced open the middle of the rearguard and Robbie Winters raced through before lifting the ball over the head of the unprotected Gould. Larsson had created a stir even before kick-off by appearing without his trademark dreadlocks, replaced by a shaven head. The fans might have wondered about the 'Samson effect', but they had no need to concern themselves as their pin-up Bhoy covered the ground in his usual zippy fashion throughout the ninety minutes.

The Swede claimed the equaliser eight minutes from the end when Petta and Moravcik combined at a short corner-kick, the Slovakian picked out Larsson with another of his measured crosses and Esson had no chance as a header zoomed past him. A minute later, Petta was shown the red card after picking up his second booking. It didn't stop Celtic surging forward in search of a winner, though. At the end, O'Neill declared himself satisfied and said, 'All things considered, especially the recent strains that have been put upon us, we are very pleased with a point.'

After a break for internationals, Larsson was at it again when he scored the second and killer goal in the 2-0 win over St Mirren in Glasgow on October 14 with a remarkable crowd - this time 60,002 - lapping up another excellent performance against a Paisley side that attempted to shut up shop right from the kick-off. O'Neill introduced Didier Agathe, his 'steal' from Hibs, for his debut now the manager believed the player was properly match-fit. The winger lit up a drab afternoon in the east end of Glasgow with a scintillating display, his electric pace continually shredding the Saints' five-man backline.

The manager was suitably pleased with Agathe's first appearance and was moved to say, 'Maybe I went overboard in the dressing room with the praise, but I thought his debut was the best I have ever seen; he was absolutely brilliant. He is prepared to get at players with a bit of strength and pace and he is a brilliant option for us. I was absolutely delighted for him.'

Moravcik had been hinting this would be his last season before bowing to the demands of Father Time. Until then, though, the Celtic supporters were determined to wring every last piece of enjoyment out of watching the little magician. He set up the opening goal in the thirty-third minute with another precision corner-kick and Sutton applied the finishing touch. Larsson made certain when he flashed in a low eighteen-yard free-kick eight minutes from time. The victory kept Celtic six points ahead of Rangers at the top of the table.

And the club were also overtaking their Ibrox rivals off the pitch, too. O'Neill had been searching for a new keeper from day one and had just failed to land Mark Bosnich on a year-long loan with the Australian opting to remain at Manchester United and fight for his first team place. Ipswich Town's Richard Wright had also been on his wishlist, but he eventually moved to Arsenal for £6million. O'Neill turned his sights to Newcastle United's Shay Given, who had been on Celtic's books as a youngster. Given admitted to being a massive fan of the club, but he wasn't tempted when the St James's Park outfit handed him a lucrative new offer and a long-term contract that locked him up tight on Tyneside. The Celtic boss had been impressed by Dundee's Rab Douglas' performance at Parkhead in September and accelerated his interest when it became known Dick Advocaat was prepared to pay £1.2million for the Dens Park No.1. O'Neill matched the fee and, once again, Douglas had a choice to make and he was delighted to join up at Celtic Park.

Jonathan Gould, though, was still in possession of the gloves when Celtic beat St Johnstone 2-0 in monsoon conditions in Perth on the storm-ravaged Tuesday evening of October 17. It was a tricky fixture in such slippery conditions. O'Neill took one look at the McDiarmid Park playing surface and told Moravcik, 'I think you can have the night off, Lubo.' Joos Valgaeren powerfully headed in an Alan Thompson free-kick for the barrier-breaking goal just before the interval. Henrik Larsson sent an assured penalty-kick wide of Alan Main in the eighty-sixth minute after Bobby Petta had been cleared out by Alan Kernaghan.

Referee John Rowbotham had a busy evening and booked nine players and sent off the Perth side's Stuart Malcolm. The second-half substitute had barely time to get soaked when he was caught firing a stiff arm into the face of Johan Mjallby with play held up as Celtic waited to take a free-kick. Seven of his team-mates were also yellow-carded, ironically, including two future Celts, Momo Sylla and Paul Hartley. The two visiting players to fall foul of the match official were Stilian Petrov and

Larsson. The victory pushed the Bhoys five points clear of Hibs and nine ahead of Rangers.

'I would have been disappointed if it had been called off, especially when we were ahead' said O'Neill. 'We went into this one knowing it was a game where we could drop points. Rangers are capable of winning their games in hand and there are miles to go yet. If you told me at the start of the season that we would have been in this position I would have smiled.'

Irish eyes were smiling again four days later when Celtic beat Dundee United 2-1 in front of 59,427 fans at Parkhead. The win left Rangers in the Hoops' slipstream, twelve points adrift. Dick Advocaat's side had already lost 1-0 to Alex McLeish's strong-going Hibs team in Edinburgh earlier in the month and, a day after this latest Celtic victory, they would flop 2-1 to St Johnstone in Perth. Almost unnoticed, Henrik Larsson scored the opening goal against the Tannadice side - another neat header from a cunning delivery by Bobby Petta in the thirty-fourth minute - which was exactly a year to the day since his left leg was shattered in the UEFA Cup-tie against Lyon in France. It was also the Swede's sixteenth goal in fifteen games and his forty-ninth in SPL history. What a legacy Wim Jansen bequeathed Celtic.

The goal that wrapped up the points came from a typical Celtic manoeuvre worked on every day in training by Steve Walford and Tommy Burns. Johan Mjallby fired over a long crossfield ball, Chris Sutton knocked it down to the edge of the penalty area and Alan Thompson, so adept with his left foot, demonstrated the right wasn't just for standing on when he hit a perfect volley past Alan Combe. United hadn't scored an away league goal on the travels since April, but Paul Lambert duly obliged when he misjudged a clearance at a free-kick and fired the ball past an astonished Jonathan Gould twelve minutes from time. The midfielder said, 'It would have been one hundred times worse if it had been 0-0 at the time.'

O'Neill didn't exactly go overboard at the end. 'We can play much, much better than we did today. We won't get carried away. I'm just glad we've done our bit by picking up all three points in this one. I don't think there is any doubt we deserved to win.' Someone mentioned Celtic hadn't scored more than two goals in each of their last eight games. That was met with a shrug of the manager's shoulders. There was also a report stating out-of-favour Eyal Berkovic had instructed his lawyer, Yoel Goldberg, to write to O'Neill demanding an explanation about the Israeli's continued exclusion from the first team. 'Well, good luck to him with that,' was the swift retort.

The Celtic manager had a lot more to say in the countdown to the next league outing, the match against Motherwell at Fir Park the following Saturday. There wasn't even the hint of blarney as he surreptitiously turned up the pressure on Dick Advocaat and Rangers. O'Neill had selected the precise moment he wanted to go public with his thoughts. He said, 'We are a long way yet from the finished article. I mean that. I really do. And I am also telling you the truth when I say that we don't have as strong a squad as Rangers. I know they have had injuries, but we could not bring in players of the same quality as they did if we had the same number of injury problems. That is why I intend to strengthen the squad before the winter break.'

The Ibrox side were due to play Kilmarnock in Glasgow on October 28, the afternoon before Celtic would travel to Motherwell. The bookies had Advocaat's side as 3/1 on with the Ayrshire men rated 7/1 against. A 3-0 win for the visitors was placed at 80/1. If anyone had been brave/daft/clever enough to accept those odds they would have cleaned up. Rangers, after missing out on Rab Douglas, spent £2.1 million in bringing in Jesper Christiansen from Odense and the big Dane was forced to pick the ball out of the net twice in just over half-an-hour of his debut in front of a stunned audience of 49,659 in Govan. Killie, managed by ex-Ranger Bobby Williamson, tore up the form book and Christophe Cocard netted in the sixth minute and Gary Holt added a second before half-time. Arthur Numan completed a grim day for the faltering champions when he put through his own goal to clinch the visitors' 3-0 triumph. Before the game, Advocaat said he saw no reason why his team couldn't win their next fourteen games in succession. Not exactly a prophetic statement.

Celtic's opportunity to open up a massive fifteen-point gap was wrecked by yet another weird refereeing decision. And, once more, Hugh Dallas was the man in the middle. The game at Fir Park fairly fizzed along and in the end O'Neill and his troops had to be content with a single point from a 3-3 draw, but TV and pictorial evidence clearly proved they had been robbed of a 'goal' that would have made the scoreline 4-2 in their favour at one stage and would almost certainly have ended the game as a contest. It didn't help, either, that Motherwell claimed a point with an extremely dodgy penalty-kick twelve minutes from the end.

Goals from Johan Mjallby, Joos Valgaeren and Jackie McNamara - with Henrik Larsson involved in all three - had given Celtic the advantage while Derek Adams and Lee McCulloch had replied for the home side. The moment of controversy arrived when, after some penalty-box ping-pong, Mjallby stabbed an effort over the line from close range. Martyn Corrigan, practically standing in the back of the net, swung at the ball more in instinct than anything else. In frustration, he booted it down the park and, inexplicably, Dallas, in a good position, and his assistant both failed to spot the ball was at least a yard over the line. Celtic players were still fuming when Mjallby and Don Goodman, a big, awkward, old-fashioned centre-forward, got involved in a tangle of limbs in the box. The visitors claimed a free-kick, Well's players screamed for a penalty-kick and Dallas duly obliged by pointing to the spot. Ged Brannan gratefully battered the ball past Jonathan Gould to his right.

O'Neill, wisely, refused to comment on Dallas' bewildering second-half calls. He said, 'That was a great game for the fans and it was a great advert for Scottish football. We would have loved to have taken all three points, of course, but you accept these things happen in football. What I will say is that those people who say all the decisions go in our favour will have to think again.'

Celtic dismissed Rangers' conquerors Kilmarnock and St Johnstone before warming up for the second Old Firm encounter of the season with a dazzling six-goal destruction of Hearts. A solitary strike on the hour mark by the diligent Alan Thompson was enough to earn the points against a fired-up Rugby Park side who had their eye on an unlikely double Old Firm giant-killing act in Glasgow. Thompson, who was never slow to take the responsibility at set-plays, found himself all alone in the Killie penalty area when a cross from Didier Agathe threaded its way across to him. The Englishman didn't hesitate as he plonnked the ball behind keeper Gordon Marshall. Agathe had come on just before half-time for the limping Paul Lambert whose injury was diagnosed as a stress fracture which could keep him on the sidelines until the turn of the year.

Chris Sutton was booked in only two minutes by referee Willie Young for a clattering challenge on former Ranger Ian Durrant. If it was possible, his stock rose even higher with some of the cheering home support. This was a rare off day for Henrik Larsson who missed two opportunities he would normally have stuck away while blindfolded; proof that even the greats can struggle on occasion.

'I'm delighted with the result,' declared O'Neill. 'This was a very big win. A draw would have been a good enough result for us, but, obviously, it's great to get a win. The players had told me before the game that Kilmarnock always make it tough for us here. Also, they were on a bit of a roll, but, so, too, were we. There is a resolve about the players, but that comes from the confidence that we have in the dressing room at the moment. I have to say, though, that I am not best pleased that we could not kill the game off with a second goal. Their goalkeeper was superb and made a couple of breathtaking saves when we had a bit of a blitz. I wasn't over-worried because I know my team are always capable of scoring goals.'

Killie boss Bobby Williamson added, 'We have to give credit to Celtic. They didn't allow us to create anything. My players gave everything, but we didn't get any breaks. No complaints, really. Celtic deserved it. They are grinding out results and that's the real difference at the moment.'

O'Neill's team went into breeze mode a week later as they overcame St Johnstone 4-1 in front of 57,137 fans. Celtic were leading by three goals before the interval with Chris Sutton, Henrik Larsson and Lubo

Moravcik on target. The Swede added a fourth before Craig Russell ruined Rab Douglas' hopes of a debut clean sheet with a strike eight minutes from the end. Before the game, Moravcik again reiterated it was his intention to hang up his boots in June, but it was obvious he wasn't going to take the anonymous route to retirement. O'Neill said, 'Lubo was marvellous again and I think Alan Thompson might just have run him close for the Man of the Match award. I was happy, too, for Henrik. It's the same with any striker. If you miss a couple of chances, the next time you might be slightly hesitant. So, when his first goal went in, it gave him the confidence to chip the keeper for his second.'

Hearts may have made the trip from Edinburgh to Glasgow in a slight state of trepidation on November 18. Sherlock Holmes qualities were not required to detect the reason for their nervousness - they had been beaten 5-2 in a thrilling League Cup encounter earlier in the month by O'Neill's men on their own ground. However, even the Celtic manager, maintaining his fair-minded attitude, admitted the final scoreline flattered his club after the game went into extra-time tied at 2-2. Remarkably, there was no scoring as the tie edged towards the interval. O'Neill had taken the decision to give Henrik Larsson the evening off and brought in youngsters Jamie Smith, Colin Healy and Stephen Crainey. It might have looked like backfiring when the Tynecastle outfit took the lead in the thirty-sixth minute when referee Kenny Clark awarded a spot-kick after Vidar Riseth had brought down Juanjo. Colin Cameron expertly tucked the ball behind Jonathan Gould to the keeper's right.

Cameron, in fact, had been linked with Celtic while Leicester City played hardball in O'Neill's efforts to entice Neil Lennon to Parkhead. He reckoned someone at his old club had a sense of humour when they slapped an £8million price tag on the Northern Ireland skipper's head. At least, Cameron, a wiry, little midfielder, proved he could take a spot-kick that night because his side were awarded another with Celtic leading 2-1 following a fine equaliser from Crainey in the forty-first minute and another from Smith just before the hour mark. This time the match official ruled Joos Valgaeren had handled a cross from Andy

Kirk and, once again, Cameron was nerveless as he scored the goal that ultimately took the encounter into an extra half-hour.

Cup-tie frenzy then kicked in. Eight minutes into the added-on period, keeper Antti Niemi made a splendid save as he sprawled full-length to tip a header from Tommy Johnson onto the post. Healy saw his opportunity and raced in to belt the ball into the net. Lubomir Moravcik, still sprightly and sparkling in extra-time, netted three minutes from the end and, sixty seconds later, Jackie McNamara put the gloss on the final scoreline. O'Neill said, 'The scoreline does not reflect the game at all. Hearts were in it right up to a couple of minutes from extra-time when we scored our last two goals. It was very, very tight until then. I thought our three young players - Crainey, Smith and Healy - took their goals really well. Indeed, I thought Healy was outstanding, quite apart from his great goal. He played with a lot of confidence throughout the game.'

Hearts' Finnish No.1 Antti Niemi, the former Rangers keeper who had been beaten twice by Lubomir Moravcik in the 5-1 game that somersaulted the veteran into the hearts of the Celtic support two seasons earlier, was back between the sticks at Celtic Park and might not have been too happy to see his nemesis lining up at the kick-off that fresh November afternoon. However, he must have dared to wonder if his luck was changing when Colin Cameron, looking as though he was doing his damndest to impress O'Neill, opened the scoring in the thirteenth minute. Cameron exchanged passes with Scott Severin, lined up a drive from just outside the box and flashed an unstoppable effort high past Rab Douglas.

Three minutes later, normal service was resumed and the cheers from the travelling support were stifled in an instant. Bobby Petta, continuing to revel under the guidance of O'Neill, was creating havoc on the left wing while Didier Agathe was doing likewise on the opposite flank. The Dutchman set up an opportunity for Joos Valgaeren and the Belgian defender bent an exquisite shot wide of the bamboozled Niemi. O'Neill joked later, 'What a strike from Joos - he must have been taking lessons from Lubo!'

In the space of eight spellbinding minutes, Niemi was invited to retrieve the ball from the back of his rigging on three more occasions. No-one was surprised when craftsman supreme Moravcik got in on the act in the thirty-sixth minute as he seized upon a loose headed clearance from Gary Locke, took a step to his left and curled the ball low into the corner with the utmost precision. Agathe turned on the afterburners to leave Steve Fulton and Grant Murray in his wake as he set up the third for Henrik Larsson. The Swede's first effort was bravely parried by Niemi, but he followed up to ram home the rebound. A minute from the turnaround, Petta worked a swift corner-kick routine with Moravcik who picked out Johan Mjallby and he powered in a fourth from close range. As expected, Celtic eased up, but still claimed two more goals in the fading moments through Larsson and Stilian Petrov.

When the dust settled, the statistics proved Niemi had to deal with nineteen shots on target during a hectic afternoon. Caretaker boss Peter Houston, stepping in to take charge following the dismissal of Jim Jefferies, sighed, 'Niemi is an international goalkeeper who did his job well. But you have to ask, where were the other players around him?' He added, 'I have to be honest and say Celtic absolutely murdered us, especially in the opening forty-five minutes.' O'Neill concurred. 'Our performance in the first-half is as good as I have seen from any football team in a long time,' he beamed. 'Regardless of our excellence today, we still need to strengthen.'

Celtic were now a humongous fifteen points ahead of their Ibrox rivals as they prepared to travel across Glasgow for the second Old Firm fixture of the campaign on November 26. The vast majority of the fans in the 59,813 applauded their heroes off the pitch following the hammering of Hearts and the Parkhead stands reverberated to the cocksure, clamorous chants of, 'Bring on the Rangers.'

No-one saw it coming. The confidence and belief that had been two of Celtic's most formidable and resourceful allies in their previous sixteen unbeaten league games simply evaporated at the home of their greatest rivals. The devastating double-act of Henrik Larsson and Chris Sutton, the partnership that had been terrifying defences since they got together at Tannadice in July, just didn't click; they could have been two strangers meeting for the first time. Lorenzo Amoruso, whose reputation was ravaged in the previous derby, ruled the Rangers rearguard and even had time to help himself to a rare goal. Barry Ferguson, Albertz and Ronald de Boer, on his Old Firm debut, took command of the midfield and Celtic's cause wasn't helped when Alan Thompson departed the scene after two yellow cards in the sixty-fourth minute with the Ibrox side already 2-1 ahead.

Leading up to the hour mark, it was deadlocked at 1-1, but, in truth, Celtic were struggling to find any sort of rhythm. Rangers, unbelievably, might have been two goals ahead in the opening minutes. Tore Andre Flo, newly-signed from Chelsea for £12million - double the previous Scottish highest transfer fee of £6million that Celtic spent on Sutton - missed a sitter from close range after being allowed a free shot at Rab Douglas' goal. Moments later, De Boer put one over the bar with the empty net gawping in front of him. Celtic awoke from their trance to attempt to get their passing and moving game together, but they were undone in the thirty-fourth minute and Martin O'Neill was apoplectic. No-one could blame him.

Rangers were awarded a free-kick at the touchline just in front of the dug-outs. Arthur Numan took it quickly, but was clearly about twelve feet away from where the incident took place. The Celtic manager screamed at referee Kenny Clark who simply turned his back and waved play forward. The ball was worked to Claudio Reyna on the opposite wing with Celtic still in disarray. The American international switched it inside to Ferguson, striding away from Lubomir Moravcik, and he sent a crisp twelve-yarder low past Douglas. It remained that way until the fifty-sixth minute when Larsson thumped a header from a right-wing Thompson corner-kick past Stefan Klos. That was one of the last actions of the day from Thompson. He had previously been booked for a late tackle on Ferguson and when he slid in again on the Rangers skipper, smack in front of the match official, the yellow card was produced in double-quick time and he was banished.

Just before that, though, the Ibrox side had taken the lead for a second time on the sixty-minute mark. In a sequence of three corner-kicks from the right wing during a disastrous sixteen-minute spell, Celtic gifted Dick Advocaat's men a trio of goals. Unfortunately, new keeper Douglas would have no reason to look back on his baptism in this fixture with any fondness. He was left flapping frenziedly at the first set-play, delivered by De Boer to the near post. Albertz hit the face of the crossbar with a header and Flo, unmarked in front of goal, knocked the ball over the line with the heel of his right boot. It didn't matter whether it was accident or design; the ball was in the Celtic net and Rangers were in front. Then came Thompson's expulsion followed four minutes later with another corner-kick on the right. This time Albertz took it, swung it to the back post and, with Douglas failing to cut it out, De Boer was given the invitation to knock the ball over the line from close range. Eight minutes after that, Albertz clipped over another ball and Amoruso, with no-one near him, raced in unchallenged and sent a header wide of the Douglas, blameless on this occasion and given no cover from the players in front of him. With five minutes to go, Michael Mols drilled in the fifth.

Martin O'Neill made no attempt to hide although he must have been bitterly disappointed to see the club's unbeaten record obliterated in such an awful and unexpected manner. 'Rangers deserved to beat us, but I don't think any manager likes to concede goals as cheaply as we did today,' he said. 'We defended poorly from corners, but Rangers were the better side.

'Their first attack came in the first minute and was made up of a breakdown by our players in the penalty box and they moved sweetly across. Flo, who is an excellent player, missed it, but we might have found ourselves a goal behind and the tone of the game could have been set from that. We didn't play well enough to cause any problems in the first-half. Of course, Rangers were up for the game, but we can play much better. At 1-1, we needed a period of ten minutes without conceding. If we had managed that, Rangers might have got anxious. We had full intention of winning this game and we were full of confidence. It's not the end of the world - or maybe it is. The run is over, let's get started again. It's going to be tight, but I believed that before the season started and, in fact, would have been delighted if we had made it tight.

'Rangers mean business and have showed that by spending £12million on a player and they won't give up lightly. We came into the game with plenty of confidence and that got wounded today. However, I've always said that Rangers are a very strong side, there is no doubt about that. If you had said at the start of the season that we'd be anywhere near Rangers at this stage, I would have been delighted. Now if we go into the winter break a point ahead at the top, that's fine.'

As the rout was nearing its end, the Rangers fans were urging their players, 'We want six.' They would have to be content with five. And, by the same token, the Celtic supporters would have to live with the fact their team were twelve points ahead of the Ibrox side at a crucial stage of the campaign.

Martin O'Neill refused to press the panic button after the Ibrox collapse when he took his side to Easter Road in midweek to face second-placed Hibs who had been maintaining their good early-season form. The encounter failed to ignite and petered out to a goalless draw, which left Celtic seven points ahead of Alex McLeish's team and thirteen in front of Rangers. The main talking point came when referee Stuart Dougal ruled out a Johan Mjallby 'goal' in the tenth minute while indicating a foul on keeper Nick Colgan after a penalty box fracas.

O'Neill wasn't entirely convinced. 'I am not one to criticise referees, but TV evidence showed there wasn't too much wrong with that goal. The referee said there was a melee in the box, but it only involved two of our players going for the ball. This was the first time we have failed to score all season, so we're a bit disappointed. But I don't think we created enough chances to take all three points. In the course of time, though, it might turn out to be a vital point for us.'

Celtic went into December and faced five league games before the turn of the year. After dropping five points from a possible six, O'Neill urged his players to attempt to recreate their early season run and begin notching up the victories. The players responded by winning all five fixtures while scoring seventeen goals and conceding two. Into the bargain, the Celtic manager finally persuaded Leicester City to part with their captain and midfield inspiration Neil Lennon in a £6million move and, a week later, he fixed up Spurs' Swiss international defender Ramon Vega on a loan deal until the end of the season.

The winning run got underway in the most unusual fashion - by losing a goal in fifty-three seconds! Dunfermline attacker Jason Dair caught out the Celtic back lot with a low shot past Rab Douglas, but that merely brought about instant retribution and Lubomir Moravcik equalised in the seventh minute and Henrik Larsson netted a second midway through the half. The Swede missed his second penalty-kick of the campaign after the break when he saw his effort scooped over the bar by the Fife club's elongated Dutch keeper Marco Ruitenbeek. However, he was spared embarrassment when Tommy Johnson headed in from the resultant corner-kick.

Alan Thompson was one of Celtic's top performers and he said, 'We needed three points from this one. I wanted to make a contribution because I felt I let the rest of the lads down when I was sent off against Rangers and then had to miss the Hibs game. Now we've got to think about putting another run together in the league games ahead.'

After the transfer saga that appeared to be in danger of being transformed into a TV soap opera, Lennon got his wish and moved to his boyhood heroes. O'Neill rushed him straight into the team for the midweek game against Dundee at Dens Park. The midfield enforcer hardly had a chance to draw breath as the home side, with former Argentinian World Cup star Claudio Cannigia in their line-up, attempted to storm the barricades after Stilian Petrov had scored in only four minutes. Ivano Bonetti, the Tayside club's excitable Italian player/manager, urged his men to make life distinctly uncomfortable for their former goalkeeper Rab Douglas and they went about their task with relish and purpose.

They had to wait until ten minutes after the interval before they got the goal they richly deserved, but it came from an unusual source - Celtic defender Tommy Boyd. Cannigia, who threatened all night with his penetrating, darting runs, flashed over a cross intended for team-mate Juan Sara. Boyd attempted to head for a corner-kick, but, his precision wasn't all that he might have expected to be and he sent an effort roaring into his own net. The points were heading back to Glasgow, though, when Celtic grabbed a fortuitous goal in extra-time. Didier Agathe was right in line when Petrov curled in a corner-kick and Chris Coyne thumped a clearance against defensive colleague Steven Tweed. The ball fell perfectly for the winger and he prodded it home from practically under the crossbar.

O'Neill was big enough to admit, 'Dundee can consider themselves unlucky not to get something out of the match. I thought they thoroughly deserved their equaliser and I have to admit I was impressed by them. I thought it was a fantastic game and we kept going for the win right up until the end and, fortunately, we got the goal.'

The Irishman was still looking for cover in his three-man back-line and moved quickly to sign Ramon Vega to team him up with Johan Mjallby and Joos Valgaeren. Tommy Boyd, who had a torrid time at Dens Park, dropped out for the visit of Aberdeen on December 16. Once again, it turned into an afternoon saunter in Glasgow against the Dons; Vega scored two on his debut, the irrepressible Henrik Larsson rattled in a hat-trick and youngster Jamie Smith, a substitute for midweek matchwinner Didier Agathe, made it 6-0 with only ten minutes left to play.

O'Neill said, 'I've told Ramon that it is not always this easy in Scotland.' He added, 'People keep asking me if Henrik is back to his best after last season's injury. Well, the way he is playing just now is good enough for me.' The Swede's third against the Pittodrie side was his twenty-seventh of the season.

A week later, he was on target again on the hour mark as he scored the second in the 2-0 win over St Mirren at Love Street. Agathe, with an exhilarating burst of pace along the eighteen-yard line, had opened up the Saints defence before he turned sharply to hammer a low effort past keeper Ian McCaldon to net the opener in the thirteenth minute. O'Neill was satisfied. He said, 'We have won the game without being outstanding and we have ground out another win away from home which is vital.'

Celtic were on their travels again on Boxing Day when they headed for Tannadice to take on a Dundee United team that had taken a point from Rangers only nine days earlier. After forty minutes they realised there was no likelihood of such an achievement against the other half of the Old Firm. Two goals from Chris Sutton and one from Henrik Larsson, still entrusted with penalty-kick duties, had the Parkhead side easing to a 3-0 half-time lead. Stilian Petrov scored the fourth goal twelve minutes from time.

The Celtic support hadn't become accustomed to seeing their team top of the league at the turn of the year. As Martin O'Neill continually told anyone willing to listen, 'The trick is still being there after we've played thirty-eight games.'

Just another fifteen to go, then.

CHAPTER TWENTY-TWO
MAKE MINE A TREBLE

With panther-like grace, Henrik Larsson eased onto the slide-rule pass from Jackie McNamara, drifted behind the unsuspecting Fernando Ricksen, lured Stefan Klos from his goal-line, gracefully pirouetted around the keeper and, with the ease and confidence of a masterly marksman, deftly stroked a left-foot shot into the net from the tightest of angles.

This consistent creator of fantasies, with a smile to match the occasion, held up both hands to the adoring supporters creating joyous bedlam in the Broomloan Road stand; the five fingers were extended on the right hand and the tips of the forefinger and the thumb on the left touched in a circle and, put together, they signified the number 50. The Swede had just rolled in Celtic's third goal in a formidable 3-0 triumph over Rangers at Ibrox and, incredibly, the lithe and cultured attacker had just claimed his fiftieth strike of a memorable campaign, a sensational feat which would see him honoured with the coveted Golden Shoe award, the prize for European football's top goalscorer.

The date was April 29 2001, it was Celtic's fourth triumph over Dick Advocaat's side - including a League Cup semi-final success - in five meetings and the title had already been won three weeks earlier when Tommy Johnson claimed the only goal of the game against St Mirren in front of a season's best attendance of 60,440 at a Celtic Park awash with euphoria. The Premier League championship was duly delivered in style with the total points tally of ninety-seven setting a new record, seven better than the previous best.

Martin O'Neill's side already had the League Cup in the trophy cabinet following Larsson's hat-trick in the 3-0 success over Kilmarnock at

Hampden on March 18. After the win over St Mirren, Celtic were one step removed from their first domestic treble since the heady days of the legendary Jock Stein in 1969. Hibs barred their way to the milestone, the Edinburgh side lying in wait after reaching the Scottish Cup Final, which would bring down the season's curtain at the national stadium on May 26.

Back at Ibrox on a memorable spring afternoon, Larsson and his colleagues had a point to prove. Dick Advocaat and his Rangers players had to be taught a lesson on the art of being humble and there was no better place to do it than Ibrox stadium in front of over 50,000 fans, most of them backing the fallen champions. They needed to be silenced and, at the same time, accept their fate. Celtic went into the encounter knowing they had not won at this ground in seven years, but it was time to set the record straight. Rangers, led by their somewhat arrogant Dutch manager, had hardly been gracious in acknowledging the superiority of Celtic in relieving them of their championship. On the day of the game, Advocaat declared vaingloriously that Rangers, at their strongest, were 'more than a match' for Celtic.

There can be no doubt the home side were more than a little eager to take the gloss off O'Neill's achievement. And this was most certainly a line-up pieced together by the Irishman with six of the starters in Govan being brought to the club by the new manager since the summer; Rab Douglas, Ramon Vega, Joos Valagaeren, Didier Agathe, Neil Lennon and Alan Thompson. Chris Sutton would surely have represented a seventh, but injury ruled him out. At the start of the campaign, O'Neill had gone on record as saying, 'If you told me we will win the league and not beat Rangers, I would take that.' Possibly, after the highs of August's 6-2 victory, he might have been persuaded to have a change of mind.

The rough and tumble of a typical no-holds-barred Glasgow derby ensured only seven minutes had gone when referee Stuart Dougal was called upon to reach for a yellow card as punishment for Barry Ferguson after the Rangers skipper had gone into a challenge on Alan Thompson with his studs dangerously close to the Englishman's shin.

Later, Thompson was clattered by an out-of-control Fernado Ricksen as they went for a high ball. It was obvious the defender had led with an elbow into the Celt's jaw and the match official motioned as such. The Dutchman was more than a trifle fortunate to get away with a booking; it should have been a straight red without argument.

It was deadlocked at 0-0 until the sixty-first minute when Lubomir Moravcik accepted a cute pass from Larsson, burst into the box and almost casually lifted the ball away from Klos. The Slovakian's second thirteen minutes later was even more accomplished. A low trajectory kick-out from Douglas was headed on by seventeen-year-old Shaun Maloney, making a surprise debut appearance as a second-half substitute for Tommy Johnson. Moravcik, roaming on the left, checked inside the unfortunate Ricksen and thumped the ball in at the near post from eight yards. And, thus, the little conjuror had bagged two goals against the Ibrox side, just as he did in his first Old Firm game in the autumn of 1998. Larsson completed the rout three minutes from the end with his delicious finish for his fiftieth goal of a mesmerising personal campaign. The victory equalled most Celtic wins over their bitterest rivals since 1983.

Martin O'Neill had offered Moravcik a one-year extension in an attempt to persuade him to remain and enjoy the forthcoming party nights in Paradise. He hoped the Slovakian, who would be thirty-six years old by the time the new season came around, might agree life in the hoops would be too enjoyable for him to turn his back on it. O'Neill, playing the crafty Irishman, also got in touch with Jozef Venglos to have a word with his protégé. The good doctor was happy to do so. He asked, 'Lubo, do you feel you can still make a contribution at this level? If you believe you can, you must stay. Are you happy? If you are, you must stay. Playing is the best part of football. Carry on while you can because these days will never be repeated.' Moravcik telephoned O'Neill early in the pre-season to say he would be delighted to remain a Celtic player for another twelve months.

'He is such a brilliant player,' enthused Larsson, after the Ibrox triumph. 'It's not often you get to play with players like that and I am so pleased

I have been fortunate to perform in the same team as Lubo. He is just unbelievable. Look at him today. For the first goal he does really well, but the second is all about class. He played against Ricksen and turned him inside out. I was in a good position in front of goal and I was actually thinking he might square the ball for me, but he just looked at me and scored at the near post. Brilliant! For me, it's a great feeling being able to score fifty goals in a season, but I am more pleased with this result. It is the first time I have won here since I came to Scotland. I've had a draw or two, but never a win. Today changed that, thankfully. We played well, particularly in the second-half and showed we deserved to win the championship.'

O'Neill was equally effusive. 'That was just fantastic! To come here and win at any given time is a great achievement. To win in these circumstances plus our performance just add to it. Lubo, quite rightly, will get most of the headlines, Henrik, too. But I thought Johan Mjallby was absolutely and utterly outstanding as he has been throughout the season. I can't give him enough praise. He has been great for us. I'm delighted for him. And all the boys, of course.'

In the previous Old Firm head-to-head on February 11, a goal from Alan Thompson in the sixteenth minute was enough to separate Scottish football's main protagonists. Celtic had beaten their adversaries 3-1 in the League Cup semi-final - sponsored this year by CIS Insurance - on the Wednesday and O'Neill made three changes when he brought back Rab Douglas and Didier Agathe, both Cup-tied with Dundee and Hibs respectively, at the expense of Jonathan Gould and the suspended Stilian Petrov while Bobby Petta came in for the injured Jackie McNamara.

Celtic had the ball in the net as early as the eighth minute when Ramon Vega headed in a corner-kick, but referee Hugh Dallas ruled it out for a foul that wasn't too apparent to anyone else in the 59,496 crowd. Fernando Ricksen, who didn't appear to require too much encouragement to wade into these confrontations, was booked two minutes later for a late tackle on Alan Thompson. Rangers appeared riddled with nerves as they were hemmed in during the early stages and that was exploited when Larsson won a header against Scott

Wilson, knocked it down to Chris Sutton, took the return on the gallop and squared it to Thompson, running free and unmarked, and he tucked it behind Klos.

O'Neill's men were now in a position to play containing football and hit their opponents on the break. At that stage they were twelve points ahead of Advocaat's ailing team and, with just a minute to go until the turnaround, the men from Govan did themselves no favours when Ricksen dived into a crazy challenge on Tommy Boyd to leave the defender writhing on the turf. Match official Dallas had no option but to show the Dutch defender a second yellow card and off he went. Fans were beginning to wonder if the £4million right-back would ever last a first-half at Parkhead after being substituted early in the 6-2 massacre. Thompson had the best chance to kill the game in the seventieth minute when he was sent through by Larsson, but he blazed over the bar from eighteen yards. A 1-0 win would have to suffice on this occasion.

Thompson, of course, had scored on his debut in the 4-0 victory over Raith Rovers when the League Cup campaign got underway in September. That was followed by the nail-biting 5-2 extra-time success over Hearts in Ednburgh the following month. Celtic, Rangers, Kilmarnock and St Mirren went into the semi-final draw and there were no prizes for guessing the ballot the sponsors wished would be avoided. Unfortunately, the fates insisted the Old Firm would be in action at Hampden on the evening of Wednesday, February 7 in their last-four meeting while the Ayrshire and Paisley outfits would meet the previous evening. A crowd of 9,203 sparsely populated the giant stands in the Mount Florida stadium while 50,019 crammed into place twenty-four hours later.

There was the most explosive finish imaginable in the third duel of the Glasgow giants. Celtic were leading 3-1 with only a few minutes left to go in what had been a high-octane conflict. Claudio Reyna sparked the shameful incident when he raced after Bobby Petta and floored the winger at the second attempt with a wild lunge on the touchline. Referee Willie Young didn't hesitate as he flashed a thoroughly deserved red card, but the American's antics acted as a cue for the players from both sides to begin piling into each other. Lubomir Moravcik and Michael Mols, two of the unlikeliest brawlers, were also banished, but, in truth, they could have been joined by a couple of their team-mates as tensions simmered. As soon as the free-kick was taken, Bob Malcolm, in a moment of sheer indiscipline, raced out of defence to have a swipe at Petta and send him flying. He seemed hell-bent in joining his colleagues Reyna and Mols in the dressing room, but Young, for reasons only known to himself, thought a yellow card was sufficient punishment.

The raw, twenty-year-old centre-half had been brought in by Dick Advocaat to square up to Henrik Larsson, but it was a catchweight contest. Larsson's know-how, not to mention his ability, had the young Ibrox player chasing shadows under the floodlights most of the evening. It took Celtic only seven minutes to take the lead. Alan Thompson, with that gifted left foot, teased over a free-kick from the right and Ramon Vega outjumped Tore Andre Flo to hammer in a pulverising header that Stefan Klos somehow tipped onto the bar. The keeper was out of position as the ball dropped to Chris Sutton and he reacted swiftly to hook it straight into the net. Ten minutes later, Larsson doubled the advantage. Vega punted a long clearance down the middle and the Swede hared after it with Malcolm looking indecisive. As the defender was caught unawares, Larsson darted in, took control, lofted the ball over the head of the outrushing Klos, raced round the keeper and toe-poked it home right on the line. He picked up the ball, released the tongue in his usual celebration and did his airplane spin as he ran back to the halfway line. The arm-waving Dick Advocaat on the touchline didn't look impressed.

Willie Young had already made his usual quota of bewildering decisions before he awarded Rangers a penalty-kick in the thirty-seventh minute. Scott Wilson challenged Sutton and Vega in the box for a loose ball before falling over. There looked nothing in it, but the referee indicated a tug of the shirt by one of the Celts and Jorg Albertz, after his customary run-up starting from outside the box, hammered the ball into the net with Jonathan Gould guessing the wrong way. The match official balanced that decision when O'Neill's men were given one of their own in the sixty-ninth minute. Larsson was clever enough to manoeuvre himself in front of the lumbering Wilson, an ungainly defender at the best of times, in a chase for a ball in the box. Wilson clearly leaned on the Swede and he crashed under the weight. By the time the furore had died down - and Klos had been booked for his trouble - Larsson dusted himself down and drilled the ball true and low to the keeper's right as he dived to his left. Then came the flashpoint incident that led to the trio of dismissals.

It had been a little more sedate at the same ground the previous evening when goals from Andy McLaren, Craig Dargo and Peter Canero eased Kilmarnock to a 3-0 win over St Mirren to book their Cup Final place against the Parkhead side on Sunday March 18. It is now known as The Larsson Final as testimony to one of the finest individual performances witnessed at Hampden, both the old one or the revamped model. Martin O'Neill, ironically winning his first trophy as Celtic manager as the last one Kenny Dalglish lifted the previous season, gushed, 'I think Henrik's a fantastic player, a truly great player and his second one was the most important goal. His third goal was absolutely world class. It was sensational finish and he just keeps getting better. I've always said that Larsson would score goals in any league and that last goal would grace any Cup Final at any given stage, in any century - he is a marvellous footballer.'

Stilian Petrov, who suffered a sickening broken leg in the 2-1 win over St Johnstone only four nights earlier, was told the news he would be out for the remainder of the season. O'Neill had to plot the victory without the skills of the Bulgarian who had become such an important player in his set-up. Young Irishman Colin Healy would deputise. O'Neill also had concerns over Bobby Petta whose entrancing form made him a target for opponents. O'Neill, after much deliberation, went with this formation: Jonathan Gould; Johan Mjallby, Ramon Vega, Joos Valgaeren; Colin Healy, Paul Lambert, Neil Lennon, Lubomir Moravcik, Bobby Petta; Henrik Larsson and Chris Sutton. Petta lasted ten minutes before having to go off following three bone-shaking challenges, two from Alan Mahood and one from Gus McPherson. Stephen Crainey went on in his place.

It was goalless at the interval and then Larsson decided to step up a level. Two minutes into the second period, Vega knocked down a Moravcik cross and, with the most amazing athleticism, the Swede launched himself into the air, appeared to hover and then lashed the ball past Gordon Marshall. Celtic were slipping into cruise control when, without warning on the hour mark, they found themselves a man down when referee Hugh Dallas dismissed Sutton after a clash with Gary Holt. Once again, O'Neill had to reorganise and, once again, Larsson stepped into the breach. In the seventy-fourth minute, Moravcik lobbed the ball forward, Larsson was the swiftest to react and hit an effort at goal. It took a touch off the challenging Chris Innes before flicking high past Marshall.

Larsson kept the best for last. With Kilmarnock trying vainly to claw their way back into the encounter with only nine minutes to play against ten men, the Swede collected a pass and had only one thought in mind - to plonk the ball beyond his former team-mate in the opposing goal. His pace took him into the box as Marshall tried to read his intentions. He was left face down on the turf as Larsson swivelled his hips, dragged the ball wide and rolled it into the net. No wonder Martin O'Neill was purring. Neil Lennon applauded and said simply, 'It was Henrik again - he's the man. It was a tremendous performance again from him'

O'Neill applauded his team and added, 'The players were absolutely magnificent from start to finish. It's been a long, hard season for them. They have been leading the league for months and months and it was difficult for them today, but they were fantastic.' Rival manager Bobby Williamson agreed. 'Celtic have got a lot of strong players, ' he said. 'It's very hard to do anything against them. I felt we did reasonably well in the first-half, but the first three minutes of the second cost us. You have got to concentrate very hard against Celtic. They are very well organised with a lot of intelligent players who know the game inside out. They made us look really ordinary.'

So, with the Premier championship and the League Cup safely deposited in the Parkhead trophy room, O'Neill could now turn his attention to the Scottish Cup. Such was the glamour of the national trophy, a crowd of 5,660 was in attendance at quaint, little Stair Park when the Irishman took his bow in the competition. Celtic were drawn against Stranraer and goals from Joos Valgaeren, Jackie McNamara, Lubomir Moravcik and Keith Knox (og) gave them a 4-0 win. It was a bit more problematical at the next hurdle, a trip to East End Park to take on Dunfermline. It ended in a 2-2 stalemate with Larsson (2) scoring for Celtic and Andrius Skerla and Barry Nicholson replying. Celtic routed the Fifers 4-1 in the replay with Larsson again scoring two as did Ramon Vega. Scott Thomson got his side's consolation.

Celtic, having handed Hearts their exit cards in the League Cup, were required to carry out the same duties in the Scottish Cup at the quarter-final stage. A goal from Larsson did the trick. On the same day, Rangers' grip on the trophy was released when a goal from former Celtic midfielder David Hannah gave Dundee United a 1-0 win at Tannadice. Hannah faced many of his old team-mates in the semi-final on Sunday, April 15, but discovered the side had now inherited a slightly more belligerent outlook with a back-three who actually knew how to defend. Goals from Larsson (2) and McNamara carried Celtic into the Cup Final where they would meet Hibs, who triumphed 3-0 over Livingston in their semi-final.

O'Neill's men gave their Edinburgh opponents a hint of what was in store at Hampden when they bulldozed their way to a 5-2 victory in the capital three weeks before the battle for silverware in the south of Glasgow. Larsson netted his thirty-fifth league goal of the campaign to equal the previous best held by ex-Celtic striker Brian McClair, which was set in the 1986/87 season. McNamara claimed two first-half strikes while Alan Stubbs and Lubomir Moravcik added two more after the turnaround. An exceptionally fussy referee, John Rowbotham, sent off Didier Agathe, playing against his old mates. The visitors were coasting at 5-0 with five minutes to go when Marc Libbra hit two in quick succession to make the scoreline not quite so lopsided.

Worryingly, Celtic then lost back-to-back league games in the run-in to Hampden. Dundee won 2-0 at Parkhead and Kilmarnock claimed a 1-0 triumph at Rugby Park. The results didn't matter, of course, with the silverware long since locked away in its new home at Celtic Park, but Martin O'Neill was only too aware that losing could become a bad habit to shake.

The Scottish Cup Final of May 26 between Celtic and Hibs had been daubed the 'Green Party' which was fairly inaccurate because neither team were allowed to wear their normal strips and both had to play in their change strips; the Parkhead men in their gold tops and the Easter Road side in white shirts. O'Neill didn't concern himself with the SFA's newly-found fixation with colour clashes and, instead, sent out this team as he attempted a clean sweep in his first season in Scotland: Rab Douglas; Johan Mjallby, Ramon Vega, Joos Valgaeren; Didier Agathe, Neil Lennon, Paul Lambert, Lubomir Moravcik, Alan Thompson; Henrik Larsson and Chris Sutton. Moravcik lasted only eighteen minutes before limping off to be replaced by Jackie McNamara.

It was the substitute who pushed the Hoops towards a half-time advantage when he was set up by Larsson who sent him free into the box with a neat pass. McNamara took a clumsy first touch, but recovered in an instant to spear a low shot wide of the motionless Nick Colgan. O'Neill said, 'Jackie took the first goal brilliantly and, naturally, I was very pleased with that. It was a great pass from Henrik, but he still had to put the ball in the net.'

Three minutes after the break, Larsson whipped a first time effort from the edge of the box high into the net for the second goal and, with ten minutes to go, the marauding Swede was hauled to the ground by a panicking Gary Smith for Stuart Dougal to award a stick-on penalty-kick. Larsson took it with his usual excellence and as the ball thudded behind Colgan, the astonishingly prolific hitman realised he had notched up his fifty-third and final goal of an incredible season. Celtic had also claimed their thirty-first Scottish Cup.

Didier Agathe enjoyed scampering down the right in the wide, rolling spaces of the Hampden playing surface and teased and tormented Ulrik Laursen, the Easter Road left-back. O'Neill must have seen something in the Danish defender because he invited him to join Celtic that summer. The thought of never having to again face Agathe in public under the gaze of thousands might have hastened his answer in the affirmative.

Larsson said, 'We won the league early, then the CIS Insurance Cup and everyone had been going on about the treble and how much it would mean to the club. Now we can talk about it, now there are no problems. This was the one I hadn't won yet in Scotland. However, I've won it today and I'm very, very pleased. The second goal gave us a bit more breathing space and then we could sit back a little bit and try to pick them off. When we got the penalty-kick that was it finished.'

A smiling O'Neill said, 'It's been an enormous season for everyone and to finish it off today in front of our supporters at a packed Hampden is just sensational. Today is about the players and the supporters. I'm so, so pleased for both sets. The players have had to rouse themselves again for another big occasion, but I never thought there would be a problem because there is no sign of tiredness. As I said, Jackie took his goal magnificently and the second from Henrik so soon after half-time settled everything. Now I just want time to enjoy this before I even think about next season.'

Neil Lennon added, 'It's been unbelievable since I came up here in December. Honestly, I did not expect this to happen. Not at all. I thought I was coming up to join a team to give Rangers a run for their money in the league. We've surpassed everything that has been asked of us. I'm now going to take it easy for a few weeks and reflect on this season. Mind you, we have now set ourselves exceptional standards and we'll just have to do it all again next season.'

CHAPTER TWENTY-THREE
THE CRUELLEST CUT

John Hartson revealed, 'I couldn't possibly in my wildest dreams have wished for it to work out better.' Just under a year after he failed a medical and saw a proposed move to Rangers fall through, the strapping, burly Welshman was back in Glasgow for signing talks and this time there were no hitches as he joined Celtic in a £6million deal from Coventry City.

On the same day in early August, Martin O'Neill unveiled two other signings, utility defender Momo Sylla, at the cost of £750,000 from St Johnstone, and Steve Guppy, the left-winger from his former club Leicester City who was priced at £600,000. The Irishman hadn't quite kept his promise to himself about having a stress-free summer following the rigours of his first season in Scotland. Man-mountain central defender Bobo Balde also arrived when his French club, Toulouse, went bankrupt. He replaced Ramon Vega, who had been impressive during his loan spell from Spurs. However, the Swiss international couldn't agree personal terms and eventually signed for Watford. Joining him in England would be unsettled midfielder Eyal Berkovic, who had cost John Barnes £5.75million from West Ham two years earlier. O'Neill offloaded him to Manchester City for a cut-price £1.5million. It must be said the little Israeli, with the obvious disdain for hard work, never looked a good fit right from the first day the Irishman arrived in Glasgow.

Olivier Tebily, old 'Bombscare' himself, was never likely to cut it, either, under the scrutiny of O'Neill and he rejoined his former Sheffield United manager Steve Bruce at Birmingham City. Bruce sold the centre-half with the capacity for creating panic in his own penalty area to Barnes for £1.2million and bought him back for £700,000 and undoubtedly believed he had done a good bit of business. Old favourite Alan Stubbs joined his boyhood heroes Everton on Freedom of Contract, striker Mark Burchill, not happy at falling further down the frontline pecking order, was sold to Portsmouth for £600,000, Tommy Johnson was given a free transfer and joined Sheffield Wednesday while keeper Stewart Kerr, who had seen his career stall as fourth in the queue behind Rab Douglas, Jonathan Gould and Dimitri Kharine, agreed a move to Wigan. French left-back Stephane Mahe, who played in the first five league games during the kick-off to the O'Neill revolution, accepted a two-year deal at Hearts.

As ever, Martin O'Neill made no promises at the start of the season while stating, as was his well-practised mantra, that he 'would give his all for Celtic and so will the players. The supporters can be assured of that.' However, after conquering the domestic scene, he had cast his eyes and ambitions in the direction of Europe. Those hopes were given a fair bit of impetus when Celtic were drawn against former European Cup kings Ajax in the third round qualifier for the Champions League in August, the first leg due at the futuristic Amsterdam Arena. O'Neill could hardly believe it when Celtic, firing on all cylinders right from the start, were two goals ahead in the opening twenty minutes with strikes from Bobby Petta and Didier Agathe. It was blistering stuff from the visitors, but the momentum wavered a bit just before half-time and Shota Arveladze, who would later join Rangers, pulled back a goal with a scrappy effort after Rab Douglas had failed to hold a shot. Chris Sutton, though, restored the two-goal advantage with a flying header from an Agathe cross that cannoned in off the inside of the bar.

Petta, performing magnificently on a rare return to his homeland, revealed he wasn't surprised by the result. He said, 'We played extremely well and created so many chances. Throughout the team we have quality players. There's Didier Agathe on the right and Henrik Larsson and Chris Sutton through the middle and it's very easy to play with players of that calibre. There is a great understanding, especially between myself and Henrik. That's why it is so easy for this team to play together.'

There was a scare a fortnight later as Celtic attempted to protect their 3-1 lead. The Dutch side pulled one back through lively Brazilian attacker Wamberto on the half-hour mark and O'Neill and his men were on a tightrope for the remaining hour as they eyed a place in the group stages of Europe's elite tournament for the first time in their history. Rab Douglas, who had failed to convince a large percentage of the support since replacing the popular Jonathan Gould, decided this was as good a time as any to answer his critics and the keeper pulled off a series of excellent stops as Celtic held out with anxious fans in the 58,575 attendance imploring Italian referee Stefano Braschi to blow for time long before the ninety minutes were up. When he did eventually put them out of their fevered state, Celtic's name would be placed in the hat for the draw the following day.

The ballot paired them with Juventus, Porto and Rosenborg. Martin O'Neill might have guessed the team were in for a rocky journey through the group stages when Juventus beat them 3-2 in the first game at the Delle Alpi stadium, in Turin, with the help of a 'phantom' penalty-kick in the last minute. The game was balanced after David Trezeguet had given the Italians a two-goal lead by the fifty-fifth minute, but a deflected free-kick from Stilian Petrov in the sixty-seventh minute somersaulted Celtic back into the tie and Henrik Larsson levelled with a penalty-kick with five minutes remaining. Then came the late controversy when German referee Helmut Krug, who had earlier dismissed Juventus' 'pitbull midfielder' Edgar Davids, awarded the home side a highly debatable spot-kick. Joos Valgaeren didn't appear to touch Nicola Amoruso, who took off in flamboyant fashion across the rain-sodden pitch. Amoruso, though, was fit enough to hammer in the award for the winning goal.

O'Neill said, 'I would put up with it if there had been a bit of wrestling, but their guy was at least a foot away. I had actually turned away, I thought it was a goal-kick. The referee has seen something no-one else did.' His opposite number, Marcello Lippi, wasn't in the least bit sympathetic. 'It might have been a draw. But that's the way it goes,' was his take on the dodgy award that failed the screen test. It was a clear dive; Celtic were robbed of a point.

O'Neill and his players would get their revenge on the last evening of October when they overturned the Italians 4-3 in another special European night under the floodlights in the east end of Glasgow. Chris Sutton, with two, Henrik Larsson and Joos Valgaeren were on target with Trezeguet (2) and Alessandro del Piero responding for Juventus. That was the sixth group game and Celtic had left it too late to reach the next stage and had to accept a place in the UEFA Cup. The Italians topped the group with eleven points, Porto were second on ten and Celtic were a point adrift. Rosenborg brought up the rear on four, unhappily their only win came against the Parkhead side when Harald Brattbakk - would you believe? - scored two in the Norwegians' 2-0 success on October 23. Celtic also went down 3-0 in their other away game to Porto, but a goal from Larsson gave the Scots a 1-0 triumph over the Portuguese in Glasgow and Alan Thompson was the man who made the difference in an identical victory over Rosenborg. It was clear, O'Neill's men suffered from travel sickness. They could win all their games in Glasgow, but, unfortunately, they couldn't replicate those results away from home.

And so it proved, too, in the UEFA Cup. A heroic performance from Rab Douglas against Valencia at the Mestalla Stadium on November 22 restricted the Spaniards to a one-goal advantage, with Vicente Rodriguez managing to beat the one-man barricade with an unstoppable effort twelve minutes from time. John Hartson came closest to getting a goal for the visitors when Santiago Canizares, the colourful Spanish No.1, denied him at the second attempt. O'Neill said, 'Valencia have proved they are a very good side, but, in two weeks' time, we are going to give it everything we have in an attempt to get through.'

Celtic had genuine hopes of playing in European competition beyond Christmas for the first time in twenty years and there was optimism when Larsson made it all-square when he snapped up a pass from Valgaeren to expertly sidefoot an effort low past Canizares just before the interval. The Swede had an effort kicked off the line in extra-time as Celtic swarmed forward in an effort to get their just reward. However, it went to penalty-kicks and, almost unbelievably, Larsson missed and so, too, did Petrov. Hartson, Paul Lambert and Chris Sutton scored with their efforts before Valgaeren saw his wretched attempt saved. That left the way open for Ferrer Mista to score the winner which he duly did, Rafeal Benitez's side squeezing through.

'I'm exceptionally proud of my players,' said O'Neill, 'I couldn't have asked for any more effort.' Larsson followed up, 'We definitely had the better of them, but the ball just wouldn't bounce for us.' It had been an interesting interlude and the performances had given hope to many that, at long last, a Celtic team was coming together that may just be a match for the best in Europe. But season 2002/02 was not one that offered too much in the way of joy for the Parkhead side in knock-out competitions. Rangers, desperately attempting to claw back some dignity, beat Celtic 3-2 in the Scottish Cup Final after already knocking them out of the League Cup at the semi-final stage. On both occasions, Martin O'Neill was left wondering about the justice of football. He might also have had cause to look again at his tactics.

The Irishman had always maintained his priority - even above Europe - was to retain the Premier League title and he achieved that feat with a certain amount of flourish and swagger. O'Neill and his charges bludgeoned all before them as they roared to the championship with an awesome total of one hundred and three points, dwarfing last season's previous best of ninety-seven. The Parkhead men went eighteen games undefeated until they slipped to their solitary loss against Aberdeen at Pittodrie, 2-0 three days before Christmas where, unfortunately, Rab Douglas played the unwitting role of Santa Claus. To be fair, though, the underfoot conditions that day were nothing short of treacherous.

The League Cup loss to the Ibrox side at a frozen Hampden Park on the evening of February 5 had to be seen to be believed. Alex McLeish had quit Hibs to take over from Dick Advocaat with the Dutchman being spirited into one of those 'upstairs' positions which don't actually exist before the individual can disappear under cover of the night. O'Neill realised how important it was to put the frighteners on his new adversary early in his career in the dug-out over at Govan.

Jock Stein had sought to do the very same thing when David White replaced Scot Symon in the sixties. Big Jock managed that with a 4-0 Scottish Cup Final walloping in 1969 from which the younger man never recovered. If history was to repeat itself, O'Neill would want to inflict maximum damage on McLeish as swiftly as possible.

Celtic went into the contest seeking their sixth successive victory over Rangers; the last time that had happened was 1972. Henrik Larsson squandered the easiest chance of the lot early in the game as he broke through with only Stefan Klos to beat. It looked an absolute certainty, but the Swede attempted to put the ball between the keeper's legs and his precision was off slightly; his attempt struck his opponent's heel and bounced to safety. Larsson then hit the outside of the post with a cunning free-kick and John Hartson had one scrambled off the line by Amoruso before sending a header just a few inches wide. Unbelievably, Rangers took the lead on the stroke of half-time when Arveladze sent Lovenkrands racing through with a neat flick and he finished low past Rab Douglas. It was one of those rare occasions when both parts of Hampden appeared to be struck dumb; momentarily, of course, as far as the Ibrox contingent were concerned.

Bobo Balde scrambled the inevitable equaliser in the seventy-second minute after Lubomir Moravcik, who had just replaced Paul Lambert, carved out the opening. O'Neill sent on Chris Sutton for Hartson as he tried to force the issue before the game entered extra-time. Against the run of play, it was McLeish's outfit who squandered the best opportunity to settle it in regulation time when Arveladze struck the bar with a late spot-kick after referee Kenny Clark had penalised Douglas following a clash with Lovenkrands. Unfortunately, Celtic didn't make the best of their good fortune. With almost the last kick of the first period of extra-time, Bert Konterman, much maligned by even his own supporters, scored the goal of a lifetime. No-one bothered to block the Dutchman as he ran onto a loose ball twenty-five yards out, but his timing, on this rarest of occasions, was absolute perfection itself and he launched a screamer high past Douglas into his top right-hand corner. Moravcik and Sutton came close, but, at the end of a mystifying encounter, Celtic had relinquished any hope of back-to-back trebles.

O'Neill said, 'I was never talking about a domestic clean sweep and neither were my players. I thought they were excellent tonight and should have been two or three up early on. We dominated for large parts of the first-half and all of the second-half, but it just wasn't to be, so well played to Rangers.'

The Irishman must have been equally frustrated three months later when he witnessed McLeish getting the upper hand once again in the Scottish Cup Final. Celtic led twice with goals from John Hartson and Bobo Balde, but their opponents replied with efforts from Peter Lovenkrands and Barry Ferguson. O'Neill was forced to replace the limping Paul Lambert with Jackie McNamara, but he kept his other outfield substitutes, Tommy Boyd, Lubomir Moravcik and Steve Guppy, on the bench as the game wore on. The tie was a few seconds from going into extra-time when Neil McCann threw over a cross from the left and Lovenkrands was completely unmarked smack in front of goal. As Douglas, getting his angles completely wrong, took off to his left, the Dane met the ball square on his forehead and directed it into the middle of the goal.

O'Neill said, 'Obviously, I am disappointed to lose the game in the last ten seconds, but that's part of football. Some of our players just didn't have the energy and that's understandable. On reflection, though, I will be disappointed tonight and tomorrow morning, but the players have been fantastic again this season. We've won the league and that means we have another crack at the Champions League.'

The Celtic manager defended his decision not to make substitutions towards the end of the match with the Final locked at 2-2. He said, 'I thought, and I'm sure Alex McLeish thought, as well, that the game was heading for extra-time and I was conscious of the fact some of my players were tiring. But I have no regrets.'

McLeish, after turning over Celtic twice in three months since arriving from Hibs, was asked the secret of his success over O'Neill. He smiled at his inquisitor and said, 'I could tell you, but then I will have to kill you!' Actually, his tactics weren't too difficult to fathom. However, if the Celtic manager had an Achilles' Heel - and he was the first to admit he was far from infallible - it was the stubborn streak that made him stick to what he perceived as his tried and trusted formation. McLeish, all too simply, encouraged wide players to drag Celtic's back three across the pitch. O'Neill's system relied heavily on 'wing-backs' such as Didier Agathe and Bobby Petta tracking back to fill in the void positions in an effort to transform a back three into a back five in an instant. The truth is both the players were at their most forceful going forward and neither possessed a keen defensive mind. Agathe, in particular, was vulnerable at identifying the threat of long, diagonal crossfield passes that could wreak havoc behind a defence. McLeish stretched Celtic and Lovenkrands became a key player with his acceleration against the likes of Johan Mjallby and Joos Valgaeren, neither of whom had been blessed with blistering pace.

It had been an entirely different story in the league outings against the club's ancient foes. Goals from Alan Thompson and Stilian Petrov gave the champions a 2-0 victory at Ibrox in September while Joos Valgaeren and Henrik Larsson, with a penalty-kick, guided the team to a 2-1 success in November which pushed them ten points clear of the Ibrox men. By a strange quirk, the managers found themselves disagreeing at the end of the game. Dick Advocaat opened with, 'A ten-point gap is very difficult. They may drop points, but not that many.' O'Neill, however, countered with, 'I don't go along with that. There is no break and there is still everything to play for.'

Advocaat, of course, was missing from the Ibrox dug-out when the next Old Firm game rolled round on March 10, but his words still rung with authenticity. It ended 1-1 and Celtic were still ten points clear after ninety tumultuous minutes. Stilian Petrov gave Celtic a twenty-third minute lead, but a spectacular thirty-yard drive on the hour mark from Arthur Numan, not known for his regularity in bothering opposing goalkeepers, gave the home side a point. TV evidence later proved John Hartson had a perfectly good goal early on ruled out by referee Hugh Dallas. The Welshman was played onside by Numan after Larsson had scuffed a shot in his direction and he walloped it home from close range. The linesman erroneously raised his flag and Dallas didn't bother to debate the point.

Hartson didn't have much luck, either, when he was sent off in the next Glasgow derby, which also ended in a 1-1 stalemate. There was an almighty melee four minutes from the end of a raw, blood-and-thunder occasion. The Welsh striker thought he had won it for Celtic with a powerful header, but Klos managed to palm the ball down and then throw himself on top of it. There was the usual barging and shoving and referee Kenny Clark insinuated himself on proceedings to flash red cards at Hartson, fellow-Celt Mjallby and Rangers' Ricksen. The Hoops frontman protested his innocence vehemently, but the match official was not impressed. After TV evidence, the red card was rescinded. O'Neill's side surrendered their one hundred per cent home record after Lovenkrands, once again a menace to the back four, scored inside the first minute. Alan Thompson levelled just before half-time and, in the end, the draw meant more to the home side than Rangers.

With four games still to play, Martin O'Neill's second successive league title was wrapped up on a pleasant April 6 afternoon in front of 59,752 cavorting fans when Henrik Larsson fired in a supreme hat-trick and John Hartson added two in a rampant 5-1 success over Livingston. The championship was delivered with style and panache against Jim Leishman's enterprising line-up that was sitting fourth in the league and determined to gatecrash the party. Larsson wrecked their plans inside three minutes when Paul Lambert and Hartson combined to set up the Swede and he did the rest with his customary aplomb from six yards. Hartson added a second in nineteen minutes when he viciously volleyed a cross from Didier Agathe behind Javier Sanchez Broto, the Spanish keeper who would join up with the champions in the summer. His Livingston team-mate Davide Fernandez, a sprightly, clever frontman, would also take the same route in a £1million deal.

Broto was helpless again when Hartson headed in No.3 six minutes later when he got on the end of a clever delivery from Steve Guppy and the ex-Leicester City winger was the provider again for Larsson to knock in the fourth just beyond the half-hour mark. Larsson claimed the matchball with his third goal in sixty minutes and it was left to Barry Wilson to give the small travelling support something to cheer by steering an effort past Rab Douglas late on.

Larsson attempted to play down his contribution to the runaway championship campaign. 'I have never made a secret of the great service I and the other strikers get from our team-mates. Alan Thompson has been playing well and Paul Lambert provided me with two goals on this occasion. We have players who can score goals from back to front and that is what you need in football. It is very hard to rely on one or two players. John and I got the goals today, but the service was absolutely tremendous.' He added, 'You never get used to winning trophies. It feels absolutely fantastic. The title is the trophy we have been playing for all season and the way we did it was tremendous.'

Hartson, in his first season in green and white, said, 'It doesn't come much better than this. To play in front of this crowd every other week is a dream come true for me. It is fitting that we won the league here - the fans have been unbelievable. The service in the team is just different class. The players just keep on providing for their colleagues, irrespective of the score. We always want more. Look at Didier Agathe today, for instance. He was still bombing down the right wing in the last minute while we're winning 5-1. Which striker wouldn't want to play in this team?'

Celtic's league form had been nothing short of breathtaking. They scored ninety-four goals in their thirty-eight games, clocked up thirty-three wins, four draws and that solitary, irritating blemish at Pittodrie prevented them from going through undefeated. Rangers, their nearest rivals, were eighteen points adrift. As the club prepared to repel all boarders for a third consecutive season, the wary words of Martin O'Neill came to the fore, 'The trick is to keep on winning.'

Compared to the previous summer, the Celtic manager had been relatively quiet in the close-season transfer market. He released goalkeeper Dimitri Kharine, who made only one league appearance the previous term, and spent £1million on a replacement, Swedish international Magnus Hedman from Coventry City. Javier Sanchez Broto and Davide Fernandez came in from Livingston and, of course, Ulrik Laursen, despite being run ragged by Didier Agathe in the Scottish Cup Final, arrived in a £1.5million deal from Hibs.

In any season, there can be a solitary and clearly defining moment that determines the fine line between success and failure. It can be one fleeting instant of magic; it can be a split-second of madness. Inspiration can be weighed against consternation. It can often be an occasion when destiny intervenes to shape events. For Rab Douglas - and Celtic - the magnitude of his performance against Rangers on a sunny afternoon at Parkhead on October 6 went a long way to the league title being agonisingly wrenched from the grasp of the champions in the cruellest possible manner. The display of the goalkeeper in this occurrence can be measured seven months and twenty-eight games later on the day Rangers won the flag by a superior goal difference of one.

It didn't matter that Celtic would later beat Rangers twice to accumulate seven points while their age-old antagonists had to be satisfied with a total of four on the back of their one win, 3-2 at Ibrox in December. The opening Old Firm game of the season was crucial on so many levels. O'Neill had not bested Alex McLeish on the previous four meetings, had lost a Scottish Cup Final, been beaten in the League Cup and been forced to accept stalemates in two league conflicts. The Ibrox side arrived in the east end of Glasgow that autumn day on the back of a shock UEFA Cup exit the previous Thursday, embarrassingly failing on the goals away rule against Czech unknowns Viktoria Zizkov. They were top of the league by a point from Celtic and O'Neill saw it is an ideal opportunity to turn them over and leapfrog over his main rivals into pole position with the resolute aim to remain there for the remainder of the campaign. There was little wrong with the thought process of the Irishman. Alas, there was little he could do to eradicate the dramatic intervention of his goalkeeper.

Rangers plundered a point in an unlikely 3-3 draw and, unfortunately, Rab Douglas was culpable for all three of their goals during his wretched ninety-minute presentation in front of a disbelieving attendance of 59,027 at Celtic Park and millions worldwide on television. The last line of defence is well known as the Aunt Sally of the beautiful game and that mantle comes with their selected position in their chosen profession. They are there to be shot down and they willingly accept they are more likely to be remembered for their mistakes than their moments of excellence. Such is the lot of Rab Douglas, his extraordinary generosity being greedily accepted by the grateful visitors, exceedingly thankful for the outrageous largesse of an opponent.

The parade of calamities began as early as the sixth minute when the bungling goalie allowed a twenty-five yard effort from Mikkel Arteta, half-hit and straight at the keeper, to squirm and trickle over the line. 'It wasn't the hardest shot you'll ever see,' said the TV commentator, well-practised in the art of the stunning understatement. The goalie seemed to be rescued when Henrik Larsson, with a wonderful touch, spin and hit, crashed an unstoppable effort into the roof of the net for the equaliser after a searching pass from Momo Sylla just before the interval. The Swede must have considerably eased his colleague's concerns when he rocketed in a header for a second goal eight minutes after the turnaround. Larsson met Stilian Petrov's heavily-driven left-wing corner-kick and his effort raged high past Klos.

A minute later, Douglas blundered appallingly once again. Sylla erred when he failed to cut out a pass from Amoruso from travelling up the left touchline to McCann. With a considerable amount of time, the winger could measure a cross into the danger zone. It drifted in and Douglas' timing was horrendous, allowing Ronald de Boer to leap uninterrupted in front of him and bang a header into the exposed net from eight yards. Could it get any worse? Indeed, it could - and did. In the seventy-fifth minute, Arthur Numan hit a speculative left-foot shot from fully thirty yards that didn't have enough puff to get off the ground. Douglas miscalculated again, allowed the ball to break free from his chest and a surprised and delighted Shota Arveladze bundled his effort over the line. 'Rab, you've got to hold that,' chided the TV man. The philanthropy of the keeper obviously knew no bounds on this outing, but, once again, he was bailed out when Chris Sutton first-timed a third goal from close-range in the seventy-eighth minute. It finished 3-3 and O'Neill tagged it 'the result that got away.' If only he had realised the savage repercussions on the final day of a fateful season as the direst of consequences awaited the Celtic manager and his players. From that match onwards Douglas was known as "Dropsy" to the Celtic support.

'Rab is very downcast,' commented O'Neill afterwards. 'It wasn't his best day. I felt we controlled most of the match and it was surreal to find ourselves 3-2 down, but we showed a lot of character and, although I'm disappointed with the result, I was pleased with the performance. I can't help thinking, though, that this was a result that got away.'

Celtic had gone into the Glasgow derby with one defeat already registered against them following their 2-1 loss to Motherwell at Fir Park on September 10. The Parkhead side turned up for the Tuesday evening encounter on an unbeaten league run of twenty-four games having last sampled defeat from Aberdeen at Pittodrie in December the previous year. Ironically, Douglas, who had made way for Magnus Hedman for the previous game - a 2-0 win over Livingston - was given the nod to start this one. With thirteen minutes to go, it was goalless, but Stevie Hammell then sent over a cross for Shaun Fagan to try his luck with a header from ten yards and the ball went under Douglas on its way into the net. Two minutes later, he was retrieving the ball from behind him for a second time when referee Willie Young awarded the home side a penalty-kick after ruling Ulrik Laursen had brought down James McFadden. The maverick Motherwell frontman took the kick and sent Douglas the wrong way. John Hartson pulled one back three minutes from time, but Celtic could not get the ball past Stevie Woods for the leveller.

O'Neill dropped Douglas for the next game and reinstated Hedman in a 1-0 victory over Hibs where John Hartson claimed the only goal. The Swedish international might have been forgiven for believing he would retain the No.1 position after keeping two clean sheets in his two first team appearances, but O'Neill brought back Douglas for the next game, another single goal win, this time over Dundee where Henrik Larsson hit the points-clincher.

It was December 7 before the champions were defeated again and once more it was in the strangest of circumstances. Chris Sutton scored the quickest goal in Old Firm history by netting on only nineteen seconds against Rangers at Ibrox, but by the interval O'Neill's men were trailing 3-1. Unfortunately, Douglas must again shoulder a fair portion of the blame for the effort that allowed Alex McLeish's side back into the contest. In the tenth minute, he was lured from his line in an attempt to deal with a left-wing corner-kick from Ricksen. His timing was flawed and Moore jumped above him to head into the unprotected net. John Hartson thought he had restored his side's lead when he crashed a low shot past Klos, but the ball battered off the inside of the upright, rolled along the line and swerved out.

Douglas had no chance in the thirty-fourth minute when McCann was allowed too much time to send in a near-post cross and Ronald de Boer lashed it into the net. Five minutes later, Mols found space in the penalty box to prod the ball under the exposed keeper. Henrik Larsson set up Hartson in the sixty-first minute to blitz a low drive into the net, but try as they might, the equaliser just would not come. In fact, it was Rangers who came nearest to scoring again when a drive from Amoruso, from fully forty yards, was lost in flight by the despairing Douglas only for the ball to thud against the crossbar and rebound to safety.

It was another thirteen games before Celtic sampled a league loss, their third and last of the campaign. A goal deep in injury-time by Hearts full-back Austin McCann gave his side a 2-1 victory at Tynecastle on April 19 after Henrik Larsson had given Celtic the imitative with his thirty-ninth goal of the season when he opened the scoring on the hour mark. Phil Stamp nullified that effort thirteen minutes later and it looked as though the game was destined to end in deadlock until McCann stormed forward, with Didier Agathe ignoring his defensive duties, and the left-back hammered in a screamer that raged over Rab Douglas and entered the net via the inside of the post. The reversal left O'Neill's men eight points adrift of Rangers although they had a game in hand with the potential to cut that back by another three points with the teams due to meet at Ibrox a week later.

There was a school of thought that inferred Celtic's European aspirations were blurring the club's focus on the championship. After this defeat in Edinburgh, O'Neill was due to take his team to Portugal for Thursday's UEFA Cup semi-final against Boavista with the score tied at 1-1 from the first leg in Glasgow. The Parkhead gaffer said, 'I am devastated, the players are devastated and this is a huge blow. We now have two massive games coming up. We have a semi-final and we know what we have to do. We have to score for a start. And then we've got Rangers at their place on Sunday. I wouldn't write us off just yet.'

Celtic, of course, got the win in Portugal that led them to Seville and they were celebrating again when they overturned Alex McLeish's team in Govan. Ironically, Rab Douglas missed eighty-one minutes of the 2-1 win after going off with a thigh injury to be replaced by Javier Sanchez Broto. It was the day Iberia came to Ibrox with the Celtic fans turning out in sombreros while the pitch was awash with colourful beach balls to signify the Parkhead side would be playing Porto in the glamorous UEFA Cup Final in Seville on a sun-graced evening of May 21, but that story is worthy of a chapter of its own. 'We'll be in Seville while you're watching The Bill,' chorused the travelling support, good-natured humour emphasising the Rangers fans could be at home that night with the TV cops and robbers programme for company. All the Celtic following required now to complete the picture was a win in enemy territory. They duly got their wish.

At long last, O'Neill changed his system and went with four at the back to counter-act Alex McLeish's basic tactics of employing wide men. Jackie McNamara, Bobo Balde, Ulrik Laursen and Joos Valgaeren were the last line in front of the keeper with Didier Agathe given more freedom on the right. Neil Lennon and Alan Thompson patrolled the midfield with Chris Sutton deployed in a role just behind Henrik Larsson and John Hartson. It worked a treat.

Celtic were two goals ahead by the break with some fabulous play by Larsson, robbing Barry Ferguson and setting up an attack in an instant. He swept the ball wide to Hartson coming into the box from the right. Amoruso looked awkward as he barged into the Welsh striker and slid his right leg across him just for good measure. Hugh Dallas awarded the obvious penalty-kick and Thompson completely foxed Stefan Klos by taking a run up from well outside the box and for all the world looked as though he wanted to rip the net from its stanchion. At the last moment, he eased up and rolled the ball to the keeper's right as Klos took off for his left. Two minutes from the interval, Larsson back-flicked a ball inside from Agathe and it rolled perfectly for Hartson to send it wide of Klos. McNamara almost claimed a freakish third when he launched a free-kick downfield from just inside the Rangers half. Klos was distracted by the antics of Moore and Larsson in front of him and, alarmingly for the Rangers fans in the Copland Road stand immediately behind him, allowed the ball to bounce past him, but he got lucky when it nudged against the woodwork and rebounded back into play.

There was an anxious moment when Ronald de Boer headed in a McCann left-wing cross in the fifty-seventh minute, but Celtic overcame exhaustion to take control again and were well in command in the last fifteen or so minutes. Klos thwarted Larsson twice with superb saves and Agathe flashed one inches wide of the post. There was one unsavoury moment when Hartson and Moore went for a high ball and the central defender fell to ground holding his face. He proved to everyone watching that Paul Hogan, of Crocodile Dundee fame, wasn't the worst Australian actor on the planet. Undoubtedly, he wanted Hartson red-carded, but Dallas was having none of it and motioned for the player to get back to his feet.

The talismanic Larsson, out with a broken jaw, missed the 1-0 win over Rangers on March 8 where Hartson was guilty of two glaring misses before thundering in the winner in fabulous fashion just before the hour mark. A diagonal cross from Thompson was headed down by Sutton to his frontline partner and, from just inside the eighteen-yard box, the Welshman volleyed a ferocious drive high past Klos. O'Neill enthused, 'That was just sensational. It was a wonderful strike from a wonderful player.' Paul Lambert chipped in, 'His ratio of goals to games started is unbelievable. He helped us to the win we deserved and needed to keep the title challenge going.'

Even Alex McLeish admitted the best his side could hope for from this confrontation would have been a draw and Neil Lennon put it this way, 'We outfought them, we out-tackled them and we outplayed them. In fact, we out-everythinged them!'

Unfortunately, only eight days later on Sunday, March 16, Celtic lost 2-1 to the Ibrox side in the League Cup Final in the most stressful and suspenseful circumstances. Neil Lennon was sent off, Chris Sutton was stretchered off, John Hartson had a perfectly good goal ruled by referee Kenny Clark and the Welsh striker also missed a last-minute penalty-kick. The gods of fortune were spitting venom at Celtic at Hampden that dramatic afternoon.

They could have no complaints, however, as the Ibrox side powered towards a two-goal half-time lead in front of a crowd of 50,034. Lovenkrands set up the opener in the twenty-third minute when a burst of pace carried him past Johan Mjallby and his low cross was deflected into the path of Claudio Canningia, the Argentinian forward bought from Dundee in the summer, and he tucked it behind Rab Douglas. Twelve minutes later, the Celtic defence was exposed again by the speed of Lovenkrands and this time the Dane, played onside by Mjallby, finished the move with a low drive into the corner. There was no chance of O'Neill's men, despite their hectic schedule, lying down in the second period. In the fifty-seventh minute Henrik Larsson zipped a near-post header past Klos after another superb inswinging corner-kick from Alan Thompson. Five minutes later, the ball was in the Rangers net again when Larsson pounced on a Mikkel Arteta error to set up Hartson and he drilled the ball away from Klos. Astonishingly, the match official deemed it was offside and there was no consolation for Celtic afterwards when TV pictures conclusively proved otherwise. 'I was two yards onside,' claimed Hartson. Former Ibrox captain Terry Butcher, providing match summary, gave his verdict, 'Definitely onside.'

Sutton had to be helped off ten minutes from time and replaced with Shaun Maloney and, two minutes from the end of a game that pulsated from start to finish, Lennon was booked for pushing Ricksen in an off-the-ball incident. Moments later, the midfielder blocked Arveladze and this time the referee produced a red card. In the fading moments, the ungainly Amoruso tripped Bobo Balde and it was a certain penalty-kick. Hartson placed the ball on the spot and realised he could put his team in with a chance of lifting the trophy in extra-time with their opponents practically on their knees. Alas, the striker didn't even hit the target, sending the ball whistling low past the left-hand post.

Celtic didn't enjoy much luck in the Scottish Cup, either, when they went out to Inverness Caley Thistle 1-0 in the quarter-final in the Highland capital on Sunday March 23 - only three days after beating Liverpool 2-0 to reach the UEFA Cup semi-finals on a 3-1 aggregate. Three years earlier, there were ructions far and wide when Caley Thistle won in the competition in Glasgow. On this occasion, it was almost met with a shrug of the shoulders with bigger prizes on the horizon. O'Neill made eight changes from the team that won on Merseyside the previous Thursday and the Highlanders took full advantage. Bizarrely, they had only one shot on target all night - Dennis Wyness' effort on the stroke of half-time - and that was enough to win the tie. Even Henrik Larsson proved he could struggle against these opponents and he missed when he was clean through and crashed the ball off keeper Mark Brown, who would later sign for the Parkhead men.

Anxiety levels were heading for the stratosphere when Celtic, disappointed by the outcome in Seville, headed for Rugby Park for the final league encounter of the season against Kilmarnock. Martin O'Neill had to hope for any sort of win and for Rangers to shed something against Dunfermline at Ibrox. If both won - the most likely outcome, everyone concurred - it would come down to goal difference. So, the champions realised that simply winning might not be enough on this fraught occasion; they would have to pile on the goals if they hoped to lift the title for the third successive season. The moment the game in Ayrshire went into motion on a bone-dry Sunday afternoon, May 25 - precisely thirty-six years to the day of Celtic's European Cup triumph in Lisbon - the match in Glasgow kicked-off, too. For some, it was synchronised torture.

The history books tell us Rangers won 6-1 against the Fifers while Celtic could only manage a 4-0 success against their opponents. Chris Sutton, with two, Alan Thompson, who scored and missed a penalty-kick, and Stilian Petrov were the marksmen for the Parkhead side. The width of the victories allowed the title flag to fly over Govan the following season by the slenderest of margins. Both teams completed the campaign on ninety-seven points with Rangers showing a goal difference of seventy-three as opposed to Celtic's seventy-two. However, O'Neill's gritty group of battlers were ahead at one stage that unimaginable day in Scottish football history and there was one moment, for me, anyway, that underlined this was not going to be a day of celebration for anyone with Celtic persuasions.

A writer of fiction would undoubtedly be pilloried for suspending belief beyond the most far-fetched of horizons, but at exactly the same time as Henrik Larsson hit the post at Rugby Park, Ronald de Boer rose to head past Dunfermline keeper Derek Stillie to make it 4-1 in the sixty-ninth minute at Ibrox. If the Swede's effort had been a couple of inches to the left, the Celtic score would have changed to 4-0. If De Boer had passed up his opportunity, Rangers would still have been stuck at 3-1. Supporters usually talk of Mikkel Arteta's injury-time penalty-kick being the goal that mattered that improbable afternoon, but, for me, that will be the abiding memory of the moment the championship was won and lost.

Like Martin O'Neill and his Celtic players, I was blessed with the belief you could not keep a good man and a good team down for long.

CHAPTER TWENTY-FOUR
SMILES AMID SORROW IN SEVILLE

There is such a thing as glorious failure. There could only be one winner in Seville on the epic evening of May 21, 2003 in the most dramatic of UEFA Cup Finals and the fates decreed, alas, the ultimate destination of the glistening trophy would not be the east end of Glasgow.

The most amazing and colourful support in the world of football staged a friendly invasion on the Spanish city as they looked forward with unprecedented enthusiasm to the meeting of Martin O'Neill's Celtic and Jose Mourinho's Porto at the vast arena of the Olimpico Stadium where the official attendance would be given as 52,972. Days before the kick-off, there were estimates of between eighty thousand and one hundred thousand Celtic supporters in the capital of southern Spain's Andalusia region. Around forty thousand are thought to have been in the ground.

Vivid, brilliant sunbeams smiled on the sparkling setting of gaiety and merriment. The blazing greens and the whites and the golds that fluttered in the welcome breeze and adorned the stadium hours before the commencement of the contest added to the breathtaking kaleidoscopic scenery. The heavily-outnumbered Portuguese supporters indulged, too, with their blue and white flags prominent in their designated areas. But the Olimpico Stadium belonged to Celtic supporters the moment Paul Lambert led out the team with the knowledge they were one game away from the club winning their second European trophy, adding to the spectacular success of the Lisbon Lions thirty-six years earlier.

With painstaking precision, O'Neill, as ever, had agonised over his final selection. The strengths and weaknesses of all the players at his disposal would be poured over time and time again. The Irishman was rarely given to spontaneity in such circumstances. He worked overtime on his strategies, especially in the competitive European arena. Celtic had played twelve games to reach this terminus. The challenges of FK Sudova, Blackburn Rovers, Celta Vigo, Stuttgart, Liverpool and Boavista had been met and answered, all interrogations of Celtic's ability repelled. The ultimate prize was now within touching distance.

After the anxiety, the self-questioning and the soul-searching, O'Neill went with this line-up: Rab Douglas; Johan Mjallby, Bobo Balde, Joos Valgaeren; Didier Agathe, Neil Lennon, Paul Lambert, Stilian Petrov, Alan Thompson; Chris Sutton and Henrik Larsson. Over the course of the one hundred and twenty minutes, Ulrik Laursen, Jackie McNamara and Shaun Maloney would replace Valgaeren, Lambert and Petrov. Magnus Hedman, Momo Sylla, Davide Fernandez and Jamie Smith would remain on the substitutes' bench. John Hartson, unfortunately, was out altogether with a debilitating back injury. It was a line-up enriched with many talents and fused with a multitude of fluctuating skills, not least those the gods had bestowed upon the incomparable Henrik Larsson, who would score his two-hundredth goal for the club against the Portuguese. The passion, desire and ambition among the Celtic players came to the fore as soon as the game went into motion.

There was the usual sparring until the stroke of half-time when a dreadful piece of defending from Belgian left-back Valgaeren undid Celtic. Goalkeeper Vitor Baia actually miskicked the ball forward and it was helped on its way by a colleague. Valgaeren collected the ball and, with no-one pressing him, sliced a clearance that ricocheted off the startled Balde. Deco seized on the opportunity, swept a cross to the unmarked Dmitri Alenichev at an angle ten yards out and the Russian rammed in a low shot to Douglas' left. Unfortunately, the keeper couldn't hold onto the rasping effort and pushed it sideways where Porto had the Brazilian Derlei lurking to fire in from close range. It was a sore one to take at such a crucial stage of the encounter.

Two minutes after the turnaround, Larsson got his magical double century for the club. Didier Agathe provided a superb diagonal cross from the right and the spring-heeled Swede leapt above Ricardo Costa to send a soaring header away from the helpless Baia. Unfortunately, O'Neill's side could not hold on for longer than seven minutes when some trickery from Deco allowed him to set up Alenichev who tucked it beyond Douglas to restore the Porto lead. Unusually, lenient Slovakian referee Lubos Michel allowed the Porto players a full minute of celebrating with their fans on the far corner of the running track. O'Neill, through gritted teeth, later observed, 'I thought they were all going into town for a drink.'

Back came that man Larsson, though, and his strength in the air proved masterful again as he rose to a Thompson right-wing corner-kick in the fifty-seventh minute to bury another searing header away from the much-vaunted Baia. Both teams had chances before the action stretched into extra-time. A moment of rashness from Balde, with a tackle on Deco, saw the match official flourish a second yellow card and banish the centre-half. The advantage passed to the Portuguese but with five minutes remaining of an exhausting occasion, and Porto seeming increasing content with a penalty shoot-out, they scored the winner. Once again, fates conspired and, unfortunately, Celtic were on the receiving end of a snarl.

Douglas slid out at the feet of Marco Ferreira and required strong hands and complete concentration. He didn't make a clean contact and the ball rolled back to Derlei, who stepped inside and clipped a weak shot at goal. The ball took a nick off the scrambling goalkeeper and that was enough to deflect it past Mjallby and then Laursen on the goal-line. Ironically, if Douglas hadn't got a touch on that occasion there was every chance either the Swede or the Dane would have cleared. It wasn't to be Celtic's night. Referee Michel balanced the red card count when he sent off Nino Valente in the last minute for a cynical foul on Thompson as he cut in from the right to bring the ball to his lethal left foot. Substitute Maloney thumped the resultant free-kick high over the bar and Celtic's last chance of carving something from this game was gone.

O'Neill had been far from impressed with the antics and play-acting of Mourinho's players throughout the two hours. He said, 'I will probably get into trouble for this, but there was a lack of sportsmanship. The rolling over, the time wasting. But they have beaten us, well done to them and it's up to us to learn from this. It is a steep learning curve, but this was a wonderful, wonderful experience. The players put everything into it. We came roaring back every time they scored a goal and, when we had eleven against eleven in extra-time, I think we were the more mentally strong. But it was not to be with Bobo getting sent off. It was a massive blow.'

Henrik Larsson - hailed as 'world class' by O'Neill - insisted his two goals meant little to him. He said, 'It is no consolation whatsoever. I've said before, I'd much rather not score and be able to lift the UEFA Cup, than to score twice and finish up on the losing side. There's nothing to be happy about, but now we have to find a way to lift ourselves.'

A distraught Stilian Petrov, fighting his emotions, said, 'I thought we deserved to win. It was really hard to walk past the UEFA Cup without being able to pick it up. But I think our performance will have made the supporters proud of us and we did Scotland proud as well.' Didier Agathe, equally inconsolable, said, 'It's very hard to accept because we put so much effort into it, coming from behind twice, but that's football. However, it's good to know that Scottish football is good enough to compete at a high level in Europe.'

And, yet, at some stages of the colourful procession towards Seville, there were critics only too willing to write off O'Neill and his players; mainly, unsurprisingly, from across the border, principally Blackburn and Liverpool.

Celtic only featured in the UEFA Cup after failing to manoeuvre their way past Basle in the Champions League Third Round qualifier. The entire European campaign got off to a shocker when the Swiss side scored after only eighty-one seconds at Parkhead on August 14 in front of a stunned crowd of 58,530. Joos Valgaeren failed to cut out a through ball from Julio Rossi that ran to Christian Gimenez and the Argentinian striker made a mess of his shot. But it was enough to leave Rab Douglas flat-footed as it rolled gently towards the net. Within two minutes, the Scottish champions were level when Henrik Larsson thumped home a penalty-kick after Stilian Petrov had been felled in the box by Marco Zwyssig. Six minutes after the interval, Neil Lennon tried his luck from thirty yards and Chris Sutton spotted keeper Pasacl Zuberbuhler moving to his right to deal with the danger. Instinctively, he shot out his foot and directed the ball into the other corner. Larsson spurned the chance to claim a third in the sixty-third minute when Spanish referee Manuel Gonzalez awarded another spot-kick after Murat Yakin's handball. The Swede drove the ball down the middle and the keeper scrambled it to safety. Two minutes from time, Momo Sylla volleyed in the third from a Steve Guppy cross to allay some of the anxiety.

Thirteen days later, the Champions League trip was over, Celtic losing 2-0 at the St.Jakob Stadium to go out on the goals away rule. Gimenez and Yakin struck in the first twenty-two minutes to extinguish any hopes of the club picking up the welcome £15million bounty that came with qualification to the group stages. O'Neill said, 'I'm obviously very disappointed, but we didn't play well enough in the first-half. In the second-half, we threw everything at them, but it wasn't to be. Now we will see what happens in the UEFA Cup.'

Celtic cleared the first hurdle with effortless ease, winning 8-1 at home against the earnest Lithuanians of FK Suduva in the first leg and 2-0 in the return. It was deemed fitting Henrik Larsson should score the first goal in the run to the Final when he netted in sixteen minutes. Before half-an-hour had passed, the Swede had collected a hat-trick and, in doing so, hoisted himself level with Ally McCoist on the European record of twenty-one goals. He would render the Rangers player's feat obsolete in the next round. O'Neill's men were coasting in Glasgow against opponents who appeared to appreciate the guile and expertise of the Scottish team. Stilian Petrov and Chris Sutton scored to make it 5-0 at the interval and Paul Lambert, John Hartson and Joos Valgaeren chipped in to take the score to 8-0 with a minute to go. The fans wondered if Celtic could match their all-time best of 9-0 against the Finns of Kokkola in 1970, but a mistake by Rab

Douglas, with a sloppy pass, cost the side a goal, Tomas Radinevicius claiming the consolation.

It was chilly and overcast in the second leg, but David Fernandez, the Spaniard making a rare appearance, got the opener in the twelfth minute and Alan Thompson added a second before half-time. The game was played at walking pace in the second period, but Didier Agathe decided to illuminate proceedings with an eye-catching slalom run down the right touchline while beating five defenders in a mazy, solo surge into the penalty area. Unfortunately, he didn't get past a sixth opponent who flattened him. John Hartson might have made a better attempt with the resultant spot-kick to, at least, give his team-mate some sort of consolation, but, alas, the Welshman's weak effort from twelve yards didn't even hit the target.

As the luck of the draw would have it, Graeme Souness and his Blackburn Rovers team were the next obstacle to be placed in Celtic's path. The former Rangers manager grimaced when he heard the ballot and, in a moment of light-hearted badinage, quipped, 'I'll need to look out the old tin helmet for Parkhead.' On his club's visit on October 31, Souness made all the right noises in public, but away from the TV cameras and the reporters' notebooks, he was supremely confident of the outcome; the Celtic players would not be requiring passports for football journeys beyond the middle of November. In truth, O'Neill's men failed to spark in the first leg and had to rely on a goal from Larsson five minutes from time for a slender advantage to take across the border for the second meeting on November 14.

Souness made the usual soothing, middle-of-the-road noises in Glasgow in the aftermath of his side's defeat, but his cover was blown by his own captain, Garry Flitcroft, when he talked to the press. Dodging the niceties that are normally observed on these occasions, the Englishman blabbed, 'The gaffer has just said that was men against boys out there.' Martin O'Neill didn't have to work too hard on his player motivational skills when that quote became public. A Celtic team, with the likes of Larsson, Sutton and Hartson, were well up for the second tie. Once it was known what Souness really thought of the opposing team, he went on record on the day of the game. 'If Celtic score one, then we can score three,' he postured. 'Hopefully, by 10pm tonight, people will be saying, "Bloody hell, that Blackburn Rovers are a good side" and we'll be in the next round.'

Seldom have the acoustics been so good at Ewood Park where vast swathes of green and white embraced a grey, old ground. Around ten thousand Celtic fans brought colour to a drab part of Lancashire and they had every reason to enjoy their visit to the home of Souness. There were quizzical looks swapped among the Blackburn Rovers players as the Parkhead side dominated proceedings. They had faced a ghost team in Glasgow, but they were now asked to deal with the real thing. They weren't up to the task. Inside fifteen minutes, they were a goal adrift and two on aggregate when Didier Agathe and Chris Sutton combined to set Henrik Larsson free and he nimbly lifted the ball over Brad Friedel. The Darwen End of Ewood Park resembled the east end of Glasgow as the entertainment flowed from Celtic. Sutton, a former Rovers player, put the finishing touches to his old team's hopes of progression when he claimed the second with a header in the sixty-eighth minute.

At the time, there had been a lot of informed reporting about Celtic wanting to move across the border to play their football. The Rovers fans taunted, 'You'll never play in England' and by the end, on the evidence of this confrontation, Souness and Blackburn Rovers should have been grateful. There were gleeful cries of 'Ole!' and 'Easy...easy!' as Lennon passed the ball to Sutton who touched it to Hartson who knocked it to Larsson who switched it to Thompson. 'Can we play you every week?' resounded round the ground. Souness had watched his team being out-played while the home fans were out-sung. It was a very comprehensive, sound beating for the English team.

Celta Vigo, a skilful Spanish outfit, came out of the ballot for the Third Round, the first tie again in Glasgow due for November 28. French referee Claude Columbo spoiled the game as a spectacle with some bizarre decisions and Martin O'Neill was eventually banished to the stand by the incompetent match official after the Irishman could contain his frustration no longer. Henrik Larsson was the man who mattered again with the only goal in the fifty-second minute in front of a crowd of 53,726. It was typical Larsson as the Swede reacted more quickly than anyone else to rise above defenders and head home after Bobo Balde had nodded on a Steve Guppy corner-kick.

O'Neill said, 'The referee's performance left a lot to be desired. He tried to ruin what was a brilliant evening for us. But that's enough talking about it because the referee did detract from our performance. Our players, however, were terrific against a top-class side. We got the goal we deserved and we should have scored a few more. I couldn't have higher praise for the team.' Celta Vigo coach Miguel Angel Lotina sniffed, 'I wasn't very impressed by Celtic. I knew it would be more or less like this, but I was more impressed by the atmosphere.'

It was taut and tight in the return and Celtic urgently required a superb strike from John Hartson to get through on the goals away rule after the game had been tied at 2-2. A wicked deflection from Ulrik Laursen sent a shot from Jesuli past Rab Douglas to hand the initiative to the Galician team in the twenty-fourth minute. Celtic, however, recovered heroically and Hartson plundered his so-important goal in the thirty-sixth minute. The brawny frontman got on the end of a Chris Sutton flick before defender Eduardo Berizzo to slide a low drive beyond keeper Jose Pinto at his far post. In a match without respite, the Spaniards took the lead on the night in the fifty-fourth minute when Benni McCarthy stole ahead of Bobo Balde to get to a Gustavo Lopez cross and clip the ball away from Douglas. The last half-hour was frantic and O'Neill took off Hartson to replace him with Jackie McNamara who went straight into the backline. The tactic worked and Celtic went into the draw for the last 16 the following morning.

The Celtic manager said, 'It was a terrific effort from the players to beat Celta Vigo over two legs, but I have to admit it was a long last forty-five minutes. They have some useful players, so we needed a great performance to get through. We conceded a bad goal at a bad time, but we did well to get the equaliser and we hung on in the second-half. It was backs-to-the-wall stuff near the end. It's a great night for the club to be in Europe beyond Christmas for the first time in twenty-three years. Full credit to the players - they created a bit of history tonight.'

Going for the 'Sore Loser of the Season' award, Celta boss Lotina moaned, 'They gave us a very good game, but we should have scored a third goal and gone ahead to win the round. Celta Vigo would have been better winners and deserved to win more than Celtic.'

The Parkhead side were given a February double date with Stuttgart in the next stage. And O'Neill faced the Bundesliga outfit without the talismanic Henrik Larsson, out with a double fracture of the jaw sustained in the previous game, a 2-1 home win over Livingston. John Hartson, too, was sidelined through suspension. However, it looked as though things were swinging the Glasgow side's way when Brazilian Marcelo Bordon, the German club's strongman centre-half, was sent off for a professional foul on Shaun Maloney in only sixteen minutes by Italian referee Pierluigi Collina. Incredibly, they took the lead ten minutes later through a header from their highly-rated frontman Kevin Kuranyi.

Immediately, Celtic stepped up the tempo and Paul Lambert levelled in the thirty-ninth minute with a controlled drive into the corner of the net. On the stroke of half-time, Maloney, Larsson's deputy alongside Chris Sutton in central attack, snapped onto an Alan Thompson pass and stroked the ball wide of Tino Hilderbrand. The keeper was beaten again in the sixty-eighth minute when a shrewd pass from Lambert released Stilian Petrov and he squeezed a shot between the keeper and the near post to wrap it up at 3-1. O'Neill welcomed the win, but, at the same time, realised such a scoreline did not guarantee progress in Europe. 'We know what we have to do in Germany,' he said tersely.

There was an unlikely scenario after only fifteen minutes in the Gottlieb-Daimler stadium on February 27 with the visitors leading 2-0 on the night and 5-1 on aggregate with goals from Thompson and Sutton. Stuttgart, who were sitting third in the German top flight, were rattled, but, with right-back Andreas Hinkel, a future Celt, forcing them on, they came back into the contest and Christian Tiffert hauled one back with a header in the thirty-eighth minute. Fifteen minutes from time Alexander Helb made it 2-2 and three minutes from time

Michael Mutzel gave Felix Magath's side a victory on the night, but Celtic advanced 5-4 on aggregate much to the delight of their manager.

O'Neill said, 'We're through and that's what matters. We also deserve to be in the quarter-finals. This was another marvellous effort and, although I became more nervous than necessary for us late on, I thought, by and large, we were in command. The start was excellent and exactly what we wanted and from there we should probably have won the game. But Stuttgart are a quality team. We have achieved another excellent result over two legs.'

Europe was beginning to take notice of the upstarts from Scotland who had now knocked out teams from the English Premiership, Spain's La Liga and Germany's Bundesliga to get within two rounds of the UEFA Cup Final and a date with destiny in Seville. Liverpool were next to attempt the derailment of the steady progress being shown by O'Neill and his team. Singer Gerry Marsden led 59,759 fans in a highly-charged version of 'You'll Never Walk Alone' before kick-off. And, in one hundred seconds, Larsson, returning ahead of schedule after being out for five weeks with a broken jaw, put Celtic ahead with the roof threatening to be lifted somewhere in the direction of George Cross as the decibel level reached a deafening intensity. John Hartson mishit a ball across goal, Alan Thompson turned it into the goalmouth and the eager Larsson was lightning swift as he diverted an effort beyond Jerzy Dudek. However, the Anfield side quickly recovered, regrouped and settled into a game of containment.

Having weathered the early storm, with Hartson also clipping the bar with a fierce drive, Gerard Houllier's side stealthily moved forward and left-back John Arne Riise raced away before setting up Emile Heskey at an angle in the box. The striker's finish was meticulous as he rolled it wide of Rab Douglas at the far post. Dudek was the busier of the two goalkeepers throughout the remainder of the tie as there were no alterations to the scoreline. The evening was somewhat marred by the filthy actions of Liverpool's disgusting El-Hadji Diouff, a Rangers player in the making, who spat at Celtic fans as he went to collect the ball for a throw-in. His needless act would have been deemed even more despicable if there had ever been any shred of evidence the Senegalese actually possessed even the most infinitesimal quantity of grey matter.

Liverpool were favourites to finish the job at Anfield, but Neil Lennon well remembers the speech that Martin O'Neill delivered to his players in the dressing room just before kick-off. 'Everyone, but everyone, had predicted our demise, but at that point Martin showed his mettle. He gave us an unforgettable talk. Personally, I didn't think we needed much motivation as we were all sure of ourselves and positive that we would compete and get a result. Yet Martin's words inspired us to even greater heights of determination. He looked around the dressing room and pointed out young Shaun Maloney. "This is a European quarter-final and this boy is only nineteen, but he might never get this opportunity again." He looked around the older guys and added, "You guys in your thirties probably won't get the opportunity again to prove a point, to prove to England and Europe that you deserve respect and that you are worthy of a place in the semi-finals." He made his points tellingly in his usual manner and did so in two or three minutes, yet by the time he had finished, we were ready to go out there and run through brick walls if we needed to.'

The Anfield side, with Steven Gerrard the main man in the middle of the park and with the 'Litte and Large' striking team of Michael Owen and Heskey leading the attack, didn't make much headway in the opening minutes although Dietmar Hamann let Rab Douglas know he was on the pitch with a rasping drive that carried just over the crossbar. Dudek made a glorious save from a Henrik Larsson free-kick, John Hartson twice missed the target with headers and, at the other end, Rab Douglas made a breathtaking stop from a vicious effort from Gerrard.

However, as the game flowed towards half-time, Celtic were beginning to grow in confidence. On the verge of the interval, defender Djimi Traore tugged at Larsson's shirt and German referee Michael Merk awarded the free-kick twenty-five yards out. Everything now depended on the educated left foot of Alan Thompson and, also, no little cunning from the perceptive midfielder. As the wall of red line up in front of him, the Englishman decided to vary his deadball routine. Goalkeeper Dudek stood crouched on his line, no doubt having already studied videos of his opponent's technique on such occasions. Larsson ran over the ball and Thompson left the Pole standing open-mouthed in anguish and horror as he speared a low drive underneath the leaping wall, the ball going under the feet of Gerrard, as it reached its destination at the left-hand post.

Near the end, Hartson scored the goal of a lifetime. He played a swift combination with Larsson and moved off to his right, eluding a challenge from Hamann. The Welsh heavyweight hardly glimpsed at Dudek before he summoned up awesome power into the crucial moment of impact and his twenty-five yard pulverising drive raged over the keeper's left shoulder as it screeched towards the top corner of his net. Lennon, in his excellent autobiography, 'Man and Bhoy', recalled it like this, 'About half-an-hour into the second-half, Big John Hartson was going through a wee dodgy period and gave the ball away a couple of times. So, I said, "Hey, you, hold that ball." Then he turned round and to me and said, "You shut up or I'll rip your head off". Something like that. Words to that effect, anyway. Two minutes later, I played it into him and he shrugged off Hyppia, played a one-two with Henrik and lashed one into the top corner. That was the best moment for me in the whole tournament, that goal. Just to see the Big Man wheel away to our fans and looking at our bench and you know that you are 3-1 up with ten minutes to go and there is just no way back for Liverpool.'

O'Neill was breathless at the end. He remarked, 'That was an extraordinary result. It was hard for us early on, but I just told the players to hang on. They deserve all the credit in the world.' However, without getting carried away, the Irishman added, 'Certainly, we have a chance of going through to win the competition, but all the teams left in are capable of beating us.'

Celtic, Boavista, Porto and Lazio went into the semi-final draw. The Parkhead side were paired with Boavista, Portuguese opponents they had beaten 3-1 on aggregate in the European Cup-Winners' Cup in season 1975/76, while Jose Mourinho's side were due to face the Serie A outfit. Porto made short work of disposing of their opponents, winning 4-1 at home and drawing 0-0 in Italy. It was a bit more problematic for O'Neill in their bid to reach the UEFA Cup Final. The first game, yet again, would be at home and a difficult task became even more daunting when the unfortunate Joos Valgaeren diverted a cross from Joaquim Martilenho past Rab Douglas three minutes after the break.

Celtic's reply was instantaneous. A cross from Lennon was knocked into Larsson's path and he drilled the ball home from eight yards for his twenty-sixth European goal for the club and his thirty-seventh for the season. However, the Swede passed up an outstanding opportunity to send the Parkhead side to Portugal a fortnight later with a lead. Fifteen minutes from time, Belgian referee Frank de Bleeckere awarded them a penalty-kick after a shot from Thompson was handled by panicking Portuguese defender Eder. Larsson lined up the kick and thumped it low to Ricardo's right, but the keeper's guess was accurate and he got across his line to beat the ball to safety.

O'Neill was upbeat afterwards. 'All I know is that we have to score over there and I think we will. We are still well in this game, there is no doubt about that. After we had drawn with Liverpool here, there was an air of despondency in the dressing room and around the stadium. But we resolved that problem and we can do it again, I'm sure.'

There were only twelve minutes left in the second game with Boavista content to keep the ball, safe in the knowledge Valgaeren's own goal would be enough to get them through to an all-Portuguese UEFA Cup Final. It had been a fairly dour affair, but no-one with a Celtic connection was too upset when, almost inevitably, Larsson struck yet again. The Swede attempted a one-two in the packed penalty box and his pass hit Filipe Anunciacao and rebounded back to him. This time his predatory instinct revealed itself and he clinically stabbed the ball past the astonished Ricardo. The ball was over the line and nothing the desperate Boavista players could do in the remaining minutes would prevent Celtic from reaching their first European Final in thirty-three years. The travelling fans enveloped the Do Besso stadium in the midst of pure euphoria, emotion and elation at full-time.

Larsson agreed there was a little bit of good fortune at his goal. 'I tried to slip the ball to John Hartson, but, thankfully, the defender slide-tackled and the ball came back to me. I didn't get much on it and it certainly didn't go in the right direction, but it doesn't matter, we got one in the end.'

A relieved O'Neill commented, 'Over the two games, we deserve it. They were so negative with their diving and time-wasting and eventually it came back to haunt them. I'm delighted for everyone at the club, the players and the supporters. I've always said it's about those who pay and those who play. We know it will be difficult against Porto, but there is no reason we can't win it.'

And, so, to Seville and a never-to-be-forgotten spectacle that brought the magnificent Celtic support to the world's attention. Martin O'Neill's mentor, Brian Clough, admitted he felt sorry for his former Nottingham Forest player, but also added he believed Celtic had been robbed. Clough, who was by this time retired and delightfully dotty at the age of sixty-eight, had his own unique take on the game. He said, 'I would have handed the UEFA Cup to Celtic in Seville. What was the referee thinking allowing the Porto players to run off the pitch for minutes on end to celebrate their goals? You can't do that. One player leaves the field to celebrate a goal with his fans and he will get booked. Porto had an entire team disappearing to celebrate. If I had been the referee, I would have taken a note of all the players who had already been booked and I would have waited for them when they came back onto the pitch. I would have said, "Sorry, son, that's another yellow card, now off you go." All the others would have been booked. And if they disappeared into the horizon after a goal, I would have been waiting for them again. "Sorry, son, you've got to go, too." I've no idea how many players would still have been on the pitch by the end of the game wearing Porto colours. I think UEFA would have had to present the trophy to Martin and Celtic.'

It wasn't a completely barren evening for Celtic. The supporters, marvellous throughout their stay in Seville and, in fact, the journey all the way to the Final, won the coveted FIFA Fairplay Award and Seville's mayor, Alfredo Sanchez Monteserin, gave them this ringing endorsement, 'You should feel proud to have such fans as these in Glasgow who give their city and country a good name.'

Yes, there is such a thing as glorious failure.

CHAPTER TWENTY-FIVE
FLAG HAPPY - AGAIN

If ever an individual and a football team had something to prove in season 2003/04 it was Martin O'Neill and Celtic. Completing a campaign without a solitary piece of silverware wasn't in the script. The Irishman had had enough of the hard luck stories. 'We start again, ' he said. The steely glint was in the eye, the fire back in the belly. Somewhere from within, the Irishman felt he owed Celtic.

There had been the usual spate of so-called 'informed' reports O'Neill was seriously thinking of moving on and a link to Leeds United had resurfaced. Reports indicated the Yorkshire club had wanted him in 2002, just two years into his reign at Parkhead. His friend David O'Leary had been sacked in June that year and the position was up for grabs. The Elland Road side, apparently, targeted the man who had created such an impression south of the border in his years at Leicester City and had continued to set standards in Scotland.

Amid the innuendo, O'Neill, of course, remained at Celtic and former England manager Terry Venables got the post. Inside a year, Leeds were searching for a replacement and Peter Reid received the call in March 2003, but was clearly struggling and lasted a mere eight months. O'Neill appeared to have a permanent place on a faltering club's radar, but was always more than happy to distance himself from speculation.

He acknowledged, though, he had a job to do at Celtic and the entire Seville experience had had a genuine effect on him. He was ruthlessly determined to achieve success on a grand scale for his club.

Unarguably, O'Neill had been embarrassed by a trophyless, barren nine months. The last-day league defeat to Rangers bordered on the insufferable. In fact, the Irishman had completed last season as he had started it - with the utmost conviction his side were superior to the men from Ibrox. And, yet, the fact all three domestic honours now resided in a trophy cabinet at a ground across the city tended to suggest otherwise. The Celtic manager was never comfortable with disputes. Or failure.

With the greatest of ironies, O'Neill won the third title in his four years as Celtic manager at Rugby Park, the very location of the surrender of the championship the previous year. Celtic, in an almighty backlash, had made Rangers pay a terrible price for their uninvited intrusion on the progress of that term. The Parkhead side won all four of the Premier League confrontations and completed the whitewash for the first time in over thirty years by knocking Alex McLeish's men out of the Scottish Cup at the quarter-final stage. If revenge is, indeed, a dish best served cold, O'Neill and his team had dined in some fine style and enjoyed a veritable feast.

On April 18 in Ayrshire, Henrik Larsson set up Stilian Petrov for the only goal of a tough game against Kilmarnock to clinch the championship with six assignments still to be faced. It was a far cry from last year's nerve-shredding last-minute finale. O'Neill said, 'It was nice to win it here, especially after what happened last season and I think I sensed even then an inner-determination to go for it this time. Now that we've won it and been terrific throughout, I think we've deserved this success. All sorts of players have been exceptional through this run. I would like to go through the league undefeated, but I'm not sure that will happen. We've now got the opportunity to bring in a few youngsters and we'll see how it goes.'

The romping, frolicking squad went on a lap of honour in front of fans who refused to leave without a hearty round of applause and, as the players returned to the tunnel, each and every single one of them was given a warm and massive hug by O'Neill. Yet, even as those supporters drifted from the ground to take their celebrations elsewhere, there remained a nagging doubt among them that this might be the Irishman's last hurrah. There was the annoying thought their charismatic, not to say well loved, manager may say his farewells in the summer. They knew he would enjoy this moment, and, probably, another if Celtic won the Scottish Cup, but more than a few of them were aware he craved success on the European stage. Clubs across the border offered him the best chance of him achieving that ambition.

Of course, O'Neill had already made the appropriate noises about plans for next season and the urgent requirement of at least half-a-dozen new quality and decent recruits to elevate the team to a new level on the most illustrious and competitive stage. There would be no Henrik Larsson next time around, either. The talisman, after seven sterling years of service in the east end of Glasgow, had revealed he would be leaving at the end of his contract. It would be a tearful parting of the ways, but the headstrong Swede, closing in on the age of thirty-three, had made the decision and there would be no turning back. No-one was surprised when he fetched up at Barcelona and even won a Champions League medal after coming on as a substitute and inspiring them to a 2-1 victory over Arsenal in 2006. Larsson and class went hand in hand.

O'Neill had introduced young Irish midfielder Liam Miller during the term, but realised he would also be without his precocious talents when the stylish twenty-three year old signed a pre-contract deal with Manchester United in January without the knowledge of anyone at Celtic Park. History now tells us he would have been far better staying at Celtic. What was I saying about hindsight all those chapters ago? Colin Healy, too, was about to jump ship under Freedom of Contract and the twenty-four year old was heading for Sunderland. Long-term injury victims John Kennedy, already an international centre-half, and Shaun Maloney, a bright, enterprising midfield talent, wouldn't be available, either.

Chairman Brian Quinn had been quoted as saying he would like O'Neill to sign a new long-term contract, but, at the same time, he also hinted the transfer budget would be limited. A successful season was already beginning to fade, but O'Neill would have been looking at cast-iron guarantees on the level of cash he would be allowed to invest in new players before dismissing possible interest in his managerial expertise from down south. He was shrewd enough to realise he would not be bereft of a suitor.

A year earlier, though, the overwhelming desire to prove himself all over again propelled him into the new season. First up, there was a visit to face Dunfermline at East End Park on August 9. Yes, the same Dunfermline team that had lost 6-1 to Rangers at Ibrox to enable them to run up the sort of scoreline required to wrest the title from Parkhead. Chris Sutton, live on television, accused the Fifers of 'lying down to Rangers' and the SFA found him guilty of bringing the game into disrepute and were swift to act by imposing a suspension upon the Englishman. He wasn't available for selection for the first game of the term. It didn't help matters that John Hartson was also injured and O'Neill went into the new programme with Larsson and Maloney leading the attack. It was a frustrating afternoon that ended with Celtic failing to score in a league game for the first time in twenty-one months. Dunfermline didn't score, either, but they were just delighted to have ended a thirteen-game losing sequence against the Glasgow team.

Rangers had won all seven of their league games prior to the meeting with Celtic at Ibrox on October 4. Alex McLeish's side had also scored twenty-six goals into the bargain and were coasting along quite nicely. O'Neill's men had responded well to their initial blank and had picked up maximum points in six successive triumphs while amassing eighteen goals. It all shaped up quite nicely for another clash of the titans, but problems were piling up at Parkhead and O'Neill faced playing McLeish without three central defenders with Bobo Balde banned and Joos Valgaeren and Johan Mjallby injured. Striker Chris Sutton would be pressed into playing at the heart of the defence. It was hardly ideal, too, the manager had to rejig the formation when Alan Thompson limped off after only twenty-three minutes to be replaced by Michael Gray, a left-back who had just agreed on a four-month loan from Sunderland.

However, a mere eighteen seconds into the second-half, John Hartson nodded on a long ball to Henrik Larsson, moved intelligently into space to take the return, clipped in a right-foot shot which flicked off Zurab Khizanishvili, the Georgian defender newly signed from Dundee, hit the underside of the crossbar and bounced down behind Klos. It was his fiftieth goal of his Celtic career with the special significance of it coming against the team who rejected him on medical grounds.

By the time the old adversaries locked horns again on October 4 at Celtic Park, Celtic were leading the table by eleven points and a win over Rangers would give them their record eighteenth successive league victory. Stilian Petrov got the party started with a full-length diving header in the nineteenth minute as he turned a left-wing lob from Larsson low past Klos at his right -hand post. Stan Varga, signed from Sunderland, thundered in a close-range header in the fifty-seventh minute after Hartson had headed on an Alan Thompson right-wing corner-kick and a piece of mesmerising impudence from the English midfielder proved to be the coup de grace five minutes from time when he swirled in a thirty-yard free-kick with the utmost precision. Only the most optimistic of the Rangers support in the 59,087 crowd that afternoon believed there was another destination for the league title outwith Celtic Park.

As ever, Martin O'Neill read from his well-thumbed script. 'Yes, absolutely delighted and I thought the players did really well,' he said. 'It's a great win for the players and the fans. However - and I realise I always state this - there is a long, long way to go. But I am happy where the team is at the moment.'

Rangers got some welcome respite in between losing league points to their greatest rivals when they were drawn to face them in the Scottish Cup quarter-final on March 7, 2004. Once more, though, Henrik Larsson put them to the sword. The Swede scored the only goal of the encounter and, in doing so, claimed his fourteenth strike in twenty-eight games against the Ibrox club. It was also his twenty-eighth of the season. England manager Sven-Goran Eriksson had been persuaded to cross Hadrian's Wall to have a look at Alan Thompson and he must have been impressed by the inventive and industrious midfielder's craft and precision with set-plays. It was Thompson who set up the winner with a right-wing corner-kick, Bobo Balde headed down, Stephen Pearson, a £350,000 addition from Motherwell in January, had a shot blocked bravely by Klos, but punishment was only delayed a mere heartbeat away when Larsson latched onto the rebound and fired home.

O'Neill said, 'We have had a busy and tough schedule and I thought that showed even in the first-half when we were a bit laboured after our midweek European trip to Teplice. But it was an important win and one which I felt we deserved.' Alex McLeish acknowledged, 'Their team has been together now for effectively three or four years and that shows. They are a powerful side.'

Three weeks later across Glasgow at Ibrox, McLeish was experiencing the same sinking emotions after the fourth consecutive Old Firm defeat, this time a 2-1 reverse in the league. By the time the debris had cleared, O'Neill's men were an unassailable nineteen points clear at the top and had just registered their thirtieth league game without defeat. It was a familiar tale. In the twentieth minute, Thompson clipped over an inviting free-kick and Larsson swooped to head in the opener. Thompson added the second in the fifty-seventh minute and Celtic came close to a third when Varga shuddered the bar with a shot from four yards. Steven Thompson got his side's consolation goal near the end and, remarkably, it would be his team's solitary effort against Celtic in five meetings throughout the season.

Rangers drew a blank again on the afternoon of May 8 when Celtic completed the season-long humiliation when Sutton scored the injury-time goal in the 1-0 win. It was a real 'Do-It-Yourself' manoeuvre from the rangy Englishman. Young keeper David Marshall fired an accurate goal-kick deep into Rangers territory and Sutton rose to glide it down to Larsson and raced off to accept the return. The Swede shifted the ball into his partner's path, Sutton positively bullied Frank de Boer - who had joined his twin Ronald at Ibrox - out of the way before curling a spectacular eighteen-yard lob high over Klos. Asked why he didn't carry the ball into the penalty box, Sutton answered truthfully, 'Are you kidding? I was too knackered. I just decided to give it a whack and I was mightily relieved to see it go into the top corner.'

The domestic blip came on an Arctic evening in Auld Reekie when Hibs won 2-1 to knock Celtic out of the League Cup at the Fourth Round stage at Easter Road on Thursday, December 18. Stan Varga gave Celtic the advantage in the fifty-sixth minute, but eight minutes later the home side were awarded a penalty-kick when John Kennedy was adjudged to have handled and Grant Brebner fired the ball past Rab Douglas. It was heading for extra-time until Kevin Thomson, with eight minutes to play, struck a happy-go-lucky effort at goal and he was as surprised as anyone to see the ball fly high over Douglas' shoulder for the winner. It was his first goal for the club and, at least, the eighteen-year-old midfielder had the good grace to admit his shot could have gone anywhere. Unfortunately, for Celtic it arrowed straight into a top corner of their net. There is one satisfying postscript. Hibs beat Rangers 4-3 on penalty-kicks after their semi-final ended 1-1. They met Livingston in the Final and our old friend Davie Hay masterminded a superb 2-0 win for the underdogs.

In the Champions League group section, Celtic disappointingly lost all three of their away games to Bayern Munich (1-2), Anderlecht (0-1) and Lyon (2-3). Goals from Liam Miller - being watched by Alex Ferguson for the first time - and Chris Sutton downed the French outfit 2-0 in Glasgow while Miller and Sutton, along with Henrik Larsson, were on target again in the 3-1 success over the Belgians. The Germans ground out a goalless draw and O'Neill observed, 'They're out there taking a lap of honour in front of their fans. You would think they had just won the trophy. But their reactions do tell you something - that's how much a draw at Celtic Park now means to our opponents.'

Lyon topped the group on ten points, one ahead of Bayern and three in front of Celtic. Once more, the UEFA Cup beckoned. O'Neill's men joined the competition at the Third Round stage and were paired with Teplice, of the Czech Republic. Celtic eased to a three-goal advantage with Larsson claiming two and Sutton another on a misty Thursday evening in February at Parkhead. Teplice won 1-0 a week later, but there was never any danger of a banana skin. O'Neill was rubbing his hands in glee when the draw paired them with Barcelona at the next stage with the first leg due in Glasgow on March 11. A volcano erupted in the east end of Glasgow that night.

The game had simmered along as the first-half came to a close. Just before the interval, Barcelona's Thiago Motta jumped for a high ball with Bobo Balde, who was having his finest performance for the team. It looked as though Motta attempted to punch the central defender and the feud continued in the tunnel after German referee Wolfgang Stark blew to call a halt to proceedings for the time being. There were ugly scenes in the tight confines and Celtic emerged for the second-half without goalkeeper Rab Douglas while the Spaniards were missing Motta. The match official showed both players a red card during the break for their part in the fracas. O'Neill said, 'Douglas is protesting his innocence. He felt he was going in to intervene.'

The Celtic gaffer had to think fast as he sent on nineteen-year-old rookie David Marshall in place of Douglas and he chose to withdraw Craig Beattie, who was making a rare appearance with Chris Sutton and John Hartson both ruled out through injury. Unfortunately, some of the half-time nastiness followed a few of the players back onto the pitch and the worst offender by far was excitable Argentinian forward Javier Saviola, who was getting involved in the unacceptable side of the game and was eventually red-carded for a petulant hack at the legs of Alan Thompson.

The only goal of a fiery affair arrived a minute before the hour mark and was good enough to win any game. Didier Agathe started it with a trot down the right before pushing a pass in front of Stilian Petrov, practically on the touchline. The Bulgarian teed it up and sent over a cross to the backpost. Henrik Larsson leapt prodigiously above Carles Puyol to nod the ball down in front of the unmarked Thompson and he took to the air to twist his body into shape to catch the bounce of the ball with his left foot and acrobatically fire his effort behind Victor Valdes from six yards. It was all set up perfectly for the second leg in the Catalan capital a fortnight later.

'One day people will realise we have one or two decent players,' observed

O'Neill, rather caustically after his team had stretched their remarkable unbeaten run at home in all competitions to seventy-four games.

Before the return, there was good news and bad news for the Celtic manager. Balde, after an awesome performance against Ronaldinho and his multi-talented team-mates, had picked up a booking which would keep him out of the game in the Nou Camp, but that was balanced with the fact Sutton had overcome his ankle problems and was fit for selection. O'Neill, with a goalkeeper poised to make only his fifth start in the first team, went for youth in the shape of John Kennedy as Balde's replacement with the twenty-year-old reserve teaming up with Stan Varga in the heart of the back four.

Marshall was immense in front of a noisy, partisan crowd of 77,108 and illustrated he would not be overawed inside the first minute when he clawed the ball away from the feet of Gerard Lopez who had been sent scampering through on a delightful pass from Ronaldinho, the Brazilian artist who was acknowledged at the world's best player at the time. The youngster made another brilliant swooping save from a Lopez header shortly afterwards and it looked as though he was going to enjoy the occasion. He kept up his level of excellence right until the end and one save from Luis Garcia bordered on the unbelievable as he touched over a raging, close-range drive. It ended goalless and Martin O'Neill, having gone through his entire 'Jack-in-the-box' routine for an hour-and-a-half must have been as exhausted as his players.

In the immediate aftermath, he praised his extraordinary teenage keeper. 'I said to him it's all downhill from here, he should pack it in and retire tonight,' he joked, as much in relief as anything else. 'He has a terrific presence and calmness, he's not fazed at all. He did an interview for TV after the match and was last into the dressing room. When he came in it was to enormous applause from the rest of his team-mates.' On the game, O'Neill said, 'It was a terrific performance. We were driven back all night and it was a fabulous effort. My players are out on their feet and they were amazing to keep going the way they did. Some of our younger players really came of age out there tonight.'

Hero of the moment Marshall commented almost matter-of-factly, 'We just thought if we got a goal, we would have a chance. However, to keep a clean sheet in the Nou Camp is just unbelievable. In the first-half, I made saves I would expect to make, but I made a good one in the second period. I was just happy to help the team. It was a long day in the hotel, especially when you know you are starting. But you have just got to deal with it as all the lads have done over the years.'

Larsson laughed, 'I think he is too young to have any nerves - he just didn't realise how big this occasion was. He was tremendous, from the first minute onwards. The save he made from Luis Garcia in the second-half was outstanding. I don't think you can have a better full European debut, so I am very pleased for him.'

O'Neill added, 'Over the two legs, we have knocked out a very, very good team. I still think we are punching above our weight. But this is not about credit; I know what this side is capable of doing.'

Unfortunately, Celtic, drawn against a Spanish team who were inferior in quality and stature to Barcelona, went out to Villarreal in the quarter-final. On the evening of April 8, in front of 58,493 at Parkhead, Henrik Larsson scored his thirty-fifth European goal for Celtic, but the occasion was a little flat with O'Neill's men being held 1-1 by a team prepared to work hard for each other and one who also rode their luck and lived to fight another day. The Swede rose with his usual precision to meet a cross from Didier Agathe to direct a header past Jose Reina for the equaliser in the sixty-fourth minute, but he also had a very good effort ruled out ten minutes earlier with a Greek linesman the only person in the vicinity to notice any apparent wrong-doing. Larsson was chasing a ball towards the penalty box when the keeper raced out to bang his clearance against him. The Celt, thinking swiftly, controlled the wayward ball and rolled it into the net. Referee Kyros Vassaras immediately awarded a goal, but his assistant kept his flag up and insisted Larsson had deliberately handled the ball. Nonsense, of course, but the ref took the word of the linesman.

Villarreal shook Celtic with an opening goal in only the ninth minute when Josico allowed a cross from Garcia Roger to brush off the side of his head and the ball drifted away from Marshall, completely helpless on this occasion. At the other end, Reina was fortunate to get a touch to a drive from Stilian Petrov that pushed the ball onto a post and, with the ref about to blow for full-time, the anxious keeper spilled a free-kick from Larsson, managed to recover to block Chris Sutton's follow-up shot, the ball flew into the air to be met with the brow of Didier Agathe, but his header was hacked clear off the line by Sergio Ballesteros. And with that clearance went the team's hopes of a lead to take to Spain a week later.

As they had done in Glasgow, Villarreal, watched by a meagre crowd of 15,964 at the cramped El Madrigal, snatched an early lead when Sonny Andersson pounced on a moment's hesitancy from Bobo Balde to score in only six minutes. Celtic, with Alan Thompson suspended and Chris Sutton injured, couldn't get their normal fluency going on the night and Roger hammered in a sixteen-yarder in the sixty-eighth minute to derail the European ambitions of O'Neill and his players for another season. The Irishman commented, 'It shows how far we have come in the last few seasons that we are disappointed to lose in the UEFA Cup quarter-finals. Expectations are now very high at the football club after reaching the Final last year. We conceded a poor early goal, but we play as a team and we missed that sparkle that would turn the tie. After the goal, we had control of the game and I was pleased with the effort shown. In the second-half, we had to go for it and we had to run the risk of losing a second goal. And that's exactly what happened.'

The season did end on a spectacular high, though, with the Swede known as the 'Magnificent Seven' bowing out in his accustomed swashbuckling style. Henrik Larsson's parting gift, after seven years as a Celtic player, was a two-goal salvo as Martin O'Neill watched his club claim their thirty-second Scottish Cup at Hampden on May 22 in front of 50,846 fans. The fairy tale was complete as Dunfermline were beaten 3-1 and Larsson said farewell with the glorious Glasgow sunshine embellishing the moment. The Swede had been in tears the previous week when 58,364 supporters remained in place long after the final whistle had gone on the 2-1 victory over Dundee United. The footballing aristocrat, of course, had scored both goals. It was an emotional afternoon and Martin O'Neill summed it up best when he observed, 'He says it has been a privilege being here, but the privilege is all ours.'

Larsson's goals against the Tannadice outfit took his total for the season to thirty-nine, bringing the overall figure for the club to a phenomenal two hundred and forty. The ice-cool exterior of the Swede dissolved amid the raucous applause from his adoring supporters. His career in the green-and-white hoops may well have got off to an awkward start when he set up Hibs' winning goal for Chic Charnley all those years ago at Easter Road, but, thankfully, he veered back on path fairly swiftly after that. One faux pas in seven years is surely allowable.

Larsson, known to the support as The King of Kings, was charged with emotion when he said, 'I am going to miss all of this. But, as I have said many times, it is time for me to go.' But he wasn't about to depart without a word of praise for O'Neill. He added, 'My whole career here has been brilliant. We have had our ups and downs, but the last four years have been tremendous. It has been fantastic and, once the gaffer arrived, things started to go forward and happen. It has been a pleasure to be at a club like this. The fans have been tremendous and it is great to have been part of something so special like this. I want to thank you all.'

Dunfermline were desperate to be partypoopers in Mount Florida on the afternoon of the Scottish Cup Final. Celtic's outstanding unbeaten home run fell at the seventy-seventh hurdle when Australian David Zdrilic scored an injury-time winner for Aberdeen in a surprise 2-1 scoreline for the visitors. Of course, the championship trophy was already bedecked in green-and-white ribbons and proudly on display in the Celtic Park boardroom at the time, but it is a measure of the team's professionalism and their desire to win that they were pushing upfield at the time and were hit by a breakaway. There were only six games remaining in the campaign and only four were left when Jimmy Calderwood brought his Fifers to Parkhead on May 2. Despite Larsson scoring to cancel out a Barry Nicholson opener, Gary Dempsey hit the winner just before the hour.

Heartened by the fact they had already proved they could win against Celtic in Glasgow, there was a hint of bravado as the manager and his players prepared for the big game. Possibly, they thought they were going to catch their opponents on another off day when Andrius Skerla gave them a half-time lead with a looping header from a right-wing corner-kick swung in by Dempsey in the fortieth minute. David Marshall was distracted by Derek Young as he was challenged on his line, but referee Stuart Dougal, who had earlier cancelled a Stilian Petrov 'goal', deemed it fair and awarded the goal.

The second-half was the perfect setting for Larsson to take centre stage. In the fifty-eighth minute, Chris Sutton, back helping to defend a left-wing corner-kick, took possession in his own penalty area before taking a couple of strides and firing a raking ball downfield in the Swede's direction on the left. He went for it along with his constant companion that afternoon, Aaron Labonte, who slipped as he tried to cut out the pass. Larsson was off and running, carrying the ball in at an angle before sweeping a right-foot shot low past Derek Stillie into the far corner of the net. With the Larsson repertoire in full swing, it was only a matter of time before he struck again and he duly did in the seventy-first minute when he accepted a pass from Alan Thompson, rolled the tortured Labonte and zipped a left-foot drive low and unerringly past Stillie. The final flourish arrived six minutes from the end when substitute Ross Wallace set up Petrov for the third goal, the Bulgarian making no mistake from close range.

Afterwards, Martin O'Neill and his players lined up to pay tribute to Henrik Larsson. The manager said, 'Both of his goals were magnificent and so important for us. I thought we did well in the first-half and were in control, but you still have to score and that's where Henrik made the difference.'

Larsson, typically, played down his individual role, but admitted he was delighted to have finished his Celtic career on such a high note. 'Winning this Cup Final means everything,' he said. 'I didn't want to leave as a loser. It was great to get the two goals to end a fantastic seven years here. I never dreamt this could happen when I signed.'

Alan Thompson said, 'This shows what a loss he's going to be for us - he's a genius. I'm delighted for him. He deserves everything he gets.' An equally-appreciative Neil Lennon added, 'He was tremendous again. It's a fitting way to end his time here. He's a great loss as a friend and as a team-mate.'

On May 25, 2004 - thirty-seven years to the day Celtic had conquered Europe in Lisbon - Henrik Larsson said one last goodbye in front of a capacity crowd at Parkhead in his Testimonial Match against Sevilla. He didn't score as his team won 1-0 - Chris Sutton did the honours - but it was still a rather special leaving party for a rather special man.

BLACK SUNDAY

403

CHAPTER TWENTY-SIX
BLACK SUNDAY

Momentarily, Martin O'Neill appeared to be suffering from posttraumatic stress. Head bowed, chin almost sunken onto a slumped chest, the distraught manager was motionless on the Fir Park touchline. Perplexed, confused, disoriented; he was all of those things. Two minutes earlier, he was preparing to celebrate the fourth Premier championship of his five-year reign at Celtic Park. Now, though, he was a beaten man; a mere also-ran. And second best was nowhere for a fiercely competitive and committed Celtic boss.

Celtic, leading through Chris Sutton's opportunistic twenty-ninth minute goal against Motherwell, were seeing out time as the clock ticked away, every second edging them closer to the trophy that had been their priority since the opening-day encounter against the same opponents way back on August 8 2004. Now, on the afternoon of May 22 2005, they were only moments from claiming their glittering prize. As it stood, they had a two-point superiority over nearest challengers Rangers.

However, nervousness had crept in and the players who had earlier squandered precious goalscoring opportunities to make the outcome inevitable had now decided retreat might be the best way to succeed. Fatigue gnawed at their weary limbs after another ferocious, gruelling campaign at home and abroad. And there was still the task of next week's Scottish Cup Final against Dundee United to contend with before a welcome break and rest from the rigours of a demanding and unrelenting profession. Two minutes to go. O'Neill was aware Alex McLeish's Ibrox side were leading 1-0 against Hibs at Easter Road, but he was not concerned with events in Edinburgh. Why should he be? If it stayed the same, the crown would remain in Paradise. And time, apparently, was on Celtic's side.

And, then without warning, catastrophe intervened. Scott McDonald, an Australian who had never hidden his affection for Celtic, chested the ball down and Bobo Balde, standing off him, was both clumsy and slow to react. It was a calamitous hesitation. The Motherwell striker turned to hook the ball goalward and Fir Park was suddenly as quiet as the grave as his effort swept onward through the still air. Rab Douglas was struggling, caught totally unawares by the speed of the reflexes of the little striker. Frantically, the Celtic goalkeeper pawed at the ball until it was beyond his reach, still sailing inexorably towards the net. Thud! It landed at its destination and the full implication struck O'Neill, his players and the supporters in a sickening instant. Rangers could now win the title on goal difference. It would be the cruellest of coincidences if Celtic's greatest rivals could lift two championships in such a charmed manner in three years. Now, though, both Glasgow clubs were locked on ninety-three points and the swing to Ibrox gave them a five-goal advantage.

Disbelief and panic descended on a tiny part of Lanarkshire. Celtic had a minute to readdress the situation before the unthinkable occurred. One goal had been enough for Celtic to lose the championship two seasons ago. Could it possibly happen again? A dazed Sutton kicked off and Celtic moved straight down into their opponents' half, anxiously attempting to draw on reserves of energy that were clearly already spent. Defensive inhibitions were abandoned as players piled forward. A frantic attack was repelled and another wayward ball was hoofed up the park to drop into the Celtic penalty box and once again McDonald moved menacingly forward. He clipped an angled shot at goal as Stan Varga lunged full length to try to block the effort. The ball flicked off the Slovakian defender's outstretched leg and spiralled crazily up over the bewildered Douglas and, with horrible finality, it dropped into the net. In the space of two minutes, Celtic's league campaign had been wrecked.

If Seville had been a glorious failure, this had been nothing short of an incompetent collapse.

'We had enough chances to win the game by six or seven goals,' remarked O'Neill, once he had pulled his jumbled thoughts together. 'We always felt it would be difficult without the second goal. We had unbelievable chances to get that goal and spurned them all. It didn't matter if

Motherwell got beaten 2-0, so they started to come forward. We hadn't killed the game off and you pay the consequences. It's very painful and disappointing for the players. It's been a terrific effort right through the whole season and we've just come up short in the final game. There's nothing to say to the players. They are absolutely gutted and it's a very disappointing day.'

It was also already a puzzling day for the Celtic support before it turned to disaster. Since the early morning of the game, reports throughout the many strands of the media, newspapers, TV and radio, had circulated that O'Neill would be leaving the club after the Scottish Cup Final. However, the manager refused to confirm or deny the stories that stated he desperately required time away from football to attend to his wife Geraldine's poor health. There were other tales that insisted Gordon Strachan, who had lost out to Walter Smith for the Scotland job the previous year, would be named the new boss of Celtic.

'I've absolutely nothing to say about it,' remarked O'Neill firmly. 'There's absolutely no word whatsoever coming from me.' And yet, forty-eight hours before the Fir Park debacle, he had given his strongest suggestion yet he could be on his way. Once again asked about his future, he repeated, 'These five years have been pretty decent and there's as good a chance of me being here next season as not. But, if you are asking me if I'm going to join another football club, the answer would be no.'

It was a lot for the Celtic following to comprehend and too many questions were being left unanswered. The urgency of their players in the most crucial and defining game of the season had been practically non-existent. On a muddy surface, hardly conducive to free-flowing, attractive football, Celtic were dominant up until the point of putting the ball behind their former keeper Gordon Marshall, who, by a strange quirk of fate, had been in Kilmarnock's goal two years earlier when the Parkhead side could only win 4-0 at Rugby Park while Rangers were gifted six by Dunfermline at Ibrox. Unwittingly, Marshall played his part in Sutton opening the scoring when he attempted to shovel away a low cross from Alan Thompson. It wasn't cleared properly and the Celtic hitman snapped up the gift to turn the loose ball over the line.

John Hartson headed past and Craig Bellamy, playing his second last game before his loan period from Newcastle United expired, also missed the target. Stilian Petrov had a drive blocked. And so it went on. Motherwell were there for the taking, but Celtic's finishing on the afternoon was abominable. Bellamy was through one-on-one with Marshall and Celtic fans with keen memories could reflect on such occurrences when Marshall was at Parkhead and there was a guy called McCoist at Rangers. The outcomes were practically inevitable and not too well appreciated. The Welsh striker had the whole goal to aim at as Marshall, as he often did in his days at Parkhead, blinked. The keeper went early to his left and, inexplicably, Bellamy elected to shoot towards the same corner and smacked the prostrate veteran with the ball from six yards. It looked a simpler task to put the ball in the net. The painful procession continued right up until the eighty-eighth minute when the roof fell in.

At the start of the assault on the championship on a blisteringly hot August day in the east end of Glasgow, Celtic, looking just a little odd without the presence of crowd-pleasing pin-up Henrik Larsson, took on the same opponents, Motherwell, and sauntered to a 2-0 victory. Jackie McNamara steered in the opener in the eighth minute and, in a fairly relaxed atmosphere, Chris Sutton slid in to claim the second goal ten minutes after the interval. There was even some mild and polite applause when the Fir Park side sent on their substitute on the hour mark, a player who had gone very public in his intentions of some day playing for Celtic, a chunky, little Australian forward by the name of Scott McDonald.

Martin O'Neill sprung a surprise before the first Old Firm head-to-head of the campaign when he signed Brazilian World Cup star Juninho on a free transfer from Middlesbrough. The tricky little South American was immediately launched into the Parkhead tussle on August 29 in front of 58,935 fans who really didn't know what to expect. The Celtic followers were well pleased with their latest box of tricks, but it took until five minutes from the end before the team could celebrate their seventh straight win over the Ibrox side. Juninho, the diminutive playmaker, was being encouraged with his every touch and just before the interval he spotted Stefan Klos off his line and attempted an audacious angled chip. Unfortunately, the ball ended on the top of the net with the keeper scrambling. Juninho's warm welcome to the Glasgow derby came from right-back Hutton who clattered into him from behind while leaving his knee in a vulnerable area.

Moore also gave him a cheery slap on the cheek.

However, Alan Thompson won the game for the champions with a shot struck with phenomenal power and accuracy in the eighty-fifth minute. Celtic's attack down the right came to nothing when the ball was cleared by the Rangers defence. They didn't get much chance of a breather, though, as it fell kindly for Thompson, lurking with predatory instincts twenty-five yards out. One touch tamed the ball and, as two Rangers defenders attempted to converge on him, he pulled back his lethal left foot and walloped in a dipping, swerving drive that completely outfoxed Klos and hammered into the rigging.

Celtic contrived to make every error possible as they crashed to their first league defeat of the season against Aberdeen at the end of October. The Dons were two goals up in six minutes and eventually claimed the points with a last-minute effort in an amazing 3-2 win in Glasgow. Darren Mackie and Fernando Pasquinelli were the men on the quickfire trigger for the visitors, but John Hartson pulled it back to 2-2 with two excellent low drives by the sixty-ninth minute. O'Neill's men chased the winner, but, four minutes into stoppage time, John Stewart broke clear to fire the winner behind David Marshall.

On November 20, Ibrox was transformed into a madhouse during x-certificate scenes of uproar and pandemonium as Celtic had Alan Thompson and Chris Sutton sensationally dismissed while Rangers won 2-0. The brutal confrontation simply exploded and the Ibrox side's substitute Bob Malcolm was spoken to by the police and six others were booked. Thompson was red-carded after a slight head movement that brought about a shameful exaggeration from Lovenkrands as he toppled backwards holding his face although TV evidence later showed he hadn't been touched.

O'Neill said, 'Players square up to each other all the time in football - hardly a game goes past without people "locking horns", if you will - and, providing there is no butting involved, it never results in a sending-off. To say what Alan did was worthy of a red card is just nonsense. He was hard done-by as Lovenkrands made a meal of it. I don't think Lovenkrands will be too pleased to have a look at the outcome again. I think there are grounds for appeal and I fully expect Alan to be cleared.'

Sutton followed the midfielder eleven minutes after the break for two handballs in quick succession. Nacho Novo angered O'Neill with wild challenges on Jackie McNamara and Stephen Pearson, both of which could - and should - have brought instant dismissal. 'Novo lashed out at Jackie McNamara early on,' he said. 'The second incident, stamping on Stephen Pearson, was really terrible.' When the uproar eventually died down, Rangers had won with a fifteenth-minute penalty-kick from Novo and a header from Dado Prso twenty-one minutes later that narrowed the gap at the top to a slender point. After the first goal, the Ibrox side's young defender Malcolm was led up the tunnel by police for what appeared to be viewed as an obscene gesture in celebration.

In fairness, the Celtic boss did concede that another incident showed one of his players in a poor light. Striker Henri Camara, on loan from Wolves, had been booked for thrusting an arm into Alex Rae's face, but escaped punishment after kicking Gregory Vignal. 'Henri Camara was very lucky to survive as that was in retaliation,' admitted O'Neill, who also blamed referee Kenny Clark for letting the game get out of hand. 'I was not best pleased, to be honest,' he said. 'I thought he was poor.'

O'Neill added to the controversy by parading midfielder Neil Lennon, who had been involved in a verbal bust-up with Rangers manager Alex McLeish during the game and was booed constantly by the Rangers fans. He answered, 'Neil Lennon, for whatever reasons, suffers dogs abuse at every single away ground and, in particular, here, obviously. He is well thought of by the Celtic fans for what he has done for us over the last four-and-a-half years. It was to show that Neil Lennon is very popular with our fans and I didn't want anyone to forget that.' The SFA were quick to absolve the Celtic manager of any wrong-doing and issued a statement that said, 'Martin O'Neill will not be charged with bringing the game into disrepute.'

Rab Douglas captured the headlines after the 2-0 defeat from Rangers on February 20 at Parkhead and, sadly, once again for all the wrong reasons. The keeper blundered appallingly as the reigning champions fell three points behind, but, at least, still possessed the safety net of a game in hand. Douglas practically presented Alex McLeish with his first win as manager at Celtic Park and ended the club's eleven-game unbeaten run at home in Old Firm derbies.

Rangers had rarely threatened when on-loan Liverpool left-back Gregory Vignal attempted a thirty-five yard drive more in hope than expectation. Douglas, alarmingly, made a mess of trying to hold the straightforward shot and allowed the ball to squirm from his grasp and drop over the line. With eight minutes remaining, Belgian midfielder Thomas Buffel, deep in his own half, fired a simple through ball down the middle. There were three Celtic defenders watching Novo, but, unfortunately, Ulrik Laursen slipped at the vital moment and the ball ran into the path of the Spaniard who lofted his effort over the head of the advancing Douglas.

Sportingly, Martin O'Neill admitted Rangers were worthy of their victory. 'We dominated in the first-half, but Rangers were better than us in the second-half and deserved it. Rab Douglas is obviously disappointed with the first goal and it was possibly a turning point. Rab has been playing very well and with a lot of confidence, but that is naturally a setback. In a big game like this, it was a poor goal from our viewpoint, but I'm sure he'll recover. Now we obviously need to win our game in hand, but I always said nothing was going to be decided here. I'm disappointed, of course, but it's just one of those things.' O'Neill also declared he was satisfied with the performance of debutant Craig Bellamy who squandered the opportunity of opening the scoring when he was clean through on new Rangers keeper Ronald Waterreus, on loan from Manchester City. 'Overall, I thought Craig did well,' summed up the manager.

Celtic collapsed to their third home league defeat of the season when they went down 2-0 to Hearts at the start of April and manager O'Neill was swift to blame his international players suffering from lack of proper rest. He said, 'We didn't see the majority of the squad together again until the day before the game. In fact, Stilian Petrov didn't get back until Friday night. But in a month's time no-one will remember these sort of things and only remember the result.'

The champions once again gave themselves a mountain to climb by allowing the Tynecastle side to leap into a nineteenth two-goal lead with Lee Miller and ex-Celt Mark Burchill on target. Celtic had their chances, but they found Hearts keeper Craig Gordon in unbeatable form. One save, in particular, from a close-range flick by John Hartson, was applauded as 'world class' by his manager John Robertson.

The pressure was getting to Rangers, too, and on April 12 they lost at home for the first time in the season when Dundee United beat them 1-0 with a headed goal from Stuart Duff in the eighth minute. Celtic had the opportunity to add to the misery twelve days later and wonderful goals from Stilian Petrov and Craig Bellamy did just that. The travelling fans who sang and danced the night away didn't realise it, but they would not see Martin O'Neill in a dug-out at Ibrox again. At least, he went out a winner in this instance. Petrov powered a header into the net in the twenty-first minute and Bellamy curled in an exquisite long-range, angled drive for the second only thirteen minutes later. Celtic were in command and the only surprise was that they allowed their hosts an opening to score and Steve Thompson took advantage to knock one past David Marshall in the fading moments.

The victory pushed Celtic five points clear, but O'Neill refused to accept the race was finished. 'I am delighted to have won here,' he said. 'But I wouldn't say it is over - there are still twelve points to be played for. We had to be very, very strong, we had to be good and we had to believe we deserved to win. I would have been disappointed if we had not taken all three points. But Rangers put pressure on us and it was a long three minutes at the end.'

Remarkably, Celtic opened the door for Rangers a week later when they faded to a 3-1 defeat against Hibs at Parkhead on April 30. After allowing Aberdeen and Hearts to take early initiatives, they did so again when Garry O'Connor scored in the seventh minute with a close-range volley. It took until the fifty-ninth minute, with the 58,322 support in a ferment, for Celtic to level when substitute Craig Beattie hammered one past Simon Brown. However, it was the keeper's namesake and future Parkhead captain Scott who did the damage with the killer third goal nine minutes from the end. Ivan Sproule put Tony Mowbray's men back in the lead in the seventy-ninth minute and it was all over when Brown lobbed David Marshall for the points-snatcher. It was the Edinburgh side's first win at Parkhead in thirteen years.

O'Neill said, 'Hibs came here and played very well, but we gave away some poor goals. These games are tough and championships are difficult things to win. We were missing some key players, but that's not an excuse. After beating Rangers, I thought we could allow one more slip up, so we need to win our remaining games.'

Martin O'Neill got that right. They beat Aberdeen 2-0 at Parkhead and Hearts 2-1 at Tynecastle. And, if the game against Motherwell had finished two minutes earlier, they would have won that one, as well. Alas, the time-keeping was perfect.

Europe turned out to be a major disappointment, too, when Celtic could manage only one win from six games in their section that contained Barcelona, AC Milan and Shakhtar Donetsk. Henrik Larsson had joined the Spanish giants in the summer and clearly didn't expect to making such a rapid return to Glasgow. The news about the draw was broken to him by Magnus Hedman, the Celtic keeper and his Swedish international team-mate. 'I couldn't believe it,' said Larsson. 'Magnus heard the draw on the radio and phoned me immediately. I was stunned.' It would be fair to say the Celtic support weren't far removed from that emotion, either, when their hero scored the third goal for Barca on the night they triumphed 3-1 in Glasgow.

The Spaniards opened the scoring through Deco, the former Porto playmaker, in the twentieth minute and then David Marshall made a stunning penalty-kick save to thwart Ronaldinho. Chris Sutton levelled on the hour mark, but the game turned three minutes later when Barca introduced Larsson for Ronaldinho. The Swede set up Ludovic Giuly from eighteen yards and he netted with a deflected shot off Jackie McNamara in the seventy-eighth minute. Then Larsson did the unimaginable and scored to silence Celtic Park. There were only eight minutes remaining, when he latched onto a poor passback from Alan Thompson, guided the ball past Marshall with his chest and rolled it home. It was a surreal moment. Larsson was almost apologetic at the end. He said, 'Of course, there were mixed feelings. I have had seven great years here, but I am a Barcelona player now. It was very difficult to celebrate. Celtic will always have a big place in my heart, but life goes on. You have to do what you have to do.'

It was Celtic's first defeat at home in a Champions League match and Martin O'Neill said, 'Now we have to go out and get something away from home.' A goal from John Hartson gave O'Neill's side a praiseworthy 1-1 draw in the Nou Camp, but chances of qualifying from the group had long since gone. Hartson stabbed home a Stilian Petrov free-kick on the stroke of half-time after Samuel Eto'o had given the Catalans the advantage. However, this time there was not even the consolation of the UEFA Cup with Celtic finishing bottom of the heap on five points. AC Milan, who beat O'Neill's men 3-1 in the San Siro and drew 0-0 at Parkhead, clocked up thirteen points with Barcelona runners-up on ten. Shakhtar, who notched six points, swamped the Glasgow side 3-0 in the Ukraine before a goal from Alan Thompson gave Celtic their solitary win.

The flirtation with the League Cup came to an abrupt halt in extra-time on the evening of Wednesday November 10 at Ibrox when Rangers, with goals from Nacho Novo and Dado Prso, beat Celtic 2-1, John Hartson scoring for the visitors. Martin O'Neill's team were a mere six minutes from the semi-final after the Welsh striker's header from an Alan Thompson corner-kick had given Celtic the lead in the sixty-fifth minute. But David Marshall failed to hold a long shot from Hamed Namouchi and Croatian striker Prso swept in to fire home from close range. In the third minute of the extra half-hour, Craig Beattie squeezed between two defenders and toe-poked the ball under Klos, but French central defender Jean-Alain Boumsong scrambled the effort off the line. Arveladze's well-drilled low shot seven minutes later gave the Ibrox side their first win over their ancient rivals since the Final of the competition in 2003.

The only piece of silverware to make it to Parkhead in Martin O'Neill's departing campaign was the Scottish Cup. A freakish free-kick goal from Alan Thompson gave Celtic a 1-0 victory over Dundee United at a wet and miserable Hampden Park on Saturday, May 28 with 50,635 fans looking on. It was almost a solemn occasion, the action matching the miserable conditions, with the confirmation the charismatic Irish manager would be leaving the club after five enthralling, never-dull years.

There was a lot more excitement about the competition when Celtic beat Rangers 2-1 at the opening hurdle at Parkhead on January 9 2005. John Hartson had just agreed a new lucrative two-year deal and celebrated with the winning goal thirteen minutes from time in typical fashion. Didier Agathe sent over a cute cross from the right that was beautifully flicked on by Chris Sutton to Hartson at the back post. He nipped in behind Marvin Andrews on the Rangers defender's blindside and sidefooted the ball past Stefan Klos from a tight angle. And the Welsh powerhouse had been instrumental in the opening goal in the thirty-fifth minute when he jostled with Zurab Khizanishvili as they went for a kick-out from Rab Douglas. Sutton's anticipation was excellent and he hared onto the ball as it broke clear and gave Klos no chance. Rangers replied a minute after the turnaround when Fernando Ricksen planted a solid header behind Douglas after good work on the right wing by Alan Hutton.

Ibrox boss Alex McLeish was sporting enough to acknowledge, 'John Hartson and Chris Sutton are quality strikers and Celtic have pushed the boat out to keep John. The way they get on the end of free-kicks has haunted us for years. They can score goals and they have troubled bigger and better teams than us.'

Martin O'Neill added, 'That is the first pay-off from the Hartson deal. I felt we had the better chances and I'm delighted with the victory. It's true both Hartson and Sutton are strong and physical, but they can also play, as well. We should never lose sight of that fact.'

In all, John Hartson would score over one hundred goals for Celtic while winning three league titles, two Scottish Cups and a League Cup in his five years with the club. Not bad for a guy with dodgy knees.

The man known as 'Big Bad John' was on target twice in the next round of the national competition as Celtic beat Dunfermline 3-0 at East End Park. He was joined on the scoresheet by Chris Sutton. O'Neill watched his side breeze past Clyde 5-0 at the quarter-final stage at ice-bound, chilly Cumbernauld on a raw February afternoon. Hartson had the day off and Sutton was replaced at half-time while the club relied on goals from Stan Varga (2), Alan Thompson, Stilian Petrov and Craig Bellamy to annex a semi-final spot where they would play Hearts at Hampden in April. Early goals in both halves guided Celtic to a 2-1 victory while booking their Cup Final place against Dundee United in the emotion farewell to an eventful campaign at the end of May.

Chris Sutton scored in the third minute against the Tynecastle side and

Craig Bellamy hit the second four minutes after the turnaround. Deividas Cesnauskis got the Edinburgh side's consolation with a deft flick on the hour mark. Martin O'Neill said, 'We deserved our two-goal lead and we were in absolute control until they scored. The natural reaction is to fall back and we allowed Hearts possession in midfield and they put us under pressure there. It was uncomfortable towards the end, but we got there in the end.'

On May 28, O'Neill, after a trying, testing week, plotted his last goodbye as manager of Celtic. He had no intention of leaving as a cup final loser. He thought long and hard over his final team selection to face Dundee United. He went with, Rab Douglas; Didier Agathe, Bobo Balde, Stan Varga; Jackie McNamara, Stilian Petrov, Neil Lennon, Alan Thompson; Chris Sutton; John Hartson and Craig Bellamy. Joos Valagaeren replaced Hartson in the seventy-third minute and Aiden McGeady played the last four minutes in place of Thompson. David Marshall, Paul Lambert and Craig Beattie remained on the substitutes" bench.

The Scottish Cup Final of 2004/05 will never figure in reruns of classic Hampden encounters. In truth, the Celtic players looked more than little jaded and weary, their strength sapped after a strenuous and debilitating crusade. A crowd of 50,635 turned out to witness the contest for the oldest national trophy in world football. Thompson claimed the only goal of the afternoon in the eleventh minute with a weird effort. Garry Kenneth, an uncompromising central defender in United's back four, was enticed into a wide area to clatter into the dashing Bellamy. Referee John Rowbotham immediately awarded the foul. Thompson eyed up the proposition on the left-hand side of the Tannadice side's penalty box while there was the usual scrum of players jostling for the most advantageous positions.

The match official blew to resume hostilities and the midfielder stepped forward to arrow a ball low towards the near post. Balde stepped over it, the effort, hit with pace, appeared to take a nick off Kenneth as it bamboozled keeper Tony Bullock on its way into the net. Fluke? That would have been a harsh assessment given the fact Thompson had proved in every single game since he had been bought by O'Neill five years ago that he possessed football's version of a magic wand in his left foot. I believe he meant it and he was rewarded for his moment of ingenuity. The nearest Celtic came to another goal was in the second-half when they were awarded a penalty-kick, the unfortunate Kenneth tangling again with Bellamy. Sutton strode forward with purpose, but at the vital moment of impact, he lost his footing on the treacherous conditions and mishit his shot well off target. In the fading seconds of injury-time, United defender Alan Archibald attempted a last-ditch speculative long-range drive at the Celtic goal. Hampden was hushed as the ball flew over Douglas' left hand, but the effort kissed the top of the crossbar and flicked off to safety. Football is a cruel spot, but possibly NOT that malicious.

The final whistle went and the Celtic players insisted Martin O'Neill go up to be first to receive the Scottish Cup, the seventh trophy of his tenure. Skipper Jackie McNamara said, 'It was something all the players felt was right. It was just a small token of our appreciation for what he's done here over the past five years. He's been great for Celtic and Scottish football, in general.'

O'Neill, albeit reluctantly, stood with assistants Steve Walford and John Robertson and lifted the trophy to be greeted with a crescendo of warm applause from a Celtic support. It was a poignant image. The Irishman admitted it was a 'fantastic moment'. He added, 'We were desperate to win, but, like last week, we couldn't put the game away. We missed some great chances and 1-0 is never enough. They hit the bar and that would have been harsh on us if it that had gone in. It was a great final effort from what is a terrific bunch of players. At least, we had the opportunity to put it right again and where better than the Scottish Cup Final?'

He paused, wiped his brow and continued, 'It has been a pretty hectic week. It has taken me a bit of time to get over the defeat and my only regret is, due to circumstances, I don't have the chance now to try to regain the championship next season.'

Within days of Martin O'Neill's departure, Gordon Strachan was installed as his successor. In his first three years, the League championship set up residence in the Parkhead boardroom. He would be only the third Celtic manager - following the legendary Willie Maley and Jock Stein - to win three successive titles.

We all like a happy ending.

EPILOGUE
REMEMBER, REMEMBER THE FOURTH OF NOVEMBER

This book went to print on November 5, 2015. The day after HMRC's appeal against Rangers use of Employee Benefit Trusts (EBTs) was upheld by the Court of Session. The Court found that while locked in an exhaustive arms race for resources and trophies with Celtic, the 'former Rangers Football Club' unlawfully avoided tax between 2001 and 2010.

When the club finally went into liquidation, HMRC's unpaid bill topped £75m, a liability which, between the EBTs and another illegal Discounted Options Scheme, accrued from 1999 and funded resources, such as title 'winning' football players.

As well as running an unlawful tax scam, Rangers failed to correctly register EBT-holding players with the SFA and Scottish Premier League. In an investigation into the non-disclosure of side-letters relating to the EBTs, an SPL Commission fined the club but, as at that time, the EBTs were regarded as legal, they found that no sporting advantage took place. The Commission wrote:

"The Tax Tribunal has held (subject to appeal) that Oldco was acting within the law in setting up and operating the EBT scheme.

"The SPL presented no argument to challenge the decision of the majority of the Tax Tribunal and Mr McKenzie (solicitor acting on behalf of the SPL) stated expressly that for all purposes of this Commission's Inquiry and Determination the SPL accepted that decision as it stood, without regard to any possible appeal by HMRC.

"Accordingly we proceed on the basis that the EBT arrangements were lawful. What we are concerned with is the fact that the side letters issued to the Specified Players, in the course of the operation of the EBT scheme, were not disclosed to the SPL and the SFA as required by their respective Rules."

No illegal activity approaching this scale has a precedent in Scottish sport. As we go to print, the SFA and Scottish Professional Football League (the renamed SPL) have yet to react against the conspirators behind the tax scam, or decide what historical notes should be made against Rangers record during that period.

Paul Brennan
Celtic Quick News